APES, ANGELS, AND VICTORIANS

APES, ANGELS, & VICTORIANS

THE STORY OF
DARWIN, HUXLEY,
AND EVOLUTION

by William Irvine

WITH A NEW
INTRODUCTION BY
SIR JULIAN HUXLEY

RTP Time Reading Program Special Edition

TIME INCORPORATED · NEW YORK

TIME INC. BOOK DIVISION
EDITOR *Norman P. Ross*
COPY DIRECTOR *William Jay Gold*
ART DIRECTOR *Edward A. Hamilton*
CHIEF OF RESEARCH *Beatrice T. Dobie*
EDITOR, TIME READING PROGRAM *Max Gissen*
ASSISTANT EDITOR *Jerry Korn*
RESEARCHER *Page Spencer*
DESIGNER *Lore Levenberg*

PUBLISHER *Jerome S. Hardy*
GENERAL MANAGER *John A. Watters*

TIME MAGAZINE
EDITOR *Roy Alexander*
MANAGING EDITOR *Otto Fuerbringer*
PUBLISHER *Bernhard M. Auer*

COVER DESIGN *Richard Rosenblum*

For Richard Foster Jones

Contents

Editors' Preface   xi

Time Reading Program Introduction   xvii

Part One

1. Revolution in a Classroom   1
2. A Scientific Odyssey   9
3. A Prophet in His Own Country   30
4. The Tale of an Unlikely Prince   49
5. A Premeditated Romance   68
6. Barnacles and Blasphemy   82
7. The Most Important Book of the Century   101
8. Convulsions of the National Mind   123
9. An Interlude: Huxley, Kingsley, and the Universe   155
10. Human Skeletons in Geological Closets   164
11. Orchids, Politics, and Heredity   184
12. The Subject of Subjects   217
13. "I Am Not the Least Afraid of Death"   247

Part Two

14. An Eminent Victorian   283
15. The Metaphysical Society   301
16. The Educator   322
17. Triumphal Progress   353
18. The Pleasant Avocation of War   381
19. "Il Faut Cultiver Notre Jardin"   406
       Notes   441
       Index   481

Illustrations

Thomas Henry Huxley, 1857
The *Beagle*
Emma Darwin, 1840
Charles Darwin, 1840
Charles Darwin, 1854
Charles Darwin, portrait, 1875
Vanity Fair's Darwin, 1871
Vanity Fair's Huxley, 1871
Thomas Henry and Henrietta Huxley, 1882
Thomas Henry Huxley, 1890

Editors' Preface

Apes, Angels, and Victorians is in that small company of books that set themselves the task of re-creating a world assailed by an idea. Battles, political intrigues, scandals—these are easy for the social historian to come to grips with. But he faces a special problem when he tangles with ideas: they change one's way of thinking so profoundly that it is almost impossible to recall the way one used to think. Thoughts, unlike monuments, do not lend themselves easily to examination by tape measure.

Thus, a landscape viewed from the perspective of another century may look quaint without being unfamiliar. The America of 1750, an agrarian colonial society clinging to the edge of an unexplored continent, must certainly have seemed small and strange when viewed from the vantage of 1850 by a rambunctious new republic that was growing by leaps and bounds and bursting into industrialization. However, that early America must have been understandable to the later one, because the concepts of life on which both societies were based had changed relatively little. This is not true of the century that followed—in America, in England or in any advanced Western society. The years since 1850 have unleashed a series of ideological blockbusters that have made it impossible for human beings to look at themselves as they had previously done for thousands of years.

In 1850, Charles Darwin had not yet spoken. Neither had Sigmund Freud. Today, steeped as we are in the doctrines of these two, it is almost impossible to recapture the innocence of that other time. It is the virtue of William Irvine's book that it succeeds in this most difficult intellectual feat.

Irvine has chosen to tell the story of the Darwinian controversy in the form of a joint biography of the two men: Darwin himself, and T. H. Huxley, who became evolution's foremost public champion. The book sketches in the background of the social and intellectual attitudes that prevailed in Western Europe in the 18th and 19th Centuries, and at the same time picks up its two main characters, carrying them through their parallel careers, up past the peak of their powers and down to their deaths—by which time each man was shining in a glow of fame that penetrated to every corner of the civilized world.

Irvine's account is an ambitious and absorbing one, with some surprises for 20th Century readers. First, it reminds us that the idea of evolution, far from being new with Darwin, had been quietly bubbling for centuries; in the 1700s the "great chain of being" was considered a proper topic for discussion within any group of enlightened and philosophically minded men. Unfortunately for the idea, it began to appear dangerous to the society of the time once it attracted the interest of scientific minds, for they threatened to promote it from the status of a mere idea to something more concrete and hence more troublesome. Georges de Buffon, the great French naturalist, was one of those who thought about evolution— and worse, wrote about it. In England, in the latter half of the 18th Century an eccentric physician and inventor named Erasmus Darwin read Buffon and composed a long poem,

Zoonomia, in which was buried the concept of a kind of evolution based on animal reactions to lust, hunger and the need for security. "Buried" is the proper word, for Erasmus Darwin was prudent enough to realize that his thesis, if too clearly expressed, would cause a scandal. The Darwins were a rich and prominent family. Erasmus' son, a portly physician, may well have found it best to ignore the Zoonomia, but his grandson Charles read it.

Charles also read a book on geology by a Scot named Charles Lyell which contained a startling heresy: it argued that the earth was thousands, if not millions, of years older than the Bible said. Despite the heresy, others read Lyell too. There was in England a small group of men of independent means and independent opinions who constituted what was then the world of science. There was as yet no proper world of "scientists"; the profession as we know it scarcely existed. There were botanists, there were geographers, there were zoologists, but most of them pursued their bent as amateurs and out of pure curiosity. The idea of supporting oneself by studying polyps or pine cones was almost unthinkable.

At the same time the world lay open for young Englishmen. Avid for knowledge in a dozen fields, society waited complacently on the brink of the very pit, heedless of the danger that may come from an onslaught of knowledge, while intelligent and adventurous men shot off to all corners of the globe to collect that knowledge. Among them went Huxley, to New Guinea and the unexplored north coast of Australia as a surgeon in the Royal Navy, and Darwin, to South America in the Beagle.

It is this era that Irvine's joint biography illuminates. It gains its drama by building on the extraordinary contrast that existed between Huxley and Darwin. Huxley was poor, Darwin was rich. Huxley was restless, forceful, a born controversialist. Darwin was timid and slow and modest; in Huxley's

own words, he had a "marvelous dumb sagacity . . . like that
of a sort of miraculous dog. . . ."

The storm Darwin let loose is almost incomprehensible
today. Kinship with apes was not so frightening as it was out-
rageous. It punctured Victorian pomposity, routed Victorian
composure. In the best clubs and regimental messes we can
sense the general tendency to swell up and turn purple. In the
drawing room we can hear the Victorian lady whisper: "Descended from the apes! My dear, we hope it is not true. But if
it is, let us pray that it may not become generally known."

All this Irvine sketches with great wit and style against a
somber background of the deeper, more important moral,
social and religious convulsions that the *Origin* also set off.
Reform was riding fast in England, and every enclave of privilege, every backwater of inherited linear thought set out to
destroy Darwin, believing, as conservatives will, that if some
particular entrenched edifice were destroyed, the country
would somehow fall in ruin. The edifice in this case was, of
course, the Church of England. That Darwin should roam
about free to hack at its foundations was clearly a national
peril, to be combated as vigorously as the late Senator
McCarthy once sought to combat "Communists" in the
United States government. It is from this essentially political
context that Irvine has taken the title of his book, going to a
speech made by the Conservative politician Benjamin Disraeli
in 1864 at Oxford: "What is the question now placed before
society with a glib assurance the most astounding? The question is this: Is man an ape or an angel? My Lord, I am on the
side of the angels."

It was inevitable that the glare of Darwinism should center
on Darwin, and perhaps inevitable that what it illuminated
was something quite different from what Darwin really was.
That is largely due to the behavior of Darwin himself, who was

a nervous invalid and a recluse. Irvine makes this point clearly: "While an unparalleled outburst of acrimony, ridicule, hatred, admiration and professional envy beat down upon the Origin, Darwin was far away in the somnolent depths of Ilkley and a water cure. He responded not a word, nor was it in his nature to respond. With the passage of years his meekness grew legendary. The bright-eyed, fabulous-bearded sage of omniscient calm and inscrutable detachment is a myth suggested to a garrulous age by a romantic portrait and a long newspaper silence."

Pottering about in his slippers at his country house, his whiskers flowing a foot below his chin, Darwin reminds us of nothing so much as that 20th Century legend, Albert Einstein, pottering in Princeton with his flowing hair and his slippers. Bathed as we are in this warm glow of antique wisdom, we have a tendency to forget Huxley—to regard Darwin as the genius and Huxley as the mere popularizer. This is an unpardonable oversimplification which Irvine corrects in his many long and admiring chapters on Huxley.

If anything, Huxley was a more interesting man than Darwin. He was certainly far more approachable, far more involved in the doings of the world, partly by temperament, partly by circumstance, since he was forced to spend much of his energy and time teaching. He had little left over for pure research. This, however, should not tempt us to conclude that if their situations had been reversed Huxley might have been the enunciator of the theory. As Irvine makes clear—and as Huxley's distinguished grandson Julian emphasizes in his Introduction to this special edition—their positions never could have been really reversed. For all his brilliance, which enabled him to grasp the significance of the Origin instantly and exclaim: "How stupid of me not to have thought of that!" Thomas Huxley lacked Darwin's patience. He was not a collector; it was not in him to hoard scores of facts, thousands of barnacles, and brood timorously over them for years. He did what he could, as did Darwin. Together, they changed Western thought. In *Apes, Angels, and Victorians*, William Irvine has done well by both of them.

—THE EDITORS OF TIME

INTRODUCTION

In the relatively short time since this classic experiment in double biography by Professor Irvine was first published, scores of the biologists, anthropologists, psychologists, teachers, writers, broadcasters—and even theologians—of the world have celebrated the landmarks in time that were both the crux of the career of Charles Darwin and the start (perhaps blast-off would be a more appropriate word) of the career of Thomas Henry Huxley, my grandfather.

In 1958 the 15th International Congress of Zoology met, most appropriately, in London, where a century before, Darwin and Alfred Russel Wallace had, through their friends Charles Lyell and J. D. Hooker, offered to the Linnean Society of London their joint paper "On the Tendency of Species to Form Varieties; and on the Perpetuation of Varieties and Species by Natural Means of Selection." This notable contribution to science, which included Darwin's first publication on evolution, was precipitated by Wallace's independent discovery of natural selection, in the jungles of the Malayan Archipelago. And it led to Darwin's making a still greater contribution to science by stimulating him to publish in 1859 The

Origin of Species, a book that shook the world and was supposed by some to degrade man. In 1959 universities, societies,
groups of like- and unlike-minded evolutionists published a
spate of essays, reviews and reassessments of Darwinism for the
centenary of the *Origin's* publication. Professor Irvine says it
was the most important book of the century: I would go further and say that it has altered the substance and the direction
of human thought more profoundly than any other publication
of the age of print.

In 1960 another centenary was celebrated: that of the
famous June meeting of the British Association for the Ad-
vancement of Science, in Oxford. In England the British
Broadcasting Corporation ranged theologian and humanist in
debate, and recalled with cameras and scholarship the famous
scene in which my grandfather earned his name of "Darwin's
bulldog," in a superbly timed piece of artistry and cold logic
in refutation of "Soapy Sam" Wilberforce, the Bishop of Oxford. It was perhaps this encounter (from which Darwin, who
shunned public meetings and public controversy, was notably
absent) which really persuaded the thinking public that in the
Darwinian theory of evolution by natural selection, the working process of all life had been at last discovered, its underlying
mechanism identified and its principles clearly promulgated.

I am glad that Professor Irvine's tender and rational biography starts with the Oxford meeting and Wilberforce's question as to whether my ancestor was descended from a monkey
through his grandfather or his grandmother. His book is so
skillfully arranged, and written with such knowledge of the
scientific and social educational background of the time, that
it still stands, in my opinion, as the fairest general statement
on the lives of the two great men and their influence on human
thought, and this after all the centennial publications. (These

are so formidable that my own very incomplete collection weighs the best part of a hundredweight.)

In spite of many differences, there were, and indeed still are, striking resemblances between the Darwins and the Huxleys. Family life, homes and gardens were their roots; all their private background was deeply respectable, with a strong moral tone; curiosity was a virtue; religion and ethics were examined— discussed in the same breath and often in the same tone as plants, animals, physiography (my grandfather's word), politics and investments. To Darwin and Huxley the world was real. But though the two great men shared the unlimited curiosity of Kipling's elephant's child, they accepted and lived their lives in utterly different ways. Darwin was an introspective, valetudinarian recluse, a great naturalist who satisfied his curiosity within the limits of the one subject of life and its biological manifestations; Huxley was the Faustian and impatient polymath, the brilliant, lucid writer with the lawyer's dramatic forensic touch, the capable organizer and committeeman, the teacher and moralist, the philosopher and preacher, the thinker with a passion for truth, who could invent a new word like "agnostic" when the situation called for it.

Now that all the tumult, shouting and stocktaking of a hundred years of stable evolution theory have settled down a little, we see that what Darwin began, without conscious formulation, was humanism as it is now understood—humanism on an evolutionary basis. And Thomas Henry Huxley was the first great prophet of this new humanism. In spite of their violently unorthodox views, they both were accepted as members of what is now called the Establishment: indeed Darwin was perhaps the most respectable revolutionary the world has known.

Huxley recognized Darwin's massive talent for intellectual

argument, but he himself was more overtly and disputatiously Socratic. In another age he might well have been given the hemlock; as it was, though his views on religion precluded him from being buried in Westminster Abbey, as Darwin was, both the great evolutionists were heaped in their time with all the honors they cared to accept. They were the leaders of the great Victorian revolution of thought. Darwin not only sparked it off with his brilliant discovery of natural selection as the effective agency of biological evolution but also set the new edifice of ideas on a firm basis by his laborious and single-minded amassing, verifying and marshaling of ever more and more facts. Huxley plunged into the controversial heart of things and, in his quest for truth, pushed on into every territory of human inquiry and learning, from anthropology and theology to education and ethics.

Professor Irvine has captured the personalities of two men of genius and with them the spirit of an age. In some important ways, the age was more benign and liberal than ours: we could well cultivate the rational humanity and the respect for learning of the intellectual Victorian families.

—SIR JULIAN HUXLEY

Author's Note

I wish to thank the Imperial College of Science for allowing me to read the Huxley Papers, and the American Philosophical Society for allowing me to read the Charles Darwin Papers. I wish also to thank the Cambridge University Library for sending me microfilms of many unpublished Darwin letters, as well as of the manuscript of his "Autobiography." I am grateful to all three of these institutions for permission to quote from their collections of unpublished materials.

I am indebted to Lady Nora Barlow for aiding me to gain access to Darwin letters and manuscripts, to Professor Arthur Giese for checking some of my expositions of biological principles, and to Dr. Walter C. Alvarez for a valuable letter on Darwin's ill-health.

What is the question now placed before society with a glib assurance the most astounding? The question is this: Is man an ape or an angel? My Lord, I am on the side of the angels.

—BENJAMIN DISRAELI,
IN A SPEECH AT OXFORD, 1864

PART
ONE

1

Revolution in a Classroom

In June, 1860, the British Association met at Oxford. Science was not very much at home there, and neither was Professor Huxley. Beneath those dreaming spires, he always felt as though he were walking about in the Middle Ages; and Professor Huxley did not approve of the Middle Ages. At Oxford, he feared, ideas were as ivy-covered as the buildings, and minds as empty and dreamy as the spires and quiet country air. Professor Huxley's laboratory was set squarely in the middle of the nineteenth century, in the narrow downtown London thoroughfare of Jermyn Street, which was as crowded and busy as Professor Huxley's own intellect.

Reciprocally, Oxford did not feel in the least at home with such people as Professor Huxley. In fact, she felt rather desperately at bay between a Tractarian past and a scientific future. Newman's conversion to Roman Catholicism had opened an abyss of conservatism on one side; now Mr. Darwin's patient and laborious heresy had opened an abyss of liberalism on the other. The ground of sanity seemed narrow indeed. But sanity can always be defended. After all, there was something obviously ridiculous in a heresy about monkeys.

Mr. Darwin himself was too ill to attend the meeting of the Association—as on a former even more important occasion, when Joseph Hooker and Sir Charles Lyell had acted in his place. A portentous absence from crucial events which deeply concerned him was already making Mr. Darwin a legend. It was just six months since his *Origin of Species* had appeared. Of course Darwinism was in everybody's mind. It was also on the program.

In Section D of the meeting, Dr. Daubeny of Oxford read a paper "On the final causes of sexuality in plants, with special reference to Mr. Darwin's work on *The Origin of Species*." Huxley was invited to comment by the president but avoided discussion of the vexed issue before "a general audience, in which sentiment would unduly interfere with intellect."[1] Thereupon, Sir Richard Owen, the greatest anatomist of his time, rose and announced that he "wished to approach the subject in the spirit of the philosopher." In other words, he intended, as in his anonymous review[2] of a few months before, to strike from under the cloak of scientific impartiality. "There were facts," he felt, "by which the public could come to some conclusion with regard to the probabilities of the truth of Mr. Darwin's theory." He then declared that the brain of the gorilla "presented more differences, as compared with the brain of man, than it did when compared with the brains of the very lowest and most problematical of the quadrumana."

Huxley rose, gave Owen's words "a direct and unqualified contradiction," pledged himself to "justify that unusual procedure elsewhere,"[1] and sat down. The effect was as though he had challenged Owen to a duel, and infinitely more dramatic than an immediate refutation, however convincing, would have been, though that duly appeared in the dignified pages of *The Natural History Review*.[3]

Between Darwin and anti-Darwin the lines of battle were now drawn. The program of the Association encouraged peace on Friday, but the air was filled with rumors. A general clerical attack was to be made on Saturday, when a somewhat irrelevant American was to speak on the "Intellectual Development of Europe considered with reference to the views of Mr. Darwin." The Bishop of Oxford was arming in his tent and

THOMAS HENRY HUXLEY IN 1857.

Owen was at his elbow, whispering the secret weaknesses of the enemy. Quite unaware that his larger destiny awaited him in a lecture room next day, Huxley had decided not to witness the onslaught. He was very tired, and eager to rejoin his wife at Reading. He knew that the Bishop was an able controversialist and felt that prevailing sentiment was strongly against the

Darwinians. On Friday evening he met the much reviled evolutionist Robert Chambers in the street, and on remarking that he did not see the good of staying "to be episcopally pounded," was beset with such remonstrances and talk of desertion that he exclaimed, "Oh! if you are going to take it that way, I'll come and have my share of what is going on."[4]

Perhaps revolutions often have their quiet beginnings in the classroom, but they seldom have their turbulent crises there. Saturday, June 30, 1860, was the exception. The Museum Lecture Room proved too small for the crowd, and the meeting was moved to a larger place, into which 700 people were packed. The ladies, in bright summer dresses and with fluttering handkerchiefs, lined the windows. The clergy, "shouting lustily for the Bishop,"[5] occupied the center of the room, and behind them a small group of undergraduates waited to cheer for the little known champions of "the monkey theory." On the platform, among others, sat the American Dr. Draper, the Bishop, Huxley, Hooker, Lubbock, and, as president of the section, Darwin's old teacher Henslow.

Dr. Draper had the compound misfortune to be at once a bore and the center of this exciting debate, having chosen to pick up the burning question of the day by its biggest and hottest handle. His American accent added a quaint remoteness to his metaphysical fulminations. "I can still hear," writes one witness, "the American accents of Dr. Draper's opening address when he asked 'Air we a fortuitous concourse of atoms?' "[6] But had he luxuriated in the combined gifts of Webster and Emerson, he would still have seemed an irrelevance. The audience wanted British personalities, not Yankee ponderosities; and they had already smelled blood.

Dr. Draper droned away for an hour, and then the discussion began. It was evident that the audience had tolerated its last bore. Three men spoke and were shouted down in nine minutes. One had attempted to improve on Darwin with a mathematical demonstration. "Let this point A be man and that point B be the mawnkey."[7] He was promptly overwhelmed with cries of "mawnkey." And now there were loud demands for the Bishop. He courteously deferred to Professor Beale and then, with the utmost good humor, rose to speak.

Bishop Wilberforce, widely known as "Soapy Sam," was one of those men whose moral and intellectual fibers have been permanently loosened by the early success and applause of a distinguished undergraduate career. He had thereafter taken to succeeding at easier and easier tasks, and was now, at fifty-four, a bluff, shallow, good-humored opportunist and a formidable speaker before an undiscriminating crowd. His chief qualification for pronouncing on a scientific subject derived, like nearly everything else that was solid in his career, from the undergraduate remoteness of a first in mathematics.

Huxley listened to the jovial, confident tones of the orator and observed the marked hostility of the audience toward the Darwinians. How could he make an effective reply? He could hardly expound *The Origin of Species*, theory and evidence, in ten minutes. But Huxley was not the man to brood on disadvantages. He was encouraged to find that, though crammed to the teeth by Owen, the Bishop did not really know what he was talking about. Nevertheless, exploiting to the full the popular tendency to regard every novelty as an absurdity, he belabored Darwinism with such resources of obvious wit and sarcasm, saying nothing with so much gusto and ingenuity, that he was clearly taking even sober scientists along with him. Finally, overcome by success, he turned with mock politeness to Huxley and "begged to know, was it through his grandfather or his grandmother that he claimed his descent from a monkey?"[8]

This was fatal. He had opened an avenue to his own vacuity. Huxley slapped his knee and astonished the grave scientist next to him by softly exclaiming, "The Lord hath delivered him into mine hands." The Bishop sat down amid a roar of applause and a sea of fluttering white handkerchiefs. Now there were calls for Huxley, and at the chairman's invitation he rose, a tall, slight, high-shouldered figure in a long black coat and an enormous high collar, which seemed to press the large, close-set features even more tightly together. His face was very pale, his eyes and hair were very black, and his wide lips were calculatingly, defiantly protruded. His manner, gauged with an actor's instinct, was as quiet and grave as the Bishop's had been loud and jovial. He said that he was there only in the interests of science, that he had heard nothing to prejudice his client's case. Mr. Darwin's theory was much more than an hypothesis. It was the best explanation of species yet advanced. He touched on the Bishop's obvious ignorance of the sciences involved; explained, clearly and briefly, Darwin's leading ideas; and then, in tones even more grave and quiet, said that he would not be ashamed to have a monkey for his ancestor; but he would be "ashamed to be connected with a man who used great gifts to obscure the truth."[9]

The sensation was immense. A hostile audience accorded him nearly as much applause as the Bishop had received. One lady, employing an idiom now lost, expressed her sense of intellectual crisis by fainting. The Bishop had suffered a sudden and involuntary martyrdom, perishing in the diverted avalanches of his own blunt ridicule. Huxley had committed forensic murder with a wonderful artistic simplicity, grinding orthodoxy between the facts and the supreme Victorian value of truth-telling.

At length Joseph Hooker rose and botanized briefly on the grave of the Bishop's scientific reputation. Wilberforce did not reply. The meeting adjourned. Huxley was complimented, even by the clergy, with a frankness and fairness that surprised him. Walking back to lodgings with Hooker, he remarked that this experience had changed his opinion "as to the practical value of the art of public speaking," and that from this time forth he would "carefully cultivate it, and try to leave off hating it."[10] Huxley had just enough of the sensitive romantic in him to imagine that he hated public speaking. How he actually felt at the time, he himself indicates in another sentence, "I was careful . . . not to rise to reply till the meeting called for me—then I let myself go."[11]

Huxley's destiny had thus been captured by another man's book, and discovering almost with astonishment how many talents for action he possessed, this young professor of paleontology became the acknowledged champion of science at one of the most dramatic moments in her history. He defended Darwinian evolution because it seemed to constitute, for terrestrial life, a scientific truth as significant and far-reaching as Newton's for the stellar universe—more particularly, because it seemed to promise that human life itself, by learning the laws of its being, might one day become scientifically rational and controlled.

He had no doubt that his victory over the Bishop was one of light over darkness. That scientific freedom might be bought at some cost to the human spirit, that an absurd theory about the origin of the world could be a valuable repository of spiritual energy, that it could somehow be psychologically linked with the soundness of contemporary morals, Huxley was too optimistic to believe. In so far as selfish motives are necessary for goodness, he felt that science could provide far solider and more tangible ones than religion. Of course he was too busy to develop a scientific ethics of his own. His ethics proceeded directly from his controversial position and from the commonplaces of his age. Truth-finding was the greatest glory of the thinker and spiritual leader; truth-telling, his most solemn

obligation. Judged by these standards, the Bishop richly deserved his fate. Huxley had enlisted the Victorian moral
sense against Victorian theology.

Theology usually gave Darwin indigestion. The stories of
these two men are joined not by similarities of taste and character, nor even by continual and intimate transaction. Hooker
and Lyell, far more than Huxley, shared Darwin's research.
Tyndall and Spencer, far more than Darwin, shared Huxley's
warfare in the world. But Darwin and Huxley are united by
joint preeminence in a great tradition. They are also united by
an idea, which one developed and the other defended. Darwin
is the quiet, sedentary cause; Huxley, the brilliant event.
Darwin caused history and Huxley made it.

2

A Scientific Odyssey

In his "Autobiography," Huxley notes with a biologist's interest in heredity that he inherited a quick temper, tenacity, and artistic aptitude from his father, and from his mother, swiftness of apprehension, which he seems to have valued most—and rightly, for, joined with the clarity which he later made a test both for truth and for style, it lies at the very basis of his mind and character.[1] He had the coolness, the sureness, the self-confidence which clarity and swiftness bestow. He was always mobilized for action. He never hesitated, was never less than himself. In fact, he was not so much the patient solver of problems as the prodigious performer—the rapid and voluminous reader, the ready and eloquent speaker, the facile and felicitous writer. He possessed the obvious virtues in nearly as much splendor as Macaulay, and was almost as magnificently adequate to his age. Like Macaulay also, he remained personally modest but gratified his self-esteem by taking his duties and his world very seriously. In fact, he had some of Macaulay's faults, but he had them in less extreme degree. He was less inclined to formularize himself and his goods for mass production. He felt somewhat less, one suspects, the need of having a stream of ready-made thoughts going through his head at all times like a Fourth-of-July parade. He was probably more patient in groping for an idea or in grappling with a problem. He certainly did not retreat from difficult subjects. Metaphysics was one of his natural elements. Here he differed from Macaulay and resembled Voltaire. He had Voltaire's combativeness, his eager curiosity about facts and theories, his heroic but often negative and incredulous common sense, which sometimes closes the mind to large and daring conceptions.

At any rate, the obvious virtues turned his youth into a rather obvious Victorian success story. He was born in 1825 at Ealing near London, and went to Ealing School, of which his father was an assistant master. But the school had fallen on evil days, and he gained little from it but a practical demonstration of the struggle for survival and a post-bellum friendship with a boy who turned up years after as a transported convict in Australia. When he was ten years old, the family moved to Coventry, where his father became manager of a small bank. After that time Tom had very little formal schooling.

But he went to church. The warfare between Huxley and religion was essentially fratricidal, for he was a born preacher and sermonized from nearly every platform but the pulpit. As a little boy he greatly admired the local rector, and once, turning his pinafore around backwards to represent a surplice, he delivered a sermon in the manner of his hero to the maids in the kitchen.[2] Somewhat later, sitting in church, he heard dark horror-stricken allusions to skeptics and infidels. At eleven or twelve he began insensibly to move still farther from orthodoxy by plunging into that course of amazingly rapid desultory reading, which, growing always more intensive and systematic and continuing throughout life, made him one of the most learned of Victorians. "Not satisfied with the ordinary length of the day, he used . . . to light his candle before dawn, pin a blanket round his shoulders, and sit up in bed to read Hutton's Geology."[3] He had a boy's eye for big titles and big subjects, from Guizot's History of Civilization in Europe to Sir William Hamilton's "Philosophy of the Unconditioned"; nor was his eye bigger than his stomach. He now noticed that village parsons frequently used bad grammar and used it to little purpose but to express ignorance of nearly everything except the Bible. He also began to resent long sermons—so fiercely that in later life he could hardly see a surplice without wanting to snub the reverend gentleman inside of it.

It was Hamilton's article on the "Unconditioned," which he found in an old volume of The Edinburgh, that finally explained everything. Employing the skeptical intellect, Sir William ponderously undermined all conditioned and finite knowledge in order to establish the Scottish Kirk, by intuition, in the sublimity of the unconditioned and the infinite.[4] Huxley abandoned the Kirk and embraced the skepticism. By the age of fifteen, he saw, probably with some secret misgivings, that he was himself very close to being a skeptic and an infidel, and merited the horror-stricken tones of the preacher. But the preacher had left an indelible mark. In all but doctrine, Huxley remained a staunch Victorian Christian throughout his life. He was as morally earnest, as devoted to practical virtue, as suspicious of elaborate theological dogma as the most pious evangelical. He felt justified by the grace and sanctity of scientific method and doubted with the deep and passionate sincerity of conviction.

At thirteen or fourteen, he had suffered a more lurid illumination. Two of his elder sisters had married physicians, and he had been thrown a good deal with medical students. Having through his reading acquired a knowledge of the human body, he went with some of his new friends to a post-mortem examination, which probably took place in a typical close, dark, village dissecting room of the period. Mr. Huston Peterson recreates the scene:

He suddenly finds himself in the presence of a naked human corpse. He is almost stifled by the mortuary & medicinal odors. He shudders inwardly as he sees the first large incision made in the torso. He sees exposed the lungs and heart, the stomach and bowels. The knives work quickly, cruelly. The dissectors are casual and matter of fact about their business. Now a serious remark, now a little joke. And young Huxley stands there—not for a few minutes—but for two or three hours, gratifying his scientific and morbid curiosity.[5]

Immediately afterward he sank into "a strange state of apathy," which seemed so serious that his father sent him away to friends in Warwickshire. There he soon recovered, but for the rest of his life suffered from "internal pain" and "hypochondriacal dyspepsia." Though he had exhibited no physical symptoms, he always believed that he had been "poisoned somehow." No doubt he had suffered a severe mental shock. Still believing in God and immortality, he had suddenly been confronted, at the sensitive period of adolescence, with a bloody and nauseating spectacle of physical death. Apparently, he had identified himself with the corpse. Recovery was a return to life.

I remember staggering from my bed to the window on the bright spring morning after my arrival, and throwing open the casement. Life seemed to come back on the wings of the breeze, and to this day the faint odour of woodsmoke, like that which floated across the farm-yard in the early morning, is as good to me as the "sweet south upon a bed of violets."[6]

Mr. Peterson maintains that as Huxley's later outbursts of temper and virtuous indignation were probably produced by the nervous strain of a strenuous sense of duty, so his aggressiveness was the result of a fear neurosis springing from his early encounter with a human corpse. Whether due to this or other causes, there is an undertone of anxiety in his many expressions of courage or trust in the face of the unknown. Perhaps he distracted himself by pommeling bishops. Perhaps he wanted to make bishops and archdeacons face the gruesome fact he had faced. Like Marx, he regarded religion as an opiate.

But of course Huxley's whole career cannot be derived from a single experience. In an age morbidly preoccupied with belief in personal immortality, he found himself imprisoned in a universe of uncertainty and death. He felt loss of faith more deeply than many have supposed. As late as 1847, in the first year of his long cruise on the *Rattlesnake*, he wrote: "*Ich kann nichts anders! Gott hilfe mir!* Morals and religion are one wild whirl to me—of them the less said the better. In the region of the intellect alone can I find free and innocent play for such faculties as I possess." And in 1849 he adds, beside the same entry: "Is it better with me now? A little."[7]

But his religious problem never came to an acute crisis. He found a substitute for religion in Carlyle, from whom he also gained, as he acknowledged, sympathy for the poor, hatred of shams, devotion to work, and the impetus to study German language and literature.[8]

Probably Carlyle also awakened the young man's literary sense. That he did not turn so fine a talent permanently to literature, is not surprising. Huxley was too little attracted to the characteristic subject matter of the writer. He became interested in man as a physical mechanism, as an anthropoid ape, as a social unit and a citizen, as a delicate machine for the discovery of scientific truth, but never to any appreciable extent in man as a personality and a human being. With all his splendid talents for friendship and affection, he remained, from the psychological point of view, largely indifferent to people. He was not even interested in himself. Seldom has so vivid and articulate a writer had so little of importance to say, even in his most intimate letters, about himself. It is the absence of human knowledge that gives his prose, with all its verve and humor, an arid, antiseptic quality. For him, writing was an instrument, never an end. It meant the art of clarity, of controversy, which he cultivated for the purposes of the scientist and the philosopher.

Huxley wanted as a boy to be a mechanical engineer, but no opportunity for training appeared. On the other hand, he did receive some instruction in medicine from his brother-in-law Dr. Cooke, and when in 1841 his parents moved to Rotherhithe, in east London, he was apprenticed to a Dr. Chandler, who served a parish in the dock region. Here for the first time he crossed the frontier of middle-class life and came to know the great Victorian wilderness of metropolitan poverty, about which he had read in Carlyle. The spectacle itself was even more eloquent. Huxley was not haunted by it, but he never forgot it.

At first he did not like medicine and comforted himself with voluminous reading on all subjects, from chemistry to ancient history. A natural linguist, he was constantly improving his knowledge of French, German, and Italian. After a year with Dr. Chandler, he was apprenticed to his brother-in-law Dr. Scott, at whose house in northern London he went to live. There, under the care of his favorite sister Elizabeth, he grew more interested in medicine.

One day, having as usual threaded through the narrow alleys of the London jungle to the library of the College of Surgeons, he saw the notice of a public competition for medals in botany. It seemed ridiculous to enter his name, for the other competitors were older and university-trained. Yet he looked longingly at the notice, and someone asked, "Why don't you try for it?"[9] He did. Soon he found himself studying from nine in the morning till midnight, often till sunrise. At last, the day of examination came. There was a nine-hour fever of writing, a longer, more terrible fever of waiting. Then the whole family was astonished. Tom had won second prize—a silver medal. His later career was paved with gold medals, but none ever shone so brightly as this silver one.*

Soon after this time Tom won a scholarship for Charing Cross Hospital. Here again he drifted into the boyish pursuit of universal knowledge, but was soon rescued by his professor of anatomy, who not only captured his imagination but gave a permanent direction to his life. This heroic individual was a pale, dry-looking little man, who lectured "with downcast eyes, and fingering his watch chain."[10] What he said was cold, lucid, logical, and severely exact, indicating a great and precise knowledge. "Quite to my taste," wrote Huxley.[11] From Wharton Jones he learned exact scientific method in the search for truth, which he pursued with so much zeal that his window, framing an inevitable silhouette, became known among students as The Sign of the Head and Microscope. Thus wooed, truth finally appeared. At the age of nineteen Tom made an original discovery, and in a first contribution to the *Medical Gazette*, reported the existence of a membrane in the root of the human hair which is still known as "Huxley's Layer." It is curious that Jones had to correct numerous errors in composition, as Huxley "detested the trouble of writing, and would take no pains over it."[12]

After three years at Charing Cross Hospital, Huxley passed his M.B. examination with a gold medal in anatomy and physiology. Still too young for the College of Surgeons, he took

---

* The prolonged study preceding this examination brought about "a sort of ophthalmia" (*Life and Letters of Huxley*, I, 19), which prevented him from reading at night for months afterward. Dr. George M. Gould believes that Huxley's later headaches, dyspepsia, and depression are traceable to eyestrain produced by a lifelong habit of intensive reading coupled with astigmatism and anismetropia. According to Dr. Gould, vision remained normal; and the strain upon the eyes was transferred,

service in the Navy, and was soon appointed assistant surgeon to the *Rattlesnake*. In 1847 this twenty-six gun frigate was ordered to chart the waters of northeastern Australia, a region then totally unknown to science and all but unknown to exploration of any kind. Huxley's medical duties were to occupy only a small part of his time. By far the greater part was to be employed in such scientific work as he thought important. Wharton Jones had provided him with a method. The Navy had provided him, under Spartan conditions, with infinite leisure and an inexhaustible museum.

The nineteenth century was of course the heroic age for voyages of scientific discovery, as the Renaissance had been for those of geographic. Equipped not with diving bells, helicopters, and floating laboratories but chiefly with a simple mariner's compass of scientific conscience and common sense, a series of great men—Humboldt, Darwin, Hooker, Huxley, Wallace, and Haeckel—had embarked on seas of ripe and boundless possibility, where every ability and strength won a fabulous reward. Each man was weighed, quite accurately perhaps, by infinite opportunity. Each brought back a famous store; and one—Darwin—high on a peak in theoretical Darien, had glimpsed with industrious and somewhat prosaic excitement his own particular Pacific. Of these sedate and meditative *conquistadores*, Huxley was by no means least—a very young man setting out in search not only of truth, but of the world and of his own life. He found a wife, uncovered nearly all his talents—including that for literature—and almost discovered himself.

---

through Nature's "perfect wisdom," to organs less vitally important to the human machine (*Biographic Clinics: The Origin of the Ill-health of DeQuincey, Carlyle, Darwin, Huxley, and Browning* [Philadelphia: P. Blakiston's Son & Company, 1903], p. 119). This theory may have some truth, but eyestrain would seem an aggravation rather than the primary cause of Huxley's ills.

For this famous voyage and intricate surveying mission, the Royal Navy had provided a distinguished crew and an antiquated vessel. Young Captain Owen Stanley, the son of a bishop and brother of the famous dean, was kindly, energetic, conscientious, idealistic, and full of ambition to be a great savant and a great explorer. He was backed by a large staff of surveyors, magneticians, and other experts, including the naturalist Macgillivray, an avid if unenlightened collector with a flair for primitive languages. But no doubt in its wisdom the Royal Navy had decided that too much shining equipment belittles and depersonalizes heroes. A complement of 180 men were therefore crowded into a slow, clumsy wooden sailing vessel of the type known to the service as a "donkey frigate." There was an almost complete lack of scientific instruments for biological research and when, at Huxley's suggestion, Captain Stanley requested one hundred pounds' worth of reference books, the response was a persistent and dignified silence.

Huxley was shocked at the crowded, stuffy, smelly wooden world in which he found himself. His first impression of the ship's company, however it bristled with technicians, was that he had never seen so many stupid, ignorant fellows in his life. Because of bad refitting, the lower deck of the Rattlesnake was under water throughout the voyage. Huxley's most modern reference work was Buffon's Suites; his laboratory was a small corner of the chartroom; his bedroom, storeroom, and library was a cabin not much larger than one of Louis XI's torture cages; he could never stand upright in it and he could scarcely turn around. Most disturbing of all, he was treated by "regular officers" as a crank unworthy of serious consideration. If he left specimens lying on the deck for an hour or two, he was only too likely on his return to find them swept away as an offense to nautical neatness. But at least he had a cabin to himself. At least the ocean was roomy and the air bracing.

Madeira, Rio, and Mauritius were beautiful. Captain Stanley was helpful and sympathetic. Huxley began to reproach himself with injustice. The crew were fine fellows after all. He even liked some of the officers.

According to the elaborate plan which he had drawn up, Huxley was to dissect mollusks and Radiata, study the coral animal, search for Epizoa on the eyes and gills of fish, and at the suggestion of Professor Owen, collect as many fish brains as possible. Actually, he never collected anything. Unlike Darwin, he lacked the patience and the acquisitive instinct to be a good collector. Nor did he have Darwin's catholic eagerness in observation. He had to be piqued and aroused by particular problems, and inevitably these lay in the range of his medical preparation. He therefore carried out only the anatomical studies on his program, being guided by his impulse for clarity and his "engineer's instinct for . . . the essence of construction."[13]

One of Huxley's principal achievements on the voyage out was to bring some order out of the chaos of invertebrate zoology—and particularly of the mollusks, coelenterates, and tunicates. Most of these were tiny, fantastic creatures stalking and eluding each other under the concealment of transparency in the brilliant light of the ocean surface. Their transparency made them admirable subjects for a scientist without delicate instruments: they could often be studied without being dissected or cut into sections. A notable triumph was the classification of Appendicularius, a minute and ingenious animal that manufactures gelatinous houses in which to trap microscopic plants. Its translucent secret of identity had defied even the discerning eye of the great Johannes Müller. Huxley gave sound reasons for locating it among the tunicates, a branch of which was later proved in startling fashion to be related, far back in its long past, to the vertebrates. But in those pre-Darwinian days organisms had, from the structural point of view, neither past nor future. Huxley's method was peculiarly congenial to the clear, platonic kind of intellect: he tried to get behind particular adaptations to a generalized structure or "archetype" which would be basic, and therefore critical, for all actual species of a class. That the archetype is but the static conception of an evolutionary prototype—in short, of Darwin's idea of a common ancestor—need not be explained.

These discoveries were made on shipboard. In Sydney Huxley discovered quite incidentally, parties, dancing, and young ladies. More particularly, he discovered Miss Henrietta Heathorn, the sister-in-law of Mr. Fanning, a leading merchant of the city. He loved her almost at first sight with that decision and strength of mind which is so admirable in the Victorians. Miss Heathorn was a person of equal decision, and she needed to be, for they were engaged seven years. Of course they would have waited forever—and in their case loyalty to love was but loyalty to reason, for they were ideally suited—alike in much and different only that need might find and admire strength. Both were intelligent, efficient, and well educated. Both loved nature, art, and literature. Henrietta had even gone to school in Germany, spoke his favorite German, and knew his beloved German authors. He never could decide whether she was beautiful, but suspected, quite happily, that she was not. Much better, she was small, very fair, pale, and fragile-looking in order that he might be tall, dark, strong, and tenderly protective. He was ambitious, moody, sometimes despondent in order that she might be constant, encouraging, and sympathetically understanding. She was delicate, inexperienced, and a little naïve and sentimental in order that he might be wise, superbly capable, and sternly realistic. In short, consciously or unconsciously, they had fallen in love as sensibly as Jane Austen herself might have wished.

Theirs was a romance only possible in an age when etiquette

was awful and camellias and handkerchiefs were eloquent. Henrietta remembered every bit of it and as a very old lady wrote down some of the best parts as freshly as a girl might confide them to her diary on the day they happened. She and Tom had met toward the end of a dancing party. He promptly asked for a dance, but her brother-in-law felt obliged to intervene. Netty's sister and chaperone had already gone for her wrap. "Never mind said Mr. Huxley, we shall meet again & then remember you are engaged for the 1st dance."[14] They did meet and Tom had his dance. From that time forth, whenever he entered the ballroom, she would think, "There is that wonderful doctor!"

"What an evening of glamour it was," the old lady wrote of another party. "Before I left he begged of me the red camellia I wore—which after my darling died I found preserved among his papers! labelled The First."[15] But romance is savorless without adversity. As a climax to all the festivities surrounding the visit of the H.M.S. *Rattlesnake*, there was to be a great party given by the ship's company itself—a picnic on an island in the afternoon and dancing on board in the evening. At last the incredible event materialized, but the wonderful doctor did not. "Everyone said they had had a lovely time," wrote the old lady, "but I—my heart was sick and weary of it all. I began to think that all that had gone before was my imagination, or that it was just a sailor's way."

The next day, from her bedroom at her sister's house—just as she finished dressing and the lunch bell sounded—she heard the clatter of a horse in the drive! Could it be he?—Her hair! Her dress! Luncheon was over when she finally brought her toilette to perfection and came downstairs. There were seven people in the drawing room, and miraculously, Dr. Huxley was one. Then Dr. Huxley eliminated four of the unnecessary six: he would accompany Henrietta and two other girls on an expedition to a nearby farm. Then he eliminated the two girls.

As he hadn't "3 arms to offer us, and it would be invidious to offer one . . . to two of us, leaving out the 3rd young lady," he offered only one, and invited Henrietta to take it. During the walk she slipped on a loose branch. He removed it, saying, "So would I remove all hindrances from your path in life." "His eyes had an extraordinary way," she noted, "of flashing under strong emotion, when they seemed to be burning." He even managed to explain his absence from the picnic. He had been ordered to accompany an excursion party which could not return in time.

The situation now seemed quite simple and cheerful to Huxley. They were engaged. Soon he would make his fortune and they would be married. "I tell Netty," he wrote his sister, "to look to being a 'Frau Professorin' one of these odd days, and she has faith, as I believe would have if I told her I was going to be Prime Minister."[16] Perhaps he would have been surprised to know some of the thoughts that were passing through his Netty's mind—in part just because he was so mesmerically determined and confident. Deeply as she loved and trusted him, she had moments of fear and hesitation in allowing herself to be absorbed in so masterful and compelling a personality. "You draw out my thoughts and feelings—and appropriate them most tyrannically," she wrote him later, "and yet 'tis perhaps one of the things which has bound me with stronger love to you. You are a tyrant still conquering by strength where influence fails."[17] Moreover, her faith in the *Frau Professorin* was by no means so implicit as he imagined. She was far from seeing the infinite practical wisdom of writing essays about jellyfish and salps. "I had only the dimmest idea . . . of how a description of a marine creature should win for him fame, or help in any way, to bring about his obtaining a position that would enable us to marry."[18]

And then, after three months in Sydney, the *Rattlesnake* sailed north to perform its mission, which was to chart the

inshore waters of the Great Barrier Reef and find a passage
through the Torres Straits to India—in short, to trace with
a clumsy wooden sailing vessel and a tender the vast labyrinths,
visible and submerged, of the Coral Sea. It was a little like
trying, blindfold, to pass a camel through the eyes of a great
many needles, with death the penalty for a single blunder: a
trial by danger and by tedium.

Sometimes a small boat put off to explore a bay or an inlet—
and disappeared for days. Sometimes a few men landed and
traveled inland, as did Huxley and the ship's naturalist Macgillivray on bleak Facing Island. Such excursions were long
disciplines of unceasing watchfulness, though on Facing no
savages appeared. But mostly, the Rattlesnake sailed mo-
notonously to and fro beneath a bright, hot sky or hovered,
tantalizingly and without ever putting a boat out, off an inscrutable, dark-jungled shore "always mute," as Conrad says,
"with an air of whispering, Come and find out."*

But on this cruise Huxley had no time to stare nostalgically
at seacoasts. He had become interested in jellyfish, and the
coastal waters of eastern Australia were brilliant with these
creatures. It was a unique opportunity, for the more delicate
specimens were unfit for examination after a few hours and a
constant fresh supply was essential. Huxley now did the work
for his most famous paper of the Rattlesnake voyage—"On
the Anatomy and the Affinities of the Family of the Medusae."
Here he shows that the Medusae, or jellyfish, are related not
to other Radiates like the starfish or sea urchins, but to extremely dissimilar groups like the polyps and siphonophores,
being formed of two fundamental membranes, an outer and
an inner. At the end of his article, almost casually, he observes
that the archetype Medusa is constructed on the same plan
as the embryo chick. In those days a biologist could hardly

* "The Heart of Darkness."

make a discovery without staring evolution in the face. But Huxley was still thinking about nineteenth-century facts with eighteenth-century ideas.

After some three months at sea, the *Rattlesnake* returned to Sydney. Tom stayed with the Fannings, under the same roof with his Netty. Even so, he managed to finish his paper on the Medusae, which Captain Stanley then forwarded to the Royal Society.

The *Rattlesnake* was nine months on its second cruise northward, surveying the Inner Passage as far as New Guinea and the Louisiades. It then convoyed the bark *Tam o' Shanter* to Rockingham Bay, where the smaller vessel landed thirteen men to explore northeastern Australia as far as Cape Yorke. The leader of the expedition, Edmund Kennedy, had become friendly with Huxley and had invited him to come along. He would certainly have done so, had the rules of the service permitted. At the time appointed for picking up the explorers once more the *Rattlesnake*'s tender, the *Bramble*, was sent ahead to exchange signals with Kennedy. No signals were observed. The *Bramble* waited ten days, then proceeded with the *Rattlesnake* to Cape Yorke. Again no news of Kennedy. His fate was not known until the *Rattlesnake*'s fourth visit to Sydney. The expedition had been a nightmare journey through nearly impassable bush. Rations had run short and the men had sickened one after another. Kennedy had pushed forward with three, then only with his faithful black, Jackie. Actually in sight of the vessel that was waiting for them, he was speared to death by natives, and Jackie barely escaped. Of twelve whites, only two were eventually rescued. Naval regulations—Huxley's own private fate in those days—had for once proved beneficent.

The third cruise northward took Huxley into the heart of the Coral Sea. Here was an unparalleled opportunity to study the coral animal, which he had listed prominently in his program of research. Here were green-jungled islands, ringed round with white surf, beckoning silently on every hand—with their strange life, their primitive peoples and cultures to be observed. Yet time and again he remained in his cabin, complaining of the heat and refusing to go ashore. Sometimes he wished he could sleep the whole voyage out and sometimes he felt "like a tiger fresh caught and put into a cage."[19]

Quite clearly, he had sunk into a prolonged depression. Throughout his life he seems to have been subject to manic alternations of furious hard work and lethargic despondency. In the present instance, he had just spent a month or more in Sydney, where he had labored hard on his Medusae paper and had the constant excitement of living in the same house with Netty. Now, in separation and loneliness, the reaction had set in. Soon he was to leave Netty perhaps for several years. He had asked her to marry him, but when would he be in a position to marry? He had heard nothing of the scientific papers he had sent back to England. Were they utterly negligible? Was a scientific career beyond the reach of his abilities? Back there was the great world—the big, really important world of London—waiting to be conquered not only for his own practical satisfaction but for the benefit and admiration of a wonderful earnest-eyed, yellow-haired girl; and here he was trapped in an irrelevant abyss of hot sunshine and steamy ocean.

A sense of responsibility and of frustration had at once sharpened ambition and awakened self-doubt. He longed to prove himself and at the same time half feared the contest. Naturally, he thought a good deal about the vanity of human ambition. After a moonlight revery on the ship's deck, he wrote:

That great sea is Time and the little waves are the changes and the chances of life. The ship's side is Trouble, and it is only by meeting with this that the little creatures in the water shine and grow bright. They are men. If it were calm they would not be bright. See, there is a big one; he shines like a fiery glove. He is some great conqueror. He keeps on shining for full a minute—that is Fame—and then gives place to darkness like the rest. Oh brave! who would not be great.[20]

Scientific work reminded him of the oblivion into which his papers had fallen. He therefore escaped into literature, improving his Italian and reading *The Divine Comedy*.

An ocean voyage transpires in a microcosm and a macrocosm, in the narrow ship and the wide world; and often the first becomes a good deal stranger than the second. Up till now Huxley had been chiefly occupied with the macrocosm. The microcosm had been simply an annoyance. But now the annoyance mounted sufficiently to elicit some vivid descriptions:

I wonder if it is possible for the mind of man to conceive anything more degradingly offensive than the condition of us 150 men, shut up in this wooden box, being watered with hot water, as we are now. . . . The lower and main decks are completely unventilated: a sort of solution of man in steam fills them from end to end, and surrounds the lights with a lurid halo. It's too hot to sleep, and my sole amusement consists in watching the cockroaches, which are in a state of intense excitement and happiness.[21]

That ships are fantastic little despotisms floating in a void, that men dissolved in steam and the acid of each other's eccentricities become stranger and stranger, that they reveal this strangeness more and more, opening up long vistas of complex and bristling individuality to curious analysis—Huxley began to see vividly, in the long and painful ruminations of his third cruise. But he saw the fact without seeing into it, developing sensitiveness without insight. Of course he never did need to understand people. He led and managed them. When himself, he felt and was so strong that he had no motive to brood enviously and analytically about the strength of others; and, though at this time still very young and sorely perplexed, he was obviously admired by all the most admirable men on the boat.

Returning to Sydney and seeing Netty evaporated much of Huxley's low spirits. The last cruise northward did the rest. As subjects of study, he abandoned the jellyfish for man. Most of his encounters with the natives were tense, dangerous, rather opaque little farces. Once a fine-looking young fellow received a hatchet for a pile of yams and was so delighted that he seized Huxley and waltzed him a quarter of a mile down the beach. Huxley guided the waltz toward the village, so that he could examine the huts. On another occasion, a fat sailor, suddenly finding himself surrounded by savages, succeeded in diverting them only by giving away all his clothes and then by doing an impromptu dance in the broiling sun until help came.

But Huxley owed his most informative experience, in part at least, to Macgillivray's knowledge of primitive languages and ideas. Australian natives believed that white men were reincarnated ghosts of the dead. During an extended stay which he and Huxley made among the friendly inhabitants of Mount Ernest Island, Macgillivray convinced an old man, Paouda, that he was the ghost of the latter's recently deceased father-in-law. Paouda then became very open and hospitable. Macgillivray now pleaded pathetically to see his daughter and grandchildren, for the women of the island had been hidden away. The old man, after many pledges of secrecy, finally took the two white men to the family who received them with a mixture of awe and affection. Forty years later, in his campaign against demonology and animism in the Bible, Huxley told of this lesson in human credulity at length.[22]

His diary of the voyage contains no systematic account of native life. He lacked the training to write such an account. He knew no native languages. The standardized methods by which skin color is gauged and skulls are measured had not yet been established. He was trying to be an anthropologist before anthropology had really been invented. What he could do, he did diligently and well, narrating incidents, describing people, dwellings, canoes, and implements, and illustrating with the vivid drawings for which he had an extraordinary talent. His schematic sketch of an outrigger canoe is a model of descriptive draughtsmanship. Beyond this, Huxley's anthropology suffered from the same want of human insight which was later, though in lesser degree, to characterize his social and political criticism, and one is tempted to think that savages aroused his sense of humor more than his impulse to understand. But such a judgment is unfair. If he did not take them quite seriously, if like many Victorians he thought of them as children, at least he regarded them steadfastly as human beings. Against the occasional violence and impulsiveness of the Papuans must be set "their invariable gentleness towards each other; the kind treatment of their women; the cleanliness of their persons and of their dwellings; their progress in the useful arts; . . . [and] the perseverance and grace of design displayed in many of their carved works."[23]

On the fourth cruise, the great island-continent of New Guinea, "shut out," as Huxley wrote, "from intercourse with the civilized world, more completely than China, and as rich if not richer in things rare and strange," unfolded its green, mist-shrouded coasts before them.[24] And one day the men of the Rattlesnake saw the low mists and thick clouds suddenly roll away and beheld with astonishment the lofty blue mountain range which, till then unknown to white men, thereafter bore their captain's name. But Owen Stanley himself, though equally exalted and still consumed with ambition to be a great explorer, remained securely on his ship or went through timid and tentative motions of exploration. He felt too responsible to let his men run avoidable risks, and he was too humanitarian to let natives be shot at even in self-defense.

As a matter of fact, his world had turned to glass at the very moment when he was preparing to discover it. Three years of guiding his fragile, populous little wooden kingdom through the steamy waters and sharp labyrinths of the Coral Sea had changed an ambitious, idealistic young commander into a fearful, snarling, boasting, scruple-ridden neurotic. The whole atmosphere of the ship altered, and the study of the captain's character became the absorbing preoccupation of the crew. Huxley's solution at the time was simple. "Funk," he pronounced, after another instance of extreme caution with the natives. "What does the man want? I suppose nothing would satisfy him of the security of his little body but seeing all the bows and arrows in the boat and all the men bound on the beach."[25]

The crisis came when the *Rattlesnake* once more turned southward toward Sydney. The captain suffered a complete prostration. Even in convalescence his mind was uncertain, and he dreamed and talked continually of great fame as a scientific explorer. He had to put himself in Dr. Thomson's charge and Lieutenant Yule took command of the ship. In March, 1850, one month after his arrival in Sydney, the captain died. He had not scaled the summits of the Owen Stanley range, but at least he had done his surveying job: he had discovered a broad deep passage through the Coral Sea and the Torres Strait.

When at last the fourth cruise was over, Huxley made a final entry in his diary:

Could the history of the soul be written for that time [the voyage] it would be fuller of change and struggle than that of the outward man, but who shall write it? I, the only possible historian, am too much implicated....

I have besides no talent for writing on any such subject.... I am not of a 'subjective' disposition and unless I have some tangible object for my thoughts they all go woolgathering.[26]

He had discovered himself as little as Stanley had discovered the rivers of New Guinea. He had contemplated the broad reaches of the obvious, but failed to move upstream.

Late in the evening of May 7, 1849, Netty Heathorn made an entry in her journal:

This morning I woke to sorrow. Scarcely could I believe in dear Hal's departure yet the bitter parting of the previous night was too vivid to let me doubt about it. So much did I struggle to suppress my grief that when he was gone I almost feared my parting had not evinced sufficient feeling, but . . . after he had gone . . . it burst forth in all the vehemence of despair—such anguish inexpressible convulsed me. . . .

Still his last dear words murmured in my ear—'God help you Menen dear.' I felt his arm round me as he patted poor Snap and bade me pet him for his sake—his last dear kiss ere he sprang upon his horse and was (oh how soon) out of sight.[27]

3

A Prophet in His Own Country

Huxley came home nerved to rational patience. He expected no more than a brilliant and moderately remunerative success in a moderately short period of time. The project began well. The two papers he had sent home from the *Rattlesnake* had both been published and already won considerable recognition, particularly from Edward Forbes, professor at the Government School of Mines, a genial and talented geologist with a romantic weakness for assuming lost continents to explain peculiarities of plant and animal distribution. On the recommendation of Forbes and Sir Richard Owen, Huxley was granted six months' leave by the Royal Navy with the possibility of another six months thereafter. But though Huxley was rationally moderate, the Royal Navy was only moderately rational. It was willing to donate Huxley's time, but, despite its declared policy, not its own money, for the publication of the remaining material he had gathered on the cruise of the *Rattlesnake*. Eminent men interceded with eminent men, even within the ministry itself, but to no avail. That inscrutable abstraction, the Royal Navy, was adamant, either in neglect or hostility.

And now his rational expectations suffered another blow.

One could be paid for classical knowledge but, only in rare instances, for scientific knowledge. The classics were necessary to the cultivation of gentlemen and the manufacture of clerics, but science was essential only to a few rather vulgar and utilitarian professions. Therefore it remained in large degree, like cricket and football, the pursuit of amateurs, of whom Sir Charles Lyell was the most famous.

There is [Huxley writes his sister] no chance of living by science. I have been loth to believe it, but it is so. There are not more than four or five offices in London which a Zoologist or a Comparative Anatomist can hold and live by. Owen, who has a European reputation, second only to that of Cuvier, gets as Hunterian Professor £300 a year! which is less than the salary of many a bank clerk.[1]

To reform his own position, Huxley needed almost to reform English intellectual life. Eventually he did both, but at the moment he could do little more than fret and complain. He was beginning to feel imposed upon.

Meanwhile honors appeared with ironical swiftness. Before he was quite twenty-six he was elected a Fellow of the Royal Society and a year later was awarded the Royal Medal, over the heads of many far older men who had done a greater quantity of work. Best of all, he was received at once into the most distinguished scientific society in England, dining with men like Lyell and Owen and discovering with refreshing surprise that Sir Richard was human enough to smoke his cigar and sing his song "like a brick."[2]

"I take all these things quite as a matter of course," he says, "but am all the while considerably astonished."[3] He was immensely, delightfully astonished. At twenty-six he could not have been otherwise, with all his rational expectations. When Forbes told him that he was "all right for the Royal Society," Huxley "spoke and looked as cool as a cucumber," but afterward he "wandered hither and thither restlessly half over

London."[4] What a sense of power—to keep the tightest grip on himself in the midst of so much exhilarating recognition!

Having plunged into the struggle, he had a moment of youthful revulsion, which took the form of extravagant idealism and considerable misconception of his own nature. He was burning with ambition, yet he wrote his sister, "The worst of it is I have no ambition. . . . A worker I must always be . . . but if I had £400 a year I would never let my name appear to anything I did."[5] He loved the personality of conflict and the excitement of crowds, yet he aspired "to be a voice working in secret and free from all those personal motives which have actuated the best."[6] "The real pleasure, the true sphere, lies in the feeling of self-development—in the sense of power and growing oneness with the great spirit of abstract truth."[7] He asserted with suspicious iteration that his only care was to leave his mark "free from the abominable blur of cant, humbug, and self-seeking," and denied passionately that he had obtained his membership in the Royal Society by intrigue. To be sure, he announced elsewhere with genial frankness that he was going to a meeting of the British Association "to do a little necessary trumpeting."[8] Huxley was of course neither an intriguer nor a hypocrite. His moral aspiration was very genuine. If he trumpeted judiciously for himself, he was later to trumpet heroically for Darwin. He advanced himself almost by instinct but served the ideal by conscious choice.

At the Ipswich meeting of the British Association in 1851, Huxley met some of the gifted young scientists of his own generation—notably Hooker and Tyndall. Belonging to the inner circle of England's scientific families, Joseph Dalton Hooker was born with botanist's drying papers in his mouth and a small volume of Linnaeus in his hand. His life was a brilliant foregone conclusion. He diligently performed the lessons set before him by his father Sir William and others, voyaged adventurously to the Antarctic and later to the

Himalayas, accumulated specimens, grew learned and shrewd, remained plodding and somewhat unimaginative—and at thirty-two discovered without much astonishment that he was one of the ablest botanists in England. His one extravagance was a hot temper; his one indulgence, a tendency to reprehend the same fault in his new friend.

Tyndall was of atmosphere all compact, having devoted much of his life to studying it scientifically and to describing it poetically. He was Huxley rarefied and intensified, Huxley without the solidity and the mass. He was at once more fanciful and more logical, more impulsive and more restrained. He had all of an Irishman's generosity with all of an Irishman's jealous insistence on his rights. He took himself very seriously and, for humor, was capable only of a boisterous and farcical playfulness. His courage, both moral and physical, was rash and quixotic. His loyalty was absolute, being coupled with an almost feminine intensity of devotion and gentleness of manner which made him the life-long friend of men so unlike as Carlyle and Faraday. His admiration of Carlyle had led him not only to read the Germans, but to study among them, at Marburg and Berlin, where he had already made discoveries in magnetism and radiant heat. If Huxley became the statesman of nineteenth-century science, Tyndall became its knight-errant. His popular writing was in a sense even clearer and simpler than Huxley's but narrower and slighter, often evaporating into diluted Wordsworthian nature rhapsody. That the two should become close friends was almost inevitable.

Huxley formed another memorable friendship at this time—that with Herbert Spencer, then subeditor of the London *Economist* and one of the most remarkable men ever to write a dozen volumes of philosophy. Trained by his father from infancy to find causes for everything, he soon found cause for being a delightful eccentric, a confirmed bachelor, and a relentless theorizer about everything that came under his lynx-eyed mental vision. His massive *Autobiography*—one of those books that is very amusing in retrospect, like a bore from whom one has escaped—demonstrates that he took himself quite as seriously as he took the universe, and could explain himself as exhaustively and polysyllabically. Largely self-educated despite the desperate efforts of a pedagogical uncle and a pedagogical father to interfere, Spencer had learned much science and no Greek; invented, successfully and unsuccessfully, a great number of gadgets, from railroad speedometers to wire-drawn flying machines; embarked on several careers, from teaching school to constructing bridges; and was now gradually settling down to the comfortable and sedentary destiny of explaining everything.

He had discovered his capacities and his tastes by a calm and almost encyclopedic process of elimination. He had tried the opera several times, but was profoundly disturbed by the irrationality of people singing duets and trios while going about the business of the plot. He had tried vegetarianism and desisted for the singular reason that it took the vigor out of his style. One day George Eliot said to him that considering how much thinking he did, she was surprised to see no lines in his forehead. "I suppose it is because I am never puzzled," replied Spencer.[9] He had the faculty of automatic induction. In his *Autobiography* he explains that facts accumulated in his mind until they had arranged themselves neatly into a generalization. There it was, ready-made. Obviously, such a man would be a fool not to explain the universe.

At the 1852 meeting of the British Association, Spencer heard Huxley's paper on oceanic *Hydrozoa*, and having thereafter used some of the facts in his equally brilliant "Theory of Population deduced from the General Law of Animal Fertility," presented Huxley with a copy. The two young men were impressed with each other.

Spencer's article on "Population" was even more significant

than Huxley realized. It expounded a theory of social evolution based on something very close to natural selection. "From the beginning," wrote Spencer, "pressure of population has been the proximate cause of progress."[10] And again:

For those prematurely carried off must, in the average of cases, be those in whom the power of self-preservation is the least, it unavoidably follows, that those left behind to continue the race, are those in whom the power of self-preservation is the greatest—are the select of their generation.[11]

In *The Leader* for the same year, Spencer had published "The Development Hypothesis," in which he had subscribed to biological evolution according to Lamarck's hypothesis. He frequently argued the question with his new scientific friend, but as Huxley was as sharply critical as Spencer was resourcefully constructive, the result was a prolonged and friendly disagreement.

The two rapidly became intimate. In one sense, it was a friendship between a plenum and a vacuum. Spencer thought busily to keep his head full of speculation. Huxley thought just as busily to keep his head antiseptically free from speculation. Huxley was full of facts. Spencer was full of ideas that craved facts. In a discussion of tragedy Spencer's name was mentioned. "Oh!" exclaimed Huxley, ". . . Spencer's idea of a tragedy is a deduction killed by a fact."[12] In 1858 Spencer moved to St. John's Wood to be near Huxley.

Meanwhile, eminent men continued to intercede with eminent men in Huxley's behalf up to an apparently acquiescent prime minister, and still the Royal Navy remained inflexible in ambiguity. It granted Huxley two more periods of six months' leave, recognizing that he should not be available for further duty until his book was published, but firmly refused to provide the publication money which would render him available. At the end of the extreme interval, Huxley once more applied for both time and money. Thereupon, four letters, in a crescendo of threatening urgency, ordered him to report to the H.M.S. *Illustrious*. But his fame had by now become moderately lucrative. He had obtained from *The Westminster Review* and a publisher of scientific textbooks sufficient work to pay for subsistence. He therefore became a civilian, and immediately afterwards the Royal Society, prevented until then by its regulations, granted him the money he had requested.

He still had to find a science professorship in a country where science professorships hardly existed. In the years that followed, openings appeared—at Toronto, Aberdeen, Cork, and King's College, London. He was steadily recommended by the leading scientists in his field, and the friends and relatives of politicians were steadily appointed to the vacancies. He scarcely hoped for a place in London, though distinguished men begged him to wait for the brilliant future that lay before him there. But he couldn't be a promising young man forever, accumulating academic honors in a financial vacuum. Sooner or later, he must marry Netty or release her from her engagement. Perhaps, after all, science and marriage were simply incompatible. He began to think of giving up his profession.

At last, he appealed to Netty in desperation:

There are times when I cannot bear to think of leaving my present pursuits, when I feel I should be guilty of a piece of cowardly desertion from my duty in doing it, and there come intervals when I would give truth and science and all hopes to be folded in your arms . . . I know which course is right, but I never know which I may follow; help me . . . for there is only one course in which there is either hope or peace for me.[13]

Months passed, and no answer came. Of course the mails were slow. He realized that. But he also realized how hard it must be for a woman living so far away, in a world so different, to understand his dilemma. He tried to make up his mind to migrate to Australia as a doctor. No, medicine would be too close to his beloved scientific work. He must go as a squatter, a store-keeper. At length he recognized these follies for what they were and manfully made up his own mind. "My course in life is taken," he wrote. "I will *not* leave London."[14] And in fact the metropolis was as important to him as ever it was to any eighteenth-century wit or statesman. Science meant for him not so much retreat and inspiration, as discussion and debate, politics and action. London, he declared, "is *the* place, the centre of the world."[15] But he also wrote to Netty, "Depend upon it, the trust which you placed in my hands when I left you—to choose for both of us—has not been abused."[14] Nor had his trust in her. Soon after, he received the long-hoped-for letter of acquiescence and encouragement.

Now that he had resolved to wait her out, Destiny became, though not without some savage rebellion, the servile old woman she usually is with dominating men. In 1854 Edward Forbes accepted a chair at Edinburgh and urgently recom-mended that Huxley be appointed to succeed him as professor of natural history and paleontology at the Government School of Mines. Huxley was given one of Forbes's lectureships and then fell heir to the other when his "new colleague was sud-denly afflicted with a sort of moral colic, an absurd idea that he could not perform the duties of his office, and resigned it."[16] In the same year he was offered various temporary lectureships, as well as an assignment with the Geological Survey, which soon became permanent.

But his good fortune was filled with ironies. Soon after suc-ceeding to Forbes's post through Forbes's intercession, he was obliged, as a member of the Royal Society Council, to vote on candidates for the Royal Medal. Hooker, named first, had re-ceived his warm support. Then Forbes was named. Huxley told the Council that in his opinion neither candidate should ex-clude the other and that he would vote for both. In letters of characteristic courage and frankness, he explained to both candidates precisely what he had done, even adding to Hooker that he would have given "a great deal to be able to back Forbes tooth and nail."[17] The Medal was awarded to Hooker. "Your way of proceeding," Forbes had replied to Huxley, "was as true an act of friendship as any that could be performed." He concluded, "And so, my dear Huxley, I trust that you know me too well to think that I am grieved or envious, and you, Hooker, and I are much of the same way of thinking."[18] Huxley valued this letter as one of his dearest possessions—the more so as Forbes died within the year.

Huxley had scarcely recovered from the first shock of his friend's death when he was offered the vacant seat at Edinburgh. The salary was one thousand pounds but the duties were heavy and he had resolved never to leave London. Determined by this time that he should not leave, the London authorities equaled Edinburgh's offer. The nobler course was becoming pleasantly profitable.

Shortly before Huxley obtained his post at the School of Mines, Netty's father decided to return with his daughter to England. Huxley proposed the marriage take place early in the following summer. When at last after six years he saw Netty again, he was shocked to find her gravely ill. A year before leaving Australia, on a strenuous trip to a newly opened mining camp, she had caught a severe chill and then fallen into the hands of a doctor of the blood-letting, calomel-dosing school. A more modern practitioner had rescued her almost at the last moment. In his character of doctor, Huxley took her, as if she were simply one of his patients, to a famous London colleague, asking privately for an opinion afterward.

"I give her six months of life," said the eminent man.

"Well, six months or not," Huxley burst out, "she is going to be my wife."[19]

The eminent man was immensely indignant. The comfort-

able conspiracy of professional ethics had been flagrantly
violated.

Happily, another eminent man commuted the death sentence to very slow recovery. Determined at all events to have
a few months of happiness, the young people were married
soon after, in July, 1855, while Huxley was still in the midst of
his strenuous first lecture course. In spite of black prospects,
his spirits rose. He resisted with difficulty an impulse to howl
and crow in class. A month later they were honeymooning at
Tenby in Wales. Mrs. Huxley was still so weak that her husband had to carry her to and from the beach. When she became
ill, he waited on her with professional efficiency. "*Un vrai
mari*,"[20] pronounced the French maid admiringly.

Congratulations flowed in upon Huxley from the scientific
world. "I hope your marriage will not make you idle," wrote
Charles Darwin, a new friend. "Happiness, I fear, is not good
for work." At almost the same time, Huxley was writing
Hooker such letters as the following:

So far as I can judge there can be no doubt that this really is a
case of downward movement. The stools of the trees are in their
normal position, and their roots are imbedded and interwoven in
a layer of stiff blue clay.[21]

Darwin did not yet understand his new ally. Huxley's temptations were overwork and rigorous self-denial. His wife and
children became his greatest happiness and fully as important
to him as his science, yet he was so abstemious of their society
that he used to refer to himself as "the lodger."

"Once we were married," wrote Netty, "the whole atmosphere was scientific—his occupation, his friends, his books—
the lectures he gave that I attended. . . . It was a revelation
that ennobled the world I lived in, made everything, for me,
full of the strangest wonder and interest."[22] It was hardly a
Christian revelation. Before her marriage, she had prayed that

"Hal's" heart might be touched by faith. Afterward, she came gradually to think of herself as an agnostic. And yet to the end of her days she thanked "the Eternal Goodness"[23] for what was noble in her life and Hal's. In any case, they made a religion of each other.

Wonderful and strange as the scientific world was to her, Netty found she could instruct Hal in some of its niceties. When they came home from a party or a dinner, he would ask her what she thought of various learned colleagues. "Of one I said he was a miser, of another I gave another characteristic."

"Good heavens!" her husband would exclaim after an obviously correct diagnosis, "have I married a witch? What makes you say that?"[24] Perhaps he never learned what.

Netty was now paid the delicate compliment of respectful admiration from a philosophic bachelor. Like most celibates, Herbert Spencer never outgrew a cautious and playful interest in women, particularly when they were safely married. He would even have been capable of romance, except that tender thoughts about a lady's charms were invariably followed by sober reflections about her purse. Congenial souls he sometimes found in this imperfect world, but not congenial pocketbooks. With young Mrs. Huxley, there was no question of either pocketbook or romance, and therefore he settled down comfortably to a long friendship. She invited him to dinner, and if he foresaw no prospect of "head sensations" or "cardiac enfeeblement," he responded with polysyllabic gallantries of acceptance.

Far from making him idle, Huxley's marriage made him incredibly busy. By dispelling doubts and creating a citadel of certainty and love, it seems to have released floods of new energy, so that he laid Herculean labors on himself and accomplished them triumphantly. Besides his regular lectures, averaging seven to eight a week from February to June, he gave a supplementary night course in January, regular courses through the year to workingmen, the Fullerian series at the Royal Institution from 1856 to 1858, and a large number of occasional lectures. Many of these, delivered in halls crowded with distinguished scientists, statesmen, and men of letters, required original inquiry and meticulous preparation. He also carried on his own investigations, wrote reviews and summaries of scientific books for the journals, reorganized the Museum of Practical Geology for student use, and with Hooker and others laid for the natural history collections at the British Museum elaborate plans which were realized many years later at the South Kensington. By way of vacations, he performed his duties for the Geological Survey at Tenby or, when headaches, dyspepsia, prostration, and other Victorian ills assailed him too persistently, made mountain-climbing excursions into the Alps, which resulted in a study of glaciers in collaboration with Tyndall.

On the last evening of 1856, while his wife lay in the next room waiting for her first child to be born, he planned his future in a spirit of solemn dedication:

1856–7–8 must still be "Lehrjahre" to complete training in principles of Histology, Morphology, Physiology, Zoology and Geology by Monographic Work in each Department. 1860 will then see me well grounded and ready for any pursuits in either of these branches.

It is impossible to map out beforehand how this must be done. I must seize opportunities as they come, at the risk of the reputation for desultoriness.

In 1860 I may fairly look forward to fifteen or twenty "Meisterjahre," and with the comprehensive views my training will have given me, I think it will be possible in that time to give a new and healthier direction to all Biological Science.

To smite all humbugs, however big; to give a nobler tone to science; to set an example of abstinence from petty personal controversies, and of toleration for everything but lying; to be indifferent as to whether the work is recognized as mine or not, so long as it is done—are these my aims? 1860 will show.[25]

This amazing plan proved not only practicable but prophetic—even to the date 1860 and the reputation for desultoriness. He made contributions to each of the sciences enumerated. He seized opportunities as they came, in particular that presented by the Darwinian controversy in 1860; and here certainly he undertook work with almost complete indifference as to whether it was recognized as his own. He did raise the tone of science, and he smote humbug as heartily as Gladstone smote sinecure and extravagance. In fact, he lived according to Carlyle's dictum: he did not know himself, but he knew what he had to do.

Like many good lecturers, Huxley began by being a rather mediocre one. His first venture, made at twenty-seven before one of the glittering and monumentally starched audiences of the Royal Institution, was begun in terror and concluded in an earnest conviction of intelligibility:

When I took a glimpse into the theatre and saw it full of faces, I did feel most amazingly uncomfortable. I can now quite understand what it is to be going to be hanged, and nothing but the necessity of the case prevented me from running away. . . .

For ten minutes I did not quite know where I was, but by degrees I got used to it, and gradually gained perfect command of myself and of my subject.[26]

Nevertheless, he received two letters of criticism—one from a "working man" and another from a Mr. Jodrell, who afterward founded the Jodrell Lectureships at University College, London. Huxley was warned against "running his words, especially technical terms, together," "pouring out new and unfamiliar matter at breakneck speed," and "lecturing in a colloquial tone, suitable to a knot of students gathered round his table, but not to a large audience."[27] His manner at first seems also to have been overtense and at times belligerent.[28] He labeled the letters "Good Advice" and kept them always at hand as a reminder.

But his very fear of an audience allowed him no peace except in mastery—and mastery was inevitable for a man so quick-witted and clear-headed, so elaborately disciplined and omnisciently well-read. In those days words and reasons still settled issues and events. To speak well was to wield power and command respect, and to speak like Huxley was to be a Hector among Trojans, a famous hero in the long Victorian wars of discussion. Huxley accepted his destiny with gusto. Yet every man is the prisoner of his talents. Huxley's kept him on the battlefield rather too much of the time. The arts of peace are higher than the arts of war.

An interesting specimen of Huxley's more popular lectures is that "On the Educational Value of the Natural History Sciences," which he gave at St. Martin's Hall in the hurry and strain of his first year of teaching. It seems to have been hastily written and is rather loose in organization. Yet the exposition is always clear and vigorous, the phrasing often vivid and memorable. Here one finds the famous metaphor in which science is called trained and organized common sense, as well as others less well known but quite as striking and indicative:

To a person uninstructed in natural history, his country or sea-side stroll is a walk through a gallery filled with wonderful works of art, nine-tenths of which have their faces turned to the wall. Teach him something of natural history, and you place in his hands a catalogue of those which are worth turning round.[29]

Clearly, at twenty-nine Huxley had discovered his pen.

The lecture is equally significant in content. It reveals Huxley, at this point in his career, as a theist, a romantic, and a disciple of Carlyle. Science is recommended as much on ethical and aesthetic grounds as on intellectual and practical. It disciplines the spirit as well as the mind, and by teaching us to observe nature closely and reason about her accurately, enables us to appreciate her aesthetically. In short, natural beauty tends to be identified with scientific truth, and spiritual consolation with both:

Leave out the Physiological sciences from your curriculum, and you launch the student into the world . . . blind to the richest sources of beauty in God's creation; and unprovided with that belief in a living law, and an order manifesting itself in and through endless change and variety, which might serve to check and moderate that phase of despair through which, if he takes an earnest interest in social problems, he will assuredly sooner or later pass.[30]

The reference to social problems is significant. In another passage, Huxley aims a sharp thrust, almost in the language of *Past and Present*, against the philosophy "which exhibits the world as a slavemill, worked with many tears, for mere utilitarian ends."[31]

These tendencies are even more pronounced in another lecture, delivered in 1856, "On Natural History as Knowledge, Discipline, and Power." Here he states flatly that "nature is not a mechanism but a poem," that where Cuvier's "correlation of organs" or agreement in homologous structures fail to explain animal anatomy, biologists may have to seek a higher principle which "appeals to the aesthetic sense as much as to the mere intellect."[32] We rightly see our sense of beauty answered in the beauties of nature because nature results "from the benevolent operation, under the conditions of the physical world, of an intelligence similar in kind, however superior in degree, to our own." Huxley had evidently given himself up, for a time at least, to the rhetorical and transcendental fervors of Carlyle's theism.

The lecture "On Natural History" is a curious combination of cautious common sense and extravagant romanticism. He soberly upholds inductive logic against Cuvier's doctrine that a whole skeleton can be deduced from a single bone, and then seems quite recklessly to throw all logic overboard in favor of the aesthetic sense. He makes the most exaggerated claims for the spiritual benefits of science, and then shrewdly warns that we may expect nemesis if there are too many thinkers who have one moral faculty for science and another for daily life.

It is just possible that in making this wise reservation, Huxley was thinking of his illustrious contemporary Sir Richard Owen, then Director of the Hunter Museum and widely known as "The British Cuvier." Sir Richard had begun by being very kind, supporting the young naval surgeon for various honors, and writing more than once to the Admiralty in his behalf. But Huxley had been instinctively on his guard. The British Cuvier was so frightfully polite. He had such a ghastly smile. Moreover, he was infamous to the backstairs of science. Actually, he seems to have been a social experimenter with a penchant for sadism and mystification.

In 1852, Huxley had on Forbes's advice asked Owen for a letter of recommendation:

I . . . got no answer whatsoever—of course I was in a considerable rage . . . met him—I was going to walk past—but he stopped me—and in the blandest and most gracious manner said, 'I have received your note—I shall grant it.' The phrase and the implied condescension were quite 'touching'—so much that I felt if I stopped a moment longer I must knock him into the path [?]— I therefore bowed and walked off. Finally received 'The strongest and kindest testimonial any man could possibly wish for.' . . . I give up any attempt to comprehend him from this time forth.[33]

Plainly, Owen was both a tyrant and a prima donna: he loved power and glory. He aided promising young men so long as they did not become too promising and welcomed new ideas so long as they agreed with his own. Huxley soon became far too promising, and by 1856 his ideas had become unwelcome also. As early as 1852 he wrote his sister that his paper "On the Morphology of the Cephalous Mollusca" would be held up if he did not keep it out of the hands of a "particular friend." "The necessity for these little stratagems utterly disgusts me," he added. ". . . I do so long to be able to trust men implicitly."[34] Huxley was a little like the brilliant professional general who detests war.

Meanwhile, war was of course inevitable. In recent papers Huxley had vigorously criticized Cuvier, the tutelary deity of comparative anatomists, and had aroused much pious horror— not so much by his criticism itself as by its vigor. He had committed that last Victorian enormity, that worst of virtuous errors— he had made a mistake in tone. Even Darwin, who had for many years been quietly and decorously removing the bottom from Cuvier's universe, felt obliged to write his young friend a letter of gentle remonstrance. In the general outcry Owen took no part, but as Cuvier's principal heir, he must have decided that Huxley could do no right. He had offended first by denying Cuvier and upholding God. Soon he was to offend even more unspeakably by denying God and upholding Darwin.

In 1856, Sir Richard Owen transferred from the Hunter to the British Museum. Shortly after, having been given permission to use the lecture theater at the School of Mines, he deliberately assumed the title of Professor of Paleontology in that institution. This was a direct blow at Huxley, who though originally little interested in fossils, had through his teaching and his work with the Geological Survey become more and more of a paleontologist. The School of Mines asked Owen to explain. When he failed to do so satisfactorily, Huxley broke off all personal relations with him.

And now Owen delivered himself into his enemy's hands. He was a sacrifice to his own devious orthodoxy, for in those days bones had theological significance. They represented the final stage in a long retreat. In the seventeenth century it had been conceded that the earth was not the center of the material universe. Must it finally be conceded in the nineteenth that man was not anatomically unique? How could he be sure there was a God if God gave him no material sign of special favor? Goethe had done religion a disservice by discovering the intermaxillary bone, common to apes, in the human ear. Apparently Owen hoped to save man's soul by discovering in the human skull large areas of bone which did not exist in any other animal. Whether he really thought he had discovered them or merely pretended to do so for other people's edification is not clear, for the paper which he read before the Linnean Society in 1857 was not only as pious, but fully as ambiguous as the Thirty-nine Articles of the Anglican Church. At one point he emphasized that man and monkey were astonishingly homologous down to the last tendon and metatarsal. At another, he emphasized that man differed so much from monkey and everything else that he must be assigned to a separate subclass under Mammalia. Owen's zeal had led him to make "elementary blunders in the anatomy of the human brain,"[35] but his immense prestige silenced opposition.

Not for long. If Sir Richard could not face his own facts, Huxley was quite prepared to face them for him. He had taken Owen's measure. The man was immensely learned and he was acute on fine points, but he could "only work in the concrete from bone to bone."[36] In broad generalization he was sentimental, pretentious, and feeble—a very shaky Goliath to attack so formidable a David. Huxley possessed every honest weapon in the arsenal of controversy. Owen had little but his duplicity, his deviousness, his ill-nature, his mastery of detail, and his immense reputation—all stilettoes and blunderbusses; and of very dubious advantage in a losing battle. "Let him beware!" concluded Huxley.[37]

Having with several brief papers suavely knocked some cracks and crevices in Owen's reputation, Huxley made a heavy frontal attack in his Croonian lecture of 1858 "On the Theory of the Vertebrate Skull," delivered before the Royal Society and—with carefully premeditated cruelty—on an evening when the British Cuvier himself was in the chair. Huxley showed fundamental inconsistencies and absurdities in Owen's favorite view that the vertebrate skull is a continuation of the vertebrae, and then offered sounder views based on embryological evidence. These were almost immediately accepted by comparative anatomists. Huxley had here undertaken a course of investigation which later enabled him not only to demolish Owen, but to produce his own epoch-making book on *Man's Place in Nature*. His antagonism to Owen's theological anatomy had drawn him away from Carlyle and was preparing him for Darwin. There was little time for preparation.

4

THE TALE OF AN UNLIKELY PRINCE

In fact, Owen's defeat would probably have seemed much
sharper, had not a more spectacular event immediately followed. On June 18, 1858, the day after Huxley delivered his
brilliant lecture, Charles Darwin, the recluse author of a number of sound and laborious books and papers, received a fateful
letter from the Malay Archipelago. It was from Alfred Russell
Wallace and contained the abstract of a theory explaining the
evolution of species and their adaptation to environment by
natural selection:

> I never saw a more striking coincidence [wrote Darwin to his
> friend Sir Charles Lyell]; if Wallace had my MS. sketch written
> out in 1842, he could not have made a better short abstract! Even
> his terms now stand as heads of my chapters. . . . So all my
> originality, whatever it may amount to, will be smashed, though
> my book, if it will ever have any value, will not be deteriorated.[1]

As usual his words failed completely to express his feelings.
Thank God! He didn't want anyone to see how keenly he felt
being anticipated. Lyell had warned him that he might be. "I
fancied that I had a grand enough soul not to care," he wrote

Joseph Hooker; "but I found myself mistaken and punished."[2]

Perhaps Darwin never really faced the possibility. He was so absorbed in his work, and he made such slow progress with it. He felt weak and listless so much of the time, was so easily upset and made ill. He read so slowly, wrote so slowly, even thought so slowly, that he always felt desperately behindhand, like a tortoise concentrating every enegry on the next step, as he creeps in frantic haste toward impossible horizons. How could such a man find time to think of the world outside? And the thought of it was so unpleasant. Darwin had a gentleman's fear of being conspicuous, an invalid's sensitiveness to the idle curiosity of crowds. How could he come before the nation with theories that were not only a scandal to orthodox biology, but a blasphemy against religion and Victorian decency?

He knew how it would be, for his opinions had already leaked out a little. "You will do more harm than any ten Naturalists will do good," his old friend Falconer had grumbled to him. "I can see you have already *corrupted* and half-spoiled Hooker!"[3] He had gradually come as a matter of course to expect opposition and even contempt from his nonnaturalist relations, among whom he had been a great favorite.

For a number of reasons he had laid the world on a shelf and pretty much forgotten about it. He had already been forestalled in minor discoveries, but had not minded very much. "This is E. Forbes' theory," he wrote to Asa Gray at the end of a geological discussion, "which, however, I may add, I had written out four years before he published."[4] And so he proceeded deliberately, testing every generalization by hosts of relevant fact. And no man ever enjoyed a fact more: "I was in London yesterday for a few hours with Falconer, and he gave me a magnificent lecture on the age of man. . . . He has a grand fact of some large molar tooth in the Trias."[5] Facts were his pleasure and his amusement, but his serious business and his constant care were his ideas about evolution, which had developed him in these twenty years or more, nearly as much as he had developed them. It was almost as though the ideas had grown a brain around themselves. "Why the shape of his head is quite altered," his father had said on first seeing him after the voyage of the *Beagle*.[6] His father noticed such things.

Charles was frequently to discover kingdoms while searching for asses, and he was always cautiously following his nose to the most bizarre and extravagant destinations. His commonest reaction to experience was a well-bred ejaculation of amazement. The commonest phrases in his letters are "I was astonished," and "I was utterly dumfounded." In short, Darwin muddled into genius and greatness like a true Englishman.

His youth was a prosaic and comfortable variation on the folk tale of the unlikely prince. The role of the king, his father, was very adequately represented by Dr. Robert Darwin, a huge, energetic, formidable man, who dominated a company as a mountain dominates a landscape and who almost invariably concluded his day's work with a two-hour monologue delivered to his awe-stricken children. Unlike most talkers, he could read other people's thoughts. It is not surprising that his four children felt ever in this great taskmaster's eye.

He was inclined to be severe with his son and seems to have reduced him to an almost permanent posture of amiable and affectionate apology. Charles's elder sister Caroline, who watched over him after the early death of their mother, was "too zealous in trying to improve" him. "I clearly remember after this long interval of years, saying to myself when about to enter a room where she was—'what will she blame me for now?' "[7] But then, though a spirited and attractive girl, Caroline apparently felt obliged to be an old maid to take care of her father's household.

Growing up in the midst of so much moral sternness, Charles was a timid, rather backward child, given to unconscious rebellion. He stole fruit from the family garden by ingenious methods and sometimes gave it to certain older boys because they admired his swift running. He loved dogs, was early moved by natural scenery, and had a passion for collecting things, from franks and seals to newts and beetles.

His student career was a good-natured attempt at respectability by the member of a clan which honored neither ignorance nor idleness, however affluent and graceful. As a schoolboy he was conscientious but uninspired. As a medical student at Edinburgh, he was deterred from serious effort by the conviction that his father would leave him a comfortable property. True, he disliked medicine. He was pathologically sensitive and could not bear to watch an operation. He also thought the Edinburgh professors extremely dull. In desperation his father proposed Cambridge and the clergy. Having consulted a sensitive but docilely orthodox conscience, Charles agreed, looking forward to the prospect with some pride and perhaps some secret rebellion. He resuscitated his Greek with good-humored patience and positively enjoyed the close and cogent argument of Paley's *Evidences*. But he obviously enjoyed snipe shooting and beetle collecting a good deal more. "You care for nothing but shooting, dogs, and rat-catching," exclaimed his father in exasperation, "and you will be a disgrace to yourself and family."[8]

And yet people noticed this amiable young snipe shooter. His uncle, taciturn, hard-headed Josiah Wedgwood, hereditary manufacturer of china, mysteriously approved of him; and the great Sir James Mackintosh was pleased to say, "There is something in that young man that interests me."[9] To be sure, Charles had listened eagerly to the eminent man's conversation, but then Sir James was one of the best talkers in Great Britain. Charles could be bored with as much discrimination as he could be interested. That was what was so promising about his bitter protests against the Edinburgh professors, whose erudition left no room for their sense.[10] And he was promising in other ways. For one thing, he was a remarkably good shot. Though physically awkward, he had a capacity for enthusiastic concentration which enabled him to overcome handicaps. At the height of his rage for hunting, he used to practice throwing up his gun before a mirror, to make sure he always brought it to the correct position. He also had an insatiable appetite for tabulation and other forms of minor certainty. Shooting was almost a grief if he could not record every hit and miss. Beetle collecting, begun without the slightest intellectual curiosity, developed observation and practical knowledge. Eventually, it led to constant attendance on J. S. Henslow, professor of botany at Cambridge; so that Darwin became known among the dons as "the man who walks with Henslow."[11] And thus, entering science by the genial path of friendship, he absorbed a casual knowledge of zoology, botany, and geology.

That his science and his religion could in any way be at odds seems never to have entered his head. The scientists whom he knew were very safe. Henslow, a minister of the church as well as professor of botany, was so impeccably orthodox that he once confided to Charles he would be grieved if a single word of the Thirty-nine Articles were to be changed. Sedgewick, a professor of geology and likewise an active divine, was famous for the intricacy and soundness with which he reconciled the metaphysical claims of his two professions. Charles had no cause to doubt church dogma. He doubted only himself:

We had an earnest conversation about going into Holy Orders [wrote his old college friend J. M. Herbert]; and I remember his asking me, with reference to the question put by the Bishop in the ordination service, "Do you trust that you are inwardly moved by the Holy Spirit, &c.," whether I could answer in the affirmative, and on my saying I could not, he said, "Neither can I, and therefore I cannot take orders."[12]

These doubts—the reaction of a sensitive conscience to moderate zeal and dedication—never became sufficiently acute to provoke an overt action. Charles shot snipe, collected beetles, tapped rocks, and believed in God. But mostly, he shot snipe. "At that time," he wrote long afterward, "I should have thought myself mad to give up the first days of partridge-shooting for geology or any other science."[13]

In 1831 he took a respectable degree at Cambridge. Neither he nor his father said anything about the ministry. In fact, Charles had read Humboldt's *Travels* and was longing for tropical scenery and a trip at least to the Canary Islands. At that point Henslow recommended him for the post of naturalist on the H.M.S. *Beagle*, a tiny 242-ton brig which was to sail on a five-year voyage, chiefly to survey the coast of South America. Here was Humboldt's own adventure—the Canary Islands and heaven too! But at first his father would not let him go. Captain Fitzroy did not like the shape of his nose. Even these objections were overcome. Uncle Josiah actually wrote a letter advising he be allowed to go. Having been rather extravagant at Cambridge, Charles tried to console his father by saying, "I should be deuced clever to spend more than my allowance whilst on the *Beagle*." Dr. Darwin smiled. "But they tell me you are very clever."[14] He gave his consent.

After his arrival in Plymouth, Charles had to wait two months for the *Beagle* to sail. It was then that he suffered his first serious illness:

I was out of spirits at the thought of leaving all my family and friends for so long a time, and the weather seemed to me inexpressibly gloomy. I was also troubled with palpitation and pain about the heart, and like many a young ignorant man, especially one with a smattering of medical knowledge, was convinced that I had heart disease. I did not consult any doctor, as I fully expected to hear the verdict that I was not fit for the voyage, and I was resolved to go at all hazards.[15]

Almost certainly, he did not have heart trouble at this time, for he was to show during the voyage that he had unusual powers of physical endurance.

When on December 27, 1831, the *Beagle* set out, Charles was on board.

By far the most famous of all the great voyages of scientific discovery, Darwin's was in many respects the least heroic. Its obvious facts were seasickness, homesickness, and a quiet, amiable young man who seemed chiefly intent on putting the South American continent into specimen bottles. Yet his inward adventure is as quaintly, magnificently impressive as the rise of the House of Commons or the development of the cabinet system. As with them, success was the happy result of an alliance between talent and accident. Darwin profited even from his ignorance, for at least it was broad and catholic. He was not, like Huxley, restricted by a sound medical preparation to making all his discoveries on jellyfish and salps. He excavated the huge *Megatheria* as bravely as he dissected marine worms. He thought about continents as naturally as about rock crystals. And the big things were what needed to be thought about at that particular time. Above all, he was relatively ignorant of the theological, cataclysmic geology anterior to Lyell. Henslow's last counsel had been that he purchase, read carefully, and emphatically disbelieve Lyell's *Principles of Geology*, the first volume of which had recently appeared. Charles bought, read, and believed. He had not meant to believe. But the first bit of land that he saw, St. Jago in the Cape de Verde Islands, was an incontrovertible demonstration. He went ashore and discovered the new geology.

The *Principles* are perhaps the most important link in the long, tenuous, precarious chain that leads up to *The Origin of Species*. Lyell taught Darwin not only how to think about geology, but how to think. From him Charles learned observation in the higher sense of a thoughtful activity which suggests and tests hypotheses. Again, he learned how to construct hypotheses. In other words, he came to see nature as logical, regular, and self-explanatory. Only on very general and state occasions should it, in the words of Cardinal Newman, "be referred forward to design."[16] Otherwise, it should always "be referred backward to physical causes." Finally, he acquired the genetic or evolutionary point of view, for geology was then the most historical of the natural sciences.

The sublimities of his South American voyage are nearly all geological. Traveling up the valley of the Santa Cruz River, with the white Andes all along the western horizon, Darwin was awed by the realization that the lava capping the great cliffs must have been poured out by volcanoes deep under the sea. And yet mountains were a symbol of eternity! His tone toward the younger, higher range of the Cordillera was positively condescending. What struck his imagination was time, graphically recorded by the slow geological clocks of sand and stone. And time was to Victorian speculation what the Holy Ghost was to medieval theology—the invisible presence which rendered all miracles credible. If only it happened gradually, regularly, and impersonally enough, the impossible became perfectly probable.

What impossibility had excited Darwin? As a matter of fact, a kind of geological process was going on inside his head, for he possessed what, in his essay on "Sir Robert Peel," Walter Bagehot has called the "alluvial" mind.[17] In such a mind, an idea develops so slowly that it hardly seems to have been there at all until it seems to have been there always. During his long voyage in the *Beagle*, tiny sands of evidence had gradually accumulated some very alarming strata of thought on the very bottom of Darwin's brain.

This process of deposition can be broadly traced in his letters, notebooks, and in the first and second editions of his *Journal* of the voyage.[18] He set sail probably without fixed or definite ideas on the subject of species. Lyell's second volume, which Charles received in Montevideo in 1832, rejected evolution because of the incompleteness and ambiguity of the geological record. Vertebrates are to be found in some of the earliest rocks known. On the other hand, his discussion was full of suggestions of natural selection and adaptation to environment. Moreover, he laid down an elaborate and verifiable theory of geological evolution. But if mountains and valleys evolved, why not plants and animals? Darwin's library on the *Beagle* also contained Cuvier, who admitted a certain succession of plants and animals in terrestrial history and attempted to explain them by a neat series of scientific geneses and last judgments. Each geological epoch is marked off by a cataclysm which sweeps away all existing life, and a fresh "creation" which provides an entirely new supply, on improved models.

This theory was revered doctrine, and evolution a disreputable speculation, because Cuvier had maintained the first and Lamarck, the second. Cuvier was all that a scientist should be; Lamarck, all that he should not be. Lamarck's chemistry was an anachronism, his physiology a museum piece, and his general theory, except for a few inspired ideas, something between poetry and prophecy. Cuvier's chemistry was strictly up to date; his paleontology was at once his own creation and a valid science; his general theory, melodramatic as it seems, was a cautious modification of Aristotle in the light of new facts from the strata of the Seine basin and the Alps. Incidentally, it permitted a vague but comforting compromise with Moses. Cuvier had developed an old-fashioned idea in a modern and skeptical spirit; Lamarck had developed a modern idea in a credulous and old-fashioned spirit. Altogether, it is not surprising that on biological matters Cuvier's language pervades the first edition of Darwin's *Journal*.

And yet he seems to have accepted Cuvier for the wrong reasons. Lyell was his model of the critical spirit. Cuvier seems to have been simply a citadel of authority, scientific and theological. Darwin was too conservative ever to outlive an influence, and therefore, not only Lyell, but Cuvier, Lamarck, Genesis, and even Paley have, either positively or negatively, left their mark on the Origin.

Meanwhile, facts were continually, secretly building themselves into an idea. Soon after landing in South America, he discovered near Bahía the fossil bones of a giant sloth. Mingled with the remains of this extinct animal, he found, as he wrote Henslow, marine shells "identical with what now exist."[19] But then Cuvier's catastrophes did not make a clean sweep. They did not fit the facts. As he traveled on the continent, he noted that related species occupied similar environments in adjacent territories. This made no sense according to the creation theory, but according to an evolutionary one it meant that a single type had spread out over a wide area and in the course of time differentiated itself to cope with different environments. Darwin also observed that vegetation on the west and east sides of the Andes was markedly different, though soil and climate were much the same. Why should the Creator introduce an abrupt change at a mountain barrier? Charles was also much struck by the close resemblance between existing species and those of the geological epoch just past; and he hints that extinction may be due to failure in the struggle for existence.

The Galapagos Islands were the most illuminating lesson. His visit there seemed an actual journey into the biological past. "Surrounded by the black lava, the leafless shrubs, and large cacti," the giant lizards and tortoises, replacing the larger mammals in a normal economy, seemed the veritable denizens of an earlier world.[20] But the landscape not only suggested evolution, the facts demanded it. Here distribution reduced the creation theory to an absurdity. Each island had great numbers of species and varieties peculiar to itself, but related species and varieties, both in the archipelago and the adjoining mainland, differed from each other according to the magnitude of natural barriers between them. One could assume "a creative power" with an inveterate sense of localism or an illogical desire for busy work, but how much more illuminating to assume an evolutionary force producing, with geographical separation, increasing difference in the offspring of a common ancestor? While still in the islands he had actually described his data as "undermining the stability of species."[21] From that time on the subject "haunted" him.[22]

Many have felt that it stared him in the face, for with the heresy of biological evolution he had been familiar ever since, as a boy in his teens, he had read his grandfather's Zoonomia. But in those days, evolution stared everybody in the face. And Charles had many other matters to think about. The long voyage of the Beagle was his creative period—the withdrawal of the prophet to his wilderness, of the scientist to his laboratory. In this crowded interval nearly every important idea of his life appears at least in germ. He didn't have time to develop them all. His principal achievements were geological—a revolutionary history of the South American continent and a theory, equally revolutionary, of the growth of coral reefs and islands.

In any case Darwin was not the man to make himself notorious by heresy—at least, not until, by slow, imperceptible degrees, he had become persuaded that notoriety, no less than heresy, was absolutely unavoidable. At the beginning of the voyage, he was still earnestly religious and, much to the amusement of the officers on board, commonly settled moral questions by quoting the Bible. He also felt that a primrose by the river's brim was very far from being simply a Latin name and an aggregation of plant cells. Long after he had returned from the tropics and discovered that nature was red in tooth and claw, he continued to think of the Creator in terms of the

idyllic beauty of the English countryside. Moreover, his day-
dreams still flowed docilely in the channel of his father's dis-
pensation. "I steadily have a distant prospect," he wrote his
sister Caroline, "of a very quiet country parsonage, and I can
see it even through a grove of Palms."[23]

But as the months passed, this decorous vision underwent
subtle changes. First, hunting and fishing faded from the pros-

LARRY BURROWS

H.M.S. "BEAGLE" IN THE STRAITS OF MAGELLAN.

pect and scientific work replaced them. Once, shooting the
first partridge of the season had made his hands tremble so
violently that he could hardly reload his gun. Now, a "first
day's partridge shooting . . . cannot be compared to finding
a fine group of fossil bones, which tell their story of former
times with almost a living tongue."[24] And after climbing from
dawn to dusk up the cold, windswept trails of the high Andes,
he could "hardly sleep at nights" for thinking of the day's
geology.[25] In fact, his recondite enthusiasm retained a boyish
gusto and freshness which made it, at least in his eyes, seem

slightly reprehensible. He justified geology to himself and his father as diffidently as he had once justified snipe shooting. And no wonder! Geology, he confided from Rio to his friend Fox, "is like the pleasure of gambling. Speculating, on first arriving, on what the rocks may be, I often mentally cry out 3 to 1 tertiary against primitive; but the latter have hitherto won all the bets."[26] In middle life, it amused him that he picked up information on the variability of species by consorting with pigeon fanciers at village gin palaces.

The months lengthened into years, and the quiet parsonage itself grew dim—obscured not by a grove of palms, but by piles of un-Biblical bones. Darwin learned gradually to contain his enthusiasm for the Thirty-nine Articles. He began the voyage quoting Scriptures and ended it mildly criticizing them in argument with the pious Captain Fitzroy. Subtle changes in his ideas about species had been mysteriously accompanied by subtle changes in his ideas about Christianity. To think about evolution was to think about creation and immutability. It was to think about ethics, religion, the Bible, nature, and God. It was to think about what sound and weighty scientists, what his father and Uncle Josiah, would think about him.

Charles was also discovering with some astonishment that all his wonderful fun was actually a valuable work. Henslow had written high praise of his letters and collections. Still better, Sedgwick had called on his father and predicted a distinguished scientific career. After reading the letter which contained this news, said Charles, "I clambered over the mountains of Ascension with a bounding step, and made the volcanic rocks resound under my geological hammer."[27] Perhaps, after all, he would become the kind of man his father could admire. Both his ambition and his sense of guilt were, as Dr. Douglas Hubble points out, connected with his feeling for his father;[28] and no doubt ambition quieted guilt, and guilt strengthened ambition, so that the two wove themselves into a long, gently arching bridge between the repentant snipe shooter and the great biological genius.

One day at St. Jago, as he took refuge under a rock ledge from the glare of the sun and thought of the bold, simple geology of the island, it struck Charles with a thrill of delight that he could write something about the geology of the places he visited. Here was a book! Later, Fitzroy bade him read aloud from his *Journal* and pronounced it worth publishing. Here was another book! The quiet parsonage receded into the future.

And yet a five-year cruise can hardly be all enthusiasm and discovery. In such an immensity of time and space there must be much monotony, vacancy, loneliness, and even privation. "Everything in America," Charles wrote Fox, "is on such a grand scale—the same formations extend for 5 or 600 miles without the slightest change, for such geology one requires 6 league boots."[29] Sometimes he spent ten hours in the saddle without a rest, and when food ran short, smoked cigarettes like a Gaucho to fight off hunger. Except from his immediate family, letters grew fewer and fewer. Meanwhile, his college friends were finding their places in life. Fox had married. "I shall be an old man," wrote Charles, "by the time I return, far too old to look out for a little wife."[30]

As their sails wore thin and their tackle turned to shreds, Charles and his comrades became obsessed with dreams of home. Absence from England was a long and slow starvation. "I hate every wave of the ocean," he wrote Fox, "with a fervour, which you who have only seen the green waters of the shore, can never understand."[31] A sailor's life is a paradox of folly. He sails the sea to tell incredible tales afterward at a comfortable fireside, and talks of nothing but the comfortable fireside while enacting the incredible tales.

On returning to England in 1836, he found that Sedgwick's prophecy was already coming true. All sorts of busy, preoccupied people knew about him and took him seriously. Of course, though they had pronounced his collections priceless, they were at first too busy and preoccupied to study them, but he was soon at work on fossil bones and pickled insects with some of the most eminent scientists in England. He became a fellow of the Royal Geological and Zoological Societies, and was shortly after appointed to the council of the first and the secretaryship of the second. "I remember," he wrote many years later of his Cambridge days, "one of my sporting friends, Turner, who saw me at work with my beetles, saying that I should some day be a Fellow of the Royal Society, and the notion seemed to me preposterous."[32] In sudden realization of his debt, he wrote to Fitzroy that the voyage of the Beagle had been the making of his life.

Dr. Darwin did not mention the fading parsonage. His change of heart, if it really was such, took the form of a health measure. While in South America, Charles had been stricken with a long and severe illness, which, though he reflected long on the symptoms and after-effects, Dr. Darwin could not diagnose. Nevertheless, he pronounced his son too delicate to assume regular duties in the world. By degrees Charles became worse, so that for forty years he "suffered terribly from weakness, fatigue, headache, insomnia, sinking feelings, and dizziness." As time went on, the slightest deviation from routine became disastrous. A half-hour's conversation with a stranger could give him a sleepless night. An hour in church could produce dizziness and nausea. Most of his waking life was spent on a sofa recuperating from brief intervals of exercise or work. At times of fatigue even the weight of a book was insupportable. The worst of it was that he usually appeared ruddy and healthy. "Every one tells me that I look quite blooming and beautiful," he wrote feelingly to Hooker in 1849; "and most think I am shamming, but you have never been one of those."[33]

Dr. Douglas Hubble is convinced he was shamming, or at

least he regards the illness as psychopathic, having its cause in environmental factors and, by a pleasant irony, chiefly in the puzzled paternal physician himself. Dr. Robert Darwin's cold and gloomy tyranny had resulted in a household of "disagreeable and unfulfilled daughters, and neurotic sons."[34] His elder son Erasmus was so lamed in initiative that he was incapable of nothing but graceful bachelordom, and Charles was left with a morbid craving for affection that encouraged excessive care from his wife and so led to lifelong hypochondriacal illness. Darwin's biographers have commonly pitied him his many years of suffering and wondered that he could complete vast researches working only two hours a day. And yet, after reading the Darwin correspondence, one cannot but feel that his illness was a very useful adjustment to his career, enabling him to concentrate ruthlessly and avoid all distractions, from attending official dinners to reading metaphysics and religion. Late in life, he explained to a clergyman that physical weakness had prevented him from feeling "equal to deep reflection, on the deepest subject which can fill a man's mind."[35] Dr. Hubble believes that Darwin's ills were not only a negative but a positive benefit: "His disordered and sleepless nights allowed his laborious mind to brood in solitude over a generalization, while two hours' observing and recording in the morning would expose the night's hypothesis to realistic examination and complete the day's work."[36]

Dr. Hubble concedes that Darwin's illness may also have had some hereditary basis. In another illuminating diagnosis, Dr. Walter C. Alvarez stresses this factor, describing Darwin as an asthenic or "constitutional inadequate."[37] Nervous tension frequently expresses itself in visceral disturbances and may be due, according to Dr. Alvarez, to a neural weakness closely related to insanity. It usually occurs in families where insanity or other grave psychic trouble is also present. On his paternal side, Charles's grandfather Erasmus "stammered badly and in other ways was odd." His uncle Erasmus committed suicide; his father stammered and was hypersensitive; his brother complained—often humorously—of mental fatigue and failing faculties. On the maternal side two of his aunts were eccentric and his uncle Thomas Wedgwood suffered from fits of depression "hardly distinguishable from insanity."[38]

Soon after his return to England, Darwin called on his hero Lyell. A substantial country gentleman turned scientist, Charles Lyell was then nearly forty—a handsome, dignified man who curiously combined Scottish prudence with generous enthusiasm and unselfish devotion to science, scholarly abstraction and absent-mindedness with friendly manners and an open, social nature. He surprised Charles by actually being interested not only in his travels but in his ideas. They discussed coral islands. Lyell had already explained them as due to volcanic craters. The difficulty was that in many cases no evidence of volcanic action had been found and the coral deposits extended down to depths much greater than those at which coral organisms can live. Diffidently, Charles outlined his own theory. To be sure, when they were alive, the organisms had been in shallow water, but as they had built upward, the ocean floor had been very slowly sinking. Lyell was all attention. He put cautious questions. Charles's evidence was as impressive as his theory. Suddenly, Lyell jumped from his seat and began to prance about the room, chuckling with delight. What wonderful simplicity! The explanation was certainly correct, immensely preferable to his own craters. Moreover, it was a key to subsidence and elevation throughout the Pacific. Again Charles was naïvely amazed. He had no idea he had made such an important discovery. He also noticed that Lyell was much more tolerant of biological evolution than his *Principles of Geology* indicated.

Charles's scientific heroes seldom survived personal acquaintance. The great botanist Robert Brown, whom he met just before sailing on the *Beagle*, was ridiculously cautious about communicating his discoveries. Humboldt, whom he met at a breakfast shortly after returning to England, was unheroically cheerful and overtalkative. On the other hand, Lyell successfully maintained his pedestal for many years, but not without some desperate balancing and squirming. Charles long remembered with gratitude all that he had learned from the *Principles of Geology*. He also found more and more reason to value Lyell's practical sagacity and later, when Darwinism was becoming an intellectual empire with extensive practical affairs of its own, affectionately called him his "Chancellor of the Exchequer." Yet, a shrewd observer, Charles was never a great admirer of the Scotch and worldly virtues. "Lyell's overestimation of a man's position in the world seemed to me his chief foible. He used to discuss with Lady Lyell, as a most serious question, whether they should accept some particular invitation."[39] Charles probably also thought it a little absurd that, though Lyell rigidly limited himself to three invitations a week, he "looked forward to going out oftener in the evening with advancing years as to a great reward."[40]

Being a young man of good family and—to his never-ceasing astonishment—of considerable eminence in his own right, Charles came to know many of the eminent literary and political, as well as scientific, men of the day. He was seldom overawed by great abilities, and rather distressed by great abilities combined with serious faults. He preferred geniuses who were gentlemen, liberals, and humanitarians. He therefore much preferred Macaulay to Carlyle. Macaulay did not talk too much and he always talked facts and good sense. George Grote was so pleasant and unpretentious that Charles was quite shocked to hear Carlyle call the *History of Greece* "a fetid quagmire, with nothing spiritual about it."[41] At this time he thought Carlyle's sneers were partly jokes.

For good-natured eccentricity, on the other hand, he had an Englishman's zest. He was very fond of genial, downright old Earl Stanhope, who inflexibly wore brown to match his complexion and who firmly believed what was utterly incredible to everybody else. "Why don't you give up your fiddle-faddle of Geology and Zoology, and turn to the occult sciences?" he once demanded of Charles.[42] Charles treasured the remark for over forty years.

5

A Premeditated Romance

On November 12, 1838 Charles confided to Lyell, "I write because I cannot avoid wishing to be the first person to tell Mrs. Lyell and yourself that I have the very good, and shortly since very unexpected fortune, of going to be married."[1] If Darwin discovered evolution by accident, he arrived at marriage by logic. More than a year before the event and, it would seem, in the complete absence of any visible and possible lady, he had jotted down a series of notes on this unscientific subject. Among the advantages of matrimony he listed: "children (if it please God)—constant companion (& friend in old age) —charms of music & female chit-chat." Among the disadvantages: "*terrible loss of time*, if many children forced to gain one's bread; fighting about no society." But he reflects, "What is the use of working without sympathy from near and dear friends? Who are near and dear friends to the old, except relatives?" And his conclusion is: "My God, it is intolerable to think of spending one's whole life like a neuter bee working, working, and nothing after all.—No, no won't do.—Imagine living all one's day solitarily in smoky, dirty London house—

Only picture to yourself a nice soft wife on a sofa, with good fire and books and music perhaps—compare this vision with the dingy reality of Gt Marlboro St.

"Marry, marry, marry. Q.E.D."[2]

It was inevitable that Charles should marry a Wedgwood. His family had done so for generations. In 1837 his sister Caroline had braved her father's displeasure and terminated with an acceptance the long and reticent courtship of Josiah Wedgwood. "He was 42, and she was 37 years old. His mother had longed for this to happen thirteen years ago."[3] In marrying a Wedgwood, Charles could show his respect and affection for his Uncle Jos, his love for his Aunt Bessy, and his strong attachment for Maer itself where he had spent some of his happiest days and where life was as gay and social as it was cold and austere at Shrewsbury. What more logical than to marry a fragment of Maer and carry it off into his own studious solitude? Whether he considered the Darwin-Wedgwood heredity, one cannot be sure. Some years later, he feared "hereditary weakness"[4] for his children, though he may have been thinking simply of his own family.

The only remaining question was, what Miss Wedgwood of his own age was available? Providentially, there was just one— Emma, who was thirty and a year older than himself. From an early age she had been described by sober and reticent Wedgwoods and Allens as "good-looking," "pretty," and above all "sweet-tempered." Her life had been "crowded with incident" only in the sense of Oscar Wilde's Cecily Cardew. At five she had astonished everybody by reading *Paradise Lost* through to the end. At nine she had survived the whooping cough "more sweet and gentle than ever."[5] At twelve she was called Little Miss Slip-slop because of her indifference to dress and her ability to make a "litter," and in this character she persisted even after marriage, so that Charles, in whom the

firm inculcation of his father had made order almost a tem-
peramental necessity, was obliged to accept chaos outside the
confines of his study.

At eighteen, Emma was a pretty girl of middle height and
dignified, graceful carriage, with large gray eyes, fine brown
hair, a straight nose, a fresh complexion, considerable expanses
of forehead and chin, and a calm, kindly, resolute expression.
Her manner toward young men was frank and open, but there
were in her letters a decision and firmness of tone that, introduced into the pleasant inanities of gallant conversation, must
have seemed formidable. When at this time Emma, her sister
Fannie, and Edward Drewe, a youthful and distant relative,
were taken to Geneva for a year by Aunt Jessie and her husband Sismondi, the historian, there was some quiet hope of a
match between Edward and Emma. Her references to the
young man in her letters were as laconic and cheerfully impersonal as the reports of a vivisectionist on the reactions of a
decapitated rabbit. To her amused disgust, Sismondi, whose
Continental ebullience was the wonder of the family, thought
it wise to counsel her in the art of effective maneuver. At the
end of two or three months, Edward fell in love with a French-
Swiss girl several years older than he and much less attractive
than Emma.

On her return to England, she began a young lady's customary round of dances, theaters, and concerts. She enjoyed
herself thoroughly, but very much in her own way. Her married sisters occasionally made desperate and defeated allusions
to her toilette and attire. Apparently she was invincible in her
idea of having no ideas about dress. "If you happen to be in a
ribbon shop," she wrote one sister, "will you get three yards
of not very handsome ribbon for a turned straw bonnet. I am
quite indifferent about the colour, except not straw colour."[6]
The years passed. Little nieces and nephews appeared on all

sides, and her mother became an invalid. Emma went to fewer dances, and her natural vivacity was sobered by her responsibilities as nurse and caretaker.

At this perilous moment, which neatly coincided with Charles's return to England, destiny intervened—in the substantial shape of at least a dozen conspiring Wedgwoods and Darwins. "It is a match that every soul has been making for us," Emma confided later to her dear Aunt Jessie, "so we could not have helped it if we had not liked it ourselves."[7] Fortunately, the two young people had been thinking earnestly about each other. Perhaps, in spite of his theoretical approach to romance, Emma was one of the objects which Charles had seen beyond his grove of palms; and certainly his return from the South American void had produced in her letters a tone which the doings of other young men had entirely failed to evoke. She was expecting the chicken pox and Charles at about the same time—the one with characteristic calm and matter-of-factness, the other with an excitement which she was at some pains to conceal.

Of course, there were difficulties. Charles feared that his face was repellently plain, that he was too selfishly given up to his solitary habits; and Emma herself was afraid there might be trouble about the theater, which she thoroughly enjoyed and he particularly abhorred. Again, he must have perceived that, though extremely intelligent, she was definitely indifferent to the more recondite mysteries of nature. She felt no poetic emotion about beetles, ostriches, or megatheria. In fact, she was interested not in extraordinary animals but in ordinary ones, and for ordinary reasons. Happily, however, Charles shared this unscientific interest; and he was also fond of music and the piano, which were Emma's real talent and delight. They shared enough to know that they could share a great deal more. Above all, they had fallen in love. "He is the most open, transparent man I ever saw," she wrote Aunt Jessie, "and every word expresses his real thoughts. He is particularly affectionate and very nice to his father and sisters, and perfectly sweet tempered."[8]

One Sunday in November, 1838, having thrown off the usual fears, Charles came down to Maer and made his proposal. It was "quite a surprise," wrote Emma demurely, "as I thought we might go on in the sort of friendship we were in for years, and very likely nothing come of it after all."[9] He was as surprised by her consent as she was by his proposal, and so they spent the day in happy bewilderment. There were tears in old Josiah's eyes when he heard the news. The two fathers now exchanged brief letters of heartfelt congratulation, with solid details about a settlement. Aunt Jessie Sismondi also wrote Emma a letter of tactful advice on an old subject:

If you do pay a little more, be always dressed in good taste; do not despise those little cares which give everyone more pleasing looks, because you know you have married a man who is above caring for such little things. No man is above caring for them. . . . I have seen it even in my half-blind husband. The taste of men is almost universally good in all that relates to dress decoration and ornament. They are themselves little aware of it, because they are seldom called to judge of it, but let them choose and it is always simple and handsome.[10]

Having long known by reading Emma's palm that she would marry a Darwin, Aunt Jessie rejoiced it was Charles instead of Erasmus, whose growing eccentricity was already becoming notorious throughout the family. "Seeing Charles did not come on, which Fan and I used to speculate on and expect in every letter from Maer," she added, "I began to fear it was Erasmus."[11]

Charles and Emma had decided to live in London. In their letters, the poetry of mutual gratitude and unworthiness now gives way to the prose of anxiety and alarm at not finding a house. Erasmus prosecuted the search even more vigorously than Charles and accepted defeat with whimsical desperation, suggesting that his brother end all letters to Emma "yours inconsolably."[12] He had also taken Charles to have tea with the Carlyles. On an earlier occasion the great Thomas had praised Emma highly, and therefore on this occasion Charles thought all his sarcasms very funny, but feared that "Jenny," whom an hysterical giggle made almost unintelligible, was neither quite natural nor ladylike. Faced with the prospect of meeting Lyell, Emma began to think seriously of attacking *The Principles of Geology*. Charles earnestly counseled her against so extreme a step. "Depend upon it you will hereafter have plenty of geology."[12]

As a matter of fact, he had given considerable thought to the impact of the new science on Emma's mind. She was a staunch believer in Revelation. Should he confess his own doubts? He consulted his father, who was famous in the neighborhood of Shrewsbury as a healer not only of bodies but of souls, and particularly of feminine souls.

My father [he wrote after many years of married life] advised me to conceal carefully my doubts, for he said he had known extreme misery thus caused with married persons. Things went on pretty well until the wife or husband became out of health, and then some women suffered miserably by doubting about the salvation of their husbands, thus making them likewise to suffer.[13]

Apparently, he took his father's advice. After a few years, how-ever, he found himself obliged, for scientific reasons, to rattle his skeleton rather loudly from time to time.

Deep in his collections and his *Journal* as well as in houses and practical arrangements, Charles found that he could think about nothing very long together except Emma herself, and even there he felt hopelessly inadequate. "What can a man have to say, who works all morning in describing hawks and owls, and then rushes out and walks in a bewildered manner

EMMA DARWIN IN 1840, FROM A WATER COLOR BY GEORGE RICHMOND.

up one street and down another, looking out for the words 'To let.' "[14] And then, having had a good deal to say and covered several pages in saying it, he concluded mildly, "How provokingly small the paper is, my own very dear Emma."

Emma boasted to her Aunt Jessie about the expensiveness of her trousseau, and assured her uncle Sismondi that she would bring Charles to Switzerland many times in the future, though

LARRY BURROWS

CHARLES DARWIN, FROM A WATER COLOR BY GEORGE RICHMOND.

for the present he was too busy. He was always to be too busy or too ill—and never to reach Switzerland.

At length they found in Gower Street the best of all possible houses. It was moderately ugly outside and so exquisitely ugly inside that even Emma mildly recorded the fact in a letter. Charles called it Macaw Cottage in honor of the color scheme in the drawing room, and often laughed in later years at the happy calm and indifference with which, at the beginning of their married life, they had contemplated so much bad furniture and hideous wall paper.

Rented before the wedding, the house remained vacant for some time. But Charles could not resist. Assembling his rocks and fossils in trunks and boxes of astonishing weight, he moved in by himself and spent his days writing geology, steeling himself to the drawing room, and dreaming of the time when he would have a wife by his side as well as a fire before his feet. Meanwhile, in the shape of wedding presents, the mysteries of the conjugal board already stared him in the face. "My good old friend Herbert," he wrote Emma, "sent me . . . a massive silver weapon, which he called a Forficula (the Latin for an earwig) and which I thought was to catch hold of soles and flounders, but Erasmus tells me, is for asparagus."[15]

He thought much about future responsibilities, sometimes gravely resolving to improve and sometimes gaily predicting decay.

> The Lyells called on me to-day after church [he wrote Emma], as Lyell was so full of Geology he was obliged to disgorge. . . . I was quite ashamed of myself . . . for we talked for half-an-hour unsophisticated Geology, with poor Mrs Lyell sitting by, a monument of patience. I want practice in ill-treating the female sex. I did not observe Lyell had any compunction; I hope to harden my conscience in time: few husbands seem to find it difficult to effect this.[16]

He concluded by observing, with a mixture of alarm and satisfaction, that the drawing room had begun to look less ugly.

The wedding took place on January 29, 1839, at Maer Church. Happiness could be reached only through the awful gates of ceremony. As the excruciating moment drew close, Charles's usual symptoms appeared. "My last two days in London, when I wanted to have most leisure," he wrote Emma, "were rendered very uncomfortable by a bad headache, which continued two days and two nights, so that I doubted whether it ever meant to go and allow me to be married."[16]

But of course, Charles did not take no for an answer—and the headache succumbed to the vigorous rocking of the train. The newlyweds journeyed immediately to Gower Street, where the next day Emma "set herself up" by facing the cook in her own region and finding fault with the boiled potatoes. Charles, on the other hand, adjusted himself somewhat more slowly to the practical details of his new happiness. Looking absent-mindedly through his mail one morning, he turned up a letter and inquired with astonishment who Mrs. Charles Darwin was. Zealously dedicated, in spite of much illness, to his high resolves, he went to concerts and plays, and even pretended to enjoy shopping.

In the wider panorama, Emma's many aunts speculated sagely about her marital future. All were agreed that at the very least she had the stability and the good sense to be happy. "Her feelings are the most healthful possible; joy and sorrow are felt by her in their due proportions, nothing robs her of the enjoyment that happy circumstances would naturally give."[17] What sort of *effect* would she make in London society, Fanny Wedgwood wondered, if the word could be "applied to such simplicity and transparency?"[18]

Of course neither Emma nor Charles had any ambition to glitter, but fronted by a physically magnificent butler and backed by a fairly good cook, they did attempt a series of modest dinners for relatives and scientists. If on these occasions Emma felt any trepidation, it was on account of her relatives. On nearer view, the remoter stars of the scientific galaxy seemed to her anything but brilliant. One evening she gave a party which included Fitton, Henslow, Lyell, and Robert Brown:

We had some time to wait before dinner for Dr Fitton, which is always awful, and, in my opinion, Mr Lyell is enough to flatten a party, as he never speaks above his breath, so that everybody keeps lowering their tone to his. Mr Brown, whom Humboldt calls "the glory of Great Britain," looks so shy, as if he longed to shrink into himself and disappear entirely; however, notwithstanding those two dead weights, viz., the greatest botanist and the greatest geologist in Europe, we did very well and had no pauses. Mrs Henslow has a very good, loud, sharp voice which was a great comfort, and Mrs Lyell has a very constant supply of talk. Mr Henslow was very glad to meet Mr Brown, as the two great botanists had a great deal to say to each other. Charles was dreadfully exhausted when it was over, and is only as well as can be expected today.[19]

Emma, like Charles, had a very considerable capacity for being bored; and this, joined with great frankness, sincerity, and increasing gravity of manner, made her a formidable person. When someone asked her how she liked Tennyson's Queen Mary, she answered, with devastating matter-of-factness, "It is not nearly so tiresome as Shakespere."[20]

Though at the beginning of their marriage she had resolved to become interested in her husband's work, she soon found that science was for her, quite definitely and irrevocably, a bore. Charles was amused rather than dismayed, and often told how he had said to her at a meeting of the British Association, "I am afraid this is very wearisome to you"; and she had replied, "Not more than all the rest."[21] Emma was bored by so many things, and Charles was either bored or overexcited by so many things that they soon found themselves—from the time they sat in their armchairs after breakfast watching the clock until they sat in their easy chairs after dinner doing nothing (and Charles "in an apoplectic state")—settled into the quietest and firmest of routines.[22] Was it a little too dull for Emma? Charles wondered. For himself, he liked it immensely. Secure behind such a routine, he even liked London. It was "so cheerful," so different from the dreary country.[23]

But a domestic routine is always subject to heroic interruptions. William Erasmus was born in 1839, Anne Elizabeth in 1841. Often Charles found himself toiling desperately over unmanageable sentences with a sick child tucked up on the sofa nearby. There is much worry in the letters to Maer and Shrewsbury about wet feet and warm clothes, and particularly about the v's and w's of little William, who persisted discouragingly in asserting that his name was "Villy Darvin." Once Emma ventured to the pantomime with the Hensleigh Wedgwoods to see the children's fun:

The first thing was a most dreadful blood and thunder thing with a gibbet on the stage, and I thought it would be very bad for Bro's dreams. . . . Poor Erny put his head down on my lap when he expected any firing, or whenever the chief comic character, a beadle with a very red face, was on the stage, whom he seemed to think quite as alarming as any of the murderers. . . . I was surprised at the extreme innocence of even Snow's questions. "Whether they were really killed?" . . . "whether the wicked squire was really a bad man?" . . . The first play ended by the military coming over a wall and shooting almost all the characters dead, to our great relief.[24]

As time passed, it became clear that London was too much with them, late and soon. Emma, particularly, longed for the country. One did not have to go far to find it in those spacious days of slow locomotion and untroubled leisure. Following the railway lines, nineteenth-century civilization was a slender-tentacled octopus extended upon an immemorial rural quiet. After some search, Charles discovered at Downe in Kent, a moderate-sized, three-story house of stuccoed-over brick. It was square, unpretentious, and uninspired; but on the ground level, all along the west side, the drawing room and larger dining room looked out through sunny, wide, floor-length windows on a broad expanse of lawn which sloped gently upward, so that the flower beds made a brilliant effect. The landscape was somewhat melancholy—"waterless uninhabited valleys, bleak uplands, with occasional yews in the hedges, and here and there a white chalkpit."[25] But it was remarkable for an unusual variety of natural vegetation. Down House was a quarter-mile from the village (Downe), ten miles from a railroad station, and yet only sixteen miles in all from London, which was occasionally visible as a haze of smoke in the sky. From this vantage point, Charles saw, he could swiftly descend on Erasmus's London house of a Friday evening—listen there to Carlyle's eloquent wrongheadedness, breakfast with Lyell, attend the meetings of the learned societies—and then disappear into pastoral oblivion the following Monday.

For Down House and eighteen acres adjoining, the owner wanted twenty-five hundred pounds. Emma was doubtful, but on the whole Charles was enthusiastic—particularly when he thought how expensive other country houses were. To his sister Susan, who had an appetite for the sordid details of his illnesses and his finances, he wrote letters that bristled with considerations and counter-considerations. Of course he apologized for doing so. "How you and my Father can take so much interest about Down, as to like to hear all the foolish particulars I send you, is something wonderful. Your sympathy in other people's pleasures . . . always makes me full of admiration and envy."[26] "After many groans,"[27] he offered twenty-two hundred pounds, which was supplied by his father. The offer was accepted, and in late spring, 1842, the Darwins moved in. Charles was for a while quite lighthearted, even about the cost of improvements. "Emma seems to like the place," he wrote, "and Doddy [his son William] was in ecstasies for two whole days."[28]

The house was to grow, as the Darwin family grew, to considerable size. Henceforth, all Charles's voyages were to be intellectual, and all were to be made at the fireside of Down. Surely, his happiness was perfect. Unfortunately, he was not the man to be tranquil, even in tranquillity. He soon fell to worrying once more—about his health, the expense of improvements, about the responsibilities of his rapidly growing family, and probably about his own inability to earn money, should other income fail. When he confided to Dr. Darwin his "fears of ruin and extravagance," he got only an emphatic "stuff and nonsense" for sympathy; and when he spoke of a "dreadful numbness" in his finger ends, the mountainous Shrewsbury oracle was only a little gentler, cutting his son short with, "Yes—yes—exactly—tut—tut, neuralgic, exactly, yes, yes."[29]

Emma never made such replies. Her method was to soothe and placate all those with whom she lived in intimacy; sometimes she carried this policy to the un-Victorian length of bribing the children to act in their own best interests. In any case, Charles's complaints always aroused her love and sympathy, never her sense of criticism and her frankness. "Without you when sick I feel most desolate, . . ." wrote Charles from Shrewsbury. "I do long to be with you and under your protection for then I feel safe."[30] And others felt as Charles did. "Towards your mother," wrote Henrietta Huxley as a very old lady to one of Emma's daughters, "I always had a sort of nestling feeling. More than any woman I ever knew, she comforted."[31] Dr. Hubble observes in her the "Wedgwood devotion in illness."[32] When she married Charles, "the perfect nurse had married the perfect patient."

6

Barnacles and Blasphemy

Almost immediately on his return to England, Charles had begun to prepare his *Journal* for publication. Reconsidering his manifold observations in many fields of science, he was more than ever struck with the virtues of the transmutation hypothesis. To be sure, there was a great preponderance of gray hairs against it. Though he did not finish the *Journal* until 1837, when already far advanced in evolutionary speculations, he characteristically made no allusion to them in his narrative, but simply eliminated a few bolder expressions of his earlier creationism.

The *Journal* appeared in 1839 as the third volume of Fitzroy's *Narrative*. "If I live till I am eighty years old," Charles wrote Henslow, "I shall not cease to marvel at finding myself an author."[1] He marveled even more at finding his book a decided success. It sold steadily and a second edition was necessary in 1845. With its voluminous and graphic observations on plant and animal life, its brilliant analysis of South American geology, and its full summary of Darwin's coral island theory, the *Journal* is a worthy successor of Humboldt's *Personal Nar-*

rative, and in its turn became an inspiration to the youthful Hooker and other scientific explorers.

In spite of repeated illnesses, Darwin published his *Coral Reefs* in 1842 and his *Geological Observations on the Volcanic Islands* in 1844.[2] Both works were received with admiration, and the first is still recognized as containing the most generally accepted explanation of its subject. Rereading it seven years later, Darwin exclaimed with engaging emphasis, "*I am astonished at my own accuracy!!*"[3] Throughout this period he also contributed frequently to the scientific journals. In 1846 he published his *Geological Observations on South America, Being the Third Part of the Geology of the Voyage of the Beagle* and began his great work on Cirripedia, or barnacles. While on the coast of Chile, he had found a peculiar species for which he had to create a special suborder. At the outset he had no idea that he was to spend eight years in the study of barnacles; but the new barnacle could not be understood without a knowledge of the old ones, and Darwin found to his dismay that barnacles had been much misunderstood.

One might think that chronic indigestion could be more pleasantly employed than in the patient dissection of thousands of smelly little sea animals, yet as the years passed this pursuit became so familiar and inevitable to the Darwin family that one of the little boys, born into the midst of it, inquired about a neighbor, "Then where does he do his barnacles?"[4] Fresh knowledge led to the metaphysical intricacies of classification and the barren intricacies of nomenclature. Darwin's letters burn with moral indignation against the vanity, which he acknowledged in himself as a young man, of attaching one's name to a species simply because one has discovered it.

There were compensations. "Pure observation" was in itself a joy. To Fitzroy he writes of being "for the last half-month daily hard at work in dissecting a little animal about the size of a pin's head, from the Chonos archipelago, and I could

spend another month, and daily see more beautiful structure."[5]
And there were odd facts, satisfying to a man with an appetite
for odd facts.

The other day I got a curious example of a unisexual instead of a
hermaphrodite cirripede, in which the female had the common
cirripedial character, and in the two valves of her shell had two
little pockets, in each of which she kept a little husband; I do
not know of any other case where a female invariably has two
husbands.[6]

The fact was not merely curious. In another letter he explained, with noticeable excitement of discovery:

I should never have made this out, had not my species theory
convinced me, that an hermaphrodite species must pass into a
bisexual species by insensibly small stages, and here we have it, for
the male organs in the hermaphrodite are beginning to fail, and
[therefore] independent males [are] ready formed.[7]

But were even such facts worth eight years? "I do not doubt,"
wrote Darwin somewhat ruefully, "that Sir E. Lytton Bulwer
had me in his mind when he introduced in one of his novels a
Professor Long, who had written two huge volumes on lim-
pets."[8] In later years he was inclined to agree with the criticism
implied, but at the time he seems to have thought the barnacles
worth while. With characteristic enthusiasm for feats of scientific industry, Huxley agreed.

Your sagacious father [he wrote Francis Darwin in retrospect]
never did a wiser thing than when he devoted himself to the years
of patient toil which the Cirripede-book cost him. . . .
    It has always struck me as a remarkable instance of his scientific
insight, that he saw the necessity of giving himself such a training,
and of his courage, that he did not shirk the labour of obtaining it.[9]

Sir Joseph Hooker confirms this account: "Your father recognized three stages in his career as a biologist: the mere col-

lector at Cambridge; the collector and observer in the *Beagle*; and the trained naturalist after, and only after, the Cirripede work."[10]

As barnacles followed each other unceasingly beneath the microscope, the observer himself grew stooped and bald, and his face became deeply lined. Three more daughters were born—Mary, Henrietta, and Elizabeth—and two more sons— George and Francis.

Moreover, old Dr. Darwin's health had greatly declined. Always massive, the oracular physician had lately grown so corpulent that, when he tipped the scales at 336 pounds, he decided never to be weighed again. Some years afterward he could scarcely turn in his bed without assistance. Dressed in old-fashioned knee-breeches and a broad-lapeled coat, he spent most of his time in his wheelchair in the garden, surveying disconsolately the shrubs and fruit trees he had once enjoyed so much. He no longer delivered buoyant two-hour lectures on the day's happenings—partly because nothing ever happened. He did not want anything to happen. More and more, he pro- tected himself from experiences and recollections to which he felt unequal. His memory was as acute as his sensitivity, and he was trapped between the two faculties. He could not forget a date, and therefore the deaths of many old friends were annually recalled to him. Charles suggested that as he could not walk, he should drive out for exercise. "Every road out of Shrewsbury," he replied, "is associated in my mind with some painful event."[11]

Even so, he could still be cheerful and spirited. He could still lose his temper. The memory of his wrath remained green and awful in the minds of his middle-aged children, though he and Charles had grown much closer in these last years. They shared a taste for gossip and an interest in people. Both were good observers and had the quick, instinctive understanding which stops short of self-conscious analysis. The doctor was clairvoyant about his former patients. Charles retailed the latest news from the London scientific societies. He accepted the human side of science much more calmly than Huxley, and relished the anecdotes about Buckland's lust for notoriety, Falconer's bluntness and hot temper, Murchison's ebullient worship of rank.

Charles's own health seemed to be growing so precarious that, sitting with his father in the garden at Shrewsbury, he may have wondered which one would go first. Dr. Darwin only hoped that his end would be sudden. Sometimes they remained silent for long intervals, and then Charles made notes about barnacles or read Madame de Sévigné, with whom, following a gallant literary practice which he shared with his brother Erasmus, he had quite fallen in love.

In October he saw his father for the last time. The aged doctor died—as he had wished, quite suddenly—in November. His daughter Catherine wrote the news. "God comfort you, my dearest Charles," she concluded, "you were so beloved by him."[12] Charles's own daughter Henrietta, then a little girl, remembered "feeling awe-struck, and crying bitterly" out of sympathy with her father. As soon as he heard the news, Charles journeyed to Shrewsbury, but felt so ill that he did not take part in the funeral and refused to act as an executor of his father's large property.

During these years, Darwin's intellectual horizons were by no means confined to the rim of a barnacle shell. Barnacles were partly, as has been indicated, a preparation for a much greater subject, perhaps partly an escape from it. That subject was of course evolution.

Nobody would have been surprised if Huxley had explained evolution. Nearly everybody who has read the facts is a little surprised that Darwin did, and clever people from Samuel Butler to Mr. Jacques Barzun have demonstrated that he shouldn't have. Huxley had more talents than two lifetimes could have developed. He could think, draw, speak, write, inspire, lead, negotiate, and wage multifarious war against earth and heaven with the cool professional ease of an acrobat supporting nine people on his shoulders at once. He knew everything and did everything, and in his own time seemed a movement and an epoch in himself. In short, he enjoyed all the luxuries of genius. Darwin possessed only the bare necessities. He was a slow reader, particularly in foreign languages. He could not draw. He was clumsy and awkward with his hands, and despite his interest and belief in experiment, he was in some ways oddly careless and inefficient. He had great faith in instruments, yet his instruments were mostly crude and makeship. His children astounded him by proving that one of his micrometers differed from the other. He could not make a speech and dreaded appearing in public so much that in 1871 he could hardly sit through the church service at his daughter's wedding. "He used to say of himself that he was not quick enough to hold an argument with anyone,"[13] and his conversation was an adventure of parentheses within parentheses which often produced a stammer and sometimes terminated in unintelligibility and syntactical disaster. He wrote fairly clear and interesting English only by slowly and painfully improving the impossible, and when he took pen in hand laughingly grumbled that "if a bad arrangement of a sentence was possible, he should be sure to adopt it."[14]

How could such a man escape ordinary failure, much less achieve spectacular success? How could he possibly discover a great principle like natural selection and bring to completion a long work on organic evolution? Perhaps he succeeded —partly at least—in explaining evolution for the delightfully English reason that explaining evolution was a tradition in his family. In any case, his idea grew like a tradition—slowly, almost inevitably. The secret of his miracle is that it eventually happened. He had faith in the facts. He saw a problem and he felt that, with patience and a sincere desire for truth, the problem could be solved.

In 1837 he opened his first notebook on the mutability of species. From that moment he was a man living with an idea —a decent, safe man living with a shockingly indecent, horribly unsafe idea. The result was to turn a quiet young gentleman who wrote checks for causes into something of a fanatic and a crusader, to give a modest, uncertain young man a secret stay and sense of moral importance, and to add to a frank, open nature a touch of benevolent mystery.

I remember [said Huxley], in the course of my first interview with Mr. Darwin, expressing my belief in the sharpness of the lines of demarcation between natural groups and in the absence of transitional forms, with all the confidence of youth and imperfect knowledge. I was not aware, at that time, that he had then been many years brooding over the species-question; and the humorous smile which accompanied his gentle answer, that such was not altogether his view, long haunted and puzzled me.[15]

At first Darwin seems to have told no one his secret, though inevitably his wife knew, and feared, as old Dr. Darwin had predicted, for the salvation of her husband's soul. Quite early he confided in Lyell, who, though sympathetic, was not converted till twenty years later. In 1844, with fearful and conspiratorial reluctance, Darwin divulged his heresy to Joseph Hooker, then recently returned from his Antarctic voyage on the *Erebus*:

I am almost convinced . . . that species are not (it is like confessing a murder) immutable. Heaven forfend me from Lamarck nonsense of a "tendency to progression," "adaptations from the slow willing of animals," etc! . . . I think I have found out (here's presumption!) the simple way by which species become exquisitely adapted to various ends. You will now groan, and think to yourself, "on what have I been wasting my time and writing to." I should, five years ago, have thought so.[16]

Hooker put aside respectability and considered evolution on its merits. Hostile at the outset, he became more and more receptive; and though always critical, he was likewise always helpful, with information as well as with constructive suggestions. For Darwin he was apparently the one man with whom argument resulted in pleasure and clarification rather than in stupidity and confusion at the moment, and in brooding and insomnia afterward.

Like many amiable, charming people in ill-health, Darwin seems to have got a good deal of help from his friends without particularly meaning to. His old college chum Fox was set to observing spinal stripes on horses. Huxley reported on the embryology of fish, Asa Gray on alpine plants in North America, Hooker on New Zealand flora and a multitude of other subjects. Later, Darwin's children helped illustrate his books, Hooker and Lyell acted as his intercessors before the world of science, and Huxley became his "general agent" and champion against hostile armies of bishops and archdeacons. Darwin tried conscientiously to give as much as he received. He also tried to ask for little; but his enthusiasm carried both him and his friends along. "How I do hope you will get up some mountains in Borneo," he wrote Hooker with an eye to his own theory about the distribution of alpine plants; "how curious the result will be."[17]

To be sure, what drew so many able and brilliant men to such a recluse was not primarily a personality but an idea, or rather a system of ideas, which was to bring revolution into every field of biological science. Darwin's thinking could not be ignored. Moreover, it continued, even after the publication of *The Origin of Species*, to be done by Darwin. The strongest proof of his greatness is that he—not Wallace, Huxley, nor anybody else—was the center of Darwinism. Despite his illnesses and his limitations, he had the largeness, sobriety, and concentration of mind to retain leadership within his own

broad area of investigation. He could see the ultimate conclusions of his theory without ever jumping to them.

If we choose to let conjecture run wild [he wrote in his first
1837–1838 notebook], then animals, our fellow brethren in rain,
disease, death, suffering and famine—our slaves in the most laborious works, our companions in our amusements—they may partake
of (?) our origin in one common ancestor—we may be all melted
together.[18]

Perhaps Darwin thought just enough to be a great thinker.
Though "he often said that no one could be a good observer
unless he was an active theoriser,"[19] he seldom got more than
a stone's throw away from the facts, feeling that if facts without ideas were pitiable and unfruitful, ideas without facts were
fantastic and dishonest—a kind of insanity proceeding often
from moral causes. He was attached to the problem rather than
to his solution of the problem, and could therefore live with
the facts until they had to yield up their meaning. "It's dogged
as does it" was a saw he observed so faithfully that he sometimes had to apologize for his patience.[20]

One is tempted to see in these qualities further evidence of
the effect of his father on him—in the dogged patience, a passionate desire to win respect and love; in the reluctance to
speculate and the eagerness to return again and again to the
facts for corroboration, a sense of insecurity born of many
shattering explosions of paternal wrath. Perhaps Darwin did
not have Huxley's clarity and rapidity because he did not have
Huxley's confidence. The sons of portentous fathers usually
mature late.

Darwin may exaggerate the caution with which he approached his great subject. "I worked on true Baconian principles," he wrote "and without any theory collected facts on a
wholesale scale."[21] Actually, he began with his observations

in South America and with the strong suspicions they engendered. He also began with a literature in which evolution and natural selection were open secrets. The second volume of Lyell's *Principles* was really *The Origin of Species* without Darwinism, or at least without explicit Darwinism. In almost the same sequence, Lyell took up the problems of the *Origin* —variability, adaptation, embryological recapitulation, the significance of distribution and of the geological record—and did everything but solve them.

He had, indeed, carefully considered the evolutionary doctrine as presented by Lamarck but finally rejected it, deciding that species do not vary beyond certain restricted limits. Domestic breeds, having through the agency of man become adapted to many widely different environments, are extremely variable; but wild species, being confined to their own habitats and stations, vary little. Similarity of embryonic development simply indicates similar plan and structure. What chiefly convinced Lyell of immutability, however, was the relative sterility of hybrids. Apparently, he demanded that species change before his eyes. In fact, he seems to have exhausted all his originality and receptiveness on geology, as later and in lesser degree Darwin seems to have exhausted nearly all his on natural selection. Lyell saw that species were often almost infinitely prolific, that they competed with one another, that the increase of one might mean the diminution of another; but he was obsessed with the idea of a predestined—perhaps theological—equilibrium and stability of natural economy. "Every plant !. . ," he declared, quoting Wilcke, "has its proper insect allotted to it to curb its luxuriancy and to prevent it from multiplying to the exclusion of others."[22]

But there was one fact he could not overlook. The dodo was very dead. Lyell did not admit that extinction implied evolution, but he did attempt to account for extinction by natural causes; species might die, like individuals, of old age; or, more probably, they might be eliminated by adverse changes of environment or by the competition of more successful rivals.*

Practical observation in South America had provided Darwin with a catalytic which ultimately precipitated all Lyell's suspended facts and ideas into a coherent theory. Charles's notebooks show that he read the second volume of the *Principles* with great care, particularly the chapter on extinction.[23] He considered the suggestion that species might have a predetermined life cycle, but he must have seen that this was an explanation which did not explain, for it soon disappears from his notes. He must also have been struck with the idea of competition. If organisms become extinct through failure in competition, what is the nature of that competition? One species may be eliminated by an unrelated species or by an improved variety of itself. While still in South America, Charles had observed that the smaller Petise ostrich was rapidly vanishing under conditions favorable to its larger competitor. Extinct species might thus be the cousins or the ancestors of living ones. Extinction might thus imply improvement and transmutation.

Again, it may have been from reading Lyell that Darwin grasped the importance of domestic animals to the species question. They might illustrate, for example, why related species, like the pig and the tapir, are often so different from one another. Obviously, the intermediate forms no longer exist. In his notebook Darwin wrote: "Opponents will say—

---

* Lyell's quotation from the Swiss botanist Alphonse De Candolle must have struck Darwin. "All the plants of a given country . . . are at war with one another. The first which establish themselves by chance in a particular spot, tend, by the mere occupancy of space, to exclude other species— the greater choke the smaller, the longest livers replace those who last for a shorter period, the more prolific gradually make themselves masters of the ground, which species multiplying more slowly would otherwise fill" (*Principles of Geology*, II, 131).

show them me. I will answer yes, if you will show me every step between bulldog and greyhound."[24]

But how do varieties like the race horse and the tumbler pigeon arise? Studiously perusing stud books and fraternizing genially with horse-breeders and pigeon-fanciers, Darwin soon became as deeply erudite in their lore, both written and unwritten, as any contemplative stable-keeper or Derby-struck nobleman. The secret of animal breeding was clearly the selection of desirable variations, which then accumulate, generation after generation, into more and more pronounced characteristics. If breeds originate by man's selection, obviously species might originate by nature's. But how does nature select?

The fancier's skill had suggested the idea of selection; the problem of extinction, the idea of the struggle for existence. How long would it have taken Darwin, swimming tentatively and conscientiously in oceans of fact, to connect these two unaided? In half a dozen passages he is within an ace of the answer. Fortunately, in her evolutionary aspects nature is almost tritely mid-Victorian. In October, 1838, he happened to read "for amusement" Malthus's *Essay on Population*.[25] The mystery was solved.

Ironically, what Darwin had not quite seen in the grim anarchy of nature, he saw clearly in the modified anarchy of "civilization." Malthus emphasized two facts, both of which Darwin understood perfectly well: the infinite fertility of mankind and the limited size and resources of the planet. Malthus had studied the situation negatively, showing how population is kept down by famine, disease, and war. Darwin took a positive view. Granting that animal numbers are checked even more intensively by similar factors, he asked himself which individuals survive and procreate? Obviously, those whose variations represent a better adaptation to environment. Nature breeds a vast oversupply of experiments and then sterilizes the failures by murdering them. Malthus had led Darwin to a new application of the economic doctrine of competition.

Charles now had a theory to work with, yet he feared so much the seductions of thought that not until 1842 did he commit his ideas to paper, and then only to the erasable impermanence of a thirty-five page pencil sketch. In 1844, however, he wrote out a statement of 231 pages, which is very complete, in its earlier part closely paralleling the first half of *The Origin of Species*, and containing a discussion not only of natural, but also of "unconscious" and sexual selection, as well as of nearly every important detail of the final theory. Nevertheless, it did omit, as he discovered with astonishment, the problem of why organisms of the same stock diverge as they become modified. The solution was that "all dominant and increasing forms tend to become adapted to many and highly diversified places in the economy of nature."[26] Late in life he wrote: "I can remember the very spot in the road, whilst in my carriage, when to my joy the solution occurred to me; and this was long after I had come to Down." Apparently, this was his only sudden illumination, his single thunderclap of intellectual grace. The 1842 sketch is interesting for the emphasis which it laid on mutations or abrupt changes; and the 1844 sketch, for the importance it gave to external conditions in accounting for variations.[27]

Darwin had his moments of speculative exaltation at this time. He delighted, though with some qualms at the treachery of logic, in the logician's ingenuity with which he fitted the theory of natural selection to all facets of evolutionary phenomena. Moreover, he could not but see that his ideas, if accepted, would have a tremendous effect on contemporary thought and science. "My theory," he wrote in his early notebook, "would give zest to recent and fossil comparative anatomy; it would lead to the study of instincts, heredity, and mind-heredity, [the] whole [of] metaphysics."[28]

At such times he felt the terrible urgency of his task, the imperative need to be free and tranquil for the one absorbing thought of his life. But who was ever free or tranquil? "Eleven children, ave Maria! it is a serious look-out for you," he ejaculated with awe to his old college friend Fox. "Indeed I look on my five boys as something awful, and hate the very thought of professions."[29] Money symbolized the intrusive practicality of the world, the haunting uncertainty of all human comfort and well-being; though comfortably rich and always generous, Charles was very anxious and careful about money. He practiced many small economies, some of them quite irrational, like his hobby for saving paper. He not only hoarded partially used sheets but waste paper, objecting, "half in fun, to the careless custom of throwing a spill into the fire after it had been used for lighting a candle."[30]

Behind all his petty anxieties there were two great ones: that he was not strong enough to complete his study of species and that his children would not be strong enough to support themselves and live normal, healthy lives. "If one could insure moderate health for them," he continued in his letter to Fox, "it would not signify so much, for I cannot but hope, with the enormous emigration, professions will somewhat improve. But my bugbear is hereditary weakness."[31]

It was probably the fear of dying before his work was done which, more than anything else, made him set his theory on paper. Yet even the lengthy sketch of 1844 seemed to him a poor and inadequate record of his researches. Immediately after completing it, he wrote his wife a letter, pathetic in its suppressed urgency, solemnly requesting that in the event of his death she engage a competent editor, at a fee of four hundred pounds, to prepare his statement for the press. It should be enlarged, corrected, and documented from materials collected in his library. The list of desirable editors, beginning with Lyell and ending with Hooker, is again pathetically long.

In 1854 he noted on the back of the letter that Hooker would be much the best.

All this suggests that Darwin hardly expected to witness the impact of his theory upon the world. And in fact his problem was so staggeringly immense, it ramified into so many fields of science and required investigation of factors so tenuous and complex, that even the swiftest and healthiest worker might have despaired of doing it justice in a lifetime. "In my wildest day-dream," wrote Darwin about 1845, "I never expect more than to be able to show that there are two sides to the question of the immutability of species."[32] And yet he wanted to make the negative as strong as possible. Moreover there was his debt to the Cirripedia, boundless and morally imperative, to be discharged. Hooker and Charles's own conscience had dinned into him that no man should presume to work on the species question without first having studied and described many particular species.

In the years between 1851 and 1854 he published his study of Cirripedia in four monographs. He was now free to turn his whole energies to evolution. He might at any time be anticipated by another man. Though dubious about any theory of organic evolution, Lyell urged the immediate publication of a brief sketch. Hooker counseled against a sketch. Darwin must not anticipate himself with a trifling and undocumented paper, but must write and publish a definitive treatise as rapidly as possible. After some anxious hesitation and a false try at the sketch, he resolutely settled down to the treatise, on a scale three or four times greater than that of the *Origin*.

The years slipped past. His evidence heaped up higher, and his book became longer and longer. Of course he worked as fast as he could. In fact, like many plodders, he lived in an extended paroxysm of defeated haste. When a talk with John Lubbock showed him he had wasted two or three weeks' work, he burst out to Hooker: "I am the most miserable, bemuddled, stupid dog in all England, and am ready to cry with vexation at my blindness and presumption."[33]

He dreaded being laughed at almost more than being anticipated, for he felt that his subject had already been discredited by the extravagant though original speculations of Lamarck and "Mr. Vestiges." That he should ever have embarked on anything so unsavory and grandiose seemed to him an appalling paradox. "I have asked myself," he wrote Lyell, "whether I may not have devoted my life to a fantasy"; later on he was astonished to find that Hooker had apparently come to believe in natural selection more firmly than he did himself.[34] He never suggested an original idea even to Hooker or Lyell without the preface, "You will think all this utter bosh." His imagination was fastidiously sober and prosaic. He was permeated with the idea of theoretic economy. Forbes's fancifulness made him physically ill, and though aware that his own position was sufficiently vulnerable, he was so indignant at the freedom with which Lyell's pupils indulged in lost continents that he wrote the father of modern geology an impassioned protest, backed by subsequent letters and a great mass of evidence:

If you do not stop this, if there be a lower region for the punishment of geologists, I believe, my great master, you will go there. Why, your disciples in a slow and creeping manner, beat all the old Catastrophists who ever lived. You will live to be the great chief of the Catastrophists.[35]

Darwin also shrank from being taken too seriously by all kinds of very serious people. It gradually became known among his relatives that he was preparing for publication a lengthy and learned blasphemy. Their pious horror must have been particularly formidable as the corporate emotion of a family so large and close-knit, so affectionate and worthy of respect, as the Wedgwoods and the Darwins. But imagine the pious horror of a whole nation! And the more effective the book, the more intense and pious the horror. Subconsciously at least, he must have wished to postpone this painful dilemma, perhaps to escape it altogether. "I almost think Lyell would have proved right, and I should never have completed my longer work," he wrote Wallace when he had finished *The Origin of Species*. ". . . I look at my own career as nearly run out."[36] Later of course, when the *Origin* was in proof and he observed how much it impressed and staggered men like Hooker and Lyell, he partly forgot his fears in his eagerness to observe its effect on the thoughtful public. "You may think me presumptuous," he wrote Hooker, "but I think my book will be popular to a certain extent . . . among scientific and semi-scientific men; why I think so is, because I have found in conversation so great and surprising an interest among such men."[37]

As early as 1855 Darwin noticed in the *Annals of Natural History* a paper on species by Alfred Russell Wallace. The ideas bore an alarming resemblance to his own. "I rather hate the idea of writing for priority," Darwin wrote Lyell, "yet I certainly would be vexed if any one were to publish my doctrines before me."[38] In May, 1857 he received a letter from Wallace, then in Celebes, putting questions on varieties and the breeding of domestic animals. "I can plainly see," Darwin answered, "that we have thought much alike and to a certain extent have come to similar conclusions."[39] He was friendly but cautious, mentioning that he had been working on the species question for twenty years. In December of the same year he received another letter from Wallace putting questions on distribution. "Though agreeing with you on your conclusions, . . ." Darwin replied, "I believe I go much further than you; but it is too long a subject to enter on my speculative notions."[40] Again he mentioned that he had been at work for twenty years.

Wallace's next letter, containing the famous paper on evolution and natural selection, struck him like a bombshell. Within a single week, while lying ill with malarial fever in the jungles of the Malay Peninsula, Wallace had leaped from his earlier position to Darwin's most advanced conclusions. What Darwin had puzzled and wondered and worried and slaved over with infinite anxiety and pain for two decades, Wallace had investigated and explained—far less elaborately but still to precisely the same result—in some three years. The familiar ideas, the older man could not help noticing, were conveyed with un-Darwinian force and clarity.

Darwin met the crisis with magnanimity, but with a rather anxious, questioning, backward-glancing magnanimity. "Do you not think his having sent me this sketch ties my hands?" he asked Lyell. ". . . I would far rather burn my whole book, than that he or any other man should think that I have behaved in a paltry spirit."[41] He had begun a letter to Wallace renouncing all claims, but he could not finish it; he could not quite close the door. "If I could honourably publish," he suggested to Lyell, "I would state that I was induced now to publish a sketch . . . from Wallace having sent me an outline of my general conclusions." Of course he despised himself. "My dear good friend forgive me," he concluded. "This is a trumpery letter, influenced by trumpery feelings."[42]

Upon this recondite and esoteric tragedy the simple realities of life intervened with ironical savagery. Scarlet fever appeared in Darwin's numerous household and in a short time his infant daughter was dead. "I am quite prostrated, and can do nothing," he wrote Hooker.[43] And a little later, "I am quite indifferent, and place myself absolutely in your and Lyell's hands."[44]

Lyell and Hooker did what Darwin had suggested. While he was still overcome with grief and illness, a joint paper, containing Wallace's report and a brief sketch of his own, was read before the Royal Society. The hour was heavy with grave

Victorian suspense. Both Lyell and Hooker were present and endorsed the proceedings.

The interest excited was intense [wrote Hooker], but the subject was too novel and too ominous for the old school to enter the lists, before armouring. After the meeting it was talked over with bated breath: Lyell's approval, and perhaps in a small way mine, as his lieutenant in the affair, rather overawed the Fellows, who would otherwise have flown out against the doctrine. We had, too, the vantage ground of being familiar with the authors and their theme.[45]

Wallace declared the course taken before the Royal Society more than generous and gracefully resigned himself for a life-time to being the moon to Darwin's sun. The latter, reassured by Wallace's reply, was soon asking him to observe the stripe on horses and donkeys. He could not, however, refrain from mentioning a third time that he had written the first summary of his ideas just twenty years ago.

Darwin now began to prepare a brief paper on evolution for the Linnean Society. Characteristically, in spite of iron resolutions for ruthless compression, he allowed it to grow by imperceptible degrees to a large volume. Still insisting that he was writing a mere preliminary abstract and still meditating a greater work to come, Darwin was writing the most important book in the nineteenth century.

7

The Most Important Book of the Century

Certainly no one who began so cautiously with facts ever got quite so deeply involved in ideas as Charles Darwin. He carefully avoided issues, and issues sprang up on all sides. He gravely eschewed speculation, and speculation enveloped him. In fact, his very caution and austerity, his very contempt for mere ideas, made him an unparalleled intellectual and controversial force in Victorian England. Herbert Spencer wallowed for decades in evolutionary speculation of the boldest sort without arousing one-tenth the scandal, excitement, loyalty, hatred, and animosity. Darwin's great investigation was not only central to scientific thought in many fields. It placed him directly athwart almost every great issue in philosophy, ethics, and religion. The old questions of necessity and free will, mechanism and spontaneity, matter and spirit, realism and nominalism, relativism and the absolute were faced all over again and argued in a new light because of *The Origin of Species*.

Like nearly everything else, evolution was invented, or almost invented, by the Greeks. From Heraclitus and Anaximander came the suggestion that animal species are mutable; from Aristotle, the idea of a graded series of organisms, the idea of continuity in nature or the shading of one class into another, and a model of evolutionary process in the development of the germ into the plant.[1] From both the Stoics and the Epicureans, and particularly from Lucretius, came the doctrine that man is a part of nature and that his origins are animal and savage rather than godlike and idyllic.

But meanwhile Plato had changed the direction of occidental thought: the shifting, evanescent world of things is transcended by a more real, static world of ideas, which is comprehended and unified by the idea of the Good, or God. To be sure, Plato's God was a self-sufficient Perfection dwelling apart from the world, and at the same time a superabundant Perfection flowing down into the world and actualizing the myriad objects and creatures which He had conceived.[2] In short, He implied unity, concentration, and other-worldliness on the one hand and diversity, expansion, and naturalism on the other. Medieval thinkers developed both conceptions, but emphasized the first. Moreover, following Plato, they thought in terms of being rather than becoming. The great historical enemy of evolution has been the Platonic tendency—so congenial to logic, morals, and mathematics—to regard the universe as a fixed order, in which realities remain perspicaciously what they are while the mind thinks about them.

Renaissance philosophers emphasized the infinite creativeness of God and the infinite vastness and variety of the universe. Creation was a great "chain of being" which extended in a linear gradation imperceptibly fine from lowest to highest.* But time was a decided inconvenience. If, according to

---

* In the seventeenth century Leibnitz carried the principles of plenitude, continuity, and linear gradation to their logical extreme. God had created all things possible that could exist together—in terms of quantity and variety, therefore, the best of all possible worlds. Naturally, an infinite diversity of creatures meant almost infinite conflict and suffering. Leibnitz's universe was not so much rational because it was good, as good because it was rational.

Plato's system, every actuality depends on an eternal essence and the ground plan of the world is simply a conjunction of all possible essences—why does not everything possible exist at once? In short, the principle of plenitude called out for evolution, for a time dimension. So did the facts of embryology and paleontology.

In the eighteenth century Buffon treated the subject of evolution for the first time "in a scientific spirit."[3] He maintained that animals vary in response to changes in environment, habit, and inwardly felt need, passing the variations on to their offspring by a process of hereditary memory.* Buffon is in every respect remarkable, being himself a kind of cultural mastodon, or magnificent extinct animal—such a wonderful combination of artist, gentleman, and scientist as, preserved in the fossil immortality of literature, illustrates whole movements of thought and transitions between epochs.

Dr. Erasmus Darwin, Charles's grandfather (1731–1803), was no less remarkable. A wit who stammered, a physician who versified botany, a mechanical inventor and walking encyclopedia who fascinated women, he was in his way as remarkable as Benjamin Franklin, as quaint as a porcelain statuette savage in red heels and ostrich feathers. And yet his modernity reaches comfortably to the twentieth century; for his evolutionary ideas, though no doubt mainly inspired by Buffon, have a definitely Freudian tendency. Animals evolve, and thereby adapt themselves to a changed environment by reacting to stimuli in terms of love, hunger, and the need for security. Dr. Darwin went beyond Buffon in maintaining that all life is descended from a single, very simple organism; but fell below him in explaining inherited habit and function by conscious

---

* What Darwin and others regarded as Buffon's fluctuations of opinion may have been, as Samuel Butler maintained with delight, but skillful and daring maneuvers in a long and grave flirtation with the authorities of the Sorbonne, who finally compelled him to a public apology.

imitation rather than by unconscious memory or instinct. His grandson read his Zoonomia twice and was disappointed to find so many ideas and so few facts.[4] Certainly it contains plenty of ideas, including a very clear exposition of his grandson's theory of sexual selection.

Lamarck's reputation is greater than Erasmus Darwin's mainly because his facts are stronger. As Charles Darwin embraced evolution largely because it explained the data of geographical distribution, so Lamarck embraced it because it explained those of comparative structure. Apparently inspired by the Aristotelian principle of continuity, he asserted there are no species, only individuals. Nevertheless, individuals can usefully be grouped according to their structure, and function determines structure. Organs arise and develop with use and degenerate and disappear with disuse.[5]

What discredited Lamarck among scientists was that he explained too much and in too antiquated a manner. His theory of the nature of life itself is a strange mixture of mechanism and vitalism, by which the essential characteristics of all living things are traced analytically to the mere motion of a metaphysical fluid or ethereal fire. What discredited him among the religious was the reckless logic with which he insinuated that man himself was not exempt from the evolutionary past. "I devoured Lamarck en voyage," wrote the youthful Charles Lyell. "His theories delighted me more than any novel I ever read." Yet in proving "men may have come from the Ourang-Outang," he had in Lyell's eyes reduced himself to a fascinating absurdity.[6]

Meanwhile, the romantic movement—with its wonder at nature, its nostalgic curiosity about origins, its fascination with change, its exultation in plenitude and diversity—had caused students in every field to think in terms of evolution. Kant and Laplace found it in the solar system, Lyell on the surface of the earth, Herder in history, Newman in church doctrine,

Hegel in the Divine Mind, and Spencer in nearly everything.

In fact, biological evolution itself was rapidly becoming the commonest heresy in Europe. In England it seemed for a while likely to become orthodox without serious bloodshed, for the political and intellectual climate of the later twenties was extremely favorable. The Tory party was making itself unpopular in office; philosophical radicalism was opening up logical vistas into a reassuringly prosaic utopia; and science itself was unfolding momentous discoveries in a manner which combined the excitement of novelty with the imposing decorum of solid vested interest and responsible conservatism.

This very English exhibition of scientific tact was largely the achievement of a single man, who worthily represented the learning, the science, the statesmanship, and even the religion of the ruling classes. That man was of course Charles Lyell— a Chancellor of the Exchequer among scientists as Darwin called him—who never entered into controversy and who always wrote with a grave sense of the weight of authoritative words magisterially penned. Acknowledging the claims not only of truth scientific and religious but of error and prejudice as well, Lyell was admirably qualified for the complex and delicate task of stating the simple facts in an age of inquiry and expanding knowledge.[7] With all of Gibbon's monumental dignity and none of his secret sedition, Lyell unfolded in his *Principles* the relentless uniformity of natural causes and geological evolution as far back in terrestrial time as one could see. Yet he was careful not to assert that natural causes had of necessity always operated: the advent of man was an exceptional event in the moral, though hardly in the physical, world. With statesmanlike abandon of logic he drew, like Pope Alexander VI, a line straight across the world, proclaiming evolution in the realms of geology and botany, and a Creator in those of man and animals. He made no allusion to Hebrew cosmogony, but described similar primitive traditions, which, he pointed out at length, were a credit both to the intelligence and the moral feelings of their authors. Nearly everything he said was at variance with the Mosaic narrative, yet he contradicted it with so much tact and dignity that sound Englishmen could not long withstand him.

The Principles of Geology occasioned little scandal. Sixteen-hundred-page treatises seldom do. There was some pained regret among the Tories, some dignified suffering among the clergy. Oddly enough, there was eager enthusiasm among ordinary readers. Harriet Martineau declared that in the period after the vogue of Scott's novels the general middle-class public "purchased five copies of an expensive work on geology for one of the most popular novels of the time."[8] Behind the scenes at the Royal Geological Society, there was a sharp battle between the "Diluvialists" and the "Fluvialists," but it was good-humored, even hilarious. Within a decade, the new ideas had been accepted on their merits. Lyell had guided the advance of science as wisely and moderately as the Duke of Wellington had conducted the retreat of the British Constitution.

Unfortunately, liberalism had enfranchised its executioners. The middle classes, coming into power after 1832, were conservative and pietistic in their religion. Nearly every outstanding figure in the new generation, from Gladstone to Newman, was a fervid Christian and a dogmatic believer in Revelation. Nearly every important sect identified the validity of the spiritual life with the liberal truth of a creation story directly contradicted by scientific facts.

Under these circumstances, science could scarcely hope to advance by tact alone, however statesmanlike. Evolution crept back into footnotes and appendices, as in Patrick Matthew's Naval Timber and Arboriculture; or ventured forth anonymously, as in Robert Chambers's Vestiges of the Natural History of Creation—only to be hooted down by surpliced geologists like Sedgwick. Lyell himself was driven to complain

of the Mosaic superstitions as "an incubus on our science."[9]
Many investigators waxed prosperous and eminent by "proving" a Cosmic Intelligence with scientific discoveries which
later made it seem less likely than ever. A few carried Lyell's
politic decorum to bewildering extremes of hypocrisy and self-
contradiction. In fact, to what depths of respectability the
scientific mind could sink became evident only after the explosion of Darwinism had occurred. In the venomous and
confused counterattacks of men like Sir Richard Owen the
only certainty which emerges is that the pillars of orthodoxy
themselves did not believe literally in the Old Testament.
Owen is said to have talked as an evolutionist in private conversation; in public he defended creationism in terms so ambiguous that no one understood him and he himself, in letters
to the editor of *The London Review*, actually felt free to claim
priority over Darwin in developing the theory of natural
selection.

But even while in England the very atheists were observing
the decencies, a theological disaster occurred in Germany. At
least partly concealed in the formidable Trojan horse of
Hegelian metaphysics, David Strauss had got inside the evangelical fortress and surprised the garrison, subjecting miracles
to such devastating textual criticism as seemed to convert the
New Testament itself into a weapon against official religion.
Though Strauss published *Das Leben Jesu* in 1835, England
remained impregnable in her ignorance for several years. Those
who dared speak, spoke obscurely or were themselves obscure.*

But cautious insinuations gave place in the forties and fifties
to bold assertions. Science waxed and religion waned. From

---

* In 1838 Charles Hennell published his *Inquiry Concerning the Origin
of Christianity*, in which, an unlettered merchant entirely innocent of
the refinements of theological decorum, he expressed his disbelief as
simply and frankly as he had previously maintained his belief. The book
caused hardly a ripple. In 1840 H. H. Milman, already under suspicion

the remote empyrean of German science came the news that
Helmholtz had formulated mathematically the law of the conservation of energy, and so turned the universe into a great
account book of mechanistic causes. In his *Logic* Mill expounded universal causation with all the authority of a great
reputation and five hundred pages of closely reasoned analysis.
Comte constructed a theory of progress which made scientists
its dedicated priests, scientific method its indispensable tech-
nique, and a scientifically directed society its ultimate goal and
destiny. Carlyle proved that a deep sense of religion could be
separated from theology—and from genuine religion as well,
for that matter. At the same time, the air was electric with
evolution. Chambers's *Vestiges* was annihilated again and
again by furious clerical cannonades, and each time rose from
its ashes in the augmented strength of corrected and revised
editions.

Among the new generation of churchmen few were as
talented as their predecessors and none were as orthodox.
Maurice rejected original sin and the atonement. Martineau
went beyond and rejected the trinity. Baden Powell embraced
evolution itself as the chief argument for design. Pattison
traveled all the way from Newmanism to agnosticism. And
while liberals plunged into skepticism, conservatives embraced
the Woman of Babylon. In 1845 Newman became a Catholic.
Evangelical orthodoxy shrank back in horror within its oak-
paneled studies, and from castellated deaneries and moated
bishops' palaces emanated influences, injunctions, and jour-
nalistic thunderings that created a reign of ecclesiastical terror.
Gaitered gentlemen waited with pens poised, ready to strike

---

for his *History of the Jews*, published a *History of Christianity* in which,
for hundreds of pages, he steadily implied the view which Strauss and
Hennell had explicitly declared and saved himself only at the last moment
by a halfhearted statement of divine inspiration.

when the Arch Fiend should raise his head. It was at this juncture that *The Origin of Species* appeared in 1859.

"Get rid of your genius for a session," the veteran orator Sheil had counseled the young Disraeli after a first successful speech. "Try to be dull. . . . Quote figures, dates, calculations."[10] Darwin did not need such advice. No one—except perhaps Sir Richard Owen—has ever complained that *The Origin of Species* was "too clever by half." It does not, with dazzling clarity of phrase and plan, derive a whole science from a piece of chalk or a whole philosophy from a bit of protoplasm. It does not spin a universe out of a few dry polysyllables or charm down a theological Jericho with a dozen epigrams. Rather it masses its facts in the forefront and carefully hides its paradoxes in the rear. It begins with the humdrum and the prosaic, and moves almost imperceptibly into the vast and mysterious. *The Origin of Species* is a long and dignified argument in which, almost with reluctance, the author convinces himself that evolution is a fact and natural selection is its explanation. Sir Robert Peel himself could not have put his case more effectively.

After a quiet, cautious introduction, in which he outlines his basic ideas and their arrangement, Darwin begins with the solid and reassuring facts of horse-breeding and pigeon-fancying.* Probably because man is constantly subjecting them to new conditions, individual animals of a domestic variety differ from each other much more than do individuals of a wild

---

* For the sake of completeness, I follow the sixth edition of *The Origin of Species*, as it appears in the Authorized Edition (New York: D. Appleton & Company, Inc., 1896). Nevertheless, I indicate, in the text or in the notes, any deviation from the first edition (see Charles Darwin, *On The Origin of Species by means of Natural Selection, or the Preservation of Favoured Races in the Struggle for Life*, a Reprint of the First Edition, with a Foreword by Dr. C. D. Darlington, F.R.S. (New York: Philosophical Library, 1951).

species. Moreover, they evolve almost before our eyes. How? By artificial selection. The farmer allows only his best stock to reproduce. The expert breeder consciously plans the animal he wants. Carefully noting differences which, Darwin cunningly observes, "I for one have vainly attempted to appreciate,"[11] he mates those individuals which vary from their fellows in the way desired, and continues to do so, accumulating favorable variations by heredity through successive generations, until he approximates or achieves his purpose.

Darwin now shows that naturalists widely disagree as to what constitutes a species. As commonly used, the term implies little more than a vague conception of difference dignified by a vague doctrine of special creation. Darwin seeks a more precise meaning in a fresh approach to the evidence. Any typical classification of flora and fauna reveals that more species appear in populous genera than in those less populous, and more varieties in populous species than in those less populous. If species are the products of special creation, this striking fact has no significance; but if species are but strongly marked varieties, and varieties but incipient species, then it means that divergent evolution proceeds from large and successful species. Species containing many individuals occupy a wide territory. Coming in contact with a great diversity of conditions, they tend to produce a greater range of individual differences than do smaller species.

Do they also, like domestic breeds, evolve rapidly and by a similar process of selection? Of course Darwin answers yes, and discovers his principle of selection in Malthus:

We behold the face of nature bright with gladness, we often see the superabundance of food; we do not see or we forget, that the birds which are idly singing round us mostly live on insects or seeds, and are thus constantly destroying life; or we forget how largely these songsters, or their eggs, or their nestlings, are destroyed by birds and beasts of prey; we do not always bear in mind, that, though food may be now superabundant, it is not so at all seasons of each recurring year.[12]

In short, the natural order is a very intricate kind of war, in which, basing itself on the limited resources of the planet, superabundant life builds up into a vastly complex and inter-related structure of hunter and hunted, parasite and host, sheltered and shelterer, eater and eaten. The slightest peculi-arity resulting in better adaptation may permit an individual to survive, reproduce, and in passing on his advantage, strengthen the position of his species.

The constant pressure of fertility and selection forces species to diverge and specialize, seizing "on many and widely diversi-fied places in the polity of nature."[13] Thus plants become more complexly and efficiently adapted to many different kinds of soil and climate. Animals become powerful and ferocious, or swift and wary, or slow and impregnable; and some grow intel-ligent and adaptable in dealing with a great diversity of con-ditions. Life blindly breeds, battles, and slaughters its way up to mind and rationality. The author himself is apparently more impressed by the progress than by the slaughter. "When we reflect on this struggle," he observes, "we may console our-selves with the full belief, that the war of nature is not inces-sant, that no fear is felt, that death is generally prompt, and that the vigorous, the healthy, and the happy survive and multiply."[14] Confronted by this dilemma between progress and suffering so typical of his century, Darwin was not always cheerful. On occasion he could feel all of a humanitarian's moral indignation against man and God for the evils of the world.

Darwin explains sex as a means partly of obtaining a di-vision of labor, partly of strengthening and stabilizing a strain by cross-fertilization. He also outlines his theory of sexual selection. Females prefer gorgeous, virile, or ferocious males; therefore such males produce more progeny and are selected into even greater gorgeousness, virility, or ferocity.

Already in *The Origin of Species* Darwin is haunted by the mystery of genetics. If variations cause evolution, what causes variations? He attacks the problem in the first and second chapters, and finally at length in the fifth. The discussion is cautious and sensible but also vague and occasionally confused. He sometimes talks as though natural selection not only sifts variations but causes them. Later, when taken to task for these lapses by Lyell and Wallace, he rectified many passages but allowed a few to remain, even in the last edition of his book. In general, he holds that variations arise through unknown hereditary factors within the organism, through use and disuse, the correlation of parts, and changes in environment. Domestic animals are extremely variable because man has introduced them into many and diverse regions. The domestic duck cannot rise from the ground because it has long ceased to need or use its wings. Significantly, its young can still fly. In short, he is often, so to speak, a Buffonian or a Lamarckian on the genetic level. At his best, he simply acknowledges a complete ignorance of the whole subject.

The sixth and seventh chapters* of the *Origin* answer objections—mostly foreseen by the author but in later editions identified with the persons who urged them. Here Darwin reveals unexpected talents as a debater. Confused, stammering, and unsyntactical in the presence of triumphantly articulate people like Huxley, he is deadly in the careful and premeditated quiet of the study. As usual, his confessions of weakness are irresistible. He freely acknowledges that the objections to his theory are grave. Nevertheless, after prolonged

* The first edition devotes only one chapter (the sixth) to objections. Its remaining chapters, though closely paralleled in subject matter, number from VII to XIV, rather than from VIII to XV, as in the sixth edition.

thought, he has in each case arrived at a solution which he hopes will prove satisfactory.

An assertion frequently made by his opponents is that if species and varieties are constantly diverging, the face of nature should present a continuity of forms shading into each other by minute degrees, instead of the many gaps and sharply separated species which we observe in fact. Not at all, Darwin replies. There is a selection of varieties and species as well as of individuals. A successful breed will spread into the surrounding territory and necessarily eliminate many related varieties, including the parent stock itself.

Next come the curious histories and the animal and vegetable prodigies which, it was thought, could not possibly have been produced by any combination of happy accidents. How, for example, could natural selection have revolutionized a carnivorous land animal into a marine leviathan like the whale? The first step would inevitably be a step away from adaptation. How could it ever be taken? Darwin answers somewhat in the anecdotal vein of Gilbert White, by citing the single instance of the brown bear which swam "for hours with wide open mouth, thus catching, almost like the whale, insects in the water."[15] More convincingly, he explains the flying squirrel by calling attention to the whole squirrel family, which graduates from relatively heavy ground animals, through light tree climbers to very light gliders. Again, how could natural selection ever account for such a perfection of ingenuity and design as the human eye? Darwin frankly confesses that this organ has always staggered him. Nevertheless, he gives a possible evolution according to natural selection, and quotes a learned German to the effect that as a microscope, telescope, or common optical instrument, the human eye is, like everything else in nature, very far from perfect.

Bronn objects that many plant and animal characteristics, and particularly those that distinguish varieties and species, are of no apparent use and cannot therefore be affected by natural selection. Darwin replies that one would expect precisely the useless characteristics to be most important in classification, for, being unaffected by natural selection, they have changed little and so indicate the more distant past of the organism. Again, Mivart objects that small variations are not sufficient to account for major changes. New species probably arise all at once. This view, similar to that later held by De Vries, is in Darwin's opinion contradicted by the finely shaded differences between many species and varieties, by the close continuity of development indicated by embryology, and by the beautiful adaptation of many structures to environment, which would hardly have been possible if the organism had evolved by abrupt mutations. In fact, mutations result in impracticable "monstrosities." Darwin deprecates their importance in every way.

Instinct he explains as resulting partly from habit and environment, but much more from a natural selection of useful variations in behavior. How did the European cuckoo acquire the instinct to lay its eggs in the nests of other birds? Darwin approaches the problem by his favorite method of seeking gradations of the same characteristic in related species, and he strengthens his case by emphasizing correlations between instinct and structure. In the first place, all known varieties of the cuckoo seem to lay their eggs not in relatively quick succession, but at intervals of two or three days. Consequently, the American cuckoo, which makes its own nest, must deal at the same time with unhatched eggs and young birds of various ages. Driven apparently by this predicament, she sometimes lays an egg in the nest of another bird. The Australian cuckoo represents an advance, but with some variability of behavior, laying sometimes one, and sometimes two or three eggs in the nest of another bird. The European species has made a complete and triumphant adjustment to her egg-laying habits. Her eggs are innocently small; she lays only one in each nest; and the young bird is amazingly strong soon after birth, so that he may thrust out his foster brothers and enjoy exclusive care.

But why does an organism vary its behavior, particularly in a situation of difficulty like the cuckoo's? Darwin has nothing to say about mental factors. He will not discuss the origin of mind, any more than that of life itself. He simply asserts that behavior tends to vary. Few theorizers on the grand scale have skirted so judiciously such vast regions of the unknown, or been so shrewd in their reticences.

In Chapters X to XIII Darwin deals with the evidence from paleontology and geographical distribution. If a record of the biological past is preserved in the rocks, why does it not provide an explicit proof of evaluation? Why does it not reveal the species of living families graduating back to common ancestors? In some degree it does, says Darwin—in future years it was with increasing discoveries to do so infinitely more—but scientists must recognize that the geological record is fragmentary and episodic in the extreme. Organic remains usually decay and disappear before they can become imbedded in sand or gravel. To be preserved they must be deposited in shallow bottoms which are slowly sinking as sediment accumulates. Under these rare conditions rich fossiliferous beds of great depth may be formed, but they may then be as slowly raised and eroded away. Formations of great paleontological importance found in England are entirely absent in Russia and North America.

That the geological record should be full of crucial silences is therefore not surprising. What is surprising is that its broken story should seem at first glance distinctly unfavorable to the evolutionist. Why do new species appear quite suddenly in a formation? Why do very similar and closely related ones appear in the same formations, and therefore in roughly the same era, throughout the entire world? The answer, says Darwin, is that a new species develops in a restricted, perhaps isolated region and then spreads with comparative rapidity at the expense of antiquated competitors. The geological record tends to preserve the ubiquitous *fait accompli*, not the isolated first innovation.

The two chapters on geographical distribution are a triumphant illustration of Darwin's mental grasp, of his ability to reduce a chaos of facts to a sound and intelligible world of law. The distribution of plants and animals on the globe is to be explained in terms of natural barriers and common ancestry. For terrestrial organisms the great division is that between the Old and the New Worlds. For marine, one great division exists between the east and west shores of the Pacific Ocean, and another between the east and west shores of the American land mass. Many aquatic species on either side of the isthmus of Panama are related to each other because they originated and spread before the isthmus formed a continuous barrier.

In the *Origin* there is no nostalgic extravagance with lost continents to solve either the minor or the major problems of distribution. Darwin thought about oceans and continents with sober common sense, assuming they were pretty much what they are now. He found his explanations in observed facts, present and past, prying with sober detective cunning into many kinds of casual transport and, incidentally, into some of nature's most genial ingenuities of dog-eat-dog. For example, seeds can be eaten by a fresh-water fish on one continent, conveyed to the coast, the fish eaten by a sea bird, the seeds transported across an ocean and ultimately deposited in excrement on another continent. They can be carried across water on icebergs, on driftwood, in dirt clinging to the feet of flying birds, or in the carcasses of dead birds miraculously spared by fish. Again, some seeds can float in sea water for months with unimpaired fertility. Darwin was also one of the first to explain

the islands of closely similar alpine vegetation on mountain-
tops throughout the world as the result of a general migration
of plants from the arctic zones during glacial periods.

Chapter XIV is devoted to the problems of classification in
the plant and animal kingdoms. The principle of descent, with
its attendant concepts of divergence and extinction by natural
selection, explains similarities in embryological development
and in rudimentary organs. On the other hand, analogical resemblances are to be explained as primarily the effect of
environment. They are convergences, produced by similar
adaptation, in organisms not closely allied. Fish and whales
are not closely related, yet they have in their more recent pasts
made an analogous adaptation to environment. Discrepancies
in the habits of related larvae are also traceable to environment.
Larvae are history books to be sure, like all embryos, but they
are history books which must get up and walk, provide themselves with food and drink, and take a part in the history which
they record. Hence they develop differences where one would
normally expect similarities.

The Conclusion is a curiously Victorian combination of
cautious statement and soaring conviction, of deep sincerity
about science and diplomatic piety* about religion, of calm
realism about the terrible facts of nature and vague optimism
about the awful fact of the Unknown. Darwin once more declares himself firmly convinced that his theories are correct
and predicts they will bear abundant fruit in many fields of
thought. He concludes:

Thus, from the war of nature, from famine and death, the most
exalted object which we are capable of conceiving, namely, the
production of the higher animals, directly follows. There is

* The reference to the Creator, however, did not appear in the first
edition.

grandeur in this view of life, with its several powers, having been originally breathed by the Creator into a few forms, or into one; and that, whilst this planet has gone cycling on according to the fixed law of gravity, from so simple a beginning endless forms most beautiful and most wonderful have been, and are being, evolved.[16]

Leibnitz, Darwin observes, once condemned Newton's *Principia* as a danger to religion. His denunciation is now an anachronism. Similar denunciations of the *Origin*, Darwin implies, will one day be equally so. No doubt. The Tennessee monkey trial would now be an anachronism even in Tennessee, but not because Darwin is recognized as a bulwark of religion.

Between him and Newton, as religious influences, there is probably not much to choose. The law of gravitation concerns mechanics and—since in the long run philosophers cannot resist analogy—implies that the universe is a machine. The law of evolution concerns living things and by analogy implies that the universe is an organism. In so far Darwin might have the advantage, for a living universe suggests warmth, response, kinship—in short Deity—more than a dead one. On the other hand, a machine requires a mechanic, whereas an organism does not obviously require anything but food and water. A machine may be perfect, whereas an evolution must be imperfect in order that—to satisfy human hope—it may evolve toward perfection; and as a matter of fact Darwin's world abounds in mere approximations of perfect adaptation and even in the most grotesque of compromises—in snakes with useless limbs, insects with welded wings, birds that cannot fly, mammals that cannot walk. Finally, Darwin's explanation of evolution is mechanistic without the favorable implications of mechanical design. Natural selection represents not a harmony but a conflict and is effectuated not by the precise, mathematical idealism of invisible force but apparently by a crude, random sorting out of variations by environment. Darwin had documented the romantic, organistic universe of Schelling—and, as many felt, documented it atheistically, in terms of blind chance and purposeless mechanism.

Schelling himself had pointed out that a romantic and imperfect universe might be the work, if not of a perfect and self-sufficient, then of an immanent and evolving, Intelligence. But many who were willing to believe in an evolving Deity could not believe in one who dealt in random variations. They could accept an evolving universe but not a universe shaken out of a dicebox. As the century wore on, Darwinism fared in metaphysics as the older liberalism fared in politics. People were impressed less with the achievements of biological progress and more with its irrationality, with the expense in waste, conflict, and suffering. "Advanced" thinkers either became agnostics or, like Butler and Shaw, acknowledged an evolving Deity conceived on Lamarckian rather than Darwinian terms.

The similar fortunes of liberalism and natural selection are significant. Darwin's matter was as English as his method. Terrestrial history turned out to be strangely like Victorian history writ large. Bertrand Russell and others have remarked that Darwin's theory was mainly "an extension to the animal and vegetable world of laissez faire economics."[17] As a matter of fact, the economic conceptions of utility, pressure of population, marginal fertility, barriers in restraint of trade, the division of labor, progress and adjustment by competition, and the spread of technological improvements can all be paralleled in The Origin of Species. But so, also, can some of the doctrines of English political conservatism. In revealing the importance of time and the hereditary past, in emphasizing the persistence of vestigial structures, the minuteness of variations and the slowness of evolution, Darwin was adding Hooker and Burke to Bentham and Adam Smith. The constitution of the universe exhibited many of the virtues of the English Constitution.

As science, Darwin's work has always seemed to the more

fastidious critic less admirable than Newton's because it is so
much less exact, complete, and conclusive. In spite of his facts,
he is sometimes regarded as little more than a speculator. He
proves by appealing to the incompleteness of the geological
record, and demonstrates with "I firmly believe" and "as far as
I am able to judge, after long attending to the subject." He
explains vaguely and he explains too much. There is at the
same time too much accident and too much finality in his
theory. He seems to explain not only how but why a cat has
claws, and the why is quite simply that they are a help in the
struggle for survival. His language is felt to imply that natural
causes, the struggle for survival, and cat's claws are teleological
finalities in themselves.[18]

Part of this objection is simply that Darwin's theory is less
aesthetically satisfying, less beautiful, than Newton's. It lacks
the elegant precision of a mathematical solution. It is the prose
realism, not the poetic truth, of science. But apparently most
biological generalizations are prose realism—are less precise,
perhaps less universal, than those of physics and chemistry.[19]
In any case, natural selection has not been supplanted by a
more graceful substitute. Darwin has proved only superficially
confused and, on the whole, astonishingly right. Paleontologists have uncovered infinitely more than he knew about the
biological past. They have discovered radioactive chronome-
ters in the rocks and arrived at much more accurate conceptions of geological time. They have estimated the life span
and the comparative populations of extinct genera and species.
They have drawn conclusions about the "rate" of evolution,
tracing a great class like the reptiles, for example, from obscure
beginnings, through "explosions" of adaptive radiation, periods
of relative stability accompanied by the increased specializa-
tion of some species and the elimination of those less efficiently
specialized, to rapid decline before new competitors.[20] Some
of these discoveries Darwin foresaw in broad outline. On the

whole, his appeals to future research have been justified. Posterity has documented his arguments.

Moreover, his "simple"[21] explanation has not been discredited; it has merely shifted emphasis a little and grown infinitely more complicated. Beneath variation yawn the Mendelian profundities; beneath natural selection, the endless complexities of speciation and differential reproduction.

According to Mr. Julian Huxley, Darwin's insistence on the importance of small variations proved entirely sound. Many scientists, including Mr. Julian Huxley's grandfather, had maintained that such variations, even though useful, might be swamped and lost.* The discussion of natural selection is an instance of how shrewdly a gnat may speculate on the hide of an elephant. Darwin's chief error consists in the Malthusianism which makes Victorian economics so gloomy. He assigns too large and positive a role to death and elimination, even—in the broad history of evolution itself—to the pressure of numbers. "Ichthyosaurs became extinct millions of years before porpoises and dolphins arose," says Professor George G. Simpson, "and during the interval this adaptive zone was simply empty."[22] Contemporary scientists regard natural selection not as a fine filter but as an intricate series of rather coarse sieves. It may daily and hourly scrutinize individuals and eliminate misfits, but it may also allow thousands of the potentially strong to be slaughtered indiscriminately. It is not so much a spectacular struggle for survival as a prosaic competition in general efficiency. Failures are not only those

---

* Having conceived of inheritance as a blending, as of colored fluids, rather than a combining, as of colored marbles, Darwin faced in an acute form this problem of the swamping of useful variations. He attempted to extricate himself by assuming that acquired characteristics are to some extent inherited and that a changed environment increases the rate at which useful characteristics appear. Unfortunately, domestic plants show most variability in the countries where they are longest cultivated. More than a half century after Darwin's death, R. A. Fisher solved these

who leave no survivors but those who leave few. Natural selection is complexly determined by the organic and inorganic environment; by the intensity and character of competition; by the size, pattern, and stability of populations; and by the gene structure, mode of reproduction, manner of growth, and physiology of individuals.[23] In short, the evolution of life is determined by intricate competition in the great world without and by curiously random play on infinitesimal chessboards within.

---

problems when, applying neo-Mendelian principles, he discovered that mutant genes can remain in storage indefinitely till needed. The principle of dominance, for example, aids in preserving variants until environment is ready to select them out. They are then "unpacked" by degrees as selection reduces dominance. In the same way, the variability of domestic animals is explained by the mating of individuals with stored-up variants. T. H. Huxley and Julian Huxley, *Touchstone for Ethics*, pp. 173–185.

8

Convulsions of the National Mind

While an unparalleled outburst of acrimony, ridicule, hatred, admiration, and professional envy beat down upon the *Origin*, Darwin was far away in the somnolent depths of Ilkley and a water cure. He responded not a word, nor was it in his nature to respond. With the passage of years, his meekness grew legendary. The bright-eyed, fabulous-bearded sage of omniscient calm and inscrutable detachment is a myth suggested to a garrulous age by a romantic portrait and a long newspaper silence. Even after Darwin's death, some biographers ignored the evidence of published letters and continued to infer the man from his myth and his achievement. "The great thinker," writes G. T. Bettany, "fulfilling his duties as head of a family, charged with the burden of new thoughts and observations, slowly perfecting his life work, had neither time nor inclination for controversy."[1] Not perhaps for controversy, but for almost every other kind of partisanship.

Darwin was as sensitive to other people's opinions as he was curious about them. Praise filled him with elation, and blame plunged him into depression and uncertainty, or plagued him with indignation and insomnia. The extravagance of his language betrays the intensity of his feeling. After being thrown to the theologians by a fellow scientist, he broke out in humorous self-pity to Hooker, "He would, on no account, burn me, but he will get the wood ready and tell the black beasts how to catch me."[2]

Essentially, Darwin was an enthusiast—a sportsman, a humanitarian, a collector of rare and wonderful bugs. One of his enthusiasms was for facts; and the enthusiasm for facts, stimulating a large mind and an immense perseverance, gradually became an enthusiasm for truth. Darwin was professionally rather than temperamentally detached. Samuel Butler was in part right about him. Though a much franker, more open nature, he did resemble Gladstone in combining a somewhat devious egotism with relative unselfconsciousness. There was not, inside the visible Darwin, any more than inside the visible Gladstone, a tiny articulate spectator of crystalline intelligence who saw everything and excused nothing. Darwin's integrity was founded on dedication rather than detachment, on warmth rather than insight.

As a matter of fact, he had been thinking for months about the reception of his book. He had Lyell's example before him. Like Lyell, he avoided controversy and practiced the British art of reticent and unprovocative statement. But his book was more scandalous than Lyell's. He had reason to fear a more determined opposition. On the whole, his campaign was much more personal, more elaborate, and more skillful—a curious mixture of deliberate planning and instinctive maneuver. He early decided that his work would be safe if he could convince three judges—Lyell, Hooker, and Huxley. He could hardly have made a shrewder choice. They were not necessarily, as has often been said, the three greatest experts on their respective phases of the species question (Owen had as great a reputation as any), but, being humane, honest, and foresighted, they were natural leaders and capable, once converted, of converting others. By November, 1859, Darwin had convinced Hooker and brought Lyell a good way along the short road he had to travel. These had been not merely intellectual, but personal, victories. It must be remembered that Darwin was a very charming man, with extraordinary powers of interesting other people in his concerns and ideas.

There remained Huxley. To be sure, the case was delicate. Darwin understood both the younger man's cleverness and his audacity. He could be a formidable critic and an even more formidable ally.

What was his attitude toward the species question at this time? It is almost more difficult to explain why every able scientist was not an evolutionist by the middle of the nineteenth century than to explain why one or two were. To be sure, nobody would admit the glacier moved until he could show how it moved. But why, with his great knowledge, his quick, far-ranging mind, his intellectual daring and contempt for tradition, had not Huxley attacked this great problem? His most brilliant work pointed directly toward it. He had also read Lamarck, Chambers, and Lyell. Actually, his position was characteristic. He gave up his belief in creation but could not accept evolution. Arguing the question with Spencer, he maintained that the evidence for evolution was not sufficient. No theory adequately explained all the phenomena. Consequently he took refuge in Goethe's *tätige Skepsis* awaiting developments with a feeling that evolution might prove true after all.

The cautious and divided state of his opinions is vividly indicated by an unpublished letter of June 25, 1853, to Sir Charles Lyell. "The finite and definite limits of species, genera, and larger groups," he writes, "appear to me to be perfectly consistent with the theory of transmutation. In other words, I think *transmutation* may take place without *transition*."[3] What he has in mind, as he goes on to explain, is the analogy of chemical compounds, in which the addition or subtraction of a single atom may cause an abrupt and profound change. He then proceeds to a meticulous weighing of the evidence, concluding the negative case with the question, so pertinent both to evolution and the scientific attitude: "How much evidence would you require to believe that there was a time when stones fell upwards?"...

And yet [he continues] the difficulties in the way of these beliefs are as nothing compared to those which you would have to overcome to believe that complex organic beings made themselves (for that is what creation comes to in scientific language) out of non-organic matter.

His summing-up is at once farsighted and cautious:

I by no means suppose that the transmutation hypothesis is proven or anything like it—but I view it as a powerful instrument of research—Follow it out and it will lead us somewhere—while the other notion is like all the modifications of 'final causation.' . . .

And I would very strongly urge upon you that it is the topical development of uniformitarianism and that its adoption would harmonise the spirit of Paleontology with that of physical Geology.

But why didn't Huxley take his own excellent advice? Probably he was much less favorable to evolution than he realized. He was extremely hostile to Chambers's *Vestiges of Natural Creation*, about which he wrote the only review he ever admitted to be harsh; and in spite of the letter just quoted, he was apparently little stirred by Lyell's *Principles*, which demonstrated orderly change in geology with all the facts and sobriety he particularly admired. Rereading the *Principles* almost thirty years afterwards, Huxley was surprised to discover how strongly they implied Darwin. When an able man fails to see the obvious, the causes usually go deep. Jones, the most influential teacher of his youth, had been violently opposed to evolution. He had also infused his youthful disciple with his own skeptical attitude, which in Huxley's strongly moral nature, became a kind of intellectual asceticism. The lures and blandishments of ideas, to which he was highly susceptible, he resisted with Puritan austerity. To abstain from speculation, to insist fastidiously on absolute proof, to undertake humbler, more routine tasks was not only sound common sense, but high moral idealism. Perhaps Darwin had his friend Huxley in mind when he wrote, many years after this time:

I am not very sceptical,—a frame of mind which I believe to be injurious to the progress of science. A good deal of scepticism in a scientific man is advisable to avoid much loss of time, but I have met with not a few men, who, I feel sure, have often thus been deterred from experiment or observations which would have proved directly or indirectly serviceable.[4]

Perhaps Huxley was not only cold toward large ideas, but in too much of a hurry for them. He spent time "keeping up" with them rather than in thinking about them. In fact, he had heard species discussed so much and so unsoundly that, as he says, he had grown thoroughly bored with the subject. Momentous and pressing problems often become tiresome to alert, well-informed people like Huxley and have to be solved by patient, apologetic people like Darwin.

Perhaps also the conception of evolutionary change, with its tendency to blur outlines and undermine categories, was fundamentally uncongenial to the sharp clarity of Huxley's intellect. His enthusiasm for the archetypal idea in comparative anatomy is significant. Indeed, there was something not only Platonic, but eighteenth century about his mind. One notices this in his taste for Berkeley and Hume, his negative common sense, his somewhat attenuated and static rationalism, his habit of explaining living phenomena by mechanistic analogies.

The story of his conversion is, in part at least, the story of his growing friendship with Darwin. He was never, early or late, a mere hero-worshiper, but always independent, always critical. Estimating the foremost biologists with the ruthless eye of an ambitious beginner, he wrote in 1851, "Darwin might be anything if he had good health."[5] In the later fifties the two men seem to have grown more intimate, and Huxley's opinions, rather less settled. "When Huxley, Hooker, and Wollaston were at Darwin's last week," wrote Lyell in 1856 to Sir Charles Bunbury, "they (all four of them) ran a tilt against species—farther I believe than they are deliberately prepared to go."[6]

Apparently Darwin was preparing Huxley more than he was enlightening him. He realized that if he confided his ideas too freely, the younger man might plunge them into reckless controversy before the Origin, with its armor of solid fact and heavy guns of weighty argument, could be brought into action. Huxley was of course present at the meeting of the Linnean Society on July 1, 1858, when the famous joint paper was read, but even then, his excitement was a little perfunctory. "Wallace's impetus seems to have set Darwin going in earnest," he wrote Hooker in September, "and I am rejoiced to hear we shall learn his views in full, at last. I look forward to a great revolution being effected."[7]

But if Darwin's ideas did not surprise Huxley, Darwin's book astonished him.[8] As a matter of fact, it surprised even Lyell and Hooker, who had watched its growth almost day by day. The idea of variations selected by competition was a commonplace of Victorian thought, not likely when developed in conversation or presented in summary to impress clever men as a dazzling ingenuity. In the Origin it gained grandeur through the infinite resource and courage, even the temerity and obsessive single-mindedness, with which it was applied to a vast number of facts and problems, for Darwin's greatness consisted partly in his having, in his cautious, prosaic way, so completely accepted his destiny as a discoverer. Huxley laid down the book with a mixture of awe and anticlimax. "How extremely stupid not to have thought of that!" he exclaimed,[9] and yet "that" explained very nearly everything. It provided the working hypothesis which he had demanded. "Since I read Von Bär's essays nine years ago," he wrote Darwin, "no work on Natural History Science I have met with has made so great an impression upon me."[10] Darwin grew taller as the years passed. Von Baer became Harvey, Copernicus, and finally Sir Isaac Newton.

Once the scales of skepticism had fallen from his eyes and one or two Buffonian or Lamarckian misapprehensions had been overcome, Huxley grasped the new ideas and the new facts with his usual quickness, seeing problems and consequences which had hardly occurred to Darwin. Even before reading the Origin, he had perceived that the theory of natural selection was incomplete without a theory of what causes variations. Still meditating transmutation without transition, he felt, like De Vries afterward, that many difficulties, such as the absence of transitional forms, could be more easily met by basing evolution not so much on minute changes as on large, abrupt ones—in short, on mutations.* Vaguely anticipating Mendel, he also saw that mutations, and indeed heredity in general, might be due to combinations of definable unit-factors. He realized, as Darwin did only later, that evolution does not necessarily imply progress, and developing this point in an early lecture on "Persistent Types," he removed an objection to the Origin before that book actually appeared. On the other hand, he insisted that artificial selection does not prove natural selection. Darwin had not so much proved that natural selection does occur as that it must occur. His great achievement was in Huxley's opinion that, for the most important problem of biological science, he had provided a simple, adequate working hypothesis which did no violence to

* See p. 214.

Lyell's principle of uniformity. Fair-minded observers should give it the most serious consideration, vigilantly maintaining Goethe's attitude of *tätige Skepsis*.

However skeptical, Huxley soon became very active. Even in 1858 he had begun to emit pugnacious noises, airing the subject in the lecture room and terminating his letters with ominous postscripts. When the *Origin* came out, he saw at once what a battle it was to provoke. "I trust you will not allow yourself to be in any way disgusted or annoyed," he wrote Darwin, "by the considerable abuse and misrepresentation which, unless I greatly mistake, is in store for you."[11] And toward the end of the letter he added, "I am sharpening up my claws and beak in readiness." Six months earlier this announcement might have alarmed Darwin as much as it would his enemies, but now the anger even of this mild man had been aroused by the treatment he had received.

Though England was overripe, she was terribly unready for the *Origin*. It rose before the national mind like a Banquo's ghost terminating the long banquet scene of the Exposition decade. Inevitably, it suggested the analogy from nature to man and became a kind of anti-Bible. And as the Bible itself had long been taken for a biological and geological treatise, so the *Origin* became a treatise on religion and ethics, eventually on politics and sociology. Scientists themselves didn't know whether to reply to it with science or theology, and often maintained the most incoherent and contradictory opinions with the utmost vehemence. Seldom has scientific detachment met so severe a trial or come off so badly. A zoologist determined to read the book yet never to believe it. An admiring ethnologist would neither change nor accept a word of it. "Lyell . . . ," wrote Hooker, "is absolutely gloating over it."[12] And yet Lyell pleaded pathetically with Darwin to introduce just a little divine direction or "prophetic germ."[13] Whewell wrote that the book was too impressive to be criticized lightly, but refused to allow a copy to be placed in the Trinity College Library. The great mathematician, Sir John Herschel was shocked not so much at the atheism which natural selection implied as at the niggling slovenliness it imputed to nature. It "is the law of higgledy-piggledy," he pronounced severely, filling Darwin with bewildered consternation.[14] H. C. Watson wrote Darwin that he was the greatest revolutionist in nineteenth-century biology and at the same time rather irritated him by enclosing a dusty offprint showing that he himself had maintained very similar ideas many years before. F. E. Gray thought the Origin absolutely nothing more than Lamarck all over again and couldn't for the life of him understand what all the fuss was about.

The Origin, as I have suggested, elicited some of the keenest theology from some of the most eminent scientists, though how much this was religious zeal and how much professional jealousy was often difficult to determine. Many objections proceeded from a misconception of theoretical method. You could not see natural selection at work. Therefore it was a mere empty speculation. But in a more particular sense the sore point was natural selection itself. It seemed to substitute accident—or, as some felt, mechanism—for intelligent purpose in the natural order. Sternly confining his theology to his footnotes, Herschel declared in his Physical Geography of the Globe that he didn't in the least mind thinking of cosmic intelligence as operating impersonally through scientific laws. But neither cosmic intelligence nor anything so rationally ordered as the organic world could ever be regarded as the result of chance.[15] Natural selection was an ingenious hypothesis but of course it could not be taken seriously. It omitted its own ultimate and governing factor. The American Asa Gray, a warm and sincere Darwinian, held that, so far from

representing chance, natural selection embodied a blind necessity totally incompatible with theism, unless the stream of
variations themselves could be conceived as guided by design.[16]

In his letters Darwin countered these criticisms with the
utmost patience and showed incidentally that when practical
occasion required, he was no mean metaphysician. You could
not see natural selection at work? Of course not. Neither could
you see gravitation at work. You inferred its working from its
results. He grumbled a little that the astronomer Herschel
wanted so much divine direction in biology and so little in
astronomy. But Herschel was ill-disposed. When Asa Gray
pleaded that variations might be divinely guided, Darwin was
all sympathy and understanding. Nevertheless, he felt that the
more divine guidance in variations, the less reality in natural
selection. Moreover, his study of domestic animals convinced
him that variations were totally undesigned. Surely God had
no interest in enabling man to develop such vanities as the
fantail and tumbler pigeons. Darwin was quick to defend the
integrity of his own principles but slow to follow the argument
into theology. He was delighted to hear a clergyman endorse
the theism of his book, but reluctant to do so himself.

In an age when everybody talked religion, when atheists
dogmatized as boldly as clergymen and agnostics wrote volumes about their ignorance, Darwin maintained for a lifetime
a discreet and sensitive reticence. He shrank from wounding
delicately orthodox feelings and felt, as other Victorian gentlemen did about their property, that his religious views were
his own concern. When hard pressed, he pleaded somewhat
nervously that he was too ill, too busy, or too old to think
about religious subjects; or that, not being a specialist, he had
not reflected deeply enough upon them to have anything
worth saying. But of course when so many people talked so
much, he could not help thinking a little—or perhaps a good

deal. At the end of his life, he spoke out frankly in the "Autobiography."

As usual, he explained himself with a history. His religion had wasted away before his science in a war of attrition so gradual that, in his own words, he "felt no distress" and hardly realized that a shot had been fired. Soon after his return to England, while yet hesitating between an evolutionary and a theological biology, he had discovered—no doubt with astonishment—that he had become a complete skeptic about Revelation. His ideas of progress and evolution—secondarily, his humanitarianism—had been decisive. He saw that scriptures and mythology were part of the evolution of every people. "The Old Testament was no more to be trusted than the sacred books of the Hindoos,"[17] not only because of "its manifestly false history of the world" but because of "its attributing to God the feelings of a revengful tyrant."[18] He rejected Christian miracles because they were similar to those in other mythologies, because they rested on dubious and conflicting testimony, and because they contradicted the uniformitarianism he had learned from Lyell. He also rejected the divinity of Jesus and doubted the supremacy of Christian ethics. "Beautiful as is the morality of the New Testament, it can hardly be denied that its perfection depends in part on the interpretation we now put on metaphors and allegories."[19] Clearly, Darwin was a progressive to the core.*

For many years after this time, he clung rather absent-mindedly to a vague theism. But natural selection finished what evolution had begun. The issue presented itself as a choice between chance and design—more specifically, between

---

* To Francis Galton he wrote in an undated letter (probably 1879), "I gave up common religious belief almost independently, from my own reflections." Unpublished letters, Darwin Papers (Cambridge: University Library).

the method and the achievement of natural selection. If the achievement is emphasized, then the universe—the physical, aesthetic, and moral habitat of such a creature as man—seems too wonderful and coherent not to be the work of an intelligence similar to our own. If chance variations and the struggle for existence are emphasized, then it seems a rather unhappy accident. But surely, he felt, method has contaminated achievement. Surely the universe cannot be the product of design— unless the sawfly is expressly designed to devour living larvae, or the intestinal worm to lodge in the intestine of its victim. Darwin put finally the humanitarian question: is there more suffering or happiness in the world? He invented an optimistic answer. In the struggle for survival, pleasure is always a stimulus and a guide to success; whereas pain, though a useful admonition when limited and monetary, is a harmful depressant when protracted. Consequently, pleasure tends to be selected over pain in the evolutionary process. But he did not convince himself. Individual failure is infinitely more frequent than individual success. In fact, failure, in the sense of death, is universal. He always came back ultimately to "the suffering of millions of the lower animals throughout almost endless time."[20]

Again, neither the laws of nature nor the intuitions of man necessarily imply cosmic purpose. The law of gravitation operates on the moon, but a lifeless desert does not indicate a living intelligence. Savages firmly believe, as Tylor had shown, in the most fantastic superstitions, but their beliefs do not indicate a fantastic universe, any more than those of civilized man indicate a benevolent one.

Darwin seems also to have been aware that a belief-pattern, once suppressed as a spiritual, may reassert itself as a secular dogma. Reasoning that solar energy is limited and constantly being expended in radiation, Lord Kelvin had begun in the sixties, like a kind of cosmic actuarial expert, to calculate the future life expectancy of the sun. Some day the earth would be as cold and dead as the moon. "To think of the progress of millions of years, with every continent swarming with good and enlightened men," Darwin exclaimed in a letter of 1865, "all ending in this, and with no fresh start until this our planetary system has again been converted into a red-hot gas."[21] Expressing the same sentiment in his "Autobiography," he concluded, "To those who fully admit the immortality of the human soul, the destruction of our world will not appear so dreadful."[22]

Darwin made no serious effort to resolve the dilemma between design and chance. Perhaps there were other alternatives, of which the human mind, at best a makeshift improvement on the mentality of the lower animals, can have no conception. A dog might as well speculate on the mind of man, as man on the mind of the Creator. Basically, of course, Charles had never felt a strong will to believe. His faith had never been, like Newman's, the result of deliberate choice. He did not choose, but evolved. Probably the first step toward irreligion had been his Cambridge religious education. Paley had taught him to delight in reasoning about material phenomena and to regard the power of assent as dependent on rational argument and physical evidence. Design had thus led him to physical fact; and with facts he had soon become much more at home than with the Cambridge God of Theology. When called on to reason about such matters as the finite and the infinite, free will and necessity, or matter and spirit, Charles soon got into "a hopeless muddle." His muddle-headedness made him a modern. Reality for him was a process evolving constantly higher values in a universe bounded by cosmic question marks. For a time, perhaps, the question marks had loomed somewhat uncomfortably over his shoulder;

but he had kept his mind on his work, and now they had long since receded into a useful and beneficent fog. Slowly, almost painlessly, Charles had become an agnostic.

These views—with many protestations of bewilderment and pain—Darwin communicated at length to Asa Gray.

Only Gray could have dragged so much theology out of Darwin. "Do not hurry over Asa Gray," he told Lyell. "He strikes me as one of the best reasoners and writers I have ever read. He knows my book as well as I do myself."[23] "A complex cross," he wrote on another occasion, "of lawyer, poet, naturalist, and theologian."[24]

Gray was magnificently equipped to lead the evolutionary crusade in the United States. He was the foremost American botanist and—as a man of ready sympathy and vast correspondence—an unparalleled power among his younger colleagues. He was a vivid and indefatigable writer of textbooks and therefore a major force in general education. As a Harvard professor and a handsome, charming gentleman with open manners and an expression of shrewd benignity, he exerted a wide influence in the most important cultural city of America. As a leading scientist with a deep and personal sense of religion, he inspired confidence throughout that whole section of American liberals who were optimistically convinced that science and religion could effect a beneficent compromise. As a stern idealist who devoted to flowers the heroic strenuousness and superb enthusiasm which his countrymen commonly lavished on more remunerative pursuits, he could be as fiercely partisan after a judgment as he was loftily impartial before; and once aroused, he could wield the fork and net of controversy almost as subtly and dangerously as Huxley himself. Evolution gave him the opportunity, for the *Origin* divided Harvard as it divided the world. In a series of dramatic public debates, Gray won an impressive victory over the famous geologist Agassiz. It was during these years immediately after the appearance of the *Origin* that Gray joined the inner circle of those who shared the master's confidence and gave valued advice.

Darwin told friends that he hoped for more from intelligent laymen than from professional scientists, "who have too firmly fixed in their heads that a species is an entity."[25] Certainly laymen were interested, for the first edition was sold out in a single day. Newspaper and magazine writers jumped to every obvious conclusion: Darwin had exalted blind chance and he had exalted divine law. He had proved that might was right and therefore Napoleon was right. He had offered a vista of unlimited progress operating on the democratic principle of fruitful competition.

Among the clergy, a few liberals were ready to accept the new ideas. Long a believer in evolution and strenuously convinced it offered ultimately a noble conception of God, Kingsley declared himself ready to follow any "villainous shifty fox of an argument" into whatever bogs and brakes it might lead.[26] The great majority of his fellows, however, attacked with all the ferocity of vested interest sorely threatened. The controversial clichés of folly, madness, and atheism were worn to transparent thinness.

Probably the most formidable and wounding attack came from a man who was both a priest and a scientist. This was Darwin's old geology professor, the Reverend Adam Sedgwick, who had once predicted for him a brilliant scientific future. Condemning the *Origin* both in his published review and in his letter of acknowledgment to the author, Sedgwick maintained that "there is a moral or metaphysical part of nature as well as a physical. A man who denies this is deep in the mire of folly."[27] Ignoring causation, which is the will of God, Darwin has deceptively gone through the motions, not achieved the reality, of true induction. Natural selection is "but a secondary consequence," a sham battle maneuvered from above. By utterly repudiating final causes, Darwin has betrayed "a demoralised understanding" and done his best to plunge humanity "into a lower grade of degradation" than any yet recorded.[28] Sedgwick particularly objected to "the tone of triumphant confidence" with which, at the end of his book, Darwin appeals to "the rising generation."[29] Other passages made him laugh till his sides ached.

Quite characteristically, Darwin found Sedgwick's letter simply unintelligible. On occasion he could see the ultimate consequences of a theory as well as any man; but in general, metaphysical ideas made him uncomfortable, and unpleasant metaphysical ideas made him ill. His mind had a useful tendency to reject what was at once unpleasant and irrelevant to the scientific problem in hand. "The more I think the more bewildered I become" terminates more than one unwelcome religious discussion in his correspondence.[30] Only after discussing Sedgwick's letter with Lyell at some length did he concede, "I dare say I did greatly underrate its clearness."[31] Nevertheless, he failed to see a legitimate criticism. Now that his theory was embodied in a book and placed before the world, he suddenly felt very closely identified not only with its scientific actualities but with its metaphysical implications. The supernatural interfered with the aesthetic symmetry of his ideas. The Deity had become an epistemological inconvenience.

Sometimes criticism was uncomfortably personal:

Here is a good joke: H. C. Watson (who, I fancy and hope, is going to review the new edition of the 'Origin') says that in the first four paragraphs of the introduction, the words "I," "me," "my," occur forty-three times! I was dimly conscious of the accursed fact. He says it can be explained phrenologically, which I suppose civilly means, that I am the most egotistically self-sufficient man alive; perhaps so. I wonder whether he will print this pleasing fact; it beats hollow the parentheses in Wallaston's writing.

I am, my dear Hooker, ever yours,
C. Darwin.

P.S.—Do not spread this pleasing joke; it is rather too biting.[32]

Meanwhile, he continued to pull wires with unflagging zeal. There was hardly an eminent scientist in Europe or America to whom he did not send a gift copy, accompanied with a letter exhibiting all that talent for disarming the mighty and pedagogically awful which he may have learned as a boy from propitiating his father. To utter irreconcilables he wrote letters which began, "My dear Falconer,—" and which ended, "I remain, my dear Falconer, Yours most truly, Charles Darwin." In between he suggested, "Lord, how savage you will be, if you read it, and how you will long to crucify me alive!" And then he added, "But if it should stagger you in ever so slight a degree . . ."[33] He was grave and respectful to Agassiz, flattering to De Candolle. He encouraged Hooker, egged on Huxley, argued with Lyell, asked Henslow for corrections. He acknowledged a great debt to Carpenter's *Comparative Physiology*, cautiously sounded him out, and on finding him favorable, urged him to write a review. When the review appeared, it was highly complimentary but fell short of announcing complete conversion. Darwin was pleased, but could not refrain from complaining to Lyell, "He admits that all birds are from one progenitor, and probably all fishes and reptiles from another parent. But the last mouthful chokes him. He can hardly admit all vertebrates from one parent."[34]

To the intimate and sympathetic, he spoke of his exhaustion and his illness; to the timidly doubtful, he referred to the great men already converted; to the timidly respectable, he declared that all the theological opprobrium would fall on him as the first offender, and grumbled humorously about suffering the silent pain of his female relatives. He wanted everybody to tell him what everybody else thought: "I fear there is no chance of Bentham being staggered. Will he read my book? Has he a copy? I would send him one of the reprints if he has not."[35] He was quick to sniff out anonymities: "I am perfectly convinced . . . that the review in the 'Annals' is by Wallaston; no one else in the world would have used so many parentheses."[36] Of one intricately and obstinately doubtful scientist he writes, "X. says —— will go to that part of hell, which Dante tells us is appointed for those who are neither on God's side nor on that of the devil."[37]

Lyell, Hooker, and Huxley continued to render invaluable service. Hooker made his fine introduction to *Flora Tasmaniae* a confession of evolutionary faith. Lyell gave a lawyer's suggestions for better marshaling the argument of the *Origin*, announced his conversion, and began to think of applying the perilous new principles to the perilous subject of man. With a magnificent display of his talents, Huxley began to hurry up history to an early and triumphant acceptance of Darwinian ideas. He buttonholed formidable opponents and stultified them with superior knowledge and readiness. He delivered lectures and fired off brilliant reviews—one in particular, an anonymous marvel of clarity and apt phrases, which created a sensation in the scientific world and threw Darwin into ecstasies.[38] "Who can the author be?" writes Darwin archly to the author himself. Whoever he is, he actually comprehends natural selection. He knows and overestimates the barnacle book. He is "a profound naturalist," quotes Goethe in the original German, and writes with an admirable flair for phrases. The only man in England who could have written this article is Huxley, who "has done a great service to the cause."[39]

Darwin's delight at the review, however, was scarcely more

intense than his disappointment at the lecture which Huxley delivered February 10, 1860, before the Royal Institution. He had carried his aches and pains all the way to London to hear natural selection expounded with Huxleyan force and clarity. Instead, he heard an eloquent sermon on the advance of scientific truth, with the *Origin* serving as the point of departure. At the time he persuaded himself that the lecture was good, but later he could not repress his vexation. "It was really provoking," he wrote Hooker, "how he wasted time over the idea of a species as exemplified in the horse, and over Sir J. Hall's old experiment on marble."[40]

But as time went on Huxley proved himself a critic with whom even an author could be content. As a matter of fact, his relationship to the *Origin* was paradoxical. He did not, like Spencer, attempt to expand evolution into a metaphysics; nor, like Bagehot, to apply the concept of natural selection to other fields of thought. He did not devote his strongest effort to extending Darwin's biological research, though here he made important contributions. Rather, he tried in the last analysis to realize what was actually an ethical ideal—to constitute himself, toward both the evolutionists and their opponents, the impartial spokesman of the scientific method, the objective defender of objectivity, criticizing Darwin where he thought necessary and defending him in everything else. Naturally, he felt that both Darwin and science needed very little criticism and a great deal of defense. One cannot make objectivity an educational and political program, a religion, an ethics, and even a war cry—without some sacrifice of objectivity.

While the great anti-Darwinians were creeping down into murky cellars of anachronism and ineptitude, new champions of the light were springing up on every hand. The most notable among these was the young German zoologist Ernst Haeckel, whose "exceedingly valuable and beautiful monograph," *Die*

Radiolarien, Huxley soon discovered. He sent a warm and admiring letter together with appropriate gifts of Barbados deposit and deep-sea mud. A fast friendship was formed.

For the progress of Darwinism abroad, Huxley's friendship with Haeckel was as important as Darwin's with Asa Gray. Intellectually, Haeckel was like one of those extremely dense and fiery stars that must linger for eons on the utmost verge of explosion. He constantly threatened to fly luminously to all the horizons at once, political, scientific, and philosophical, with an appalling cosmic bang. Religious by nature and up-bringing, he had lost his faith, as well as his political conservatism, in the excitement of 1848. For a while he had relieved the dangerous accumulation of incandescent energies by denouncing, with splendid rhetorical pyrotechnics, the priests and archdukes of the reaction, until Darwinism provided him, in his own field of biology, with a positive faith and a new mission. At the scientific congress of 1863, he greatly advanced the evolutionary cause in Germany by giving a lecture on the *Origin*, identifying natural selection with the "natural" law of progress, which "neither the weapons of tyrants nor the curses of priests" could suppress.[41]

Haeckel waged intellectual war against the German enemies of evolution with a *Schrecklichkeit* which brought pallor to the cheeks of his English allies. Apparently, however, they themselves did not suffer. In the opinion of Ernst Krause, the historian of Darwinism in Germany, Haeckel "concentrated on himself . . . all the hatred and bitterness which Evolution excited in certain quarters," so that in a surprisingly short time it became the fashion in Germany that Haeckel alone should be abused, while Darwin was held up as the ideal of fore-thought and moderation."*

* *Charles Darwin und sein Verhältniss zu Deutschland* (Leipzig: E. Günther, 1885), p. 162; quoted in *Life and Letters of Darwin*, II, 251. Haeckel's *Morphologie* was everything Darwin ordinarily disliked. It was

It is part of Huxley's importance that, together with Haeckel, he brought the man of science as a cultural type into the broader arena of European civilization. The warfare between evolution and orthodoxy created a splendid dramatic opportunity, and with the quick instinct of a man of action Huxley seized it. To the cleric as the benighted and prejudiced defender of a fading superstition, he opposed the scientist, the impersonal investigator who, though somewhat satanically godless and inhumanly detached, is by virtue of his dedication and discipline devoted to truth in the field of thought, to rectitude in the field of action, and—because truth is power, and in its nineteenth-century form rectitude is sympathy—to humanitarian progress in both fields. Lecturing in defense of the *Origin* at this time, he delivered an eloquent indictment against the Divine Will as a natural cause. It has been swept by advancing science from position after position, but reappears again and again, an obstinate and illogical ghost, far behind its former lines:

But to those whose life is spent, to use Newton's noble words, in picking up here a pebble and there a pebble on the shores of the great ocean of truth—who watch, day by day, the slow but sure advance of that mighty tide, bearing on its bosom the thousand treasures wherewith man ennobles and beautifies his life— it would be laughable, if it were not so sad, to see the little Canutes of the hour enthroned in solemn state, bidding that great wave to stay, and threatening to check its beneficent progress.[42]

He then outlined the glorious role that England can play.

German, metaphysical, and so intricately obscure that even Germans complained. But Charles himself did not complain. Apparently he understood enough to see that the book propounded natural selection as something very like omniscience implicit if not explicit. If the *Origin* did not explain everything about organic life, it provided a clear basis for explanation. Naturally, Darwin felt that the *Morphologie* should be translated into English. For once Huxley disagreed strongly. He was right. The *Morphologie* was a success neither in England nor in Germany.

Will England play this part? That depends upon how you, the public, deal with science. Cherish her, venerate her, follow her methods faithfully and implicitly in their application to all branches of human thought, and the future of this people will be greater than the past.

Listen to those who would silence and crush her, and I fear our children will see the glory of England vanishing like Arthur in the mist; they will cry too late the woeful cry of Guinever:—

> "It was my duty to have loved the highest;
> It surely was my profit had I known;
> It would have been my pleasure had I seen."[43]

This is the language of the pulpit. It evoked, in many at least, the response of a congregation—both toward the new orthodoxy and its consecrated representatives.

What would the evolution controversy have been without Huxley? No doubt, sooner or later, the *Origin* would have exerted its profound effect on science and religion. No doubt Darwin's reputation would have been nearly as great. Leslie Stephen would probably have invented the word *agnostic*, and John Tyndall would have been the foremost popular preacher of naturalism. But science would not have enjoyed such dazzling prestige among politicians and businessmen, nor figured, perhaps, so prominently in the late-nineteenth-century school curriculum. Its general victory over tradition would have been slower, less complete, and certainly less dramatic. Huxley turned what promised to be a dull war of attrition into a brilliant campaign. He created a legend, both for himself and for Darwin, founded a new priesthood, and very nearly made England a scientific nation.

Looking on, fascinated at the agonized convulsions of the English mind, lay, scientific, and religious, Charles had very nearly forgotten about his suffering family. Gradually he became aware that they were with him almost to the last old maid. Had his book been universally ignored, they might have resented every blasphemous word of it. As it was, they worried a little, but devoted their main energies to hating offensive reviewers with a hearty and solid tribal loyalty. Even Erasmus took part in the great campaign of the *Origin* to the extent of sounding out Dr. Henry Holland, who was undergoing a first perusal. Erasmus happened to mention the eye before the eminent physician got to that point. Like everybody else, Dr. Holland boggled. In fact,

it took away his breath—utterly impossible—structure—function, &c., &c., &c., but when he had read it he hummed and hawed, and perhaps it was partly conceivable, and then he fell back on the bones of the ear, which were beyond all probability or conceivability.[44]

Erasmus confessed that for his own part he had been a little weak in the head of late. Nevertheless, the *Origin* seemed to him the most interesting book he had ever read. Perhaps he didn't feel enough "the absence of varieties," but he doubted "if everything now living were fossilized whether the paleontologists could distinguish them." As a matter of personal taste, he preferred a priori reasoning. "If the facts won't fit in, why so much the worse for the facts is my feeling."[45] He repeated that he was astonished at the book. Nevertheless, he predicted that the ideas would prove to have been thought up already by somebody else. He also predicted that if his brother studied ants long enough, he would discover that they had their bishops as well as their soldiers and slaves. "Ants display the utmost economy," observed Charles somewhat regretfully, "and always carry away a dead fellow-creature as food."[46]

Of his immediate family, only Emma caused him deep concern. Not long after their marriage she had written him a letter about religion in which she had stated the Victorian dilemma with an un-Victorian courage and clarity. "The state of mind that I wish to preserve with respect to you," she said, "is to feel that while you are acting conscientiously and sincerely wishing and trying to learn the truth, you cannot be wrong."[47] On the other hand, she perceived that, being constantly preoccupied with scientific ideas, he might come to regard religious considerations as a disquieting interruption. Moreover, "may not the habit in scientific pursuits of believing nothing till it is proved, influence your mind too much in other things which cannot be proved in the same way, and which, if true, are likely to be above our comprehension?"[48] Charles's science might bore her, but never Charles the scientist. "Don't think," she concluded, "that it is not my affair and that it does not much signify to me. Everything that concerns you concerns me, and I should be most unhappy if I thought we did not belong to each other for ever."

She seems to have given little sign that she was troubled by Charles's want of faith. Her letters to the children were as terse and laconic as the military dispatches of the Duke of Wellington:

Down, Brownley, Kent, Nov. 13, 1863.

My Dear Lenny,

You cannot write as small as this I know. It is done with your crow-quill. Your last letter was not interesting, but very well spelt, which I care more about.

We have a new horse on trial, very spirited and pleasant and nice-looking, but I am afraid too cheap. Papa is much better than when Frank was here. We have some stamps for you: one Horace says is new Am. 5 cent.

Yours, my dear old man,
E. D.

Begin your jerseys.[49]

Yet Emma was not imperturbable. The children remembered the publication of the *Origin* as a "time of frozen misery."[50] The whole family was shivering in icy, uncomfortable lodgings at Ilkley, where Charles, utterly exhausted, was taking the water cure. Then came a great stream of letters from eminent scientists. Both parents were much excited. Apparently, Emma read most of the letters to the children, but Sedgwick's with its "horrified reprobation" of the *Origin*, she did not show even to Henrietta.

While eminent scientists bungled and frowned and scratched their heads over the *Origin*, all the young Darwins were becoming Darwinians with the quick, clear, instinctive apprehension of intelligent children. Horace astonished his father with a theory about adders:

Horace said to me yesterday, "If every one would kill adders they would come to sting less." I answered: "Of course they would, for there would be fewer." He replied indignantly: "I did not mean that; but the timid adders which run away would be saved, and in time they would never sting at all." Natural selection of cowards![51]

Even as he anxiously studied the battlefield where Darwinians and anti-Darwinians fought in rivers of printer's ink, Charles was living another life, very full and on the whole very happy, in the midst of a numerous family already growing up. To his children, the Victorian Newton was an extremely human as well as a slightly comical hero. They early discovered his fallibility, which ranged all the way from discrepant micrometers to permanent bewilderment with the complexities of the German sentence, so that his older and more precocious children were continually astonishing him with intelligible meanings as well as with accurate measurements.

Yet the familiarity of laughter bred only love and admiration—partly because Charles dared to confess a larger fallibility. To one of his daughters he said that "if he had his life to live over again he would make it a rule to let no day pass without reading a few lines of poetry. Then he quietly added that he wished he had not 'let his mind rot so.' "[52]

"How often, when a man," wrote Francis, "I have wished when my father was behind my chair, that he would pass his hand over my hair, as he used to do when I was a boy."[53]

Himself a charming combination of man and boy, and a fabulous storehouse of knowledge and accomplishments, Charles was inevitably a hero to his children. He read them Scott's novels, explained steam engines, taught them how to covet rare beetles and stamps, and shared their youthful experiences with easy equality and at the same time a persistent suggestion of the mature view.

"What a tremendous, awful, stunning, dreadful, terrible, bothering steeple-chase you have run," he wrote Willy, who had just entered Rugby: "I am astonished at your getting in the 5th."[54] Again, addressing himself to "My Dear Old Gulielmus," he related some of his encounters with pigeon fanciers in the neighborhood gin palaces:

Mr. Brent was a very queer little fish; . . . after dinner he handed me a clay pipe, saying "Here is your pipe," as if it was a matter of course that I should smoke. . . . I am going to bring a lot more pigeons back with me on Saturday, for it is a noble and majestic pursuit, and beats moths and butterflies, whatever you may say to the contrary.[55]

Charles could make almost anything as intimate and interesting as pigeons and steeplechases. Advising Willy how to prepare for reading in chapel, he wrote, "When I was Secretary to the Geolog. Soc. I had to read aloud to Meeting MS. papers; but I always read them over carefully first; yet I was so nervous at first, I could somehow see nothing all around me, but the paper, and I felt as if my body was gone, and only my head left."[56]

Later on, when Willy was a Cambridge student occupying his father's old rooms at Christ's, Charles became less boy to

boy, giving opinions on professors and courses with courteous
deference and inviting Willy to be gently amused both at
paternal preaching and at the delightfully pious reception of it
by his younger brothers:

By the way, one evening I said to Frank, who is getting on very
well in French, that he would be very glad of it all his future life,
and a few days after Lenny was dissecting under my microscope
and he turned round very gravely and said "Don't you think,
Papa, that I shall be very glad of this all my future life."[57]

To be sure, Charles still preached. Remembering his own idleness at Cambridge, he was almost pathetically anxious about
Willy:

I do hope that you will keep to your already acquired energetic
and industrious habits: your success in life will mainly depend
on this. So much for preachment, but it is a good and old established custom that he who pays may preach; and as I shall have
to pay . . . , so I have had my preach.[58]

Remembering also that his own want of ambition had depended partly on a sense of affluence, he put the facts very
plainly: Willy must drive through to a profession. "You must
see that when my fortune is divided amongst 8 of you, there
cannot be enough for each to live comfortably and keep house,
and those that do not work must be poor (though thank God
with food enough all their lives)."[59] His letters to Willy were
full of money and the care with which it must be spent.
  One is not surprised that Charles wanted Willy to be pleasing and well mannered. "You are almost always kind and only
want the more easily acquired external appearance," he wrote.
"Depend upon it, that the only way to acquire pleasant
manners is to try to please everybody you come near, your
school-fellows, servants and everyone. Do, my own dear Boy,

sometimes think over this, for you have plenty of sense and observation."[60] Willy became the most charming as well as the most eccentric of the later Darwins. Many years afterward he testified that his father practiced what he preached:

> To be present with him . . . at a small luncheon party with congenial friends, especially if a sympathetic woman were seated near him, will not be easily forgotten by anyone who has experienced it. He put everyone at his ease, and talked and laughed in the gayest way, with lively banter and raillery that had a pleasant flavour of flattery, and touches of humour; but he always showed deference to his guests and a desire to bring any stranger into the conversation.[61]

By continual practical demonstration, Charles communicated his interest in nature, his experimental method, and his love of truth. Of course all the young Darwins became amateur biologists and insisted on helping their father. But because they were his children, he was often humbly doubtful whether they could do the bits of work that offered; and when they triumphantly succeeded, he was overcome with astonishment, and then they laughed at him because he praised them too highly. Later, they became genuinely useful and then he depended on them a good deal.

He never had much time for them. They disturbed his working hours with a moderation singular to children. Not that they were really overawed. When four years old, one of them valued his father so highly as a playfellow that he once tried to lure him away from his study with the bribe of a sixpence. "I remember his patient look," wrote his daughter Henrietta after his death, "when he said once, 'Don't you think you could not come in again, I have been interrupted very often.' "[62]

As a disciplinarian, Charles fell below the lofty standard of his time. In the opinion of relatives, the children were "decidedly spoilt."[63] When strictly necessary, however, he could approximate the stern Victorian father. A letter to Willy contains several times "You want pitching into severely,"[64] and Lenny remembered an interview about a soiled jacket as "rather awful."[63] But such occasions were rare. Charles's power depended on his extraordinary ability to compel interest and sympathy: his children would rather please him than please themselves.

They particularly dreaded interrupting him to get sticking plaster—which was kept in the study—not only because he disliked seeing they had cut themselves but because the sight of blood was so painful to him. Undoubtedly his extreme sensitiveness protected him from disturbance by infusing a sympathetic sensitiveness in the children.

In fact, when he was ill, a pall settled over the whole family. The children played half-heartedly, in a depressed hush. And sometimes, even when he was well, they seemed to sense something that lay deeper than sickness. As quite a little boy, Lenny approached his father while strolling: "after a kindly word or two," he "turned away as if quite incapable of carrying on any conversation. Then there suddenly shot through my mind the conviction that he wished he was no longer alive."[65] To be sure, particularly when speaking to his children, Charles emphasized that his life was a happy one. Emma best knew his sufferings. Charles wrote his sister Susan during a dose of water cure that "Dr. Gully has generously allowed me 6 pinches of snuff for all this week which is my chief comfort except thinking all day of myself and complaining [?] to Emma, who, bless her old soul, thinks about me as much as I do even myself."[66]

The family attitude toward sickness was unwholesome. "There was a kind of sympathetic gloating in the Darwin voices," a grandchild recalls, "when they said, for instance, to one of us children, 'And have you got a *bad* sore throat, my poor cat?' "[67] Charles was such a graceful, charming invalid, and Emma such a tireless, loving nurse, that the children could hardly resist being ill. Of course heredity made the situation doubly dangerous. All the children except William showed a

LARRY BURROWS

THE MIDDLE-AGED CHARLES DARWIN.

tendency to melancholy, and Etty, Horace, and later George suffered from their father's complaint.

In 1851 Darwin lost his ten-year-old daughter Annie. Characteristically, his grief expressed itself in terms of his powers of observation. He wrote a memorial in which he carefully described her ways and habits:

Even when playing with her cousins, when her joyousness almost passed into boisterousness, a single glance of my eye, not of displeasure (for I thank God I hardly ever cast one on her), but of want of sympathy, would for some minutes alter her whole countenance.[68]

Often Annie's nurse during her last illness, he remembered her unfailing cheerfulness and gratitude. "When I gave her some water, she said, 'I quite thank you'; and these, I believe, were the last precious words ever addressed by her dear lips to me."[69]

The letter Emma wrote the day after Annie's death is eloquent of the relation between man and wife: "I knew too well what receiving no message yesterday means. . . . My feeling of longing after our lost treasure makes me feel painfully indifferent to the other children, but I shall get right in my feelings to them before long. You must remember that you are my prime treasure."[70]

The Darwin children were surrounded by indulgent elders. There was Emma's quiet, unmarried sister Elizabeth, who was devoted to everybody but herself. There was Emma's aunt—sweet, intense, intelligent Jessie Sismondi, who took the most passionate, yet discriminating interest in the children while waiting impatiently to join her absurd, beloved, good-hearted Sismondi in heaven. Above all, there was Charles's bachelor brother Erasmus, who diminished his great height with gentleness as he diminished his talents with modesty. He spoiled legions of nephews and fell remotely and whimsically "in love" with each niece as she grew up.

The relationship between the two brothers themselves is one of the most charming in biography. Mildly astonished at everything and deeply surprised at nothing, Erasmus accepted his brother's greatness with gentle exclamations and a quiet pride that was most flattering. On his side, Charles retained for Erasmus to the end of their days something of a schoolboy's reverence for an elder brother. In her "beautiful letter" about religion, Emma guessed that Erasmus's agnosticism had made agnosticism easier for Charles. He felt a tender sympathy for Erasmus's loneliness and would often murmur, "Poor dear old Philos," using the nickname the latter had earned at school.

Meanwhile, the *Origin* exhausted edition after edition, filling Murray's coffers with money and Darwin's letters with exclamations of astonishment.

What a grand, immense benefit you conferred on me by getting Murray to publish my book [he wrote to Lyell]. I never till to-day realised that it was getting widely distributed; for in a letter from a lady to-day to E., she says she heard a man enquiring for it at the *Railway Station!!!* at Waterloo Bridge; and the bookseller said that he had none till the new edition was out. The bookseller said he had not read it, but had heard it was a very remarkable book!!![71]

When he corrected for the second edition, however, he found that two things annoyed him: "those confounded millions of years (not that I think it is probably wrong), and my not having (by inadvertence) mentioned Wallace toward the close of the book in the summary, not that anyone has noticed this to me. I have now put Wallace's name at p. 484 in a conspicuous place."[72]

9

An Interlude: Huxley, Kingsley, and the Universe

In his personal journal—at a blank space immediately below the entry recording the birth of his first child—Huxley made another significant entry:

Sept. 20, 1860
And the same child, our Noel, our first-born, after being for nearly four years our delight and our joy, was carried off by scarlet fever in forty-eight hours. This day week he and I had a great romp together. On Friday his restless head, with its bright blue eyes and tangled golden hair, tossed all day upon his pillow. On Saturday night the fifteenth, I carried him here into my study, and laid his cold still body here where I write. Here too on Sunday night came his mother and I to that holy leave-taking.[1]

Doubtless Huxley received many letters of sympathy and wrote replies more or less conventional and restrained. But one letter stirred him to the depths and elicited a whole spiritual autobiography and justification of faith—or lack of faith—in response. His correspondent was almost a total stranger: the Reverend Canon Kingsley, novelist, poet, pamphleteer—and Chaplain to the Queen. Kingsley's letter of condolence has not been preserved. He seems to have roundly declared that he could not himself face the loss of a loved one without the confident assurance of knowing that person in another existence. Fortunately, he had that assurance. The strong sense of personality proves the permanence of personality. Kingsley may also have touched on his early doubts and struggles, so similar to Huxley's, and on the consolations of work and a happy married life. Certainly he divined, with the double insight of a novelist and a kindred spirit, Huxley's state of mind in this crisis of grief.

Huxley replied:

My convictions, positive and negative, on all the matters of which you speak, are of long and slow growth and are firmly rooted. But the great blow which fell upon me seemed to stir them to their foundation, and had I lived a couple of centuries earlier I could have fancied a devil scoffing at me and them—and asking me what profit it was to have stripped myself of the hopes and consolations of the mass of mankind? To which my only reply was and is— Oh devil! truth is better than much profit. I have searched over the grounds of my belief, and if wife and child and name and fame were all to be lost to me one after the other as the penalty, still I will not lie.[2]

As for immortality, Huxley neither denies nor affirms it. He has no a priori objections:

It is not half so wonderful as the conservation of force, or the indestructibility of matter. . . . The longer I live the more obvious it is to me that the most sacred act of a man's life is to say and to feel, "I believe such and such to be true." All the greatest rewards and all the greatest penalties of existence cling about that act. The universe is one and the same throughout; and if the condition of my unravelling some little difficulty of anatomy or physiology is that I shall rigorously refuse to put faith in what does not rest on sufficient evidence, I cannot believe that the great mysteries of existence will be laid open to me on other terms. . . . I know what I mean when I say I believe in the law of inverse squares, and I will not rest my life and my hopes upon weaker convictions.

Man's first duty is to seek truth. Here science, evangelicalism—and pantheism—find common ground. To act on a false theory is to disregard nature's laws and to incur an inevitable punishment. That would seem a practical matter. But the matter is not altogether practical. To think wishfully, to rest in comforting illusion when scientific truth is conceivably within reach, is to desecrate both one's self and the universe. Doubt and ignorance are sanctified when based on a firm resolve to believe nothing but truth.

After explaining how he became an agnostic by reading Hamilton on the unconditioned, Huxley returns to the theme:

Science . . . warns me to be careful how I adopt a view which jumps with my preconceptions, and to require stronger evidence for such belief than for one to which I was previously hostile.

My business is to teach my aspirations to conform themselves to fact, not to try and make facts harmonise with my aspirations.

Science seems to me to teach in the highest and strongest manner the great truth which is embodied in the Christian conception of entire surrender to the will of God. Sit down before the fact as a little child, be prepared to give up every preconceived notion, follow humbly wherever and to whatever abysses nature leads, or you shall learn nothing. I have only begun to learn content and peace of mind since I have resolved at all risks to do this.

Intellectual humility is not basically different from religious. The ultimate mystery extends to the very borders of the known. Discovery thus becomes a religious discipline. The chemist at his bench is a priest at an altar. Huxley indignantly denies that a "system of future rewards and punishments" is necessary either to practical morality or to the moral government of the world.

I am no optimist, but I have the firmest belief that the Divine Government (if we may use such a phrase to express the sum of the "customs of matter") is wholly just.

The more I know intimately of the lives of other men (to say nothing of my own), the more obvious it is to me that the wicked does not flourish nor is the righteous punished. But for this to be clear we must bear in mind what almost all forget, that the rewards of life are contingent upon obedience to the whole law—physical as well as moral—and that moral obedience will not atone for physical sin, or vice versa.

The ledger of the Almighty is strictly kept, and every one of us has the balance of his operations paid over to him at the end of every minute of his existence.

Life cannot exist without a certain conformity to the surrounding universe—that conformity involves a certain amount of happiness in excess of pain. In short, as we live we are paid for living.

And it is to be recollected in view of the apparent discrepancy between men's acts and their rewards that Nature is juster than we. She takes into account what a man brings with him into the world, which human justice cannot do.

The absolute justice of the system of things is as clear to me as any scientific fact. The gravitation of sin to sorrow is as certain as that of the earth to the sun, and more so—for experimental proof of that fact is within reach of us all—nay, is before us all in our own lives, if we had but the eyes to see it.

This passage summarizes Huxley's basic faith for the greater part of his life. As Mr. David G. Aivaz has observed in an unpublished paper, Huxley's ultimate problem is man's place in nature, or value's place in fact.[3] His solution was to assert a simple identity. An admission of fact does not require a rejection of value, nor is any metaphysical substructure of false information necessary to sustain value. Truth thus becomes morality; error, sin; agnosticism, faith—and one might add—science, religion. If one knew enough, he would see that he was receiving precisely what he deserved—and presumably, would hasten to deserve all that his natural endowment permitted.

In more ways than one, the solution was heroic. One thinks of Darwin's intestinal worm and his accidental bolt of lightning. Huxley was faced, in the most personal and tragic sense, with a fact of just this kind. His response was a fierce reassertion of faith: he would follow scientific truth wherever it might lead, confident that it would lead to some moral or spiritual equivalent of God. As a matter of fact, he rather often, as in the famous passage of the hidden chess player, comes close to smuggling God into his immaculately impersonal universe in a metaphor:

The chess-board is the world, the pieces are the phenomena of the universe, the rules of the game are what we call the laws of Nature. The player on the other side is hidden from us. We know that his play is always fair, just and patient. But also we know, to our cost, that he never overlooks a mistake, or makes the smallest allowance for ignorance. To the man who plays well, the highest stakes are paid, with that sort of overflowing generosity with which the strong shows delight in strength. And one who plays ill is checkmated—without haste, but without remorse.[4]

A similar infusion of nature with spirit and personality per-vades the letter to Kingsley. In the hour of grief the need for clarity had become irresistible. He strove for clarity without God and attained something like God without clarity.

Probably inspired by a similar passage in Kingsley's letter, Huxley now plunges into astonishing self-accusation: "Kicked into the world a boy without guide or training, or with worse than none, I confess to my shame that few men have drunk deeper of all kinds of sin than I." The confession need not be taken literally. It represents a puritan's dissatisfaction with his instincts. "Happily," he continues, "my course was arrested in time." And then, in a famous passage, he explains what rescued him:

Sartor Resartus led me to know that a deep sense of reli-gion was compatible with the entire absence of theology. Secondly, science and her methods gave me a resting-place independent of authority and tradition. Thirdly, love opened up to me a view of the sanctity of human nature, and impressed me with a deep sense of responsibility.

Huxley concludes almost with a threat, pointing ominously to the prostrate form of his recent victim, Bishop Samuel Wilberforce:

And I write this the more readily to you, because it is clear to me that if that great and powerful instrument for good or evil, the Church of England, is to be saved from being shivered into fragments by the advancing tide of science—an event I should be very sorry to witness, but which will infallibly occur if men like Samuel of Oxford are to have the guidance of her destinies—it must be by the efforts of men who, like yourself, see your way to the combination of the practice of the Church with the spirit of science.

The correspondence between these two men continued for several years. There is something here of the encounter between Glaucus and Diomedes: two great champions of opposing hosts happen to meet at close range and discover that a deep bond exists between them. That bond was a great similarity of character and outlook. The canon was quite as much at home as the professor under the nodding plumes of oratorical and literary war. He was as amazingly energetic, as indomitably frail and unhealthy, as sumptuously talented for versatile performance, as tensely mobilized for action, and with a mind as splendidly adequate to any intellectual adventure but that of patiently groping through labyrinths of logic to a subtle and complex truth.

His Odyssey had been a parade of dazzling Victorian triumphs over Circes and Scyllas very similar to Huxley's. At a tender age he had made his voyage down into the underworld and like Huxley seen his grisly visions of suffering and death. He had performed equal prodigies of undergraduate study and taken firsts with an ease as terrible and wonderful, though with less intellectual zeal, having lusted after hounds, hunters, and a military career. His family could not afford to make him a soldier—he had to be a poet and prophet instead. Yet throughout life part of his enjoyment of nature on walks and rides consisted in planning fortifications for likely sites; and when in later years he preached for the first time in the chapel of a military school, the clank of the officers' swords and measured tramp of the men brought tears to his eyes.

He had passed through a period of doubt, and eventually achieved an affirmation at the expense of logic and clarity. His Kingdom of God, perhaps even more than Huxley's scientific utopia, became a rather mundane destination at the end of the busy road of social progress; he was secure in the domestic paradise of an ideal married life, with Carlyle and tobacco for occasional solace. He had offended orthodoxy on political grounds, as Huxley had on scientific; and he also had known the orator's bliss of swaying a hostile crowd at a moment of national crisis. In short, he illustrates strikingly that, in its essential human terms, Huxley's career could have been passed under a shovel hat as well as a mortarboard, and that life on one side of the Victorian spiritual gulf could be much like life on the other.

Even at the time of Noel's death Huxley's wife was far advanced in pregnancy. On December 11, 1860, a second son, Leonard, was born. Mrs. Huxley urged that the child be christened, and at length, in spite of agnostic scruples, her husband consented, feeling it "only fair to a child to give it a connection with the official spiritual organization of its country."[5] Nevertheless, he wrote Hooker, the prospective godfather, that he would be in a bad temper until the ceremony was done with.

In the spring of 1863 Huxley and Kingsley exchanged a number of letters. Darwin's *Fertilization of Orchids* and Bates's *The Naturalist on the Amazons* had filled Kingsley with ecstasies of enthusiasm and piety. Undoubtedly he was very curious about science and very curious about Huxley—of course not without designs of conversion. Huxley was much less curious about Kingsley, and inclined to be scientifically oracular about man's ignorance and personal immortality. And yet he was more open with this noisy, aggressive· clergyman than, one suspects, he was ordinarily with himself. Kingsley was challenging but never disconcerting. He had the sympathetic insight to understand Huxley without the depth and subtlety to be critical of him. He also spoke Huxley's moral idiom. The blunt courage with which he put questions, the colloquial geniality with which he discussed the ineffable, unlocked Huxley's most sacred interiors. "I am often astonished," wrote the latter of their first exchange of letters, "at the way in which I threw myself and my troubles at your head."[6]

What Kingsley evoked in these later letters was the philosophical skeptic. P. E. More has pointed out that Huxley's strategy against bishops and archdeacons was not free from inconsistency.[7] When on the offensive, he tends to be an uncomprising materialist, insisting on the primacy of matter and the absolute determinism of natural law. When pressed by questions and counterarguments, he falls back on the fluid defense of Pyrrhonism:

> I know nothing of Necessity, abominate the word Law (except as meaning that we know nothing to the contrary), and am quite ready to admit that there may be some place, "other side of nowhere," par exemple, where $2 + 2 = 5$, and all bodies naturally repel one another instead of gravitating together.
>
> I don't know whether Matter is anything distinct from Force. I don't know that atoms are anything but pure myths.[8]

He goes even farther: "My fundamental axiom of speculative philosophy is that *materialism and spiritualism are opposite poles of the same absurdity—*the absurdity of imagining that we know anything about either spirit or matter."[9] Then for the first time he develops the metaphor, quoted above in its most famous form, of the hidden player, with its tenuously ambiguous implications of impersonal personality. He sums up:

For, if you will think upon it, there are only four possible ontological hypotheses now that Polytheism is dead.

I. There is no x $\quad=$ Atheism on Berkeleyan principles.

II. There is only one x $\quad=$ Materialism or Pantheism, according as you turn it heads or tails.

III. There are two x's $\Big\}$ $=$ Speculators *incertæ sedis*.
    Spirit and Matter

IV. There are three x's $\Big\}$ $=$ Orthodox Theologians.
    God, Souls, Matter

To say that I adopt any one of those hypotheses, as a representation of fact, would to my mind be absurd; but No. 2 is the one I can work with best. It chimes in better with the rules of the game of nature than any other of the four possibilities, to my mind.

But who knows when the great Banker may sweep away table and cards and all, and set us learning a new game? What will become of all my poor counters then? It may turn out that I am quite wrong, and that there are no x's or 20 x's.[10]

At the close of this letter he concludes, without much humility: "Maurice* has sent me his book. I have read it, but I find myself utterly at a loss to comprehend his point of view."[11]

* F. D. Maurice, the theologian, and the intellectual leader of Kingsley's group.

10

Human Skeletons in Geological Closets

The period from 1859 to 1863 was for Huxley both a transition and a culmination. It was a transition in that he now entered on a life too broad and varied to be reconciled permanently with arduous and effective scientific research. It was a culmination in that, for the time at least, the prophet found his mission, the literary artist developed his most characteristic vein, the platform champion won some of his most notable victories —and yet the scientist did not suffer. In fact, he managed in large measure to combine all his activities and to achieve all his destinies in a single work, *Evidence of Man's Place in Nature*, which was at once excellent writing, superb Darwinian propaganda, and perhaps his most remarkable scientific achievement.

The year 1861 saw him working at the materials of this book with one hand and performing the amenities of controversy with the other. In Edinburgh he gave two lectures on the relation of man to the lower animals. Skeptical Edinburgh came to applaud. Religious Edinburgh stayed away to snub—heard incredible rumors, and suddenly filled the newspapers with shrieks of wounded piety. Quite unruffled, Huxley answered with a public letter. His two lectures, scientifically original as well as popularly exciting, were later published as the second part of *Man's Place in Nature*.

How general was the impact of Darwinism and how much Huxley was its living embodiment, may be gathered from his effect on audiences of workingmen, to whom he delivered in 1862 his lectures "On Our Knowledge of the Causes of the Phenomena of Organic Nature." "I never saw an audience more intent, intelligent, and sympathetic . . . ," wrote Frederic Harrison. "I could not but be struck with the vigour and acuteness of their looks. It was a perfect study of heads, such foreheads and such expressions of hungry inquiry."[1]

Published in pamphlet form, these lectures sold in great numbers. One can readily understand the thrill of intellectual wonder with which they were received. In easy, vivid language they reveal the great and dazzlingly intricate structure of mechanical causes which science had recently uncovered in the world of living matter, bringing the discoveries of Cuvier, Lyell, and Darwin on the one hand into relation with those of Mayer, Du Bois Reymond, Helmholtz, and Pasteur on the other. With characteristic virtuosity, Huxley explores this complicated wonderland—and here a pun is almost unavoidable—on horseback. He expounds that animal as a physiological machine, contracts him to his constituent protoplasm, ramifies him out into various types of vertebrate adaptation, traces him back to the embryo and forward to death and the chemical enrichment of the soil. He explains the life cycle, including the photosynthesis of plants and the ultimate derivation of energy from the sun. Lectures IV and V are devoted to an exposition of Darwinism, and VI, to a criticism which amounts to a judicial defense.

"The Phenomena of Organic Nature" represents the confident and dogmatic Huxley, as passages in the letters to Kingsley do the skeptical and agnostic. The constituents of reality are energy and matter, of which everything in the universe, including man, is a more or less subtle combination. There is no essential distinction between organic and inorganic. Thought is an electric current running along the nerves. These lectures, together with *Man's Place in Nature*, indicate pretty well the effect of the *Origin* on Huxley. Darwinian evolution confirmed him in the religion of matter that he learned from Helmholtz and gave to that austere creed a ray of millennial hope. Apparently, man could look forward not only to unlimited scientific knowledge but to unlimited biological improvement.

These lectures were as much admired by experts as by workingmen. Darwin looked upon his servant's handiwork and was well pleased. "Though I have been well abused," he wrote, "yet I have had so much praise, that I have become a gourmand, both as to capacity and taste; and I really did not think mortal man could have tickled my palate in the exquisite manner with which you have done the job."[2] As to the lectures themselves, "I have read Nos. IV and V," he wrote Huxley. "They are simply perfect. They ought to be largely advertised; but it is very good in me to say so, for I threw down No. IV with this reflection, 'What is the good of my writing a thundering big book when everything is in this little green book so despicable for its size?' "[3] He was so much impressed that for the first time he expressed a doubt whether Huxley's future really lay in research. Perhaps he should write a new textbook on zoology. It was much needed and would have an immense influence. Huxley repelled the suggestion.

The year 1862 saw Huxley Hunterian Professor at the College of Surgeons, the man with whom he shared the post having resigned. The new professor promptly found that twenty-four lectures were much easier to give than twelve, and contracted to publish the substance of them from year to year in a work which eventually became his *Comparative Anatomy*.

The process by which twenty-four lectures became easier

than twelve did not involve any superficiality of preparation. It was his rule, says his colleague Sir William Flower, "never to make a statement in a lecture which was not founded on his own actual observation"; and as the vertebrata were somewhat new to him, he began with the primates and made "a series of original dissections of all the forms he treated of."[4] Much of this work was valuable in the preparation of *Man's Place in Nature*. Yet only a limited number of birds can be killed with one stone, and Huxley was accomplishing a stupendous slaughter. Plagued with neuralogic rheumatism, frequently prostrated with headaches and dyspepsia, he measured skulls during free days, dissected primates every evening, sat on commissions, gave infinite lectures, wrote *Man's Place in Nature*, read metaphysics and philosophy through the small hours lengthened by insomnia, and still with unflagging ebullience could write to Darwin, "If one had but two heads and neither required sleep!"[5]

All this labor was both rapid and purposeful. Sir William Flower, who usually assisted him in his evening work, described Huxley in action:

In dissecting, as in everything else, he was a very rapid worker, going straight to the point he wished to ascertain with a firm and steady hand, never diverted into side issues, nor wasting any time in unnecessary polishing up for the sake of appearances; the very opposite, in fact, to what is commonly known as "finikin." His great facility for bold and dashing sketching came in most usefully in this work, the notes he made being largely helped out with illustrations.[6]

In the general war which followed the publication of the *Origin* in 1859, the battle over man was the fiercest. Evolution meant low origins, and low origins meant that man was a disgusting upstart. There were many who resented the imputation.

Yet long before 1859 the fact had become embarrassingly

clear. As early as 1797, in a short paper before the Societies of Antiquaries in London, John Frere had described finding flint instruments in rock strata dating from a period well before that at which an act of the Creator could be counted on. The paper was received with pain and piously forgotten. In 1847, having made a great find at Abbeville, Boucher des Perthes had published his *Antiquités Celtiques*, in which he proved that man had existed at the glacial epoch and, theologically speaking, had herded with the mastodon and the rhinoceros. Des Perthes' book was too large and his case too detailed to be ignored. Lyell, Flower, Prestwich, and others went to Abbeville and returned convinced.

In 1848 a very curious skull had been found on the Rock of Gibraltar. The brain cavity was extremely shallow, the encasing wall very thick, the forehead shockingly low and recessive, and there were heavy ridges over the eye sockets. The Gibraltar Scientific Society reported simply "a Human Skull." In 1856 a similar skull and a skeleton were found in the valley of the Neander in Germany. The paleontologist Schaaffhausen was on hand and investigated. He concluded that the bones were extremely ancient and, though human, more primitive than those of the most barbarous tribes now living.

It was upon this sequence of anthropological events that the *Origin* burst in 1859. In the ensuing battle over the nature of man, field generalship on the scientific side passed from Lyell to Huxley. However illuminated by the new ideas and determined to approach the study of man in their light, Lyell found in the moment of crisis that the religion of his boyhood had returned to him. As time went on, it became more and more evident that his conscience would allow him to do little beyond reckoning divine intervention according to geological, rather than Mosaic, time. In the evolution of man, he felt, natural selection could not be more than a secondary cause.

Darwin offered him no "consolatory view,"[7] and indeed, when Lyell was beginning to have his first uncomfortable qualms, had jauntily summed up embryological evidence for him: "Our ancestor was an animal which breathed water, had a swim bladder, a great swimming tail, an imperfect skull, and undoubtedly was an hermaphrodite!"[8] To be sure, Darwin uttered his blasphemies in strict confidence. His was still biology with the heroic theme omitted.

Huxley did not share either Lyell's doubts or Darwin's reticence. "I will stop at no point," he had warned Darwin, "so long as clear reasoning will carry me further."[9] By a happy coincidence, the cause of truth was also the case against Owen —and it was at the Oxford meeting of the British Association in this year that Huxley sacrificed the famous anatomist on the altar of Darwinism.

In February, 1862, he began a series of lectures on "The Relation of Man to the Rest of the Animal Kingdom," which had great success. "By next Friday evening they will all be convinced that they are monkeys," he wrote his wife.[10] These lectures, published in *The Natural History Review*, brought Owen to life for another controversy, and at the 1862 meeting of the British Association, he went to absurd lengths of opposition. But the sugar-of-lead smile was no longer formidable, for what lay behind it was too well understood by everybody. Huxley triumphed at every point and only gained further glory from the wild flailings of his adversary. To climax the meeting, Sir William H. Flower annihilated Owen once more and buried him afresh under a long and unanswerable demonstration of the Darwinian position. Owen had become almost an historical curiosity by the time Huxley's *Evidence of Man's Place in Nature* appeared in 1863.

That book was the natural fruit of controversy. It was a triumph of courage even more than of intellect; a contribution to scientific liberty even more than to scientific truth. Huxley said not so much what nobody had thought as what nobody had dared say—and said it so forcefully that many who hardly thought at all were persuaded. He had been warned again and again not to imperil his career by meddling with the dread theological bones, but he was more than justified by the event. People had been waiting for a strong, clear voice of scientific authority.

Not that his book was simply an act of daring. Huxley was the first to use embryology, paleontology, and comparative anatomy—his own specialties—to establish the anthropoid origin of man. He gathered together all the available evidence; laid down suitable criteria, including some new ones; and embodied his work in a biological treatise which, for style and convincingness of proof, can, in the opinion of Sir Arthur Keith, be equaled only by Harvey's *Movement of the Heart and Blood*.[11]

As published in 1863, *Man's Place* consisted of three essays. The first is a history, beginning with Pigafetta and Purchas, of what civilized man has learned about the higher apes. Throughout, Huxley emphasizes their human characteristics. The second essay marshals the evidence from embryology and comparative anatomy. Here Huxley's strategy is to show by a series of comparisons that, in biological terms, there is no gap between man and the rest of nature. In his embryological development, man is far nearer to the apes than the apes are to the dog. In the measurements of his skull and skeleton, he is closer to the gorilla than the gorilla is to the gibbon. Huxley argues that his moral and cultural achievements are not due to the weight of his brain but, primarily, to the possession of articulate speech. He is not degraded because he shares many instincts with the lower animals: he is raised up because he has developed some of those instincts and controlled others.[12] The essay culminates in a poetic expression of the unity of all living

things on the one hand and the sublimity of human development on the other:

In comparing civilised man with the animal world, one is as the
Alpine traveller, who sees the mountains soaring into the sky and
can hardly discern where the deep shadowed crags and roseate
peaks end, and where the clouds of heaven begin. Surely the
awestruck voyager may be excused if, at first, he refuses to believe
the geologist, who tells him that these glorious masses are, after
all, the hardened mud of primeval seas, or the cooled slag of
subterranean furnaces—of one substance with the dullest clay,
but raised by inward forces to that place of proud and seemingly
inaccessible glory.[13]

The third essay presents the evidence from paleontology.
Are there any fossilized remains from the past which would
indicate a transition from the higher apes to man? Huxley dis-
cusses in detail the newly discovered Engis and Neanderthal
skulls. His conclusion is cautious. These skulls—and particularly the Neanderthal—are certainly human, but more apelike
than those of any living race. Early races of men introduce the
question of present races. Still restricting himself to skull types
and employing a neat, geometrical mode of measurement
which was his own invention, Huxley finds, among a multitude
of varieties, two extremes—the straight-jawed, shortheaded,
and the "snouty" or prognathous, longheaded—which are also
opposed in geographical distribution:

Draw a line on a globe, from the Gold Coast in Western Africa
to the steppes of Tartary. At the southern and western end of that
line there live the most dolichocephalic, prognathous, curly-haired,
dark-skinned of men—the true Negroes. At the northern and
eastern end of the same line there live the most brachycephalic,
orthognathous, straight-haired, yellow-skinned of men—the Tar-
tars and Calmucks. The two ends of this imaginary line are indeed,
so to speak, ethnological antipodes. A line drawn at right angles,
or nearly so, to this polar line through Europe and Southern Asia
to Hindostan, would give us a sort of equator, around which
round-headed, oval-headed, and oblong-headed, prognathous and

orthognathous, fair and dark races—but none possessing the excessively marked characters of Calmuck or Negro—group themselves.[14]

Neither of the two extremes is necessarily lower in the evolutionary scale than the other. The Negro's jaws are more apelike than the Calmuck's, but his cerebral cavity is much longer. As a matter of fact, the lowest or most pithecoid type is the aboriginal Australian, whose skull in many respects surprisingly approximates that of Neanderthal Man.*

Huxley's researches into the structural similarities between man and ape led his friend Charles Kingsley to draw some surprising conclusions. About the time the first edition of *Man's Place* appeared, the canon wrote to his friend Frederic Maurice:

> If you won't believe my great new doctrine . . . , that souls secrete their bodies, as snails do shells, you will remain in outer darkness. . . . I know an ape's brain and throat are almost exactly like a man's—and what does that prove? That the ape is a fool and a muff, who has tools very nearly as good as man's, and yet can't use them, while the man can do the most wonderful things with tools very little better than the ape's.[15]

Huxley showed remarkably little enthusiasm when "this great new doctrine" was pressed on him as the tendency of his book. What he felt he had done was, by a bold act of vivisection, to amputate man's soul, so that the primate remainder could be subjected to scientific study.

Man's Place in Nature, despite the fears of Huxley's friends, was received with just enough vituperation to make Huxley

---

* The 1894 edition of *Man's Place* expands the 1863 edition with three periodical essays on ethnology published in the interval. The first, on "Method and Results" (1865), recommends that races be defined by their physical characters, rather than by language, arts, and customs, which evolve and migrate. The second, on "British Ethnology" (1871), is remarkable for its extensive use of Latin literary sources, for a very sensible

feel like a daring spirit. Even by 1863 orthodoxy was chastened. It hoped piously for better days. It had developed a sense of humor. The Athenaeum, reviewing Man's Place together with The Antiquity of Man, observed that Lyell's object was to make man old; Huxley's "to degrade" him. "Man probably lived a hundred thousand years ago, according to Lyell; man probably had a hundred thousand apes for his ancestors, according to Huxley." And with a somewhat edged concession to Huxley, the reviewer decides, "Thus, then, it appears that while Owen and Huxley differ, apes and men do not."[16]

What impressed The Athenaeum reviewer, as well as everybody else, about Man's Place in Nature was that there was so little of it. The Antiquity of Man enunciated an elaborate ambiguity in five hundred pages. In less than two hundred Man's Place laid down a clear-cut, far-reaching principle. Huxley astonished the cultivated Victorian world with a lesson in twentieth-century brevity.

He also filled the Darwinians with pride and superlatives. Hooker found the book "amazingly clever";[17] and Lyell, always generous and enthusiastic, thought it needed only to be a little longer in order to be perfect:

If he had leisure like you and me [he told Darwin], and the vigour and logic of the lectures, and his address to the Geological Society, and half a dozen other recent works (letters to the 'Times' on Darwin, etc.) had been all in one book, what a position he would occupy![18]

Darwin likewise wished for greater length. There might have been something about false ribs, the intermaxillary bone, the

---

little homily on the vanity of speculating about the moral attributes of Celtic blood, and for some very bold and speculative conclusions about the primitive race and language of Great Britain. The third, on the "Aryan Question" (1890), attempts, in spite of earlier cautions, to connect the Aryan language with an Aryan race.

muscles of the ear, and the habits of young orangutans in European zoos. But even so, his delight and admiration were unbounded. Pages 109 to 112 were as grand and condensed as any passage in Bacon; and "what a delicious sneer" (at Owen, of course) on page 106.[19] And how not be pleased with an author who fought one's battles so successfully, explained one's doctrine so clearly, and identified it so poetically with the cause of civilization and the march of progress?

Darwin was the more comforted by *Man's Place in Nature* because he was bitterly disappointed in *The Antiquity of Man*. The history of the friendship between Lyell and Darwin is the quiet, somewhat abstruse tale of a master who, in old age, very nearly becomes a disciple: a prolonged and subdued encounter between Sohrab and Rustum in which there is no violence, much generosity, some estrangement, more pathos, and a kind of death. We who are so much less passionately lost between two worlds find it difficult to understand the desperate tenacity with which Victorians defended the shakiest of compromises. Part of the tragedy was of course that Darwin owed Lyell so much.

Since the middle forties, when he had studied the findings of Boucher des Perthes at Abbeville, Lyell was convinced that man was far older than he—or Moses—had ever thought. After reading the *Origin* in 1859, he resolved to speak out.

Well accustomed to the view from the summit of the evolutionary hypothesis, Darwin was at first both encouraged and somewhat alarmed at his friend's audacity. "It is a good joke," he wrote Hooker; "he used always to caution me to slip over man."[20] It early became a maxim with Darwin that those who went a little way toward his doctrine would eventually go much farther, and that those who went a great way, would eventually become converts. Lyell had already gone a good way, and in those exciting days immediately after the *Origin* had come out, he seemed on the very point of conversion. He fully understood all that conversion implied:

> I am . . . well prepared to take your statements of facts for granted [he wrote Darwin in 1859], . . . and I have long seen most clearly that if any concession is made, all that you claim in your concluding pages will follow.
> It is this which has made me so long hesitate, always feeling that the case of Man and his Races and of other animals, and that of plants, is one and the same, and that if a *vera causa* be admitted for one instant, or a purely unknown and imaginary one, such as the word 'creation,' all the consequences must follow.[21]

As a matter of fact, he had reckoned with his head but not his heart. He was not, like Darwin, one of those men whose whole intellectual and spiritual life had been absorbed by a single idea. His constant geological travels were also human travels. He lived as much in the politics and culture of his own age as in the geology of the cretaceous or the oölitic. He had a more genuinely sympathetic interest in the religious thought of his time than either Darwin or Huxley and religion meant much to him:

> I plead guilty [he wrote Huxley] to going farther in my reasoning towards transmutation than in my sentiments and imagination, and perhaps for that very reason I shall lead more people on to Darwin and you, than one who, being born later, like Lubbock, has comparatively little to abandon of old and long cherished ideas, which constituted the charm to me of the theoretical part of the science in my earlier days, when I believed with Pascal in the theory, as Hallam terms it, of 'the archangel ruined.'[22]

Having gone a long way, he began, to Darwin's inexpressible dismay, to back up step by step. The more he thought about evolution, the more he liked divine interference. "I feel that Darwin and Huxley deify secondary causes too much," he

wrote Hooker. "They think they have got farther into the
domain of the 'unknowable' than they have by the aid of variation and natural selection."[23] Lyell seems also to have had a
sneaking preference for Lamarck, of which he thought Darwin
simply a modification. "I will look at Lamarck again," Huxley
promised him, "but I doubt if I shall improve my estimate."
And he continues very justly:

The notion of common descent was not his—still less that of
modification by variation. . . . Darwin is right about Natural
Selection—the discovery of this *vera causa* sets him to my mind
on a different level altogether from all his predecessors—and I
should no more call his doctrine a modification of Lamarck's than
I should call the Newtonian theory of the celestial mechanics a
modification of the Ptolemaic system.[24]

But Lyell could not see with such crystal clarity. Late in 1860
he was still brooding obstinately about such evolutionary trifles
as rodents in Australia and mice in the Galápagos.

Even so, Darwin remained hopeful:

I have had [he wrote Hooker] a long letter from Lyell, who starts
ingenious difficulties. . . . This is very good, as it shows that he
has thoroughly mastered the subject; and shows he is in earnest.
Very striking letter altogether and it rejoices the cockles of my
heart.[25]

But the mice and rodents refused to evaporate. They were in
fact theological mice and rodents. Once thoroughly awakened
and alarmed, Lyell's religious sense threatened to swallow his
uniformitarianism. Darwin wrote:

I grieve to see you hint at the creation "of distinct successive
types, as well as of a certain number of distinct aboriginal types."
Remember, if you admit this, you give up the embryological
argument (*the weightiest of all to me*), and the morphological
or homological argument. You cut my throat, and your own

throat; and I believe will live to be sorry for it. So much for species.[26]

Despite their differences the correspondence between Lyell and Darwin during these years is one of unusual charm. The dingo and the Amblyrhyncus wander cheerfully in the gloomy forests of metaphysics. "Fixed fate, free will, foreknowledge absolute" are discussed cheek by jowl with the "gestation of hounds" and "adaptation in woodpeckers."[27] Unfortunately, many of Lyell's letters are lost. The heretic's history must be traced in the saint's replies. "I rather demur," wrote Darwin, "to Dinosaurus not having free will, as surely we have."[28]

As always when his great subject was at stake, Darwin showed infinite patience and resource:

One word more upon the Deification of Natural Selection: attributing so much weight to it does not exclude still more general laws, i.e. the ordering of the whole universe. I have said that Natural Selection is to the structure of organised beings what the human architect is to a building. The very existence of the human architect shows the existence of more general laws; but no one, in giving credit for a building to the human architect, thinks it necessary to refer to the laws by which man has appeared.[29]

And in the same letter:

I cannot believe that there is a bit more interference by the Creator in the construction of each species than in the course of the planets. It is only owing to Paley and Co., I believe, that this more special interference is thought necessary with living bodies.[30]

Despite incidental disappointments, Darwin continued to be hopeful until he actually read Lyell's manuscript. In July, 1860, he wrote Gray of Lyell: "Considering his age, his former views and position in society, I think his conduct has been heroic on this subject."[31] As late as September 26, he felt that Lyell "has, perhaps unconsciously to himself, converted himself very much during the last six months."[32] Thereafter he said no more about conversion, but continued to be generous. Reading portions of the unfinished manuscript, he was enthusiastic about the precise geology and the splendid heap of facts. "What a fine long pedigree you have given the human race!"[33] he exclaims; and again, characteristically, "P.S.—What a grand fact about the extinct stag's horn worked by man!"[34]

The Antiquity of Man, like Man's Place in Nature, appeared in January, 1863. Although Lyell's book represented much more work and his name was still much more famous, time had moved past him. He was still sailing on the hither side of Pope Alexander VI's line, still practicing a reticent and dignified statesmanship. In fact, the sagacious ambiguity of his language had entered into his thought. The Antiquity of Man begins like a geological treatise and ends like an essay on liberal theology. Lyell could not make up his mind about evolution, natural selection, man, or the degree and manner of divine interference. Therefore, his book is, as Darwin observes, necessarily "a compilation."[35]

"But," Darwin adds, "of the highest class." There are elaborate analyses from firsthand observation of the Engis, Neanderthal, Natchez, and other remains, as well as of their geological sites. There is a lengthy account of the hippocampus-minor controversy between Huxley and Owen, with a decision tactfully handed down in Huxley's favor. There are chapters on the glacial period which, Darwin feels, are "in parts magnificent." Up to this point, all is firm, consistent, and full of the authority of professional knowledge. But with the discussion of species begins that protracted indecision which makes The Antiquity of Man so interesting as a human document and so ineffective as a scientific treatise. "He has shown great skill," says Darwin, "in picking out salient points in the argument for change of species"; and yet one of his strongest endorsements begins, "If it should ever be rendered highly probable that species change by variation and natural selection . . ." His application of Darwinian principles to language is exact and precise, exhibiting at once a great knowledge of evolution and a great ignorance of linguistics; but the chapter concludes, probably in answer to Huxley's emphasis on speech in *Man's Place*, with a discussion of Humboldt's "profound saying" that "Man is man only by means of speech, but in order to invent speech he must be already man."[36]

The humanism of Humboldt fittingly introduces the last chapter, which deals with the classification of man—the culminating problem of Lyell's book as it is the central problem of Huxley's. Huxley arrives at a solution largely because, for the time at least, he rules out mind. Lyell fails to arrive at a solution because he will not forget mind for a moment. To classify man as an ape may be illuminating, but Lyell refuses to profit by an illumination which implies, even provisionally and temporarily, a denial that man is formed in God's image. He opens with a survey of biological classifications, emphasizing "an immaterial principle" which, though it is "traceable far down into the animate world,"[37] takes a great leap as it ascends to humanity. Then he paraphrases Carlyle, quotes the Archbishop of Canterbury, and concludes with a rather Tennysonian picture "of the ever-increasing dominion of mind over matter."[38]

The Lyells are coming here on Sunday evening to stay till Wednesday [Darwin wrote Hooker]. I dread it, but I must say how much disappointed I am that he has not spoken out on species, still less on man. And the best of the joke is that he thinks he has acted with the courage of a martyr of old.[39]

Actually, Darwin was very far from taking *The Antiquity of Man* as a joke. A little more than a week later he wrote Lyell

straight out, "You . . . leave the public in a fog."[40] He complained of such phrases as "Mr. D. labours to show" and "is
believed by the author to throw light," which were almost
worse than direct negatives.[41] Most unkind of all, Lyell repeat-
edly referred to natural selection as a modification of Lamarck's
view. With increasing exasperation Darwin protested against
an opinion which connected his own and Wallace's ideas with
what he considered "a wretched book," and one from which
he "gained nothing."[42]

Darwin regretted his frankness almost as soon as he had
written, but Lyell replied with "a kind and delightfully candid
letter,"[43] and the correspondence quickly regained its old cordiality. Darwin was soon discussing the Duke of Argyll on sexual
selection and giving thanks for excellent advice about the footnotes in the "Dog chapter" of his new book.[44] But now, perhaps, there was a difference. "You and Hooker," he wrote
Huxley, "are the only two bold men."[45]

And yet, among Darwin's old friends, Lyell had been almost
the only disappointment. Nearly everybody else had been
"staggered." Hooker and Huxley had seen the light early and
seen it in floods. George Bentham, a more casual friend, had
been so staggered by the famous joint papers of Darwin and
Wallace that he had withdrawn one of his own, scheduled to
be read at the same time, on the fixity of species. The Origin
had converted him completely. Henslow, the botany professor
with whom Darwin had walked at Cambridge, and now
Hooker's father-in-law, had received the Origin in deep silence,
presided with alert impartiality over Huxley's famous slaughter
of the Bishop of Oxford, drifted into guarded defense of the
new heresy, and in the last days before a slow and patient death
allowed his orthodoxy to be cautiously and discreetly "shaken."

But the proselyte who gave Darwin greatest joy was the
ponderous, massive-tusked, loud-bellowing Hugh Falconer,
who had once thundered that Darwin was corrupting both

Lyell and Hooker with his accursed evolution. When the *Origin* appeared, Falconer was in the midst of a "heavy" and adventurous research on the congenial subject of elephants, living and extinct.[46] "The story has gone through all Switzerland," reported Lyell, "how Falconer threw up his cap to the ceiling when he saw" the splendid fossil *Mastodon angustidens* of Winterthür.[47] To Darwin's amazement and joy, he very nearly threw up his cap to the ceiling when he read the *Origin*. He immediately sent his elephant paper for approval.

With all my shortcomings, I have such a sincere and affectionate regard for you and such admiration of your work, that I should be pained to find that I had expressed my honest convictions in a way that would be open to any objection by you.[48]

"There is not a single word in your paper to which I could possibly object," replied Darwin with delight. Falconer was very nearly orthodox!

There follows a jovial and affectionate correspondence about elephants. When by an elaborate maneuver Owen stole the naming of an extinct American elephant away from Falconer, Darwin lay awake till three o'clock fuming with indignation. When Falconer returned from one of his paleontological forays to the Continent, he announced triumphantly:

I . . . have brought back with me a live *Proteus anguinus*, designed for you from the moment I got it. . . . The poor dear animal is still alive—although it has had no appreciable means of sustenance for a month—and I am most anxious to get rid of the responsibility of starving it longer. In your hands it will thrive and have a fair chance of being developed without delay into some type of the Columbidæ—say a Pouter or a Tumbler.[49]

The caresses of an affectionate pachyderm could be a little embarrassing. Darwin expressed profuse thanks, protested that he had no aquarium, and hastily suggested that the poor dear animal be sent to the Zoological Society. A little later, with tusks and trunk elevated and an appalling salvo of bellows, Falconer charged into print accusing Lyell, in *The Antiquity of Man*, of having appropriated without acknowledgment some of his choicest fossils. "It is too bad to treat an old hero in science thus," Darwin wrote to Hooker; but he could not deny Falconer his affection.[50]

By 1863, Darwin had made evolution credible to European science. "Darwin is conquering everywhere," Kingsley wrote Maurice, "and rushing in like a flood, by the mere force of truth and fact."[51] He had the satisfaction not only of winning his battle, but of having predicted the precise course it would take. The older generation remained divided and doubtful, but those who "were staggered ever so little" lived to be staggered more. Even the most eminent and fastidious could not carp for long. Von Bär, who, as the father of embryology, had spent a lifetime looking through a microscope at the most graphic evidence of evolution, expressed in French a reserved but respectful interest. De Candolle, a fellow student with Lamarck and a great botanist frequently cited in the *Origin*, declared himself very nearly a convert. Braun, an eminent and intelligent compiler, offered to superintend a German translation.

But what particularly pleased Darwin and best confirmed his prophecy was the enthusiastic support of the younger generation. H. W. Bates, a youthful friend of Wallace, brilliantly explained the phenomena of mimicry by natural selection. At the urging of Darwin, he also produced in 1863 the delightful *Naturalist on the Amazons*, which became a classic of scientific travel literature. "He is second only to Humboldt," declared Darwin proudly, "in describing a tropical forest."[52]

In 1864 two eminent scientists sharply criticized the *Origin*. One was R. A. Kölliker, famous for the clarity of his expositions in microscopics; and the other was M. J. P. Flourens, who, though he had done distinguished work in nerve physiology, rejoiced rather too much in being Perpetual Secretary of the French Academy of Sciences. Being very busy at the time, Huxley disposed of both men in a single review, crushing Kölliker beneath the weight of his own clear, precise misapprehensions of Darwin, and grinding Flourens between the two millstones of his fatuity and his academic position:

> But the Perpetual Secretary of the French Academy of Sciences deals with Mr. Darwin as the first Napoleon would have treated an "ideologue"; and while displaying a painful weakness of logic and shallowness of information, assumes a tone of authority, which always touches upon the ludicrous, and sometimes passes the limits of good breeding.[53]

And then after a devastating illustration: "Being devoid of the blessings of an Academy in England, we are unaccustomed to see our ablest men treated in this fashion, even by a 'Perpetual Secretary.'"

Darwin crowed with delight: "If I do not pour out my admiration ... I shall explode."[54]

11

Orchids, Politics, and Heredity

Superficially, the next decade of Darwin's life is the story of a quiet recluse with delightfully eccentric habits. But there are undercurrents—the sadness of prodigious labor and fading inspiration, the burden and strain of increasing concentration and the resulting persistence of ill-health and greater ceremony of cure.

Being the author of *The Origin of Species* proved to be a profession itself. There were always new editions to be prepared, translations to be arranged. The question of priority, rendered painful from the first by the appearance of Wallace, was a constant source of petty indignity. Erasmus's prediction not only came true—it came true again and again. Apparently, the idea which had cost Charles so much thought and perplexity had casually occurred to half the crackpots in Europe.

A few months after the *Origin* came out, Mr. Patrick Matthew wrote an indignant letter to *The Gardner's Chronicle*, claiming credit for the theory of natural selection, which, by a refinement of cruelty, he had tucked into the appendix of a work on *Naval Timber and Arboriculture* written some thirty years before. Darwin hastily procured the book. Yes, there in three scattered passages was a clear statement of his hypothesis. Of course he was astonished. He anxiously consulted Hooker, swallowed his suffering, and wrote a suitable reply, mingling dignified apology with an undertone of mild complaint that his ideas should ever have been put into the appendix of a book on arboriculture. Matthew refused to be mollified and had "Discoverer of the Principle of Natural Selection" printed on his visiting cards and title pages.

In 1865 a "Yankee" called Darwin's attention to a paper read by Dr. W. C. Wells before the Royal Society in 1813 and to his "Two Essays upon Dew and Single Vision" in 1818. Natural Selection again! "So poor old Patrick Matthew is not the first,"[1] Darwin wrote Hooker with heartfelt satisfaction. The old man would have to alter his title pages. In 1866 he prefixed "An Historical Sketch" to the sixth edition of the *Origin*. None of his other writings expresses so little gusto. Lamarck gets a grudging paragraph and grandfather Erasmus, a martyr to family modesty, is perfunctorily immortalized in a phrase at the end of a footnote.

The great book drew many visitors and occasioned countless letters. "An awful Russian bore has been here,"[2] he notes; and again, "Half the fools throughout Europe write to ask me the stupidest questions."[3] And then there were the correspondents who fervently admired the *Origin* but who had written a very similar book which "goes much deeper." A German doctor, for example, "explains the origin of plants and animals on the principles of homeopathy or by the law of spirality. Book fell dead in Germany. Therefore would I translate it and publish it in England."[4] On the other hand, Lyell wrote that he had an animated conversation about Darwinism with the Princess Royal, who, a true daughter of Prince Albert, took a keen interest in the great contemporary battle of the books. "She was very much *au fait* at the 'Origin,' and Huxley's book, the 'Antiquity,' &c.," wrote Lyell. "I have the true English instinctive reverence for rank," replied Darwin somewhat sedately, "and therefore liked to hear about the Princess Royal."[5]

In 1865, looking over the *Origin* for a second French edition, Darwin had a refreshing experience. "I am, as it were, reading the 'Origin' for the first time . . . ," he wrote Hooker, "and upon my life, my dear fellow, it is a very good book, but oh! my gracious, it is tough reading."[6]

The German translation by Victor Carus was a sterner ordeal. "I well remember," wrote his son Francis, "the admiration (mingled with a tinge of vexation at his own shortcomings) with which my father used to receive the list of oversights, &c., which Professor Carus discovered in the course of translation."[7]

The *Origin* saddled Darwin with a double task: he had to write a book and to solve a problem. The book was the great work of which the *Origin* was meant to be a mere summary. The problem was of course evolution—particularly in its unsolved aspect of heredity and its controversial aspect of man's place in nature. One cannot but feel that in his anxious, scrupulous way Darwin became a little confused at the complicated interlocking character of his purpose, that he sometimes thought writing the book nearly equivalent to solving the problem. He must have been often tempted to mistake labor for achievement. There is a suggestion of Laocoön in Darwin's later intellectual history.

He had hardly finished the *Origin* when he settled down doggedly to his longer work, which confronted him at once with the enigma of heredity; and this line of inquiry led back to an earlier study of fertilization in plants. In the summer of 1839 he had begun to investigate the cross-fertilization of flowers by insects, on the theory "that crossing played an important part in keeping specific forms constant."[8] Gradually his interest had centered on orchids. He had read Robert Brown's paper in *The Linnean Society's Transactions* and on Brown's advice had procured C. C. Sprengel's *Das entdeckte Geheimniss de Natur.*

He was soon as irrevocably dedicated to orchids as he had formerly been to barnacles. It was a briefer and perhaps a more fortunate dedication, though he had waxed nearly as lyrical over structural beauty in the sliminess and smelliness of the barnacle as he now did over that in the bright color and exotic forms of the orchid. Nevertheless, he preferred flowers:

> He would often laugh at the dingy high-art colours, [says his son], and contrast them with the bright tints of nature. I used to like to hear him admire the beauty of a flower; it was a kind of gratitude to the flower itself, and a personal love for its delicate form and colour. I seem to remember him gently touching a flower he delighted in.[9]

Like many somewhat inarticulate people, Darwin used his hands a great deal when talking "in a way that seemed rather an aid to himself than to the listener."[10] His son remembers that in explaining the fertilization of an orchid, he would use his hands as another man might use pencil and paper.

Orchids proved to be the perfect subject, so much so that he scarcely regarded them as serious work. They were a delicious waste of time:

> It is mere virtue in me [he wrote Hooker] which makes me not wish to examine more orchids; . . . Nevertheless, I have just been looking at Lindley's list in the *Vegetable Kingdom*, and I cannot resist one or two of his great division of Arethuseæ, which includes Vanilla.[11]

And a little later: "I must keep clear of *Apostasia*, though I have cast many a longing look at it in Bauer."[12]

Of course both *Vanilla* and *Apostasia* were included; of course what was meant to be a paper swelled gradually into a book. As a matter of fact, Charles found himself obliged to be more of a discoverer than he had intended to be, for in spite of the excellent work of Brown and Sprengel, orchid science was a little unsound at its foundations. Flowers did not look quite as the great Bauer drew them. What had seemed solved and simple proved all at once to be desperately puzzling and complex. "If I cannot explain the case of *Habenaria*," he exclaims tragically to Hooker, "all my work is smashed. I was a fool ever to touch orchids."[13] But eventually, of course, each variety yielded up its secrets. What ingenuities of adaptation! "I carefully described to Huxley," he wrote to a new friend, T. N. Farrer, "the shooting out of the Pollinia in Catasetum, and received for an answer, 'Do you really think I can believe all that?' "[14]

As usual, Darwin had plenty of assistance. Hooker and Lindley sent him rare specimens; his sons caught pollen-bearing moths at night; and everybody watched orchids for visiting insects. Even Lord Avebury received orders:

I write now in great haste to beg you to look (though I know how busy you are, but I cannot think of any other naturalist who would be careful) at any field of common red clover (if such a field is near you) and watch the hive-bees: probably (if not too late) you will see some sucking at the mouth of the little flowers and some few sucking at the base of the flowers, at holes bitten through the corollas. All that you will see is that the bees put their heads deep into the [flower] head and rout about. Now, if you see this, do for Heaven's sake catch me some of each and put in spirits and keep them separate.[15]

Alas! The next day he wrote in a fresh ecstasy of apology and parenthesis: "I beg a million pardons. Abuse me to any degree, but forgive me: it is all an illusion (but almost excusable) about the bees. I do so hope that you have not wasted any time from my stupid blunder. I hate myself, I hate clover, and I hate bees."[16]

He was also harassed by the incidental catastrophes which assail a numerous family in an unhygienic age. Ever since an attack of diphtheria in 1858, his daughter Henrietta had been ailing and was eventually sent to a warmer climate. In the summer of 1862 one of his sons caught scarlet fever. When the boy had recovered sufficiently, Darwin took a house in Bournemouth, but on the way his wife came down with the disease. "We are a wretched family, and ought to be exterminated," he wrote Asa Gray. "There is no end of trouble in this weary world."[17] And again he wrote:

Children are one's greatest happiness, but often and often a still greater misery. A man of science ought to have none—perhaps not a wife; for then there would be nothing in this wide world worth caring for, and a man might (whether he could is another question) work away like a Trojan.[18]

The Various Contrivances by Which Orchids Are Fertilised by Insects appeared in 1862. It is a study of nature's trap doors and spring mechanisms. Orchid fertilization is a melodrama of ingenuity which transpires in a microcosm of exotic beauty. The insect is attracted by a sweet odor. Sometimes a petaldoor opens up before him and snaps shut behind. Sometimes a ridged passageway, like the secret stairway in a haunted house, guides him to precisely the spot where he may sip nectar and at the same time release the mechanisms of the flower. When he touches a certain point on the rostellum, the pollen-masses are either shot at him like arrows, or they grip his proboscis with a clasp, or, more frequently, they simply slide through a kind of trap door and are cemented to his eyes by two viscid discs. After an interval sufficient to allow the insect to sip nectar and make his exit, the pollen-masses bend forward on their discs so as to be in exactly the right position to touch the stigma of the next flower. Most orchids are invariably cross-fertilized and completely dependent on insects. Darwin regards the few species which fertilize themselves as degenerates:

> I should like to hear [he wrote, perhaps slyly, to Asa Gray] what you think about what I say in the last chapter of the orchid book on the meaning and cause of the endless diversity of means for the same general purpose. It bears on design, that endless question. Good night, good night![19]

Certainly the book is less innocuous than it seems. Orchids were a natural stronghold of anti-Darwinians. In the first place, they were held, like other intricate structures, to be a conspicuous instance of botanical art for art's sake—or at least art for man's sake. As such, they had no relation to utility or natural selection. Darwin therefore demonstrated that orchids are not simply beautiful to men but useful to themselves, that "apparently meaningless ridges, horns" have meaning and utility.[20]

But even if God had intended usefulness rather than beauty, Darwin's book still seemed to support the argument for divine intent in nature. Actually, it undermined that argument. Asa Gray was quick to see this and Darwin was quick to respond: "Of all the carpenters for knocking the right nail on the head you are the very best; no one else has perceived that my chief interest in the orchid has been that it was a 'flank movement' on the enemy."[21]

In short, he does not directly attack the ideas of creation and divine intent, but he labors to make them untenable so far as practical science is concerned. The adaptations of orchids, varied and intricate as they are, could not possibly have resulted from a single act of the Creator. There is too much history in orchid structure for that. The little treatise concludes with a discussion of homologies in which Darwin traces all species back to a monocotyledonous flower of fifteen organs. This evolution from a general to a highly complex and specialized form is best explained by natural selection. In fact,

the more I study nature, the more I become impressed with ever-increasing force, that the contrivances and beautiful adaptations slowly acquired through each part occasionally varying in a slight degree but in many ways, with the preservation of those variations which were beneficial to the organism under complex and ever-varying conditions of life, transcend in an incomparable manner the contrivances and adaptations which the most fertile imagination of man could invent.[22]

Such reasoning might suggest that natural selection renders cosmic mind unnecessary.

When the book came out, the Duke of Argyll, writing in *The Edinburgh*, pointed out that while Darwin's argument proved natural selection, his language proved design. He constantly used phrases such as "beautiful contrivance," "the labellum is . . . *in order* to attract," "the nectar is *purposely* lodged."[23] The reviewer concluded that Darwin was unintentionally right. Wallace made a brilliant reply, and Darwin remained cheerful.

As a matter of fact, Charles did not fear the theologians quite so much as the botanists. He intended the orchid book as an example of how natural selection could be applied to the plant kingdom, and was full of trepidation at the thought of laying down fundamental law in a field not his own. But the botanists were full of praise. The book also sold widely among the general public. Charles was so astonished and delighted at his success, that he had to compose devastating reviews against himself to keep his vanity within bounds.

His orchid study remained a lifelong pleasure to him. "They are wonderful creatures, these Orchids," he wrote almost at the end of his days, "and I sometimes think [of them] with a glow of pleasure, when I remember making out some little point in their method of fertilisation."[24]

On November 30, 1864, the Royal Society yielded to history and awarded Darwin the Copley Medal. Not that British science yet ventured to endorse his ideas. Availing himself of the dignified ambiguity of official language, General Sabine emphasized in his announcement speech at the anniversary dinner Darwin's general achievement in geology, zoology, and botany, and then, carefully knocking the brains out of the *Origin*, admired it as "a mass of observations" valuable to science.[25] He also explained that the award was based more particularly on such masterly treatises as *The Fertilisation of Orchids*.

Indignant at the slur against his friend's greatest achievement, Huxley rose at once and inquired whether General Sabine had expressed the attitude of the Society. The offensive expressions were softened in the minutes. Equally indignant, Lyell also protested, though still lost between two worlds. Afterwards he reported the event to Darwin, who had been absent as usual, "I said I had been forced to give up my old faith without thoroughly seeing my way to a new one. But," he added pathetically, "I think you would have been satisfied with the length I went."[26]

As a matter of fact, a strong movement to give Darwin the Copley Medal had been defeated in 1863, and even in 1864 some members of the Society had been bitterly opposed. Who were they? Darwin had inquired of Hooker with eager curiosity. Less inclined than Huxley to expect logic either in himself or in others, he regarded the bizarre proceedings of Sabine and the Royal Society as hopeful and promising. "Sabine, through you to a large part," he wrote Huxley, "has made me very proud of myself."[27]

Within another year there was a veritable stampede of societies, royal and otherwise, to press their decorations upon him. He was elected an honorary member of the Berlin Academy and of the Edinburgh Royal and Royal Medical Societies. To be sure, he lost his diplomas and forgot which societies he belonged to:

Does the Berlin Academy of Sciences send their Proceedings to Honorary Members? [he inquired anxiously of Hooker]. I wanted to know, to ascertain whether I am a member; I suppose not, for I think it would have made some impression on me; yet I distinctly remember receiving some diploma signed by Ehrenberg.[28]

He was deeply pleased at being recognized by the Royal Society of Edinburgh, for as a young medical student he had been taken to a meeting by Lyell's father-in-law, Leonard Horner, and had seen in the chair the famous man whose novels, then and in later life, he had read over and over again:

Sir Walter Scott [sat] in the chair as President, and he apologised to the meeting as not feeling fitted for such a position. I looked at him and at the whole scene with some awe and reverence . . . If I had been told at that time that I should one day have been thus honoured, I declare that I should have thought it as ridiculous and improbable, as if I had been told that I should be elected King of England.[29]

And if he had ever been told that he would one day be introduced to the Prince of Wales—Charles would either have laughed outright or begun to think it very possible that he might be elected King of England. Yet he was not only presented but presented—as Emma wrote Fanny Allen—the first of a very distinguished and select three. It was at a soiree of the Royal Society. Charles had just grown himself a complete Victorian beard, which proved so effective a disguise that he had to name himself even to his old friends. The Prince, "a

nice good-natured youth, and very gentlemanlike,"[30] murmured something which Darwin could not hear. Charles therefore bowed very low and went on. What Bertie thought of
such a convocation of gray beards and learned foreheads, what
he thought of the notorious monkey-sage in particular—posterity has no record. Perhaps he did not feel obliged to think.

Preparing for further botanical work, Darwin decided to
have a small hothouse. With the aid of a neighbor's gardener,
it was planned and built with gusto. "The new hothouse is
ready," he wrote Hooker, "and I long to stock it, just like a
schoolboy."[31] And a week later: "You cannot imagine what
pleasure your plants give me (far more than your dead Wedgwood ware can give you*); and I go and gloat over them."[32]
Even nausea and headache could not keep him away. The
stove-plants, he said, "do so amuse me. I have crawled to see
them two or three times."[33]

A note by Asa Gray on the tendrils of climbing plants had
set him off on a fresh scent. He got a Wild Cucumber† plant
to observe in his study. He noticed that in an interval of from
one-half to two hours the uppermost part of each branch
twisted round in a circle. After two or three revolutions, it
rested a half-hour and then untwisted, revolving in the opposite direction. The movements had no relation to light. Moreover, whenever the searching tendrils touched any object, their
sensitivity, on which Gray had remarked, caused them to seize
it immediately and make fast. Darwin was astonished.

A "clever gardener" came in that evening for a talk and observed the plant. "I believe, Sir," he declared, "the tendrils can
see, for wherever I put a plant it finds out any stick near
enough."[34]

---

* Darwin had been astonished to learn, some time earlier, that Hooker
actually collected Wedgwood ware.
† Echinocystis lobata.

"The tendrils have some sense," Darwin told Hooker, "for they do not grasp each other when young."[35]

Now, of course, he was dedicated to climbing plants. They would not interfere with the great book and the great problem. "It is just the sort of niggling work which suits me, and takes up no time and rather rests me whilst writing."[35]

> My present hobby-horse I owe to you [he wrote Gray], viz. the tendrils: their irritability is beautiful, as beautiful in all its modifications as anything in Orchids. About the *spontaneous* movement (independent of touch) of the tendrils and upper internodes, I am rather taken aback by your saying, "is it not well known?" I can find nothing in any book which I have.[36]

Would Gray please tell him whether anything had been published on the subject? "I shall hardly regret my work if it is old," he concluded, "as it has much amused me."[37]

The new hothouse was soon rapidly filling up with all sorts of climbers, which Hooker sent from Kew. Darwin toiled through two long German books and lusted after the exotic climbers there described. Despite a prolonged illness, he observed and experimented in idyllic happiness through the spring of 1864.

At last he had to begin writing to keep himself from further experimenting. Then came the horrible last phase, which, temporarily, poisoned all the many months of happiness. "I finished and despatched yesterday my climbing paper. For the last ten days I have done nothing but correct refractory sentences, and I loathe the whole subject."[38]

"The Movements and Habits of Climbing Plants" was published in 1864 in the *Linnean Journal,* and in 1875 it appeared as a book. Darwin found that the ability to climb depends basically on a sensitiveness to contact with any firm support. In the more perfect tendril bearers it becomes an elaborate combination of differential growth and spontaneous, surprisingly rapid movement of the young shoots and other organs. Inevitably he preached a homily on natural selection. Plants move less than animals not because they are necessarily inferior, but because, being fixed to one spot, they could derive no advantage from great mobility.

Charles thought this book too dull and obscure for general readers, and too obvious and trivial for the experts. But all his friends liked it and said so in the warmest terms. "I think my friends must perceive that I like praise," he told his wife, "they give me such hearty doses."[39]

His next project grew out of a friendship with John Scott, a young gardener employed as head of the propagating department at the Edinburgh Botanic Gardens. A great admirer of the Origin, he first wrote Darwin to point out, very modestly and deferentially, an error in the orchid book. The letter was five long pages, bristling with botany and syntax. Though mildly flurried by his error, Darwin did not fail to notice a mind beneath the syntax and the Latinisms. "He had interested me strangely," Darwin wrote Hooker, "and I have formed a very high opinion of his intellect. I hope he will accept pecuniary assistance from me."[40] With his customary skill and eager shyness, he conspired to get Scott's articles accepted, and he conspired still more to get them noticed and reviewed.

Meanwhile the disciple bemoaned his style and the master gave shrewd and at the same time revealing advice:

Do not despair about your style; your letters are excellently written, your scientific style is a little too ambitious. I never study style; all that I do is to try to get the subject as clear as I can in my own head, and express it in the commonest language which occurs to me. But I generally have to think a good deal before the simplest arrangement and words occur to me . . . I would suggest to you the advantage, at present, of being very sparing in introducing theory in your papers (I formerly erred much in Geology in that way): *let theory guide your observations*, but till your reputation is well established be sparing in publishing theory. It makes persons doubt your observations.[41]

Scott expected a great deal of himself and a great deal of other people. When the authorities offered him what he considered a slight, he abruptly left the Edinburgh Botanical Gardens, and found himself, with some alarm, without means of support. Hooker was helpful in securing him a position with the Botanic Garden at Calcutta, and Darwin paid the passage out.

He had great hopes for his protégé. In diffident, yet enthusiastic terms, he recommends one of Scott's papers to Asa Gray: "A most remarkable production, though written rather obscurely in parts."[42] And he interposes, with anxious calculation, "He is a most laborious and able man, with the manners almost of a gentleman."[43] But launching into a full summary of the article, he can hold back his enthusiasm no longer. Scott has provided what Huxley required as a final proof of natural selection—an experimentally developed species incapable of producing fertile offspring when crossed with the parent stock. "The red cowslip is very sterile when fertilising, or fertilised by the common cowslip. Here we have a new 'physiological species.' "[44]

But Scott's passage to India was no odyssey of the creative spirit. It was a dropping off into the void. In the published correspondence there is a break of seven years, and then a kindly, yet rather formal letter from Darwin. "You have done good work," he concludes, "and I am sure will do more."[45] And thus, softly damned with faint praise, Scott passed into oblivion. He returned to Edinburgh in 1880 and died in the same year. But Scott's subject did not die with the man in

Darwin's mind. The common interest in primroses and other
dimorphic flowers led him to publish a series of papers in
which he showed that sterility is after all no test for species.
It is the simple result of a difference in the sexual organs.

Through these years his illness seemed to grow more serious.
"A succession of doctors and a plenitude of treatment," says
Dr. Douglas Hubble, "were necessary to protect him from the
suspicion of shamming."[46] He was long devoted to Dr. Gully
and hydropathy, undergoing faithfully a program of "the
lamp" five times a week, as well as a "douche daily for five
minutes and dripping sheet daily." He began to doubt hydropathy only as he came to know Gully better. "It is a sad flaw
. . . in my beloved Dr. Gully," he wrote Fox, "that he believes
in everything. When Miss —— was very ill, he had a clairvoyant girl to report on internal changes, a mesmerist to put her
to sleep—an homeopathist, viz. Dr. ——, and himself as
hydropathist! and the girl recovered."[47] Gully was followed by
Lane, Brinton, and then Bence-Jones, who half-starved Darwin and prescribed riding. But one day Charles's horse Tommy
fell on Keston Common. Severely shaken, Charles placed himself in the care of Sir Andrew Clark, that courteous, reassuring
professional presence at so many eminent Victorian bedsides.

As his fame spread rapidly through the world during these
laborious years, Darwin could feel the scope of his own life
contract. More and more, his infirmity was regulating his
tastes and habits down to the last detail. Society had become
very nearly intolerable for him. He avoided all formal occasions
and saw only close relatives and old friends. He went less and
less often to London. An evening at the Linnean Society cost
him days of suffering afterwards. Even a half-hour's conversation with a distant relative was followed by a sleepless night.
He was astonished at his susceptibility. He deplored it. But he

yielded to its tyranny—and doubtless turned the time he saved to good account.

People not only excited him; they evoked problems—and if at all possible, every problem must be solved, every shadow must be cleared from his mind, before he went to bed. Had he hurt anyone's feelings? Had he involuntarily misrepresented a fact? His conscientiousness about even the most trivial facts would have seemed fantastic pedantry in anyone less genuinely free from that vice.

One evening, when his younger friend and disciple Romanes was a guest at Down, the conversation turned to the difficulty of explaining the evolution of the aesthetic emotions, and particularly of the sense of the sublime. Darwin said that he had felt the sublime most deeply when he had stood on one of the summits of the Andes and surveyed the prospect all around. It had seemed as though "his nerves had become fiddle strings and had all taken to rapidly vibrating."[48] The talk had then turned in another direction and after about an hour Darwin went to bed. One of his sons sat until late with Romanes in the smoking room. At one o'clock in the morning the door opened softly and Darwin appeared in dressing gown and slippers:

> Since I went to bed [he explained], I have been thinking over our conversation in the drawing-room, and it has just occurred to me that I was wrong in telling you I felt most of the sublime when on the top of the Cordillera; I am quite sure that I felt it even more when in the forests of Brazil. I thought it best to come and tell you this at once in case I should be putting you wrong. I am sure now that I felt most sublime in the forests.[49]

Having said this, he returned to bed.

In a world of possible problems and threatening nervous tension, Down House was a tiny island regulated by Emma and blessed routine. Charles rose early, took a brief turn in the

garden, breakfasted alone at 7:45, and then worked an hour
and a half till 9:30. At that time "he came into the drawing
room for his letters—rejoicing if the post was a light one and
being sometimes much worried if it was not. He would then
hear any family letters read aloud as he lay on the sofa."[50]
After the letters came a chapter or two of some current work
of fiction, and thereafter until twelve, another period of work,
which was then, in the austerer sense of writing or experiment,
concluded for the day, so that he "would often say, in a satisfied voice, 'I've done a good day's work.' "[51] At midday, accompanied by his fox terrier Polly he took his constitutional,
stopping for a few minutes at the greenhouse, and then
proceeding to the "Sand-walk," a one and one-half acre strip
—planted in hazel, alder, dogwood, and privet—with a gravel
path around it. Usually he paced methodically, keeping careful count of his round trips, but sometimes, particularly when
alone he would stand still or walk stealthily to watch a bird
or an animal. "It was on one of these occasions that some
young squirrels ran up his back and legs, while their mother
barked at them in an agony from the tree."[52]

After lunch, he retired once more to the drawing room sofa
and read the newspapers. Then he answered letters. Seated
comfortably in a huge horsehair chair by the fire, he would
either write straight off in his swift, illegible hand or make a
rough draft from which to dictate later. His friends complained
piteously about his handwriting—often he could not read his
own notes—so that he commonly used an amanuensis, cau-
tioning him to write plainly and begin an important sentence
with a new paragraph. Following his father's rule, Darwin
answered and preserved every letter. He had a printed form
for troublesome communications, but rarely used it. Even the
most personal inquiry into religious principles received a polite
and evasive, sometimes a frank and open, reply. Minor celebri-
ties must have been surprised at the deference with which this

major celebrity addressed them. His first letters to a new correspondent—with their "I hope you will excuse the liberty" and "I must apologize for troubling you"—betray his shyness. Nevertheless, conscientiousness, the constant search for information, and perhaps a certain curiosity about his correspondents made him one of the most voluminous letter-writers of his time. Like many a recluse, he was positively gregarious with pen in hand.

From three until four he rested in his bedroom, listening to a novel and smoking cigarettes. Cigarettes were for relaxation in idleness, snuff for stimulation during work. Late in the afternoon—since the best rules are made to be broken—he sometimes got in another half-hour's work before dinner at seven-thirty.

After dinner came the traditional game of backgammon with his wife. He played with gusto, as he did everything he liked, "bitterly lamenting his bad luck and exploding with exaggerated mock-anger" at his wife's success.[53] He carefully kept track of the score into the thousands of games.

Charles's reading falls into two classes and was done in two postures. Strenuous or disagreeable scientific reading he got through late at night in his study. Because of his long legs he raised himself by putting cushions in the seat of his study chair; then, to neutralize the effect, he raised his feet onto a footstool. One is tempted to imagine him, in the course of a long German work, rising rather close to the ceiling. For all other reading, he lay on a sofa. Such reading consisted in lighter or more agreeable scientific works, travel books, history, and above all fiction. He held a low opinion of novels as works of art, yet he frequently blessed all novelists. "A novel, according to my taste, does not come into the first class unless it contains some person whom one can thoroughly love, and if a pretty woman all the better."[54] In later years he cared much less for music because it set him to thinking about his work.

Passing much of his intellectual life on a sofa, Darwin believed, with an almost missionary strenuousness, in easy and comfortable reading. At times he found every unnecessary movement, and even the weight of a book, intolerable. His remedy was surgery on the book. With a ruthless, unbibliophile hand he dismembered heavy and dignified tomes, in order to read them in light and manageable sections. Even Lyell's *Elements of Geology* was not exempt. "With great boldness," he coolly informed its author, "[I] cut it in two pieces, and took it out of its cover."[55]

In some respects, Charles's reading had narrowed nearly as much as his personal life. Philosophy and metaphysics almost invariably gave him indigestion. He intended to read Bishop Colenso but read reviews of him instead. He had only the most desultory interest in poetry:

Give my kindest remembrance to Mrs. Huxley [he wrote his old friend], and tell her I was looking at 'Enoch Arden,' and as I know how she admires Tennyson, I must call her attention to two sweetly pretty lines (p. 105) . . .
. . . and he meant, he said he meant
Perhaps he meant, or partly meant, you well.
Such a gem as this is enough to make me young again, and like poetry with pristine fervour.[56]

History when it flattered his preconceptions or general science when it bordered on his own researches, he could still enjoy. He liked Tylor's *Researches into the Early History of Mankind* but thought Lecky's *Rise of Rationalism* too vague and full of abstract phrases. He was so much impressed by Spencer's *Principles of Biology* that he felt ignorant and feeble-minded by comparison.

I could bear, and rather enjoy feeling that he was twice as ingenious and clever as myself, but when I feel that he is about a dozen times my superior, even in the master art of wriggling, I feel aggrieved.[57]

This praise is obviously not without edge. At about the same time he wrote Hooker, "I went this afternoon to the Lubbocks to have an interview with Herbert Spencer, and I enjoyed my talk much though he does use awesomely long words. I plainly made out that Lady Lubbock thinks him like you do, not a small bore."[58] Still, he was inclined to believe that Spencer needed only to observe more, and think a little less, to be a very great man.

The one nonscientific work that thoroughly aroused his enthusiasm was Buckle's *Introduction to the History of Civilisation in England:*

> Have you read Buckle's second volume? it has interested me greatly; I do not care whether his views are right or wrong, but I should think they contained much truth. There is a noble love of advancement and truth throughout; and to my taste he is the very best writer of the English language that ever lived, let the other be who he may.[59]

The passage speaks volumes about Darwin's nonprofessional reading. In fact, he seems to be defending himself as well as Buckle. He read not to be critical, but to be entertained, agreed with, stimulated to feeling. For these purposes, Buckle must have been admirable. He is irrepressibly curious about origins, studies the animal man broadly and naturalistically in his planetary environment, is boundlessly enthusiastic about science, progress, humanitarianism, freedom—in short, all of Darwin's favorite ideas. Science is daily reducing great chaoses of the unknown to luminance and order. It needs now only to investigate man to make morals, history, and nearly everything else as undeviatingly regular as mechanics. Again, as a writer, Buckle is often ponderous but seldom vague and abstract like

Lecky. And when he comes to narrative, the ponderosity falls away and he is simple, swift, and vivid, fighting with contagious zeal the battle of Victorian progress in a dozen historical settings.

Darwin's curiosity about the world was omnivorous. He liked all kinds of facts, even nonscientific ones. The Times was one of his most important ceremonies. It was taken up directly after lunch, and though it suffered the indignity of the sofa, was read personally and with great thoroughness. Charles was a spirited politician; that is to say, he was inclined to feel much and think little about politics.

The American Civil War confronted him with the classic dilemma of the patriotic humanitarian—complicated by some of those delicate ironies of which the infinite variety of history alone is capable. A brash, unpleasant, vulgar people were fighting for a good principle against a charming, refined, aristocratic people with a bad principle. Moreover, the bad principle meant cheap cotton for British manufacturers; the charming people augmented British wealth, whereas the unpleasant people seemed to threaten British power. To be sure, the dilemmas of history are sharp and real only in the transitory and unperspicacious logic of the moment. Time dissolves them all— often tragically—into paradox and anticlimax. The temptation to use black soldiers brought the South to the verge of emancipation; the American Union eventually became a bulwark of British security.

Darwin did not, of course, make any clear-cut choice between North and South. In fact, he expressed for both sides several shades of enthusiasm, even of fanaticism, slightly tempered at times by the detachment of the spectator who welcomes distraction from more immediate concerns. His correspondent on this subject was chiefly Asa Gray, who was both more critical and more deeply involved.

I never knew the newspapers so profoundly interesting [Darwin wrote soon after the outbreak of hostilities]. North America does not do England justice; I have not seen or heard of a soul who is not with the North. Some few, and I am one of them, even wish to God, though at the loss of millions of lives, that the North would proclaim a crusade against slavery. In the long-run, a million horrid deaths would be amply repaid in the cause of humanity. What wonderful times we live in! Massachusetts seems to show noble enthusiasm. Great God! how I should like to see the greatest curse on earth—slavery—abolished![60]

After the Confederate victory at Bull Run, Darwin is doubtful that the North can win. He also distrusts "the men of Washington" and their good intentions toward England.[61] Gray reiterates that the Union would be insane to want war with England as well as the Confederacy. On the other hand, "it is generally believed that the governing influence in England desires to have us a weak and divided people, and would do a good deal to secure it."[62] Consequently, many Americans are hostile.

In the first year of the war the Confederacy had been recognized as a belligerent, though not as an independent, state, by both France and Britain. It now sent John Slidell and James Mason to act as representatives in Paris and London. These two men were taken from the Trent, an English vessel, by a Union man-of-war. Great Britain protested. Meanwhile, a dinner to celebrate the seizure was held in Boston, where the old enemy was verbally conquered with all the ruthless violence of American hyperbole. Darwin wrote to Gray:

What a thing it is that when you receive this we may be at war, and we two be bound, as good patriots, to hate each other, though I shall find this hating you very hard work. How curious it is to see two countries, just like two angry and silly men, taking so opposite a view of the same transaction![63]

"If we do go to war," he adds—rather naïvely, in the light of facts—"it will be with the utmost reluctance by all classes, Ministers of Government and all."[64]

But a month later he decides on second thought that he is really very angry about the *Trent* affair. "I must own that the speeches and actions recently of your leading men . . . , and especially the Boston Dinner have quite turned my stomach . . . and I have begun to think whether it would not be well for the peace of the world, if you were not split up into two or three nations."[65] He had now very nearly reversed his initial stand on the American conflict. In fact, "the present American row," as he wrote Hooker, "has a very Torifying influence on us all."[66]

Gray apologized for the Boston hyperbole. "Such men should not have talked bosh, even at a little private ovation." Wiser men, "some of whom refused to attend the dinner," criticized the incident as sharply as Darwin. "It was really as bad as the speeches of some members of Parliament, and worse because it was foolish."[67] Gray continued to blame bad relations with England on the press and sends American newspapers to let a little air into the mental world created by the London *Times*.

Darwin's reply is all mildness and propitiation—the more so, perhaps, because Lincoln had in response to the English protest ordered the two Confederate agents released.

For a while the correspondence rests cautiously on the solid ground of professional interests. In August Gray sends stamps to Darwin's little boy, and in November Darwin mentions Miss Cooper's *Journal of a Naturalist*: "Who is she? She seems a very clever woman, and gives a capital account of the battle between our and your weeds." And then he adds, "Does it not hurt your Yankee pride that we thrash you so confoundedly? I am sure Mrs. Gray will stick up for your own weeds. Ask her whether they are not more honest, downright good sort of weeds."[68]

Gray insists that no compromise is possible. The war can only end in victory for the Union, whose resources and man power are almost unlimited. The country laid waste and desolate? By no means. Even while fighting the rebels it is building vast new industries and spanning and crisscrossing the continent with railroads:

> I fear it is true that the English do not really care about slavery [wrote Darwin after the Emancipation Proclamation had been published]; I have heard some old sensible people say here the same thing; and they accounted for it . . . by the present generation never having seen or heard much about slavery.[69]

He had by this time begun to distrust *The Times*. "*The Times* is getting more detestable (but that is too weak a word) than ever. My good wife wishes to give it up, but I tell her that is a pitch of heroism to which only a woman is equal."[70] And now apparently—with vigorous assistance from Gray—he comes to realize the extent of British partisanship. "Do not hate poor old England too much"[71] becomes almost a refrain in Darwin's later letters.

Almost to the end, he refused to foresee a Northern victory. In the very month Sherman took Atlanta, he once more succumbed to *The Times* and wondered whether "there will be peace and that the Middle States will join with the South on slavery and reject the Northern States.—In this latter case, I suppose you will marry Canada, and divorce England, and make a grand country, counterbalancing the devilish South."[72]

With this rather wild speculation the American conflict seems for a long interval to vanish from Darwin's correspondence. Of Gettysburg, of victory in the West, of Grant's massive attack on Richmond, of Sherman's march to the sea or Lee's surrender at Appomattox—there is not a word. Even Lincoln's death does not interrupt the steady stream of discussion about pigeons and orchids, dogs and glaciers. But Darwin must have made further comment, for in May, 1865, Gray writes, "Don't talk of our 'hating' you." Americans appreciate England's good feeling and "hearty grief at the murder of Lincoln."[73] Several years later Darwin confesses with generous frankness, "How egregiously wrong we English were in thinking that you could not hold the South after conquering it. How well I remember thinking that slavery would flourish for centuries in your Southern states."[74]

Darwin read the morning news—as he read world history—en *pantoufles*, without much attempt at analysis and criticism. In fact, he found it difficult to be critical of anything:

> I have no great quickness of apprehension or wit which is so remarkable in some clever men, for instance, Huxley. I am therefore a poor critic: a paper or book, when first read generally excites my admiration, and it is only after considerable reflection that I perceive the weak points. My power to follow a long and purely abstract train of thought is very limited; and therefore I could never have succeeded with metaphysics or mathematics.[75]

Only when thoroughly aroused by a problem was Darwin capable of the tension of close criticism and analysis. His feelings were quick and alert, but his mind was not.

His intellectual vices were curiously linked with his intellectual virtues. Perhaps, after the inspiration of the *Origin* had passed, his strong, affectionate grip on fact expressed itself too often as a timid and confused reluctance to deal with abstraction; his obstinate, unrelaxing grip on a few ideas, as a tendency to consider them and the phrases in which they were couched, inevitable and unchangeable.

Once he had finished writing a book, Darwin hated to return to it, either for criticism or revision: he had worked too hard and suffered too much; he had begun with too passionate an enthusiasm and ended with too deathly an exhaustion. At such a time, and perhaps for long after, one dares not think of error. In 1866 Wallace astounded Darwin by pointing out that in the fourth chapter of the *Origin* he frequently seemed to personify nature and used the term "natural selection" in two senses—for the preservation of favorable variations and also for the species-forming result produced by such preservation. Wallace suggested that Spencer's "survival of the fittest" would clarify much of this confusion. Did Darwin understand? Yes, for once everything was "as clear as daylight."[76] He resolved in the next edition to carry Wallace's advice into effect, though he didn't think the confusion had been very serious. Some people—particularly clever people—can misunderstand anything. Besides, he observed with foreboding, *survival of the fittest* "cannot be used as a substantive governing a verb."

Meanwhile, a reluctant and preoccupied Columbus, he had continued to sail the inscrutable seas of heredity. He had long been trying to ascertain what he was looking for, but apparently he decided only when his voyage was almost over that it was something he had sketched out twenty-six or -seven years before.[77] In 1865 he wrote to Huxley, requesting that he read the statement of a theory called *pangenesis*. "It is a very rash and crude hypothesis, yet it has been a considerable relief to my mind, and I can hang on it a good many groups of facts." Huxley must briefly give his verdict—burn or publish. Darwin concluded with trepidation, "I must say for myself that I am a hero to expose my hypothesis to the fiery ordeal of your criticism."[78]

Huxley's answer began with a cry of bewilderment, "I shall have to put on my sharpest spectacles and best considering cap."[79] Darwin's exposition of the subject has since earned a reputation for obscurity. On mature reflection, Huxley was for

neither burning nor publishing. The theory was highly speculative. Moreover, something very like it had been developed
by Buffon.

Anticipated again! Darwin thanked his friend with patience.
"It would have annoyed me extremely to have re-published
Buffon's views, which I did not know of, but I will get the
book. I will try to persuade myself not to publish."[80] Huxley's
rejoinder was generous and cheering. He did not mean to express an absolute negative. "Somebody rummaging among
your papers half a century hence will find *Pangenesis* and say,
'See this wonderful anticipation of our modern theories, and
that stupid ass Huxley prevented his publishing them.' "[81]

Darwin's spirits rebounded at once. He could even regard
Buffon with amusement. "I have read Buffon: whole pages are
laughably like mine."[82] Nevertheless, there was a fundamental
difference. Darwin feared he would publish, but he would be
humble and tentative. A year later he wrote Wallace not to
expect too much of pangenesis, and almost on the eve of publication he confided to Haeckel rather pathetically that the
book itself was hardly worth translating. "A naturalist's life
would be a happy one," he told Lyell, "if he had only to
observe, and never to write."[83]

The *Variation of Plants and Animals under Domestication*
was published in two volumes on January 30, 1868. As a matter
of fact, Darwin had already been forestalled. The primary
experiments in genetics had just been performed by a Mora-
vian monk in a monastery garden. Setting out to discover the
mechanism of heredity, with the influence of environment as
a constant, Gregor Mendel very deliberately selected as his
subject the ordinary garden pea. It was comparatively short-
lived and could be rapidly studied through several generations.
It might be either self- or cross-fertilized, so that each mating
could be controlled. Its progeny were numerous and could be

treated statistically. They also differed in clearly marked characters.

Mendel crossed yellow-seeded peas with green-seeded. The hybrid seeds were all yellow. He therefore called the yellow-seeded character *dominant*, and the green-seeded, *recessive*. Allowing 258 of the yellow-seeded hybrids to seed themselves, he obtained 8,023 seeds, of which 6,022 were yellow and 2,001 were green—or the three-to-one proportion which occurs for every pair of characters involving a dominant and a recessive. The recessive *gene* or trait-determiner re-expressed itself in the second hybrid generation wherever it was by chance combined with another recessive.

Altogether, Mendel studied seven pairs of contrasted characters in the pea. He communicated his results to the naturalists' society of Brno and his paper was published in their journal. It there suffered the supreme irony of learned publication and while pangeneticists, germ-plasmists, and Lamarckians battled furiously over their own errors, lay neglected until 1900, when it was unearthed after three scientists had rediscovered the same law.

Darwin's attack on the problem of heredity was almost as irresolute and confused as Mendel's had been bold and perspicacious. He had accepted the lore and hearsay of fanciers nearly as confidently as he had his own careful observations. He had studied not one domestic plant but scores, and he showed a decided preference not for plants but for the complex, slow-maturing animals favored by breeders. He had studied not one or two sets of characters but all that exhibited variation, and he had concentrated on minute, scarcely perceptible changes ill-adapted to elementary work in genetics. Here, of course, he was guided by his early conviction, probably correct on the whole, that such minute changes are the primary material of natural selection. On the other hand, he admitted in this book, almost for the first time, that the more abrupt changes later emphasized by De Vries might have a considerable role in the formation of species. In any case, Darwin apparently could not, even for purposes of temporary study, make a clear-cut separation in his mind between variations and natural selection, as he could not make a separation between the problem of heredity itself and his old preconceptions regarding the influence of environment and of use and disuse.

Perhaps one good thought had corrupted his mind on this subject. Animal breeders had shown him how varieties might develop in nature. Therefore he seems to have felt they could show him how variations themselves originate. Accordingly, his first volume is a very learned and astute breeder's manual. It contains chapters—bristling with facts, many of them antiquarian—on each of the common domestic animals. One learns that there were cats in ancient Egypt, mastiffs in ancient Assyria, and lap dogs in ancient Rome. Darwin not only investigates breeds, but breeders also, explaining their methods, psychology, and objectives. One seems to catch echoes of talk from the gin palaces. "Baron Cameronn challenges, in a German veterinary periodical," he cites with gusto, "the opponents of the English race-horse to name one good horse on the Continent which has not some English race-blood in his veins."[84] And he quotes with solemnity a great breeder of Shorthorns:

The eye has its fashion at different periods: at one time the eye high and outstanding from the head, and at another time the sleepy eye sunk into the head; but these extremes have merged into the medium of a full, clear and prominent eye with a placid look.[85]

Jehovah in a whirlwind, or Schiaparelli in an advertisement, could not describe a creature or a creation more impressively.

The second volume deals primarily with heredity, and here again one must admire Darwin's grip on enormous bodies of facts. He is familiar with all the phenomena that Mendel studied, and many more. He is aware that in hybrids characters do not necessarily "blend" but may contrast sharply, that they may be sex-linked, that one may be dominant, or as he says, "prepotent," over another, so that the second skips a generation and reappears thereafter. Yet these facts are not particularly meaningful to him—chiefly because he thought others more important.

What he thought important were first, his own preconceptions and second—to do him justice—certain observations on the most complex and difficult aspect of his subject. All of these elements he combined in his theory of pangenesis. He believed that acquired characteristics are inherited. He also believed—and as we now know rightly—that "inheritance must be looked at as merely a form of growth" the pattern of which lies implicit in the fertilized ovum or in the simpler organism itself.[86] Simple organisms divide and each part grows toward maturity. Certain worms may be cut into many sections and each section grows into a complete individual. A young salamander can replace a lost limb or tail. Growth thus seems connected with reproduction and regeneration, possibly with the direct influence of environment.

In seeking an explanation, Darwin was thrown off the track by his stubborn old ideas—ultimately traceable to Buffon and Lamarck—of direct environmental influence and the inheritance of acquired characteristics. He saw that if function and environment directly modify heredity, they must do so through the body cells. He was thus led to a neat inversion of Mendel's theory. The body cells secrete minute corpuscles or "gem- mules" which record and embody growth pattern in relation to the total organism. These gemmules are carried along by body juices and the blood stream to the reproductive organs, where they are packed into the ova or spermatozoa—to determine the characteristics and growth pattern of a future individual.

Darwin had picked up his problem by its most slippery and unwieldy handle. Pangenesis attempted to explain too much too crudely. It contained so many variable and intangible factors that it was very hard to test by experiment and very easy to support by argument. In fact, it called forth the parliamentarian rather than the investigator in Darwin—and he was as ready to argue it as he seemed reluctant to probe it. Even so, it did provide, as Darwin hoped, a kind of summary of what was known about heredity, and De Vries has told how Darwin's gemmules led him to the conception of unit characters and so ultimately to the rediscovery of Mendel's law.

Darwin's conclusion illustrates his growing frankness about the Creator. Asserting his belief that living forms in their wonderful multiplicity derive from one common progenitor, he asks whether such a conception can be reconciled with design. In so far as the ultimate result is order and harmony, yes. In so far as the basic means of effecting that result are accidental variations, no. The dilemma, he says, is as profound as that between free will and necessity.

It "will be called a mad dream," Darwin assured Asa Gray after seeing pangenesis published.[87] His fears were as usual exaggerated. Nevertheless, the famous chapter was certainly not greeted with shouts of intelligence and joy, even by his most faithful admirers. "Bates says he has read it twice, and is not sure that he understands it."[88] Hooker felt, with perfect justice, that the theory merely summed up contemporary ignorance about heredity, and Huxley apparently said something "so deuced clever" to Hooker on the subject that Hooker could not for the life of him remember what it was.[89] Wallace alone expressed unreserved admiration. Darwin was deeply

touched, for his ugly duckling had become his favorite child—
"an infant cherished by few as yet, except his tender parent,
but which will live a long life," he told Gray, and added,
"There is parental presumption for you!"[90]

With *Variation* finally published, Darwin began, at least for
a time, to lose the old sense of hurry and desperation. He was
no longer a tortoise creeping in frantic haste toward the horizon. If he had become less human, at least he now had more
time to be human in. In 1869, with one of his daughters, he
visited his father's old house in Shrewsbury. Too eager, perhaps, to do honor to his famous landlord, the tenant remained
with them during the entire visit. As they went away, "with a
pathetic look of regret," Charles said, "If I could have been
left alone in that green-house for five minutes, I know I should
have been able to see my father in his wheel-chair as vividly
as if he had been there before me."[91]

Charles's recollections of his father had remained very clear,
and particularly those of the last years, when they had sat
together, each with his own ailment, gossiping of the people
they knew. The paternal terrors—the vocal mountain erupting
in its wrath—had faded away. Dr. Darwin had grown ever more
kind, sensitive, and oracular in his son's memory. "My father,
who was the wisest man I ever knew . . ." prefaced many an
observation or anecdote.[92] As a young man, Robert Darwin
had hated his profession, for he had scarcely been able to
endure the sight of blood and "to the end of his life the
thought of an operation had almost sickened him."[93] Nothing
could have induced him to continue with medicine had old
Erasmus left him any choice. Such stringency, Charles reflected with gratitude, he had never known! Later Robert
discovered a genius for the psychological side of his profession
and became a psychiatrist before psychiatrists were invented.
His personal charm and quick sympathy "gave him unbounded

power of winning confidence," and he had once assured Charles of medical success for the same reason.

Charles did not think he gained much from his father intellectually. "My father's mind was not scientific," he wrote, "and he did not try to generalize his knowledge under general laws; yet he formed a theory for nearly everything which occurred."[94] Long before the fact was established, he was convinced that two different diseases were lumped under the name of typhus. On several occasions, he loaned considerable sums to strangers and never failed of payment. He once astonished a gentleman who had brought his nephew for consultation by saying, "I am sure that your nephew is . . . guilty of . . . a heinous crime." "Good God, Dr. Darwin, who told you!" exclaimed the gentleman. "We thought no human being knew the fact except ourselves."[95]

And so, after this late visit to Shrewsbury, Charles mourned his father a second time. His daughter Henrietta remembered his saying with the most tender respect, "I think my father was a little unjust to me when I was young, but afterwards I am thankful to think I became a prime favourite with him."[96] Henrietta also recalled "the expression of happy reverie that accompanied these words, as if he were reviewing the whole relation, and the remembrance left a deep sense of peace and gratitude."

12

The Subject of Subjects

Jermyn Street, Feb. 20, 1871

My dear Darwin—Best thanks for your new book, a copy of which I find awaiting me this morning. But I wish you would not bring your books out when I am so busy with all sorts of things. You know I can't show my face anywhere in society without having read them—and I consider it too bad.[1]

Poor Huxley, obliged to be omniscient on more and more subjects as he grew older! How the professorial heart goes out to him! And yet how far away he was now from that quiet, passionate, intricate world in which he was thought to be so much at home, how far away from auditory organs in the Orthoptera and possible polygamy among the butterflies!

Darwin's new book was *The Descent of Man*. He had not meant to write it. He was still toiling away at the great work: in the introduction to the two volumes of *Variation under Domestication*, he had promised more and larger volumes on variation in a state of nature. But the treatise on domestication had been a powerful argument against mere bulk, and though it had sold well, Darwin himself had been somewhat appalled by that "huge" and "unreadable" book, with all "the horrid, tedious, dull work"[2] which it had required. Meanwhile, the world had long awaited the master's word on this subject of subjects.

Yet man was hardly adapted, like the orchid, to happy and tranquil investigation. He leered mockingly with imponderables and intangibles, and towered awfully with a vast accumulation of data, humanistic and traditional as well as scientific. And though already somewhat accustomed to the teasing inquiry of the scalpel and geological hammer, he could still turn ferociously on the zealous investigator. He also remained the sacred animal of theology, history, literature, and ever so many ancient and established profundities. For a long time Darwin had hoped somebody else would write the book. Huxley had shown with great clarity and boldness that man was an animal, but he had not shown how man had evolved into such an extraordinary animal.

And what was the relation of man to Darwinian theory? From one point of view, natural selection was but the most dramatic embodiment of a master idea of the nineteenth century. As struggle for survival, this idea had appeared at least as early as the seventeenth century in Hobbes's *Leviathan*. It assumed a more elaborate and characteristically modern form in Adam Smith's *Wealth of Nations*. The competition of individuals produces an abundance of goods, services, and capital at the proper times and places. Laissez faire implied enlightened self-interest and freedom of action limited only by sanctity of contract and a criminal code. Though in practice increasingly modified by social legislation, economic law was in theory long regarded as natural and immutable. And therein lay a chief danger of extreme laissez faire: it tended in fact to establish a state of nature, to banish the higher and gentler virtues from practical life as irrelevant. It offered freedom with too little justice and judged excellence with too little reference to what is humanly and culturally excellent.

For these reasons the romantic artist was against it. Ethically confused, he attacked it sometimes in the name of Christian morals and sometimes in that of romantic eccentricity or humanitarian pity. He emphasized that it repudiated duties and that, paradoxically, it produced a narrow and uninspired conformity, for men must find common ground in order to give battle and must herd together in order to compete. From all forms of prosaic and utilitarian competition, the romantic drew back with scorn, haughtily enfolded in his proud uniqueness. He strove with none, for none was worth his strife. True, like Byron or Carlyle, he could admire a conqueror or a captain of industry, if only his triumph were violent or titanic enough. Napoleonism was the tribute which the romantic paid to the vulgar republic of hard knocks.

In the *Communist Manifesto* of 1848, Marx and Engels joined the concept of competition to one of social decadence. They asserted that history in general is produced by a Hegelian process of class struggle and that the decline of capitalism in particular will be produced by the "atomic" competition of individual capitalists. What laissez faire economists tend to regard as the immutable laws of nature are simply the rules of a game legislated by capitalists to favor capitalists, but not, it would seem, to favor them permanently; for the profit motive leads deterministically to its own destruction, after which enlightened self-interest, directed by revolution to juster and broader class objectives, is ultimately transformed into something more generous and altruistic. In the larger dialectic of history, the class conflict is in each of its phases at first economic, then political, and finally armed and violent; and out of armed violence is ultimately to materialize the idyllic vision of a classless society. Marx used competition to destroy competition.

Far more famous in its time than the *Communist Manifesto*, but unhappily far less influential today, is Mill's "On Liberty."

Published in the same year as the *Origin*, this essay resembles it strikingly in theoretical structure. As Darwin sums up the realism of Victorian conflict, so Mill sums up the idealism. For British society he lays down in effect a principle of rational selection based on discussion and public opinion. Freedom of speech is necessary in order that, in the competition of ideas, truth—or at least the half-truth best adapted to the needs of the hour—may survive and propagate itself. Freedom of action, in so far as it does not injure others, is necessary in order that new types of moral character may freely develop and then, in competition with other types, either perish or survive to enrich English life. Darwin's spontaneous variations are thus paralleled by a romantic emphasis on the value of diversified or eccentric moral character. Mill's fault is not only that he counts too much on man's rationality but that he counts too little on man's evolving moral environment. Moral excellence is the result not only of thought and competition, but of aspiration, habit, experience, and tradition. Moreover, reason seems not so much to select a new variety of moral excellence as to refine and broaden by criticism a moral tradition already established. The interminable debate of infinitely energetic but comparatively skeptical minds would be likely, in the long run, to produce nothing so much as the deathly silence of dictatorship.

The Origin of Species gave the doctrine of competition a thoroughly naturalistic setting, freeing it from the last restraint of moral law and showing how, in the plant and animal kingdoms, warfare between individuals, species, or social communities could lead to evolutionary progress. And if in the natural, why not in the human realm also? What an opportunity for an ingenious writer with a turn for paradox and a taste for sensation! Meanwhile, history itself was daily becoming more paradoxical and sensational. The time was rapidly approaching when neo-Darwinism would almost seem sober sense.

But the *Origin* encouraged knowledge before it encouraged folly. Evolutionary ideas were getting into all sorts of sedate gray heads and producing the most novel and amazing discoveries, truths, and half-truths. While the geologist was gauging man's antiquity and the anatomist was estimating to a nicety his kinship to the gorilla and the orangutan, the anthropologist and the scholar, observing him in his jungles and south sea islands and exhuming him from his old epics and law codes, uncovered depths of cruelty and superstition hitherto unsuspected in the repository of reason and the lord of creation. Nevertheless, though hardly a noble savage, primitive man was a moralist, a lawyer, a politician, a speculator on nature and the unseen—a complex, thoughtful, though dirty and scrambling biped, just conceivably capable of rising eventually to the majesty of an umbrella and a top hat. In this decade of Darwinian enlightenment about man, the advantage passed from the biologist and the comparative anatomist to the anthropologist and the historical scholar. The two former, having located man among his fellow creatures, could do little more than speculate, sometimes naturalistically and sometimes transcendentally, on remote and grandiloquent dawns and origins; whereas the latter two, facing lesser and more soluble problems, moved triumphantly from doctrine to doctrine, building up intricate structures of fact and inference. Nearly every year brought forth some classic work, and Darwin's silence on the great subject was golden with the wisdom of other authors.

The earliest of these by several years was Sir Henry Maine, who in 1861 produced his *Ancient Law*. Inspired by Savigny rather than Darwin, he showed that, in the few progressive societies in which law evolved very far, it followed the same general pattern, arising in custom, crystallizing into a code, and then breaking free for a further development in terms first of legal fictions, then of equity, and finally of legislation. In

Maine's sagacious pages, primitive man, as a legal thinker, develops a startling resemblance to the nineteenth-century English Tory.

In 1864 Wallace published a paper on man in *The Anthropological Review*.[3] Arguing that humanity derives from a single species, he inferred that physical differences among the races probably date back to the dawn of reason, for when clothing, tools, weapons, and social organization had rendered fur, claws, and fangs unnecessary, natural selection ceased to operate on the bodies of individuals and began to operate on the brains of herds and social groups, so that "the most favored races" were preserved. The severest environments, setting up high standards of ingenuity, selected the best brains.

This essay, though it contained very few facts, did contain many illuminating ideas; and Darwin was impressed. He objected only to the way in which Wallace referred to natural selection. "You ought not . . . to speak of the theory as mine," he protested; "it is just as much yours as mine."[4] Since the *Origin* had long since made it his, Darwin was probably much better able to appreciate both Wallace's magnanimity as a rival and his imaginative resource as a theorist. "I never heard anything more ingenious," he exclaimed, and farther on, "That is a splendid fact about the white moths; it warms one's very blood to see a theory thus almost proved to be true."[5] Why shouldn't Wallace write the indispensable book about man? Darwin offered all his bibliography and notes, a twenty-seven years' accumulation, but Wallace courteously refused. He was busy with a book about his travels in the Malay peninsula.

Darwin now brought himself to think cautiously of "a little essay" on the great subject. He had a theory about facial expressions and another about the origin of races. Could he not introduce both into his essay? In 1867, when *Variation* had been sent off to the printer, he began "a chapter on Man," and soon discovered with horror that it was rapidly growing into the spacious antechamber of another great verbal edifice. He decided to publish it separately as a "very small volume."[6] But then *Variation* descended on him in avalanches of proof. His consequent frustration showed him that he was already hypnotized by the new subject. He could not wait to resume it. Nothing else had any savor.

The year 1868 was a prolonged experience in the desiccation of living without science. He had hardly finished his proofs when he fell ill; and he had hardly recovered from his illness when he was carried off to Freshwater in the Isle of Wight by his family. To be sure, Freshwater offered compensations. Erasmus stayed at the same house, and their landlady, the photographer Mrs. Cameron, was an extraordinarily vivid and intelligent woman. She made a photograph of Charles which actually aroused his enthusiasm; and it was published with the inscription, in his own hand, "I like this photograph very much better than any other which has been taken of me."[7] She won the hearts of so many Darwins that when they were about to go and Charles had paid the bill, Erasmus called out to her with a bachelor's boldness, "You have left eight persons deeply in love with you."[8]

Meanwhile, the younger Darwins had begun to distinguish themselves: George was second wrangler at Cambridge, and Lenny had passed the entrance examination for Woolwich second on the list. Charles was beside himself with astonishment and joy. But so much achievement brought consequences. The children decided they could no longer use the terms "papa" and "mama." Charles was very firmly informed that henceforth he was "father." He received the news with extraordinary bitterness: "I would as soon be called Dog."[9]

While at Freshwater, the Darwins dined several times with the Tennysons, but were not amused: though better than his poetry, Tennyson was really rather absurd. Longfellow, passing through Freshwater on a European tour, was a little more interesting because he talked of Agassiz. The famous Swiss geologist, then professor at Harvard, had of late shown increasing respect, if not for the arguments, at least for the success, of the *Origin*.

Returning home in August, Charles underwent further brief incidental martyrdoms of delay, including the rather tedious immortalization of a bust by Woolner—and then gave himself up to the problems of sexual selection. To be sure, work, though not so bad as vacation, was its own special kind of torture. Darwin faced minor puzzles in his data as Flaubert faced the fearful alternatives of a relative clause and a prepositional phrase in a fallible sentence—with an eager, fascinated suffering. He was "fearfully puzzled" by protective coloring in females and "driven half mad" by polygamy and the proportion between the sexes in many animal species.[10]

Moreover, his old friends, always ready with advice and comfort in the past, could not for one reason or another follow him into this new and difficult field. A confirmed botanist, Hooker seldom wandered far from the herbarium; Huxley was busy with schools; and Lyell had declined into age and transcendentalism. Seeking inveterately the sympathy and stimulus of an interlocutor, Darwin had turned insensibly of late years to his old rival Wallace, who had once been nothing so much as an accusing reminder of a humiliating experience.

To be sure, he still anticipated ideas in the most embarrassing manner:

I have been greatly interested in your letter [wrote Charles in 1867], but your view is not new to me. If you will look at p. 240 of fourth Edition of the *Origin* you will find it very briefly given with two extreme examples of the peacock and black grouse. . . . I have long entertained this view, though I have never had space to develop it. But I had not sufficient knowledge to generalise as far as you do about colouring and nesting. In your paper perhaps you will just allude to my scanty remark in the 4th Edition, because in my Essay on Man I intend to discuss the whole subject of sexual selection, explaining as I believe it does much with respect to man. I have collected all my old notes and partly written my discussion and it would be flat work for me to give the idea as exclusively from you.[11]

Wallace replied by sending all his notes on sexual selection. Darwin returned them at once:

I earnestly . . . hope that you will proceed with your paper . . . I confess on receiving your note that I felt rather flat at my recent work being almost thrown away, but I did not intend to show this feeling. As a proof how little advance I had made on the subject, I may mention that though I had been collecting facts on the colouring and other sexual differences in mammals, your explanation with respect to the females had not occurred to me. I am surprised at my own stupidity, but I have long recognized how much clearer and deeper your insight into matters is than mine . . .
Forgive me, if you can, for a touch of illiberality about your paper.[12]

Wallace was so retiring, so reassuring, so generous.

As to the theory of Natural Selection itself [he wrote Darwin in 1864] I shall always maintain it to be actually yours and yours only. You had worked it out in details I had never thought of, years before I had a ray of light on the subject, and my paper would never have convinced anybody or been noticed as more than an ingenious speculation, whereas your book has revolutionised the study of natural history, and carried away captive the best men of the present age.[13]

Moreover, he was so receptive, so full of sympathy for an aching stomach and of suggestions for an ailing theory. What had once made him a rival now made him a friend: he had pursued the same studies, faced the same problems, lived with the same ideas. He was, at least in some degree, the masked alter ego, the mysterious and threatening stranger who turned out, in a strange, Conradesque way, to be Darwin himself.

Charles came to feel that they should agree in everything scientific.

Fortunately, they hardly ever did—except on essentials. Pointing to the incessant war among savage tribes, Darwin supposed that natural selection must operate in human evolution. Wallace countered that war only eliminated the brave and the strong. Darwin yielded, and then maintained that sexual selection explained the brilliant coloring of male birds. Wallace urged that brilliant coloring in either sex might be explained in terms of protection and mimicry. Sometimes he was a little trying.

> I agree about Wallace's wonderful cleverness [Darwin told Hooker], but he is not cautious enough in my opinion. I find I must (and I always distrust myself when I differ from him) separate rather widely from him all about birds' nests and protection; he is riding that hobby to death.[14]

Wallace's enthusiasms were a little tedious, too. Darwin must read Spencer's *Social Statics*. Later, he must read George's *Progress and Poverty*. Darwin replied that political economy always made him ill. Wallace was sympathetic. In fact, he thought Darwin much more gravely ill than his poor friend Spruce, and was naïvely astonished when Spruce died and Darwin produced two enormous books and a new edition of the *Origin* in three years. Nevertheless, he continued, in the most comforting manner, to insist against long letters and long hours of study. Darwin could not but relent. Besides, Wallace had dashed off such a wonderful explanation for gaudy caterpillars—and for brightly plumaged female birds nesting in holes. Darwin had been thinking along much the same lines. "It is curious how we hit on the same ideas."[15] Wallace responded by offering all his notes. Darwin refused. Wallace could write a much better paper on the subject.

Though very shy, Wallace opened his own heart, and confessed a broken engagement. Between inquiries about East Indian pigs and Amazonian butterflies, Darwin administered comfort. Later Wallace married, and at length announced the birth of a son, whom he named "Herbert Spencer." Darwin congratulated him, hoped that "Herbert Spencer" would write better than his namesake, and in the next sentence begged Wallace to note down the date at which the child began to secrete tears.

Still struggling with the problems of color in animals, Darwin seemed for a time in 1868 to be moving away from his own sexual selection to Wallace's protective principle. "This morning I oscillated with joy towards you; this evening I have swung back to the old position, out of which I fear I shall never get."[16] He tried, almost pathetically, to bring about closer agreement by restating the whole problem. "We differ, I think, chiefly, from fixing our minds perhaps too closely on different points."[17] And a few days later, he wrote, "I grieve to differ from you, and it actually terrifies me, and makes me constantly mistrust myself."[18] He was persuaded the truth was one; he wanted both Wallace and himself to recognize it. But Wallace remained obdurate. He was much less anxious for finality. "The truth will come out at last, and our differences may be the means of setting others to work who may set us both right."[19]

In April, 1869, Wallace published in The Quarterly Review "Sir Charles Lyell on Geological Climates and the Origin of Species," in which he dealt once more with man. Darwin was almost afraid to read the article. Apparently he feared that Wallace might reject natural selection altogether. "I hope you have not murdered too completely your own and my child," he wrote.[20] So far as Wallace on man was concerned, Darwin's worst fears were justified. Never was infanticide more blandly committed. Clearly, Wallace felt that human intelligence could only be explained by the direct intervention of Cosmic Intelligence.

The mental requirements of the lowest savages [wrote Wallace], such as the Australians or the Andaman Islanders, are very little above those of many animals. . . . How, then, was an organ developed so far beyond the needs of its possessor? Natural Selection could only have endowed the savage with a brain a little superior to that of an ape, whereas he actually possesses one but very little inferior to that of the average members of our learned societies.[21]

In the margin of his copy Darwin wrote a vehement "No," triple scored and showered with exclamation points. As often before, he was as nervously alarmed at the disagreement as he was obstinately loyal to his original convictions. He told Lyell he had been "dreadfully disappointed," and to Wallace himself he wrote, "If you had not told me, I should have thought that [your remarks on man] had been added by someone else."[22]

Wallace's article was of course primarily concerned with Lyell. Calling attention to the latter's latest confession of evolutionary faith in the tenth edition of *The Principles of Geology*, he wrote:

The history of science hardly presents so striking an instance of youthfulness of mind in advanced life as is shown by this abandonment of opinions so long held and so powerfully advocated; and if we bear in mind the extreme caution, combined with the ardent love of truth which characterise every work which our author has produced, we shall be convinced that so great a change was not decided on without long and anxious deliberation, and that the views now adopted must indeed be supported by arguments of overwhelming force. If for no other reason than that Sir Charles Lyell in his tenth edition has adopted it, the theory of Mr. Darwin deserves an attentive and respectful consideration from every earnest seeker after truth.[23]

Darwin read such passages with enthusiasm. He had almost forgotten what a great man Lyell was. "I have often said to younger geologists . . . ," he wrote Wallace, "that they did not know what a revolution Lyell effected; nevertheless, your extracts from Cuvier have quite astonished me."[24]

Wallace's *Malay Archipelago*, finished at last, came to him later in the same year. Here, implicitly at least, was the record of how his own idea had been discovered in the middle of a tropical forest by another man. And yet the tropical forest, the creatures in it, the collecting, the adventures, and the adventurer himself—were all strangely familiar. In Wallace's book Darwin rediscovered his own scientific odyssey, and much else besides. "That you ever returned alive is wonderful . . . Of all the impressions which I received from your book, the strongest is that your perseverance in the cause of science was heroic." And to catch such splendid butterflies! "Certainly collecting is the best sport in the world."[25] Wallace's book had made him feel quite young again.

In 1869 the book on man suffered further interruptions—a vacation among old haunts in North Wales, as usual reluctantly undertaken and fretfully enjoyed; and a fifth edition of the *Origin*, perhaps even more reluctantly undertaken, but much more heartily enjoyed, for now the general chorus of praise was swelled by unmistakable sounds from pulpits and vestries. But while bishops cheered, reviewers began to look askance. Having conceded that the *Origin* was a very important book, they now began to discover that it was also rather dull. Men like John Robertson in *The Athenaeum* were obviously astonished that so ordinary a composition should have produced so extraordinary an effect. Charles was to be pursued into the farthest Elysium of celebrity by this annoying kind of critical astonishment.

A new German edition, meticulously and reverently prepared from the English fifth, now came out under Darwin's benevolent eye and particular blessing. Shortly after, a third

French edition, still based on the first English and accompanied by a very critical preface nearly as long as the text, appeared unceremoniously without the author's knowledge or permission. Darwin tried hard to be amused. "I must enjoy myself," he wrote Hooker, "and tell you about Mlle. C. Royer, who translated the 'Origin' into French. . . . Besides her enormously long preface to the first edition, she has added a second preface abusing me like a pickpocket for Pangenesis, which of course has no relation to the 'Origin.' "[26] Darwin at once entered into an arrangement with Mr. Reinwald for an authoritative and up-to-date French translation.

Mlle. Royer was discouragingly typical of the whole French attitude toward his ideas. Le Darwinisme was still simply an interesting speculation, perhaps a little less respectable than that of Lamarck and well within the range of armchair refutation. To J. L. A. de Quatrefages, who had just published a polite but severe book of criticism, Darwin conceded "a wonderfully clear and able discussion" and some "strictures" with which he felt compelled to agree.[27] Nevertheless, the inaccurate French translation of which M. de Quatrefages had made use invalidated many of his arguments. Darwin could not refrain from observing in conclusion:

It is curious how nationality influences opinion; a week hardly passes without my hearing of some naturalist in Germany who supports my views, and often puts an exaggerated value on my works; whilst in France I have not heard of a single zoologist, except M. Gaudry (and he only partially), who supports my views.[28]

In 1870 Darwin received a reprint of Wallace's Natural Selection, which contained many fresh instances of the author's generosity. "There has never been passed on me, nor indeed on any one," wrote Darwin warmly, "a higher eulogium than yours. . . . I hope it is a satisfaction to you to reflect . . . that we have never felt any jealousy towards each other, though in a sense rivals." And then he added, "I believe that I can say this of myself with truth, and I am absolutely sure that it is true of you."[29]

Darwin voyaged widely into his past during this period and found much old enmity reconciled, much old friendship lost forever. In May he went down to Cambridge to see his boys. The whole family stayed at the Bull Hotel, and Charles found "the backs of the Colleges . . . simply paradisaical." With some trepidation he went to visit his old professor, Adam Sedgwick, who ten years before had, in an angry and caustic review, found such bewildering fault with the Origin. The magnificent old fellow was most hearty in his welcome, but his cordiality was nearly as formidable as his enmity had been:

After a long sit he proposed to take me to the museum, and I could not refuse, and in consequence he utterly prostrated me; so that we left Cambridge next morning, and I have not recovered from the exhaustion yet. Is it not humiliating to be thus killed by a man of eighty-six, who evidently never dreamed that he was killing me? As he said to me, "Oh, I consider you as a mere baby to me!"[30]

But Cambridge was too changed and too unchanged, too much a part of his own youth and now of his children's youth to be, even in the bright spring sunshine, an altogether cheerful place. "Cambridge without dear Henslow was not itself," he told Hooker; "I tried to get to the two old houses, but it was too far for me."

Huxley's essays, which poured in on him in a steady stream, were one of his greatest pleasures. He read them with all the envy of an awkward and painful writer for an easy and brilliant one. Huxley's style fascinated him somewhat as a large, sharp pocketknife would fascinate a small boy. One could do such things with it, but it would be oh, so dangerous! "There is no one who writes like you," he declares, in acknowledging Huxley's "Anniversary Address" of 1869 to the Geological Society, but "if I were in your shoes, I should tremble for my life."[31] To be sure, he thought that Huxley—particularly when not slaughtering anti-evolutionists—used his knife a little too freely. "I return Huxley's letter . . . ," he wrote Hooker in a revealing passage. "I think he was right *pro bono publico*; but . . . I for one could not have dared to do so disagreeable a thing."[32]

Meanwhile, several brilliant works on man had appeared. In 1865 John McLennan had published his *Primitive Marriage*, which obviously owes much both to Darwin's *Origin* and to Maine's *Ancient Law*. Fastening on weak points in Maine's patriarchal theory of the state, McLennan attempted to show that behind patriarchal society lay a long and un-Victorian evolution from anarchy and sexual promiscuity through various stages of polyandry and female relationship to tribal communities based on monogamy and descent through the father. He also showed that savages adapt themselves by tribal law to tribal environment; and he implied that such adaptation is at least in part produced by natural selection operating on communities.

The last idea, applied by Darwin to social insects and afterwards by Spencer to mankind, forms the basis of Walter Bagehot's *Physics and Politics*, which was first published in *The Fortnightly Review* as a series of articles, beginning in November, 1867. Bagehot shows how the universal war of savage life evolves into the rational peace of civilization—and thus he bridges the gulf between the realism of the *Origin* and the idealism of the essay "On Liberty." Skirting the unknown with Darwinian circumspection, Bagehot says little about the formation of races and the origin of primitive communities. A polity grows up because a polity is necessary to survival. Generally, "a cake of custom" is formed: an elaborate structure of traditions and taboos, bolstered by religious sanctions, exercises a rigid control on the fierce waywardness of savage nature. In the competition of war, disciplined communities overcome the undisciplined and impose their discipline upon them. "Civilization begins because the beginning of civilization is a military advantage."[33] Innovations, particularly when introduced by a revered leader, may be widely spread through imitation, but they are even more likely to be repressed at the outset through superstitious fear, for as a rule the cake of custom hardens sooner or later into complete rigidity. Steady progress is possible only in societies which, like the Greek, Roman, and English, have developed the moral restraint to debate and decide fundamental issues without resorting to repressive violence or civil war. Thus, not only are freedom and democracy essential to sustained progress, but a certain type of moral character—which, as it appears in the English, Bagehot calls "animated moderation"—is essential to freedom and democracy. Bagehot may not have got all of Darwin's wild animals back into their cage, but at least he had triumphantly built Victorian discussion on its roof.

In the middle sixties, Darwin's cousin Francis Galton published several articles on man and in 1869 a book on *Hereditary Genius*, which, though a little vague and more than a little inconsistent, put forth a number of startling ideas with some force and distinction. A pioneer in statistical method, Galton presents considerable evidence to show that talent and genius, as well as the inclination toward all kinds of moral traits, tend to be inherited and concentrated in families—and understandably so, for in the competition of civilized life, there is a sexual selection of the factors that make for civilized achievement. In fact, by developing the appropriate qualities, certain families adapt themselves to success in their traditional professions. Galton also suggests that as chance, natural selection, and many other factors may improve a human breed partially and temporarily, so artificial selection, guided by scientific study, might improve it greatly and continuously.

This work was full of reverence and admiration for Darwin, who on his side was much struck. "I do not think I ever in all my life read anything more interesting and original," he wrote the author.[34] But the program of eugenics he wisely thought "utopian,"[35] though he was as zealously hopeful as Galton for the evolutionary future of the human race. "To me," he had written Lyell a few years before, "it would be an infinite satisfaction to believe that mankind will progress to such a pitch that we should [look] back at [ourselves] as mere Barbarians."[36]

Eugenical speculation, with its heady fumes and its Dionysian exaltation, mounted rapidly in Galton, though, like a true Englishman, he retained his decorum of style to the end. His "Gregariousness in Cattle and Men," published in 1871, expresses Nietzschean ideas in irreproachably sturdy, common sense Anglo-Saxon. It sets up, both for beasts and men, an opposition between the leader and the herd. In the past, civilization has favored the human herd, for society represents, as Nietzsche said of Christianity, "a deadly enmity against . . . aristocrats."[37] Galton speaks of "the slavish aptitudes" of the masses, "their exaltation of the vox populi," and "their willing servitude to tradition, authority and custom."[38] He implies that leaders are by contrast bold, original, and emancipated from traditional restraint: in short, they are romantic supermen. He seems to believe that the aristocratic few and the slavish many are separate strains produced by natural selection, and that artificial selection should be employed to eliminate the latter, who are no longer adapted to the requirements of modern civilization. In this recommendation Galton presages Shaw rather than Nietzsche. He wants not an aristocracy, but a populace of supermen.

Similar ideas, expressed with a nonconformist zeal and piety

which would have made Nietzsche shudder, are to be found in
another article, published anonymously in 1868, "On the Failure of 'Natural Selection' in the Case of Men,"[39] which Darwin
attributed to W. R. Greg.[40] The author points out that the
modern state protects failures and allows them to propagate.
In fact, the two least valuable classes in the state, the extremely
rich and the extremely poor, are precisely those who have the
largest families. The author regards the middle class as the
elite that should be improved by eugenics, though he is realistic
enough to see that the British state is not likely to sacrifice the
present realities of democracy and freedom for the distant
possibility of bourgeois supermen.

In 1870 Darwin worked almost without interruption on *The
Descent of Man*. It grew longer and longer, so that he saved it
from the interminability of *Variation* only by amputating *The
Expression of the Emotions*. As the manuscript neared completion, he turned it over to Henrietta, who once more assumed
her role of Miss Rhadamanthus, questioning and testing and
simplifying the tortured polysyllables into a blessed stream
of intelligibility. Looking over the corrections, Charles was as
usual astonished, and when after its appearance the book was
admired for its "lucid, vigorous style," he attributed this unwonted virtue wholly to his daughter's efforts and presented
her with thirty pounds from his royalties.[41] "By Jove, how hard
you must have worked," he exclaimed, "and how thoroughly
you have mastered my MS."[42] By 1871, having labored three
years and driven himself to the extremity of boredom and disgust with his subject, he sent the last corrections to John
Murray, and then plunged, with passionate eagerness, into his
study of the emotions.

Murray sent proofs to Whitwell Elwin, who, like so many
intelligent men before and after him, declared the book with
cries of astonishment and exasperation to be "little better than

drivel," and prophesied that Darwinism would not long survive the criticism of "a really eminent naturalist."[43] But Murray was not deceived. His ledgers had taught him that, however dull and ridiculous clever men might think them, Darwin's writings would continue, at least in the near and practical future, to enjoy the solid repute of a wide and ready sale. Moreover, this work had long been awaited. It was published in February, 1871.

The Descent of Man is usually considered Darwin's second best book. As a matter of fact, despite much amputation and other drastic surgery, it is really two books in one pair of covers. Having dealt with man for 206 pages, the author digresses to sexual selection and persists indefatigably in that digression to the last and 688th page. Considered apart from its giant appendage, the Descent is undoubtedly Darwin at a disadvantage —Darwin at grips with an uncongenial animal in uncongenial environments, Darwin without the miracles of inspiration and discovery, in large part without even the exhaustive, first-hand research and the tireless, sympathetically understanding observation which were among his most dependable gifts. He himself says in his Introduction that if Haeckel's Natürliche Schöpfungsgeschichte had appeared before he began to write, he would probably never have completed his essay. And yet in that case we should lack one of the most important books in the nineteenth century, for the Descent is just good enough to fill up the space between a great thinker and a great opportunity. It sums up and evaluates, sometimes with authority and always with balance and common sense, a decade of brilliant anthropological thinking.

Studying man somewhat less exhaustively than the barnacle, Darwin maintains that his preeminence is due not to any one characteristic, like the acquisition of language, but to many— to his upright position, the freedom and delicacy of his hands, the use of tools and language, and above all, the mental capacity which made tools and language possible. Nevertheless, Darwin believes that increasing powers of expression must have interacted with increasing mental powers to bring intelligence to a genuinely human level. Like Spencer, he regards mind as an adaptation to environment and a weapon in the struggle for survival, but, unlike Spencer, he soberly refrains from pursuing the metaphysical implications of this view. He insists on the great gap between man and the higher mammals, and disagrees with Wallace that the savage could have discovered fire or developed language with a brain little better than that of the ape; yet he insists also that, as a product of natural selection, man differs from animals physically, mentally and morally not in kind but in degree. Monkeys use sticks and stones as tools; dogs exhibit loyalty and other moral virtues; and many of the higher species are capable of very elementary reasoning. Darwin is always at his best with animal anecdotes:

One female baboon had so capacious a heart that she not only adopted young monkeys of other species, but stole young dogs and cats, which she continually carried about. . . . An adopted kitten scratched this affectionate baboon, who certainly had a fine intellect, for she was much astonished at being scratched, and immediately examined the kitten's feet, and without more ado bit off the claws.[44]

Like a good Darwinian, he is cautious about theories which, like Bain's and Spencer's, involve inherited memory and the recording of thought patterns on the nervous system of succeeding generations. Deeply ingrained habits may transmit tendencies, but scarcely, perhaps, the habits themselves. Otherwise, absurd customs, like the Hindoo's aversion to certain foods, ought to be inherited.

Making no pretensions as an ethical thinker, Darwin does

not attempt any elaborate account of moral experience, nor is
he entirely free from confusion and inconsistency. Nevertheless, his general position is pretty clear. Broadly considered,
conscience arises from the evolutionary process; more particularly—first, from sympathy and the social instincts, which are
supported by opinion, and second, from rational reflection on
the consequences of actions and from the emergence of the
idea of *ought*, which may, in idealistic individuals, rise above
mere public opinion. Darwin had prepared himself for the
moral problem by extensive reading in Bain, Mill, Adam
Smith, Hume, Bacon, and even Marcus Aurelius. His reading
indicates that he belonged to the very English tradition of
Shaftesbury and the Utilitarians; his thinking indicates that,
like John Stuart Mill, he usually rose above the characteristic
limitations of this school. He follows Smith in stressing the
importance of sympathy, and Hume in emphasizing the non-
rational basis of conduct. Yet he avoids the speculative sub-
tleties of the Utilitarians, and particularly their tendency to
turn moral consciousness into an epicurean balance sheet of
pains and pleasures—keeping as close as possible to the broad
generalities of common sense on the one hand and the solid
facts of animal behavior on the other. In general, he sees clearly
that the moral life consists in a struggle between duty and
desire, and that virtue and happiness depend first on humility
and self-knowledge and second on effort and rational discipline.

His discussion of man in society is equally sound but less
definite and clear-cut. Within the community, physical, mental, and moral excellence tends to be preserved both by natural
selection and by deliberate cultivation. Social achievement is
spread within the community by imitation and beyond it by
Bagehot's natural selection of communities. Darwin sees only
a partial truth in the arguments of Greg and Galton that civilization preserves weaklings and failures. Successful men in all
walks of life tend to leave more offspring; and the diseased, the

pathological, and the criminal tend to be eliminated. The total result is apparently that all peoples progress biologically at a very slow rate, and a few peoples progress socially at a very rapid rate.

Undoubtedly, the Descent encouraged the trend toward naturalism, but it also pointed the way toward that more complex, cautious, and critical naturalism which recognizes salient differences, as well as a basic unity, in the immense region of organic phenomena. It emphasizes that as man grows more civilized, the natural process is in all its higher and determining phases superseded by an ethical. Darwin was no crude leveler down to origins. He may more readily be accused of making animals too human, than of making men too animal. With regard to method, he is of course extremely modern in emphasizing behavior rather than introspection.

The first part of the Descent concludes with a chapter on race, for which Darwin promises to account by sexual selection. He is thus led to his Olympian tour de force on sex, in which he explains everything in order to explain something. In short, he analyzes another kind of biological warfare, in which, for the possession of a mate, the males of a species not only fight each other physically, but compete in erotic dances, in artistic displays of plumage and other ornamentation, or in musical concerts with instruments, voice, or penetrating odors, sometimes accumulating aesthetic extravagance upon extravagance until the principle of utility seems actually to give way to that of beauty. Moreover, behind the outward display of instinctive art is the inward intensity of erotic passion. Certainly, the Descent adds new and violent colors to Darwin's picture of nature.

Returning at last to man in the final chapters, Darwin explains race differentiation by divergent masculine conceptions of female beauty. Negroes are black and flat-nosed because the remote male ancestors of Negroes preferred women with dark

skins and flattened noses. The strongest and most virile males
mated with such women, and by rearing more children than
their weaker rivals, brought their tribe, and ultimately their
race, to a closer approximation of their ideal. Darwin also
maintains that sexual selection made women more tender,
affectionate, and unselfish, and men more courageous, energetic, and intelligent—thereby proving once more that biology
was a soundly Victorian science. The three primary masculine
qualities are, in Darwin's opinion, closely bound together.
In their highest manifestations, they constitute genius, which
is essentially "patience," or "unflinching, undaunted perseverance."[45]

Darwin awaited publication in his usual state of superficial
collapse and exhaustion resting on a broad basis of latent eagerness and curiosity. He protested he hardly knew whether the
book had been worth writing. Nevertheless, he wanted Murray
to send him all out-of-the-way reviews and notices. The public
response was a very pleasant surprise. One indignant Welsh-
man, it is true, did in a personal letter abuse him "as an old
Ape with a hairy face and a thick skull."[46] But, on the whole,
having steeled himself for fresh waves of virtuous horror and
pious vituperation, he was astonished to find that everybody
was interested without being in the least shocked.

A happy change [pronounced Huxley in his most authoritative
tone as Darwin's vicar in the world outside Down] has come over
Mr. Darwin's critics. The mixture of ignorance and insolence
which, at first, characterised a large proportion of the attacks with
which he was assailed, is no longer the sad distinction of anti-
Darwinian criticism.[47]

The new politeness, though certainly a tribute to the Origin,
was perhaps scarcely so to the Descent itself. Its fame might
last longer, if at its first appearance clerical tempers had been

shorter. Sir Alexander Grant, writing thoughtfully on the side of the angels in *The Contemporary Review*, grumbled a little that Darwin thought so well of monkeys and so ill of Tories and churchmen, but exhibited no symptoms of shock or intellectual dazzlement. Darwin had given us simply "the theory of Epicurus with the atheism removed." Grant's final pronouncement, uttered with just the suspicion of a yawn, was, "There is very little that is absolutely new."[48]

Darwin feared the worst from scientists, especially from those who had one foot in religion. "I shall probably receive a few stabs from your polished stiletto of a pen," he wrote Asa Gray.[49] He was partly right. Most scientists admired his science, but a few objected to his theology. Wallace was as usual full of praise but reiterated his view that something more than natural selection was necessary to produce man. The Roman Catholic St. George Mivart, whose *Genesis of Species* had appeared shortly after the *Descent*, agreed with Wallace, adding that new types in particular must be explained by teleological forces acting within the organism. Mivart also objected that Darwin made morality too little self-conscious and rational. On the other hand, he not only accepted evolution but, citing the medieval Jesuit Suárez, declared it in accord with the doctrines of the Catholic Church.

Darwin was alarmed at Mivart's criticisms and feared they might do natural selection real harm. In the sixth edition of the *Origin*, issued in 1872, he answered them at length, and at his own expense republished as a pamphlet Chauncey Wright's article against Mivart's *Genesis*. Meanwhile, emerging dramatically from the fire and smoke of educational controversy, Huxley descended on both Wallace and Mivart for their heresies. Inevitably, from much exercise in slapping and cuffing, the corrective hand was none too gentle. Even Wallace was ridiculed for introducing an intelligent agent, "a sort of supernatural Sir John Seebright,"[50] and for reducing men to the mentality of gorillas and then pronouncing them intellectually superior to any process of natural selection. But for Mivart the punishment was made to fit the crime with a cruelly Gilbertesque appropriateness. Suspicious of any open-mindedness in the Woman of Babylon, Huxley had looked into Suárez's venerable tomes "as the careful robin eyes the delver's toil,"[51] and found that neither the learned Jesuit, nor for that matter, St. Thomas, approved of anything remotely like evolution. Huxley wielded his bludgeon, and while Mivart staggered under a massive theological blow, neatly riddled his professional armor with lighter scientific weapons.

Darwin's fears turned at once into jubilation and for a while Mivart disappeared from his correspondence. "What a wonderful man you are to grapple with those old metaphysico-divinity books!"[52] he exclaimed to Huxley, and quoted Hooker's saying, " 'When I read Huxley, I feel quite infantile in intellect.' By Jove I have felt the truth of this throughout your review."[53]

When a second edition of the Descent appeared in 1874, Mivart rose up like a decapitated knight in a medieval romance to renew the attack, indirectly accusing Darwin of entertaining degraded views about man and of fraudulently concealing a change of opinion. On this occasion, the master was defended by Wallace, who gently reprehended Mivart's language and firmly confuted his ideas.

A little later George Darwin published an article "On Beneficial Restrictions to Liberty of Marriage" in the Contemporary. In the Quarterly Mivart accused him of encouraging at once tyranny and sexual license. This was turning the Victorian Unmentionable into an assassin's dagger with which to strike at the father through the son. Beside himself with indignation, Darwin appealed to the great master of controversy for advice. Huxley entered heartily into his old friend's emotion. "If anybody tries that on with my boy L.," he growled almost hopefully, "the old wolf will show all the fangs he has left by that time, depend upon it."[54] Nevertheless he felt that Darwin's most terrible weapon was silence. "You ought," he continued in significant language, "to be like one of the blessed gods of Elysium, and let the inferior deities do battle with the infernal powers." Darwin contented himself with writing Mivart privately that he would never speak to him again.

The *Descent* was received by the Darwins and the Wedgwoods with the quiet and dignified conviction that, having been written by a master, it was clearly a masterpiece. Of blasphemy or heresy there was no question. Charles's genius had become a family dogma, and dogmas cannot be heretical. "I hope you are successfully helping the great Man out of his thorny brake," Fanny Allen had written her niece Henrietta, "and are drilling his contingencies into rank and file order—it is a great privilege, as well as honour, to be the Lion's aid (not Jackal)."[55] That was the tone. To the same "Henrietta," with whom he had apparently by now "fallen in love," Erasmus wrote admiring not only his brother's book but Wallace's review in the *Academy*. "The way he carries on a controversy is perfectly beautiful, and in future histories of science the Wallace-Darwin episode will form one of the few bright spots among rival claimants."[56]

In spite of the quiet hum of family applause, one Darwin still could not overlook the heretic in the genius. While Charles was still working at the *Descent*, Emma wrote, "I think it will be very interesting, but that I shall dislike it very much as again putting God farther off."[57] Charles and Emma shared one world and divided another. About their large household of children and animals; about Henrietta's cleverness and Charles's dyspepsia; about Polly, the terrier who, after her

young had been done away with, licked and tended Charles as
her "very big puppy" and Bobby, the dog who put on his "hothouse face" of despair when Charles delayed his walk to look
in at his experiments in the hothouse; about Louis Napoleon's
folly and Bismarck's wickedness, about the irrationality of
war and the absurdity of Americans—they were in close agreement. The world they divided was of course that of first
principles. Religion was nearly as important for her as science
for him. Yet even here she was open to argument, and changed
as she grew older. Throughout her life she remained in doubt
whether she should knit, embroider, or play patience on Sunday; and among her papers after her death was found a document in which she had listed in separate columns very sensible
reasons for and against a strict observance of the Sabbath.
What he thought of her sabbatarian scruples and quiet piety,
Charles does not say, but when the sagacious and useful Henrietta married R. B. Litchfield, a barrister and a follower of
Maurice, her father wrote to her on her honeymoon:

Well, it is an awful and astounding fact that you are married;
and I shall miss you sadly. But there is no help for that, and I
have had my day and a happy life, notwithstanding my stomach;
and this I owe almost entirely to our dear old mother, who, as
you know well, is as good as twice refined gold. Keep her as an
example before your eyes, and then Litchfield will in future years
worship and not only love you, as I worship our dear old mother.[58]

Etty and her Litchfield lived happily ever after in a very odd
way. A lifelong invalid waited on hand and foot by an indefatigable maid, she carried the Darwinian cult of illness to its
logical extreme, employing all the talents and energies of an
unusual mind to develop a fantastic and ingenious system of
precautionary measures. To these she condemned not only
herself but her husband, who submitted with great meekness
and no apparent injury to his health. One of Etty's nieces re-

membered him as, in later middle age, "a nice funny little man, whose socks were always coming down," and who "had an egg-shaped waistcoat, and a fuzzy, waggly, whitey-brown beard, which was quite indistinguishable, both in colour and texture, from the Shetland shawl which Aunt Etty generally made him wear round his neck."[59]

Etty did not at once abandon her Radamanthine role among the quiet, anxious, syntactical perplexities of her father's studies. In fact, she interested her husband in Charles's next book, *The Expression of the Emotions in Man and Animals*, and presently Litchfield made some suggestions about expression in music, which Henrietta, accustomed to anonymity, proposed that Charles insert as his own. He replied that he would not.

I used at school to be a great hand at cribbing old verses [he wrote], and I remember with fearful distinctness Dr. Butler's prolonged hum as he stared at me, which said a host of unpleasant things with as much meaning and clearness as Herbert Spencer could devise. Now if I publish L.'s remarks as my own, I shall always fancy that the public are humming at me.[60]

The Expression of the Emotions in Man and Animals, published in 1872, is written at lower tension and within a more restricted range than the *Descent*. Observation is at a maximum, theory at a minimum. There is much precise, almost novelistic description of the facial expressions, together with relatively little analysis of what lies behind them. In general, they are explained by three principles: useful associated habit, antithesis, and the direct influence of nervous excitement. Thus, an infant screams to release the nervous excitement generated by rage. But in screaming, he contracts the muscles about his eyes to prevent too much blood flowing into them. By so doing, he frowns. In later life, through association, he frowns to express many shades of anger and indignation when he has no intention of screaming. When an infant feels love and affection, he learns, partly by antithesis, to express his emotion by soft sounds and protective gestures, which are contrary to the harsh, threatening manifestations of rage. Clearly, Darwin's treatment implies, as he was aware, additional principles of evolution and adaptation to environment. From this point of view, the *Expression* was a considerable innovation. All previous works on the subject, with the exception of Spencer's *Principles of Psychology* (1855), had analyzed facial expression in terms of design and special creation.

Darwin's evolutionary theory was now living an ever expanding life of its own, reaching out into new fields and bringing about all sorts of fresh thoughts and new discoveries in other men's minds. His letters were therefore becoming more and more the business correspondence of an immortal with posterity. Distinguished scientists and philosophers wrote from all parts of the world, deferentially putting queries, asking advice, and suggesting criticisms. Weismann and Moritz Wagner differed with him on the formation of species; Hyatt and Cope outlined a theory of "acceleration"; Bastion and de Soporta speculated about the origin of life and of man.

A modest and somewhat anxiously preoccupied immortal, Darwin expressed astonishment at new discoveries, bewilderment at extreme speculation, delight at the overthrow of opponents, gratitude for intelligent compliments—and in the face of criticism, sturdily defended his old opinions. In 1875 he sat for a portrait by Ouless. "I look a very venerable, acute, melancholy old dog," he wrote Hooker when it was finished; "whether I really look so I do not know."[61]

13

"I Am Not the Least Afraid of Death"

The *Descent* was Darwin's last large-scale encounter with the unknown. It marks the end of a long dedication. Though he did not avowedly give up his Great Work until 1877, he scarcely ever mentioned it after 1871, and eliminated many of the references to it from the final edition of the *Origin*. He excused himself to his friends by declaring that his mind was weakening and that he was determined not to make a fool of himself, like some aged scientists, by spending his final years in grandiose generalization about everything. Undoubtedly he had less confidence in his abilities at this time, but he can hardly have thought himself in danger of plunging into an old age of reckless speculation. Rather one suspects that having completed the most difficult part of his program, he now felt free to become an old man and do what he wanted. That is, he gave up nearly all amusements and devoted himself unremittingly to the more congenial kinds of hard work. As much as possible, he abandoned his study and his desk for his garden and his hothouse, living more and more with flowers and facts and less and less with words and ideas. "I have taken up old botanical work," he joyfully wrote Wallace, "and given up all theories."[1] Under this congenial regimen and the sympathetic guidance of Sir Andrew Clark, whom he often consulted after 1870, Darwin's health improved considerably and remained fairly good until a few months before his death in 1882.

His last decade was valedictory, even somewhat posthumous. Living more and more withdrawn into his house and his family, he revised old books, completed old studies, saw old friends, lived with old ideas and old furniture—even with old pets, for now the aging terrier Polly, which he had inherited from his daughter Henrietta, was his constant companion.

Of course he still had to write a little. Worse, the agonized composition of a lifetime had to be passed in agonized review. He published a revised edition of the *Descent* and of the *Coral Reefs* in 1874, of *Variation, Climbing Plants,* and *The Fertilization of Orchids* in 1875. In 1876 he permitted the *Volcanic Islands* and the *South America* to be reprinted as a single volume.

Having finished with man, he fled happily almost to the other extreme of the organic world, resuming the study of his beloved Drosera, a rather messy little insect-catcher, of which in 1862 he had written to Hooker, "It is a wonderful plant, or rather a most sagacious animal. I will stick up for Drosera until the day of my death."[2] A decade later he wrote to Asa Gray with undiminished zest, "It is an endless subject"—and launched, with the freshest enthusiasm, into its intricacies. Darwin loved Drosera partly for the fine old tory reason that he had studied it a long time, partly for the liberal reason that it is a nonconformist, an evolutionary freak. Its leaves and tentacles react to 1/70,000 of a grain of nitrogenized matter. An operation severing a critical point in the nervous system of a leaf is "exactly like" an operation severing the spinal marrow of a frog.[3]

The result of these delightful labors was *Insectivorous*

Plants (1875), a work full of the gusto of painstaking detail, measurements minutely exact, and ingeniously varied experiment. Darwin arranged the insect-bearing plants in an evolutionary series of increasingly specialized adaptation, but on their paradoxical history was so cautiously reticent that Wallace expressed concern:

You do not make any remarks on the origin of these extraordinary contrivances for capturing insects. Did you think they were too obvious? I daresay there is no difficulty, but I feel sure they will be seized on as inexplicable by Natural Selection, and your silence on the point will be held to show that you consider them so![4]

The subject of plant movement was eventually rounded out by *The Power of Movement in Plants* (1880), in which, collaborating with his son Frank, Darwin attempted to prove that all plants revolve in all their parts as they grow, and that from this fundamental revolving movement they have developed all their more complex movements in relation to light, food, and gravitation. In short, like animals, plants move in order to live, though they move with invisible slowness. The imposing idea of organic unity informs this work as no comparable idea informs *Insectivorous Plants* or *The Expression of the Emotions*.

Darwin now resumed an investigation which he had begun about 1866, on observing that cross-fertilized plants were more vigorous than self-fertilized. In his orchid book he had studied the mechanisms of cross-fertilization; now, in *The Effects of Cross- and Self-Fertilization* (1876), he studied the benefits. "Nature tells us, in the most emphatic manner," he asserted, "that she abhors perpetual self-fertilization."[5] Why? Here he was once more faced with the old mysteries of sex and heredity. But apparently he had renounced mysteries. Though aware that sex was a means of diversifying heredity, he was content to make the point that cross-fertilization invigorates the off-spring when the parents are of but slightly different constitution. They differ in constitution, he supposed, taking his hint from pangenesis, because their progenitors have been subjected to slightly different conditions.

The Forms of Flowers (1877), an expansion and reworking of papers published in the sixties, deals with significant cases of cross-fertilization, particularly with that of heterostyled plants, the "making out" of which was one of his greatest pleasures.

In these later years, the moment of synthesis and composition became increasingly terrible. "I am overwhelmed with my notes," he confessed in 1879, just before writing *Movement in Plants*, "and am almost too old to undertake the job which I have in hand."[6] First drafts, which he now wrote at breakneck speed, drew from him, in the crises of revision, comic but exasperated threats of madness and suicide. Final drafts left him calm but unhopeful. "Please observe," he wrote Gray of *Cross- and Self-Fertilization*, that "the first six chapters are not readable, and the six last very dull."[7] Oddly enough, his writing at this time shows no indication of increasing obscurity. It is, if anything, a little simpler and clearer than before.

The botanical works, selling from 1,500 to 3,000 copies each, were certainly not popular. Nevertheless, all were received with appropriate if somewhat incurious awe by the public, and those on fertilization, with rare and gratifying warmth by scientists. Gray placed Darwin beside Robert Brown in botany and Wallace declared flatly that he had revolutionized the science.[8] *The Power of Movement in Plants*, however, was not generally accepted, and ponderous scientific sneers were distinctly audible from across the North Sea. Perhaps Darwin's *Methodologie* was not quite up to Teutonic standards. He was himself quick to admire German experiments, but, with all his self-deprecation, he sturdily resented German amusement.

"They may sneer the souls out of their bodies," he wrote
Thiselton Dyer, one of Hooker's lieutenants at Kew, "but I
for one shall think [plant movements] . . . the most interesting
part of Natural History."[9] On the other hand, he could write
with detached, if somewhat mournful admiration, "Wiesner
of Vienna has just published a book vivisecting me in the most
courteous, but awful manner, about the 'Power of Movement
in Plants.' "[10]

In August, 1876, while vacationing at Hensleigh Wedgwood's house of Hopedene, Charles began his "Autobiography," writing thereafter for nearly an hour every afternoon
until his last illness in 1881. He had not got the idea all at once.
He hardly ever got an idea all at once. The request of a German
editor for a brief self-portrait had sown the seed. Then he reflected how he would have prized "even so short and dull a
sketch" from his grandfather.[11] He had begun to think more
about old Erasmus lately. He may also have been thinking
more about himself.

Very properly, he entitled his narrative "Recollections of
the Development of my Mind and Character." It was to be
the evolution of Charles Darwin, treated in a thoroughly
scientific spirit. "I have attempted to write . . . as if I were a
dead man in another world looking back at my own life."[12]
Fortunately, he did not succeed in quite such unearthly detachment. "The Autobiography" was intended only for his
children, and one of its greatest attractions is its strong atmosphere of family feeling and intimacy. In fact, filial affection
leads Charles at the very outset to such a prodigious digression
on his father that he seems in great danger of never getting
back to himself. Altogether, Charles's "Autobiography" com-
bines the conscientiousness of Mill's, with the warmth and
intimacy of a prolonged family letter.

A man who could be noticeably charming about barnacles
and earthworms should be markedly charming about himself.

In Darwin this quality is partly an openness and transparency of manner. He not only explains, but depicts and illustrates himself. The result is that the eager little boy who stole fruit evolves convincingly into the eager, white-bearded sage who even at the moment guides the pen.

But not convincingly for the sage himself. He is quite frankly

LARRY BURROWS
PORTRAIT OF CHARLES DARWIN, PAINTED IN 1875.

astonished at having evolved into himself. He remarks with wonder that he once loved music, that he once enjoyed Milton and Wordsworth, that he now can do nothing but grind scientific facts into scientific generalizations. He is astonished that he ever became a serious worker, an author, a member

of the Royal Society, a celebrated thinker. He is astonished
that he ever had a revolutionary idea. His concluding words
are, "With such modest abilities as I possess, it is truly surprising that I should have influenced to a considerable extent
the belief of scientific men on some important points."[13] But
of course Darwin is not just surprised. His explanation of himself might be called Lamarckian: he was able to think successfully because he felt the need to think.

He traces in some detail the development of his ideas and
of the mind that thought those ideas. On the moral significance of his life he has much less to say:

I believe that I have acted rightly in steadily following and devoting my life to science. I feel no remorse from having committed
any great sin; but have often and often regretted that I have not
done more direct good to my fellow-creatures. My sole and poor
excuse is much ill-health and my mental constitution which makes
it extremely difficult for me to turn from one subject or occupation to another. I can imagine with high satisfaction giving up
my whole time to philanthropy but not a portion of it; though
this would have been a far better line of conduct.[14]

The note of apology is revealing: in the last analysis, he does
not expect to be judged severely; he does not judge himself
severely. Darwin was appealing in his humility, warm and human in his domestic affections; but he was neither profound
in self-knowledge nor lofty in moral aspiration. He was virtuous above the level of most men, but heroic chiefly in prodigious intellectual labor in the face of nervous and physical
suffering. About his moral life there is a distinct suggestion of
comfort and upholstery.

The want of self-knowledge revenges itself in occasional
ironies. "I cared very little," he writes of the greatest crisis of
his professional life, "whether men attributed most originality
to Wallace or to me."[15] His gravest moment of humility comes,
characteristically, when he acknowledges his debt to his wife:

She has never failed in the kindest sympathy towards me and has borne with the utmost patience my frequent complaints from ill-health or discomfort. I do not believe she has ever missed an opportunity of doing a kind action to anyone near her. I marvel at my good fortune that she, so infinitely my superior in every single moral quality, consented to be my wife. She has been my faithful adviser and cheerful comforter throughout life, which without her would have been, during a very long period, a miserable one from ill-health.[16]

Scratching rapidly each afternoon in an undecipherable hand, mixing the casualness of anecdote with the solemnity of a final reckoning, Darwin took autobiographical farewell not only of his life but of his world; and for him the latter meant chiefly the eminent men he had known. He seldom ventures on a moral judgment. Of Owen, Mivart, and Butler, who had injured him, he says little. Of literary men he says mostly good. On fellow scientists like Brown, Babbage, and Murchison, he is full of anecdote, good humor, and incidental illuminations. Falconer, now dead, is still his "poor dear Falconer,"[17] because he had loved a fact so ardently and because he had been so shaken by the *Origin*, plunging dramatically from elephants to evolution. On Spencer—whom he had heard so much admired, and had been compelled so much to admire by Wallace and Huxley—he permits himself the luxury of a frank, though cautious criticism:

Herbert Spencer's conversation seemed to me very interesting, but I did not like him particularly and did not feel that I could easily become intimate with him. I think that he was extremely egotistical. After reading any of his books I generally feel enthusiastic admiration of his transcendental talents, and have often wondered whether in the distant future he would rank with such great men, as Descartes, Leibnitz, etc. about whom, however, I know very little. Nevertheless, I am not conscious of having profited in my own work by Spencer's writings. His deductive manner of treating every subject is wholly opposed to my frame of mind. His conclusions never convinced me, and over and over again I have said to myself, after reading one of his discussions, "here would be a fine subject for half-a-dozen years work."[18]

For Huxley and for Hooker, who had so long stood upon his right hand and his left, he has almost nothing but praise. Hooker is delightful, kindhearted, acute, tireless, honorable to the backbone. He is, however, "very impulsive, and somewhat peppery in temper."[19] But, concludes Charles, "I have known hardly any man more lovable than Hooker."[20]

Darwin seems to regard Huxley as the most gifted among his intimate friends, though he says little more than the obvious in unrelieved superlatives. "His mind is as quick as a flash of lightning and as sharp as a razor. He is the best talker whom I have known."[21] The gentleness of his conversation gives no idea of the ferocity of his controversial writing. Having dwelt briefly on the length of Huxley's fangs and the massiveness of his jaws, Darwin continues, with something of a small boy's pride and awe:

He would allow me to say anything to him: many years ago I thought that it was a pity that he attacked so many scientific men, although I believe he was right in each particular case, and I said so to him. He denied the charge indignantly, and I answered that I was very glad to hear that I was mistaken. We had been talking about his well-deserved attack on Owen, so I said after a time, "how well you have exposed Ehrenberg's blunders"; he agreed and added that it was necessary for science that such mistakes should be exposed. Again after a time, I added "poor Agassiz has fared ill at your hands." Again I added another name and now his bright eyes flashed on me and he burst out laughing, anathematizing me in some manner. He is a splendid man and has worked well for the good of mankind.[22]

Huxley has been "a most kind friend"; he has been the "mainstay in England of the evolutionary principle; and he has done much splendid work in zoology, though he might have done much more, had he not been so much preoccupied with writing, education, and official duties."

Another close friend, less warmly celebrated in the "Autobiography," had already died.

I met Lyell in Waterloo Place to-day walking with Carrick Moore [Huxley had written in July, 1871]—and although what you said the other day had prepared me, I was greatly shocked at his appearance, and still more at his speech. There is no doubt it is affected in the way you describe, and the fact gives me very sad forebodings about him.[23]

To these ills blindness was added soon after.

Lyell had looked forward to old age as a time when he might reward himself for a lifetime of hard work by dining out a little more frequently than before. But dining out was not possible for a man who could scarcely talk and who could not see at all. Quite apart from physical misfortunes, which he bore without a murmur, there was about his later years something of the tragedy of a man who has not received an important invitation. Lyell had brought about a revolution in geology. He had quibbled with a larger revolution in biology. He had hesitated —and lost his entree. It was a heavy punishment, and sometimes he complained a little. When he made his last confession of evolutionary faith, he wrote reminding Darwin of the latter's own words against the foes of the new geology—that every scientific man should die at sixty, and so escape an authoritative old age of opposition to "all new doctrines."[24] Lyell hoped that he might now be allowed to live. And when in 1868 Haeckel sent him a copy of The History of Creation, Lyell thanked him warmly, and especially for the chapter "On Lyell and Darwin." "Most of the zoologists forget," he wrote, "that anything was written between the time of Lamarck and the publication of our friend's 'Origin of Species.' "[25]

But now Lyell moved into deeper shadows. In 1873 he lost

his devoted Mary, who had followed him on so many scientific journeys in Europe and America and who, as still a quite young woman, had sat patiently by while he and Darwin had vanished into geological unintelligibilities. Surely nothing more remained for Lyell? As a matter of fact, his days were passed in an eager and enthusiastic study of the ancient volcanoes of his native Forfarshire, which he explored with the brilliant young geologist Judd. The old veteran trudged patiently in his darkness, listened to descriptions of the rock formations, offered painfully articulated opinions, and rejoiced in the success of his young friend's book. The last letter of his correspondence, addressed to Darwin, was full of Judd's ancient volcanoes, and without a word of his own failing health.

He died on February 22, 1875. Hooker was stunned. He was "my loved, my best friend, . . . whose affection for me was truly that of a father and brother combined."[26] Darwin was surprised at Hooker's grief. "I cannot say that I felt his death much, for I fully expected it, and have looked for some little time at his career as finished."[27] Then he rejoiced that Hooker, as President of the Royal Society, had requested and obtained for Lyell the honor of a Westminster burial. "The possibility . . . had not occurred to me when I wrote before." He was asked to be a pallbearer but refused, fearing giddiness and collapse. His letter to Lyell's secretary Miss Buckley was less muted and remote than that to Hooker, but there was an indefinable perfunctoriness about its superlatives. "It seems strange to me," he concluded, "that I shall never again sit with him and Lady Lyell at their breakfast."[28] That was his deepest note. Lyell had never been closely identified with Darwinism. Inevitably, therefore, he had faded out of Darwin's select, intimate little world, as nearly all old friends were fading. Charles confessed that he was no longer capable of strong feeling, except for his own family.

Lubbock, now Lord Avebury and a figure in public life, was

the Mercury who usually ushered into that tiny world, hori-
zoned with applause, the brief visitations of celebrity. One
Sunday afternoon in February, 1877, he emptied nearly half
the Victorian political Olympus on the astonished somnolence
of Down, bringing not only Huxley, Morley, and Lord Playfair, but that grandly courteous and volubly declamatory Jove,
the Right Honorable William E. Gladstone. Charles emerged
from the sapient tentacles and folial stomachs of Drosera with
a jerk. Surely here was an episode, unexplored by Landor, in
which history should have ascended to the philosophic generality of poetry: the great statesman of liberalism met for the
first time the great scientist of liberalism. Gladstone was on
the very point of abandoning an heroic posture of thought for
an even more heroic posture of action. Holding himself
haughtily aloof from the low and venal noises of the forum,
he had sat for the last three years, the Bible in one hand and
Homer in the other, symbolizing the intellectual history of
Europe. But meanwhile Disraeli had committed clever follies
in order that his great rival might display a noble, simple wisdom in denouncing them, and Turks had massacred Christians
in order that he might display his zeal and eloquence by pouring out the long periods of his virtuous and cadenced wrath
against barbarism and murder.

Unfortunately, he was a little too full of zeal and eloquence.
No luminous bridge could be built between the iniquities of
Turks and the ingenuities of Drosera. Having hurled his furious thunderbolts at the Turks with inexhaustible zest and
good humor through the whole week end at Lubbock's house,
he continued to do so throughout his visit with Darwin.
Charles listened with unaffected delight. Here were all his
Brazilian slaves and maltreated horses avenged in one glorious
crusade! At length the polished, oratorical thunder died away
and the company broke up. Shading his eyes against the setting
sun, Darwin stood, with his scholar's stoop and his long white

beard, watching Gladstone's erect alert figure as he walked away. Turning to Morley, who waited to say good-by, he exclaimed with simple, heart-felt gratitude, "What an honour that such a great man should come to visit me!"[29] Gladstone remembered only the Turks. His papers simply record "a notable party" and "interesting conversation."[30]

"We have both," Emma wrote Fanny Allen, "been reading a grand sermon . . . on Darwinism. I sometimes think it very odd indeed that anyone belonging to me should be making such a noise in the world."[31] But Charles had made the noise quite a long time ago. More and more, he and Emma found themselves spectators of the story which they had begun. Now the children were making some noise of their own. George, the mathematician, was improving on Sir William Thompson and would soon explain himself to the Royal Society. Frank, a physician turned biologist, had become his father's assistant and was discovering protoplasm in the most improbable places. Lenny, whom Emma a few years before had commanded to "begin his jerseys," was soon to build forts and was even now setting forth, as photographer, on a scientific Columbiad to New Zealand. "Oh Lord, what a set of sons I have, all doing wonders," exclaimed Charles.[32] They were so obviously and gratifyingly cleverer than he had been at their age.

And yet little of this early promise was to be fulfilled. In their mature years the younger Darwins were intelligent, unself-conscious, absent-minded, innocent, eccentric, delightful. One became a major in the army; another, Lord Mayor of Cambridge. All married admirable and exemplary young woman. All lived in large houses and disposed of even larger checkbooks. They were the friends of eminent men, but not eminent men in their own right. As a matter of fact, a kind of retrospective nostalgia seems to have taken the forward direction from their lives. In a time of mounting insecurity and self-assertion, they remained placidly secure and diffident. In an age that was rapidly becoming indiscreet, they remained sensitively proper and mid-Victorian—so much so that when at a dinner party Virginia Stephen made "a slightly double-edged joke," George—to his daughter Gwen's astonishment—"actually *understood* it" and then "turned away: shocked."[33] The trouble with them, says Gwen, was that their father had been too indulgent, too easily pleased, and above all too charming. He had therefore always been their hero and childhood had remained their happiest and most significant experience. He should have been mean enough to make them rebel or deeply concerned enough to make them strike out and experiment for themselves. "At any rate, I know I always felt older than they were. Not nearly so good, or so brave, or so kind, or so wise. Just older."[34]

To the general growing-up of sons, Emma was less resigned than Charles. Lenny's New Zealand adventure did not fill her with any enthusiasm. "I feel rather flat. One is so awfully used to New Zealand," she remarked to Etty, ironically using the verb with which, as a child, Lenny had expressed boredom with bread and butter for tea.[35] Perhaps neither she nor Charles quite realized what was happening to them until they visited William in his villa at Basset. Not that the visit was in any sense a failure. "William says how quiet and dull the meals are, and how much he enjoyed our visit. I believe he quite misses us—" and here she put into words the unpleasant possibility—"though F. [father] would think that quite too presumptuous an idea, he being a man and we fogies."[36]

Every evening for many years they played exactly two games of backgammon. When fortune went against him, Charles, employing a ritual expression borrowed from *The Journal to Stella*, would exclaim, "Bang your bones!"—and no doubt Emma made a ritual reply. This solemn frivolity also exercised his passion for numeration. "Pray give our regards to Mrs. Gray," he wrote to his old friend Asa. "I know she likes to hear men boasting, it refreshes them so much. Now the tally with my wife in backgammon stands thus: she, poor creature, has won only 2,490 games, whilst I have won, hurrah, hurrah, 2,795 games!"[37]

Emma corresponded, dutifully and lovingly, with a remote past of maiden aunts and elderly widows. Of the generation of Josiah Wedgwood and Dr. Robert Darwin, Fanny Allen was now the sole survivor. She was a bright, alert, indomitable old maid in her nineties, who lived in a pretty, cheerful house by the sea and steadfastly refused to pay her cook more than twelve pounds a year, though Elizabeth Wedgwood and Fanny Hensleigh secretly augmented the amount to the contemporary standard. With eighteenth-century clearheadedness, Fanny scorned Tennyson and his "bland and mild" Shakespeare, citing the murder of Duke Humphrey in the chronicle plays as a refutation. She gave her grandniece Henrietta a volume of Burns cuttingly inscribed with the hope that it might wean her away from "Mr. Tennyson."

Emma explained modern youth to Fanny. "Henrietta . . . has been going to a workingman's ball," she wrote, "and danced with a grocer and a shoemaker, who moved and behaved exactly like everybody else and were quite as well dressed. The ladies were nicely dressed but not expensively, and much more decently than their betters in a ballroom now-a-days."[38] She and Charles several times welcomed Litchfield's class from the London Workingman's College. Some sixty or seventy in number, they wandered about the garden, sang under the lime trees, and finally had tea on the lawn. Charles got on well with them. Nevertheless, he must have moved through these afternoons with an anxious eye to his symptoms and a terrifying probability of headaches and insomnia afterwards.

At about this time Emma very quietly became very liberal in her religious ideas. Nearly forty years of evolutionary dinner conversation had taken its toll. To respect Charles's fame was to face his facts, and to face his facts was to reject the Deluge and the Garden of Eden. Emma now began to admire Bishop Colenso, though more for his exploits among the Caffres, perhaps, than for those against the Old Testament. "Dean Stanley had the courage to ask him to preach at Westminster Abbey," she wrote, "but Colenso declined, saying he had not come to England to stand up for his own rights, and he would not make a fuss."[39] She had also come to take a fond and motherly, if somewhat vague interest in Charles's science. Her husband was so much the eager and lovable boy, continually busy about his projects with earthworms and primroses. "F. is much absorbed in Desmodium gyrans," she wrote Henrietta, "and went to see it asleep last night. It was dead asleep, all but its little ears, which were having most lively games, such as he never saw in the day-time."[40]

"F. was made very happy," she wrote sometime later, "by finding two very old stones at the bottom of the field, and he has now got a man at work digging for the worms. I must go and take him an umbrella."[41] Charles had begun to investigate how stones are buried by the castings of earthworms. His adventures with these humble animals came to their logical climax in a monumental event: he visited Stonehenge. "I am afraid," wrote Emma in prospect, "it will half kill F.—two hours' rail and a twenty-four mile drive—but he is bent on going, chiefly for the worms, but also he has always wished to see it."[42] George met them at Salisbury and conducted the tour with great gusto. Charles stood about in the sun with wonderful perseverance and immunity to headache. But at Stonehenge the victorious worm had obviously failed to obliterate the works of his traditional victim. "They did not find much good about the worms, who seem to be very idle out there."[43]

All the male Darwins took earthworms very seriously. Horace observed how they buried stones; William, how they covered over ruined terraces; and Frank, how they dragged leaves into their burrows. Finally, Charles's book (1881) demonstrated that, though simple little creatures, they lead ingenious, complicated, and highly useful lives. They are blind, deaf, and dumb; yet they construct remarkable, humus-lined burrows extending sometimes six or seven feet underground and terminating in little spherical, pebble-floored chambers where they roll themselves up into balls and hibernate. They have extraordinary gizzards and esophagi that moved Charles to eloquent admiration. They are quite sagacious about picking up leaves by the most convenient end. Above all, they literally swallow, digest, and excrete nearly all the surface soil of the globe, refining and enriching it into the fertility which makes abundant plant growth possible.

In 1876, youth, in the rather terrifying form of a newly born baby, re-entered the Darwin household. Frank had married, lost his wife, and come back to live at Down House with his son. Emma took up the task with energy and courage, though the sudden loss of her daughter-in-law had left her, in Henrietta's opinion, a more fearful and anxious woman. Her references to the baby are divided between anxiety and admiration, but mostly admiration. "We think he . . . is a sort of Grand Lama," she told Henrietta, "he is so solemn."[44]

The infant and the sage were on easy and confidential terms from the first. Charles may have suffered atrophy of his organ for appreciating Shakespeare, but not of that for responding to children. It was such a pleasure to see the boy's little face opposite him at luncheon. "He and Bernard used to compare their tastes; e.g., in liking brown sugar better than white, &c.; the result being, 'We always agree, don't we?' "[45]

Meanwhile, Charles and Emma were concerned about their eldest son. A prosperous banker in Southampton, William was modest, serene, genial, and sweet-tempered. He had only one fault: he was a bachelor. Was he doomed to be another Erasmus? Like his uncle, William was devoted to solitude and reading. When Emma urged him to marry, he replied with a ritual "Why if I did I shouldn't have any time to myself."[46] But sometimes, looking over the top of his book, he must have given way to conjugal thoughts, for in 1877 he became engaged to Sara Sedgwick, the sister-in-law of that elegant Bostonian and fastidious Anglophile, Charles Eliot Norton.

Convinced that William's had been a narrow escape and that he had won a remarkable young lady, Charles wrote Sara one of his inimitable letters of personal gratitude. "For many years," he declared, "I have not seen any woman, whom I have liked and esteemed so much as you." He admitted that Southampton was dull but modestly urged that William was not. Moreover,

I can say with absolute truth that no act or conduct of William has ever in his whole life caused me one minute's anxiety or disapproval. His temper is beautifully sweet and affectionate and he delights in doing little kindnesses. That you may be happy together is my strong desire, and I thank you from the bottom of my heart for having accepted him.[47]

Sara is an index to the propriety and innocence which, beneath the informality, were rather awful in the Darwins. She was an intelligent, animated young puritan with an appetite for moral heroism which in a prosaic age could express itself in no other dedication than that of being a perfect lady. Having nothing to die for, she lived in order that her life and William's might be a monument to correctness. They inhabited a large, hideously faultless late-Victorian villa with lawns, a carriage sweep, a monkey-puzzle tree, plate glass windows, and bells which footmen never failed to answer. Unlike Sara herself the house did not excite Charles's admiration.

Happening to be alone in it for a few hours, he collected every ugly object of bric-a-brac that he could find and then arranged them all together in a single room. When William and Sara returned, he laughingly led them through his chamber of horrors.

Apparently William had his uncle Erasmus's gift for quiet and intelligent reverence. Certainly both had a way with Carlyle. One of the most delightful of the Darwin letters is an account written by William to his mother of a carriage ride with the aged transcendentalist. In the warmth of William's sympathy, the dark, dyspeptic clouds melted away from the frosty brow, the proud suspicious heart opened, and the sharp tongue ceased to be the slave of its own satiric art. Carlyle spoke of the terrible difficulty of rewriting the first volume of *The French Revolution* after the manuscript had been accidentally burnt by Mill's charwoman. Trying to write without notes or references had seemed like trying to fly without wings. He said that his friendship with Goethe had prevented him from going mad at the horror and mystery of this world. Had Carlyle ever reread any of his own works? Yes, he had actually reread *Frederick* in its eleven-volume entirety (proving thereby that such books can be read as well as written). All this and much more he said with the utmost frankness and good humor, but William was constantly losing immortal words in the rumbling of carriage wheels. In parting, Carlyle inquired after Charles's health, and showing his teeth a little, remarked with a grin, "The origin of species is nothing to me."[48]

Charles's own later relations with the prophet of hero worship were less fortunate. Carlyle could not swallow the monkeys; and Darwin could not quite swallow Carlyle, particularly after the *Reminiscences*, which devote one rapid, patronizing page to the Darwin brothers, upsetting the honest fame of the younger with the intelligent obscurity of the elder:

Erasmus Darwin, a most diverse kind of mortal, came to seek us out very soon ("had heard of Carlyle in Germany" etc.); and continues ever since to be a quiet house-friend, honestly attached; though his visits latterly have been rarer and rarer, health so poor, I so occupied, etc. etc. He has something of original and sarcastically ingenious in him; one of the sincerest, naturally truest, and most modest of men. Elder brother of Charles Darwin, . . . to whom I rather prefer him for intellect, had not his health quite doomed him to silence and patient idleness.[49]

In his "Autobiography," Darwin revenged himself by doing Carlyle justice. Carlyle was a good talker but he talked too much. Darwin recalls with some gusto how the great writer once silenced a whole dinner party, including two formidable raconteurs, with a gigantic lecture on silence. Carlyle sneered too much and the *Reminiscences* seemed to indicate that his sneers came too much from the heart. Even so, he was a sincerely benevolent man. His descriptions of men and things were unexcelled in vividness but not necessarily in truth. He was a grandly influential moralist, but one who did not know the difference between might and right.

In 1877 Cambridge shed prestige on science, and orthodoxy on evolution by conferring an LL.D. on Charles. The occasion, one of the most memorable in university history, was something between a riot and a ritual. Entering by a side door with her daughter Bessie and her two youngest sons, Emma found the Senate House an almost unendurable pandemonium of noise, stifling air, and crushed humanity. Undergraduates not only carpeted the floor and jammed the aisles but perched on the statues and stood in the windows. Sardonic catcalls alternated with deafening cheers. Presently Charles, positively Chaucerian in his white beard and magnificent red cloak, was ushered in by a squadron of brightly robed dons. For several minutes, the cheers were so stupendous that Emma half expected her husband to wilt and evaporate away out of sheer sensitiveness and ochlophobia. Quite the contrary. He sat waiting, with his most charming smile, for the Vice-Chancellor. Meanwhile, there were loud groans for an unpopular proctor, who responded with a stern, angry face, "which," observed Emma with the sageness of great experience, "was very bad policy."[50] Some undergraduates now stretched cords from one gallery to another, and Emma was not surprised to see first a dangling monkey and then a large ring tied with ribbons, which she conjectured to be the missing link. There was a fresh outburst of catcalls about "our ancestors," in the midst of which the Vice-Chancellor appeared. Charles was now marched down the aisle by two men with silver maces. The Public Orator made his long harangue, which Emma found extremely tedious and which was interrupted in the middle by a cheerful, valedictory voice calling out, "Thank you very kindly!" At length the Vice-Chancellor, in scarlet and white fur, said a few Latin words over Charles, and Charles was an LL.D. Emma conceded that she felt very proud walking through the quadrangles with her red-robed husband.

That evening Charles ate a quiet dinner with Emma in the pleasant and contented knowledge that in his honor a great many other people were eating a very ceremonious dinner with the Vice-Chancellor. Huxley as usual represented him, expressing thanks and making the principal address. Darwin's alter ego could say things that Darwin would never think of saying, and Huxley said them with relish. In fact, the actor reinforced the Puritan on these occasions. Huxley loved to dumfound, not the bourgeois, but the accepted idols and potentates of this world. In spite of his large geniality and friendliness, he liked, in an atmosphere of conviviality sickening toward social horror, to turn gala dinners into punitive expeditions. He began by expressing the gratitude of his old friend. The university had shown wise foresight and singular restraint in not bestowing this delicate academic wreath until it could run no risk of being crushed under the marks of approbation which had accumulated since the first appearance of the *Origin*. Huxley then searched scientific history in vain for a name of equal luster between those of Aristotle and Darwin. In conclusion, he was very glad to hear from Dr. Humphrey that in conferring a degree on his old friend, the university had accepted the doctrine of evolution. The younger Darwins reported the speech to their father with glee and exultation.

The red robe was timed to the snail's pace of general opinion, for from about this time forward, Charles wore an invisible red robe of celebrity wherever he went. When he attended Burdon Sanderson's lecture on movement in plants and animals, he was applauded as he entered and ushered with ceremony to a place next to the chairman. In this stooped, shaggy-browed, white-bearded old man with his earnest, bright-eyed expression of pain, people recognized an immortal who would soon vanish from the prosaic haunts of mortality.

In 1879, with characteristic piety, Charles carved another ancestral head on the top of his totem pole. A typically Victorian bit of woodwork, it was meant to represent grandfather Erasmus. Charles had recently been much struck by Ernst Krause's article on Erasmus in the German periodical *Kosmos*. Perhaps Erasmus's exuberant speculation was not so disgraceful after all. He decided to have Krause's essay brought out in English; then, finding scientific work more strenuous than formerly, himself undertook a biographical introduction by way of literary relaxation. To be sure, the introduction soon grew longer than the essay.

At that particular time Erasmus was probably best known through a footnote in the "Historical Sketch" prefixed to the *Origin*. Apparently Charles imagined he was better known through the vindictive contemporary biography of Miss Anna Seward, who had revenged the secret crime of never having been made Mrs. Erasmus Darwin by depicting a monster capable of so dastardly an omission. Collecting evidence from old family papers and letters, Charles had attempted "to refute the calumnies of Miss Seward." To be sure, one does not paint a vivid or even a veracious portrait by refuting calumnies. Nor could he even refute calumnies with a perfectly clear conscience. "Do you know her maiden name?" he had once asked Hooker about a certain lady. "I suspect she is Granddaughter of Dr. Darwin of Zoonomia; who had some illegitimate daughters who were brought up like ladies."[51] By judicious quotations and even more judicious silences, Charles succeeded, not in bringing his grandfather to life, but in making him a thoroughly edifying character. The erudite lover, the brilliant virtuoso and armchair philosopher becomes what in part he was, a scientist, humanitarian, and benefactor of mankind.

The whole Darwin family was dubious about the "Erasmus." Charles cut, revised, and agonized to no avail. Everybody was pessimistic, and for once the pessimism was justified. Less than a thousand copies were sold.

The little book was not only unpopular, it was unfortunate as well. Samuel Butler, who had spent his boyhood in developing a sense of injury and half his lifetime in detecting elderly malevolence, discovered almost at a glance that Krause's essay was an insidious veiled attack against himself. Moreover, he saw that Charles's whole scientific career was a long and dignified burglary of ideas from Erasmus Darwin, Buffon, and Lamarck. Butler could not blink at the facts. Reluctantly but resolutely, he quarreled his way into contemporary notice, demonstrating as many talents for defamation as Gladstone for oratory. He was suspicious, critical, alert, witty, devious, elusive. He also had the satirist's power of turning his victims into vivid, plausible villains who thoroughly deserved the savagery of his pen. The Darwin of Luck, or Cunning?, like the Theobald Pontifex of The Way of All Flesh, causes the reader to burn with moral indignation.

Butler's quarrel with Darwin is not an incident. It involves his total biography. In the early sixties, while still a young man, Butler made a modest fortune at sheep raising in Australia and discovered the leading idea of his life in New Zealand. That idea was evolution and he found it in the *Origin*. The theory of natural selection he hardly took in at all. What fascinated him was the thought that living things grow, develop, and evolve. Quite characteristically, he began to experiment with the idea, as a scientist experiments with guinea pigs or wrinkled peas. First he assumed that men were machines. This proved rather tame and unfruitful. Then he assumed that machines were alive. This proved delightfully exhilarating, and soon he had a sketch in a New Zealand newspaper. But despite all his skill in making out a case, Butler could not quite convince himself that machines were alive. He therefore turned to the more cautious and rather Lamarckian notion that machines are exterior and detachable limbs that men have made for themselves—and published another newspaper sketch.

In 1870 and 1871, as a prosperous dilettante bachelor in London, he used both sketches—and much else—to construct a very compact and suggestive little satire called *Erewhon*, of which he sent a copy to Darwin. Charles thought it great fun, and Butler hastened to explain that it was not, as some critics thought, intended as a satire of the *Origin*, for which he could "never be sufficiently grateful."[52] He now paid visits to Down House and struck up a friendship with Frank.

Butler resumed his chiropractic experiments on the analogy between mechanisms and organisms, twisting and pushing and wrenching it into all sorts of grotesque shapes. He had considered machines as limbs or organs. What if organs were machines? He quickly saw that animals might "invent" them through need, improve them through use, maintain them through habit, and pass them on through unconscious memory. Individuals of the same descent would then enjoy unity of personality and experience. They would live "with the accumulated life of centuries."[53] Standing on the mountain of Montreal, one magnificent summer evening while on a business trip to Canada, he viewed with exaltation the grandeur of the St. Lawrence River and of his own idea. He listened to the bells of Montreal Cathedral, and as the sounds died away they seemed to symbolize the gradual diminution of generic memories losing themselves in the abyss of past experience.

Butler hardly realized that he had evolved a new theory, much less that he differed greatly from Darwin. As he began to write Life and Habit in 1876, however, friends put him on the track of Lamarck and Hering, who had anticipated him. He also read Mivart's objections to Darwin with great sympathy, and then, looking into the sacred book once more after several years, bristled at what seemed the summary manner in which those objections were answered. Incidentally, he discovered a good deal of wool in his idol's head and therefore, of course, a good deal of clay in his feet. When was Darwin for Darwin and when was he for Lamarck? Besides, the theory of natural selection didn't explain anything if it didn't explain the causes of variations. Butler tried to be respectful but the gusto of destruction was upon him. The closing chapters of Life and Habit leave the aged prophet of evolution only the merest shreds and patches of his sage's mantle.

Life and Habit appeared late in 1877. Butler awaited bolts from the scientific empyrean somewhat as Ernest Pontifex had awaited blows from the paternal ferule. Nothing happened— except that he received two courteous and appreciative letters from Frank Darwin. He sighed with relief, then grew suspicious. Was he to be another victim of that great warfare of silence which—as he was beginning to perceive with horrified indignation—Darwin had waged so successfully against eminent predecessors? For the fact of organic evolution had been perfectly well known to Buffon, Lamarck, and Erasmus Darwin. Moreover, they had explained it much better than Charles Darwin had. Why were they so totally unknown? Butler found his answer in The Origin of Species. Darwin's "Historical Sketch" was a jewel of studied or unstudied detraction, damning many—among them his own grandfather—in little space and small type. His ambiguities, intended or unintended, were not simply baffling, but interested, deceptive, and insidious, enabling him to insinuate a claim to the discovery of evolution itself as well as of natural selection.

By a very romantic logic of his own, Butler had found Darwin to be first superhuman, then human, and finally inhuman. That inhumanity needed only to be demonstrated by an overt act. Of course it was, almost at once. In May, 1879, Butler published Evolution, Old and New, exposing Charles and restoring Erasmus, Buffon, and Lamarck to their proper glory. A few months later, Charles brought out, together with his own "Preliminary Notice," Krause's Erasmus Darwin. Clearly, Evolution, Old and New had quickly given him a bad conscience about his grandfather. Butler read the Erasmus Darwin in haste. The sole comment on the new Lamarckianism consisted of one sentence, in which Krause observed that the recent attempt to revive Erasmus Darwin's system showed "a weakness of thought and a mental anachronism which no one can envy."[54] That was all. Yet, though purporting to be an accurate translation from a German article published some time before Evolution, Old and New, Krause's essay contained several mysterious and unacknowledged echoes from that work. Moreover, Charles's preface seemed to guarantee the accuracy of the translator, and also mentioned the subsequent publication of Evolution, Old and New. Butler sent for the original article and furiously studied German. Sure enough! The article had been tampered with. Was he to be buried alive, as others had been buried dead, under these insidious emanations of silence and misrepresentation? Fortunately, he had seen the trick in time. In phrases exuding a distinct odor of villainy detected, he wrote to Darwin demanding an explanation.

The explanation was that Butler had given a very mean and ingenious interpretation to a rather complicated accident. Darwin had glanced through Butler's book when it came out, and sent it to Krause with the comment that it was not worth much attention. Engaged in revising his article, Krause had apparently used material from Evolution, Old and New and at the same time condemned its doctrine even more heartily than Darwin had. In his preface, Darwin stated that Krause had revised, but the statement had accidentally been deleted from the proofs. Now, deep in vegetable mould, and earthworms, Charles did not remember ever having written it. In reply to Butler, therefore, he merely acknowledged the revision and declared the practice so common as hardly to require mention. Explanations were already too late. In the mood of a literary David defying the scientific Goliath and all his Philistine host, Butler wrote a letter to The Athenaeum stating his case. His tone was dignified, but at intervals he made rapid and dexterous use of the slingshot, grimly noting the "happy simplicity" with which Charles used a common scientific practice to introduce "a covert condemnation of an opponent."[55]

There was a startled consultation among the Darwins. Should Charles reply or not? He drafted two letters but both were rejected by the family conclave. In desperation he appealed to the archcontroversialist himself. Huxley advised the bludgeon silence. Butler's punishment was cruel. Just a little fuss, just an angry word or two would have gratified him so much. He gnashed his teeth with increasing desperation into an awful and deepening silence, so that his later books contained more and more rage against Darwin and less and less thinking about evolution. In the extremity of his warfare, he even made frantic gestures toward his old enemy the Church, recommending his own Lamarckianism as a means of salvaging mind in a mechanistic age. Darwin, he declared, had knocked the brains out of the universe. In putting them back in, Butler emptied out nearly all the gray matter. Very few paid any attention to him in any case. What seemed to him a fearless unmasking of hypocrisy and error was to most Victorians simply a prolonged and incomprehensible violation of decorum.

Darwin's final years were as full of domestic happiness and material prosperity as the concluding chapter of a Victorian novel. In 1879 Mr. Anthony Rich, named with Dickensian appropriateness, wrote that he intended to leave Charles and Charles's descendants nearly the whole of a large property. Charles protested he was already wealthy, but Mr. Rich was obdurate. When in 1881 he inherited another large fortune from his brother Erasmus, Charles renewed the protest. To no avail. Mr. Rich absolutely insisted on carrying coals to Newcastle—and Charles looked forward to the double satisfaction of leaving more and more money to more and more descendants, for he and Emma were also wonderfully fortunate in acquiring new relatives-in-law. Having become a Cambridge don, their youngest son Horace now married Ida, the only daughter of Lord Farrer, a statesman much interested in botany. Charles had for some time been deep in *Primula* with the father. Emma now became devoted to the daughter.

Having learned in his youth how to be busy, Charles learned once more in his old age how to be idle. The sense of haste and of work to be done gradually departed. Vacations ceased to be punitive sentences of exile from his beloved hothouse. He picnicked, excursioned, and even traveled with the gaiety and enthusiasm of a schoolboy kept too long over his lessons. Twice he actually got as far from Down as the Lake country. Apparently he had been a little premature in bidding farewell to his sense of beauty. He was so devoted to the rocks about Grasmere that Emma feared he might overexert himself.

Charles's last summer was one of the happiest of his life. There were new Darwins to replace the old; there were the inexhaustible, constantly unfolding marvels of little Bernard in evolution; and there was a great deal of fine weather under the lime trees. Henrietta remembered one day in particular when there was a beautiful lady to go with it. The lady was Mrs. Vernon Lushington, who played, sang, talked, and charmed the seventy-two-year-old sage into the gayest of spirits.

Yet in the long sunshine of those late summer days Charles must have felt at times the chill of his own frailty and impermanence. His second visit to the Lake country was much less satisfactory than the first. The least exertion—even looking at scenery—tired him. "I have everything to make me happy and contented," he wrote Wallace, "but life has become very wearisome to me."[56] The worst of it was, of course, that he had no heart to undertake any important scientific task. Short studies did not suit him or they threatened to become long, and for a long study he did not have time. Moreover, the increasing swiftness of biological progress made his head swim. He could not keep up. In fact, he found it hard to concentrate, to grasp facts firmly enough to reason upon them. People should no longer expect discoveries from him. And yet he had to work, and did work—in a desultory, despondent fashion.

Erasmus had been increasingly ill of late years. On August 26, 1881, he died, and was buried in the churchyard at Downe. One of Frank Darwin's most vivid memories was of the expression of sad reverie on his father's face as he stood, wrapped in a long black funeral cloak, in a scattering of snow beside Erasmus's grave. "He always appeared to me," Charles wrote Hooker, "the most pleasant and clearest headed man, whom I have ever known. London will seem a strange place to me without his presence."[57] But Erasmus, as his brother knew, had not been sorry to leave his beloved London for a quieter residence. "He was not, I think, a happy man," Charles told Lord Farrer, "and for many years did not value life, though never complaining."[58] The real tragedy was that so affectionate a man should have been so lonely.

Though deeply engrossed in their own new lives and families at this time, all the younger Darwins mourned Erasmus as an irreparable loss, and none more than William, who resembled him in many ways:

Next to coming to Down [William wrote his mother], one of my greatest pleasures was going to see dear Uncle Eras whenever I was in London. He seems to me much more than an uncle, and from quite a little boy I can remember his steady kindness and pleasantness, always knowing how to make me feel at ease and be amused. After I grew up, it year by year was a greater happiness for me to go and see him. To me there was a charm in his manner that I never saw in anybody else.[59]

By December there was a new Erasmus, the son of Ida and Horace. Charles made a last visit to Cambridge in order to see him. Cambridge undergraduates must have seemed extremely young, extremely noisy, and extremely irrelevant. But the old buildings and quadrangles were familiar and pertinent enough, and when he listened once more to the singing at King's College Chapel, old memories flooded back upon him and gay, youthful Cambridge became a city of ghosts.

He was growing steadily weaker and could hardly work at all. Fearing for his heart, Emma took him to Sir Andrew Clark, who pronounced him reasonably sound. Surprised and reassured, Charles apparently became more venturesome. A few days later, ringing the bell at Romanes's door, he suffered a heart attack. Romanes was not at home, but his butler, perceiving that Mr. Darwin was ill, begged him to come in. It was one of those occasions when, amid the prosaic and impersonal commonplaces of a city street, one may have to choose between impropriety and death. With characteristic shyness and pride, as well as consideration for others, Darwin chose propriety. He would prefer to go home. The butler urged him to come in and rest at least until a cab could be called. But again Charles refused. The butler watched him walk painfully toward the cab stop. At about three hundred yards from the house, he staggered, leaned against the park railings, half turned as though to come back, then, as the butler ran toward him, turned once more and found a cab.

He recovered and was fairly well until the last week of February, when he was again troubled by an irregular pulse and by pain in the region of his heart. But spring came on, the crocuses bloomed, birds sang in the orchard, and Charles sat in the warm sunshine with Emma. He seldom ventured far from the house without her, but once, going as far as the Sandwalk alone, he suffered another attack. Huxley wrote in March, earnestly counseling closer medical supervision. Darwin responded with the warmest gratitude. "Once more, accept my cordial thanks, my dear old friend," he concluded, and then added, with sly reference to one of Huxley's most terrible papers, "I wish to God there were more automata in the world like you."[60]

In April it sometimes fatigued him even to look out the window. Yet he refused to be bedridden and worked whenever he had any strength. His tenderness and consideration for others seemed to grow each day. He told Henrietta and Richard that they were "the best of dear nurses"; and often assured Emma, "It is almost worth while to be sick to be nursed by you."[61] He was always begging her to spend more time with the others. On April 15th he was seized with giddiness while sitting at dinner, and fainted before he could reach the sofa. On the 17th Emma recorded, "Good day, a little work, out in orchard twice."[62] The next night he woke Emma, saying, "I have got the pain, and I shall feel better, or bear it better if you are awake." The pain increased and he fainted. When he was revived with great difficulty, he turned to Emma. "I am not the least afraid of death," he said. "Remember what a good wife you have been to me. Tell all my children to remember how good they have been to me." When the worst of the attack was over, he said, "I was so sorry for you, but I could not help you."[63]

Pain and nausea visited him at regular intervals throughout the following day. That night he had another attack. "He fainted and regained consciousness," Frank wrote Huxley, "but remained in a condition of terrible faintness and suffered very much from overpowering nausea, interrupted by retchings. He more than once said, 'if I could but die.' "[64] At three o'clock the next morning, April 19, 1882, he died very peacefully.

Emma had been wonderfully calm during the last weeks. After his death, the only regret that her children heard her express was that she had not told him how pleased she was when he had put her photograph beside his big chair in the study, so that he could look at it while working.

Emma and the children wanted him to be buried at Downe; but long before they could think of practical details, the press and the pulpit had spoken, the presidents of learned societies had taken counsel, cabinet ministers had concurred with cabinet ministers. Westminster Abbey was inevitable. Death, in fact, had canonized him; his heresies had become part of the wisdom of our ancestors, so that many English divines felt obliged to show there was no essential disagreement between God and "Professor" Darwin.[65] Huxley did not believe a word of it, nor was he one of the eminent scientists who signed Lubbock's petition to the Dean of Westminster. Nevertheless, the Dean telegraphed his "cordial acquiescence."[66]

Sorrow was the heroic emotion of Victorian domestic life. The decent black which in umbrellas and stovepipes made daily life prosaic crescendoed in velvet-palled coffins and lugubriously garlanded horses to a sable grandiosity which made death sumptuous and splendid. Emma did not approve of such displays, nor did she attend the ceremony at the Abbey. Charles was conveyed from this world with a pomp which he had never used while living in it.

Entrance to the ceremony at Westminster Abbey was through the Poet's Corner by black-edged invitation cards. Full mourning was required for admission. To the multitude of distinguished ladies and gentlemen rustling portentously in black silk and broadcloth within the Abbey, a faint singing of youthful voices became increasingly audible as the procession moved through the cloisters toward the west front. At length, the great doors were flung open, the singing grew suddenly louder, and the Choir began to march down the nave. The coffin, borne by Huxley, Hooker, Wallace, Lubbock, James Russell Lowell, Canon Ferrar, an Earl, two Dukes, and the President of the Royal Society, sent a stir of feeling through the crowd. Huxley, Lubbock, and Hooker were visibly moved. Sitting among the members of the family, William Darwin felt a draught. With the respect shown by all Darwins for the possible invasion of disease, he calmly poised his black gloves on the top of his bald head and sat thus throughout the service. Finally, the coffin was lowered into a deep grave close by those of Newton and Herschel. The white-robed choir filled the austere corner of the British scientists and sang, "His body is buried in peace, but his name liveth evermore." Soon the throng of ladies and gentlemen filed out into the spring sunshine and left the Abbey to its great population of statues, which, lying in the frozen compactness of medieval sleep or standing erect in the periwigged flamboyance of neoclassical gesture, tell from choir to west front a long and silent tale of English achievement in many strange costumes and extinct fashions.

The Times recorded the event with decorum and considerable gusto of funereal detail. Spencer, who overcame his sense of the absurdity of ecclesiastical ceremony to attend, was struck with the evident personal sympathy shown by all for the deceased. Galton was obviously moved at the time, then on second thought found the whole occasion too much like that of giving a University Degree. Nevertheless, he was sufficiently impressed to urge in a letter to The Pall Mall Gazette that the old creation window, based on a neolithic myth, be replaced by an evolutionary one in honor of his famous cousin. This doctrinaire proposal did not meet with "cordial acquiescence" from the Dean of Westminster.

Almost immediately after the funeral, Huxley wrote for the forthcoming issue of Nature a brief memorial of his old friend. It contains some of the most valuable observations he ever made on another human being. The central principle of Darwin's nature, Huxley felt, was "a certain intense and almost passionate honesty," which acted at once as restraint and propulsion, keeping "his vivid imagination and great speculative powers within due bounds" and at the same time compelling him "to undertake the prodigious labours of original investigation." In his conversation Darwin reminded Huxley of Socrates. There was the same "ready humour," the same "desire to find some one wiser than himself," the same "belief in the sovereignty of reason."[67]

PART
TWO

14

An Eminent Victorian

Huxley's later career suggests further contrast with Darwin's. Their lives embraced opposite metamorphoses. Darwin's pattern was essentially crustacean; Huxley's was, in part at least, lepidopteral or butterflylike. Beginning as an active, free-swimming snipeshooter, Darwin developed evanescent tendencies to Bible reading and theology grubbing, suddenly acquired new microscopic eyes and fresh appendages of dissecting lancets and geological hammers, ranged far and wide with great activity of all the appendages and much storing up for a future to come, and then, returning to his earlier habitat, abruptly settled down to the sedentary existence of the mature organism, living parasitically on an idea. Huxley began as an industrious scientific caterpillar chewing the prosaic vegetables of fact and creeping cautiously on the solid ground of empiricism. In certain fleeting but extra-lepidopteral phases, he became suddenly aquatic and roamed the seas, preying fruitfully on salps and medusae. At length, returning to his former habitat, he retired briefly into an academic cocoon and then burst miraculously forth, a gorgeous literary and philosophic butterfly, sipping innumerable sweet and unscientific nectars and describing all sorts of wayward arabesques in the soft, balmy airs of speculation.

In short, Huxley expanded as Darwin contracted. The two processes were of coordinate importance to evolution and science, but expansion was inevitably the more spectacular. Through his friendships, his lectures popular and academic, his writing in the newspapers and the reviews, Huxley became a figure upon every intellectual battlefield in Europe and the living embodiment of science militant.

Meetings, lectures, committees, conferences, public and scientific business of all kinds kept him in railroad trains and hotels so much through these years that he was hardly more than a visitor in his own home. He was continually returning to relate his adventures and to be astonished at new progress in his children. At long or close range he was always with immense gusto in the midst of their lives. "Catch me discussing the Afghan question with you you little pepper pot," he wrote his daughter Jessie, and then argued with her at great length in his most aggressive manner.

"Children work a greater metamorphosis in men than any other condition of life,"[1] he told Haeckel. "They ripen one wonderfully and make life ten times better worth having than it was."[2] He was constantly advising his bachelor friends to get married.

Against his own deeper melancholy and solitude, Huxley found in marriage a lifelong stay and strength. "Love opened up to me," he told Kingsley in the famous letter, "a view of the sanctity of human nature, and impressed me with a deep sense of responsibility."[3] Clearly, he experienced romantic love in all its Victorian moral earnestness, but with good practical reason. From his biography one learns little of his wife directly, except that she disliked dinner parties, wrote thoughtful notes to bachelors, and pressed copies of Tennyson's poems on everybody. ("You are subjecting poor Darwin to a savage Tennyson persecution," her husband warned her.⁴) Nevertheless, reading between the lines, one can see that in spite of children and household cares she could face any problem or confidence he might lay before her. She was eagerly interested in everything that concerned him. "I know you will be dying to know how my lecture went off to-day," he wrote her in 1875, "so I sit down to send you a line, though you did hear from me to-day."⁵ She was his better conscience in all difficult moral questions. Should he accept money for a lecture to be given at the opening of the Johns Hopkins University? They decided—no. He submitted everything he wrote to her criticism. One gets interesting glimpses of her in this role.

I met Grove who edits *Macmillan* . . . [he wrote her in 1868]. He pulled the proof of my lecture out of his pocket and said, "Look here, there is one paragraph in your lecture I can make neither top nor tail of." . . . I looked to where his finger pointed, and behold it was the paragraph you objected to when I read you the lecture on the sea shore! I told him, and said I should confess, however set up it might make you.⁶

Realizing that "Hal" habitually overworked himself, Henrietta was always conspiring to send him off on vacations, and when in the eighties his health grew bad, she actually succeeded in getting him to obey his doctor. Sir Andrew Clark had ordered him to spend four months in the South, he wrote in 1884 to his assistant Foster. "This is the devil to pay, but I cannot honestly say that I think he is wrong. Moreover, I promised my wife to abide by his decision."⁷ One strongly suspects that it was she who finally persuaded him to retire. A letter of 1884 on the subject bears all the marks of protracted argument. He pleads that he owes it to his immediate chief and the School to remain active as long as possible:

If I did not do all that I can to requite Donnelly for the plucky way in which he has stood by it and me for the last dozen years,

I should never shake off the feeling that I had behaved badly. And as I am much given to brooding over my misdeeds, I don't want you to increase the number of my hell-hounds. You must help me in this . . . and if I am Quixotic, play Sancho for the nonce.[8]

Sancho, no doubt, had been her permanent role.

But in the sixties the world and his duties were always too small for Huxley, and everything he did seemed to bring further power and influence. Finding that too many affairs and responsibilities sealed him off from his most intimate friends, he suggested to Hooker that, in order to meet regularly—as well as to plot further affairs and responsibilities—they gather their circle together into a club. Hooker eagerly agreed and on November 3, 1864, the club convened for dinner at St. George's Hotel, Albemarle Street, which became accordingly the convivial Olympus of contemporary science until the later eighties, when the dinners were shifted to the Athenaeum. Embarrassed by a superfluity of possible names, the club remained anonymous so long that, at the suggestion of Mrs. Busk, the wife of a member, it was called the X. The name soon developed the somewhat sinister emphasis of an incognito. One day in the smoking room of the Athenaeum, Huxley was astonished to hear, from two scientific colleagues, the following conversation, which he gravely ignored: "I say, A., do you know about the X Club?" "Oh yes, B., I have heard of it. What do they do?" "Well, they govern scientific affairs, and really, on the whole, they don't do it badly."

The membership—Busk, Frankland, Hirst, Lubbock, Spottiswood, Tyndall, Spencer, Hooker, and Huxley—was a very choice and exclusive constellation of the brightest scientific stars. With the exception of Spencer, all were presidents and secretaries of societies, and Royal, Copley, or Rumford Medalists—the sort of men who could not dine, however lightheart-edly, without arriving at serious decisions. They discussed, often in a systematic manner, the politics of the learned socie-ties, projects of new museums and journals, the periodical warfare with religion and the classics, the place of science in contemporary education. Moreover, they were not just nine eminent men. They knew, among them, almost every famous scientist in the world, as well as many distinguished radicals and sympathizers with science. Darwin, Helmholtz, Asa Gray, Agassiz, Youmans, John Morley, Robert Lowe, Bishop Co-lenso, and many more were at one time or another guests at their dinners. The members themselves represented so many sciences with so much distinction that Huxley boasted they could, among them, have contributed most of the articles to a scientific encyclopedia. For British science they were, in fact, a kind of fluid cabinet united by the reliable intimacy of an eating friendship.

The X was a godsend for Herbert Spencer. He delighted in their erudite conviviality—the more so as he was constantly on the lookout for new ways of getting information. In later years he was so little capable of the docile passivity necessary for getting through a long book that he could not hear more than a paragraph read aloud without launching on a disquisi-tion of supplement or rebuttal. No modern thinker has read so little in order to write so much. He prepared himself for his *Psychology* chiefly by perusing Mansel's *Prologomena Logicae*, and for his *Biology* by going through Carpenter's *Principles of Comparative Physiology*. He produced a treatise on sociology without reading Comte, and a treatise on ethics without appar-ently reading anybody. Clubs provided Spencer with an excel-lent substitute for reading. He pumped the authors themselves. Strolling about midday through Kensington Gardens to the Athenaeum, he lunched with one notability, buttonholed a second, played billiards with a third, rifled the periodicals in the library for facts—and was thoroughly crammed for the next morning's composition.

Spencer was now as deep in his own physiology as in the metaphysics of the universe outside. He had discovered that his "head sensations," with their attendant ramifications, were due to an impaired circulation of the blood to the brain. When he began in 1860 to construct his philosophical system, therefore, he hired an amanuensis and retired with him to a Highland loch. Here he rowed for fifteen minutes to make the blood flow freely to the brain and then dictated in polished and fluent polysyllables, for another fifteen minutes, on Simple and Compound Evolution and the Instability of the Homogeneous. Some of the most abtruse chapters of the *Psychology* were dictated in a similar manner during the intervals of a tennis game near London. His rational life had not become less eccentic with the passing of years.

Obviously, the dinners of the X, boisterous with high spirits and bristling with facts, must have been for Spencer a little like mastering the encyclopedia by eating it. When he received the algebraic equation that announced a dinner, he disregarded "head sensations" and "cardiac enfeeblement" in a most reckless manner, and attended.[9]

Perhaps no man has been, intellectually, so provincial on so large a scale. Building a very big, modern universe which was somewhat inconsistent within itself but perfectly consistent with his own early predispositions, Spencer found cosmic reasons for being a utilitarian, liberal, naturalist, evolutionist, materialist, and agnostic.

What he had in common with Huxley were agnosticism and a somewhat ambiguous materialism built on evolution, the nebular hypothesis, and the law of the conservation of energy. Which man influenced the other is by no means clear. After

1852 they were in constant and intimate contact, and through the later fifties they walked together every Sunday afternoon. Spencer frequently acknowledged his debt to Huxley for facts and expert criticism. Huxley expressed on several occasions a rather vague and courteous admiration of Spencer's ideas: Spencer bade fair to become a modern Bacon;[10] he was as sound in his classification of the sciences as Comte was unsound.[11]

Spencer gave expression to his materialism in a series of works beginning in 1853, Huxley, to his, in a series beginning in 1863. Perhaps he exerted some influence on Huxley, but certainly not so much as the scientists themselves, and particularly Darwin and Helmholtz. Huxley had the scientist's suspicion of philosophers. He seldom expressed anything like hearty enthusiasm for Spencer's largely verbal syntheses, and in documenting his own ideas, adhered closely to the data of science.

Huxley seems, unlike Darwin, to have read the newspapers seated bolt upright in his laboratory, with his microscope on one side and his dissecting knives on the other. He allowed himself no prejudices, no sentimentalities, no illusions. He sometimes faced facts so courageously that they bent over backwards. Moreover, he spoke out on almost every conceivable subject—from the emancipation of women to the vivisection of dogs—in the firm belief that scientific method could clarify morals and politics as triumphantly as it was revolutionizing industry and sanitation. Inevitably, he spoke with a noticeable air of authority, of special grace and illumination.

He was divided on the American Civil War, as he wrote his sister Elizabeth, who had a fifteen-year old son in the Confederate Army: "My heart goes with the South, and my head

with the North." He had "not the smallest sentimental sympathy with the negro." Nevertheless, slavery meant bad economics, bad politics, and bad morality. It must go, no matter
which side won.[12]

Much the same views he expressed in "Emancipation—Black
and White," which he published at the end of the war in *The
Reader*. This is a curiously concentrated bit of writing, full of
the sharp, geometric clarity of truth and error. A bare page dis-
poses of black emancipation. The rest of the essay deals with
white—in other words, with the woman question, which was
then just beginning to be aired and was drawing so much sentimentality from poets, melodrama from playwrights, and nonsense from philosophers. The passionately affectionate father of
many daughters, Huxley faces female inferiority as bluntly as
he faces Negro. History proves that woman is less intelligent,
less responsible, less artistic, less passionate, and less beautiful
than man: in short, she is simply man minus. Clearly Huxley
does not approve of "the new woman-worship."[13] But at least
he does not, like Tennyson, endow woman with every sentimental perfection in order to lock her up in the purdah of the
domestic hearth, nor like Mill, make her a giantess of the intellect simply to qualify her for the vote and for competition with
men. Let her compete, by all means, urges Huxley; educate
her, give her every opportunity. " 'Golden hair' will not curl
less gracefully . . . by reason of there being brains within."[14]
Woman may thus grow stronger and more intelligent, and she
will then rear stronger and more intelligent men. In any case,
she will never surpass the male.

Actually, Huxley seems to have been even a little less liberal
than his essay indicates. Five years before, in a letter to Lyell,
he had declared that female education was essential to progress,
but apparently he felt that such education need not extend
much beyond childhood. In any case, he seemed rather com-

fortably convinced that his advanced ideas would never be generally followed.

I have fully made up my mind to give my daughters the same training in physical science that their brother will get, so long as he is a boy. . . . But you know as well as I do that other people won't do the like, and five-sixths of women will stop in the doll stage of evolution; to be the strongholds of parsondom, the drag on civilizations, the degradation of every important pursuit with which they mix themselves—"intriguers" in politics and "friponnes" in science.[15]

In 1872 Miss Jex Blake, a medical student at Edinburgh, confronted him with the woman problem in the concrete—and Huxley responded with what seems a decidedly Victorian compromise. The demonstrator at the Surgeons' Hall had been conducting a separate anatomy class for women, but now the University Court refused him recognition, explaining that they had no evidence of his qualifications. At the same time, they refused to examine him. Through Miss Blake the women students therefore begged that Professor Huxley examine their teacher. Huxley replied that he fully sympathized with young women who aspired to qualify themselves for medical practice. Nevertheless, he added, "I as completely sympathize with those Professors of Anatomy, Physiology, and Obstetrics who object to teach such subjects to mixed classes of young men and women brought together without any further evidence of moral and mental fitness for such association than the payment of their fees."[16] Giving ill-health and inadequate laboratory facilities as his reasons, he declined to examine the former demonstrator.

In 1865 Governor Eyre put down a Negro uprising in Jamaica with great violence. He invoked martial law, allowed the troops a pretty free hand with the civil population, and hanged a Negro Baptist minister named Gordon. Though slavery in the Empire had long since been abolished, these events had a classic generality and took hold of the British mind at many points. Liberals, humanitarians, and noncomformists felt that justice and law were in danger. Tories, Anglicans, and hero-worshippers felt the British power and prestige were in danger. Mill headed a committee of all the talents for one party; Carlyle, a committee of all the talents for the other. Eminent Englishmen fell upon each other with an altogether Jamaican savagery. The mild and humanitarian Mill started proceedings to indict Eyre for murder. Goldwyn Smith called Ruskin "a sentimental eunuch," and Carlyle pitied poor Mill with a withering benevolence, while the father of Herbert Spencer, dying of an overdose of laudanum, spent his last moments dreaming furiously of the whole affair. It was the Dreyfus case of the British Empire.

Among the scientists, Tyndall followed his hero Carlyle, while Darwin, Lyell, and Huxley gave their support to Mill. Darwin contributed ten pounds to the Jamaica Committee, half apologized for his fanaticism to lukewarm friends, and maintained a decorous newspaper silence.

As soon as Huxley put his name down for the Jamaica Committee, controversy sought him out. The Pall Mall Gazette observed that, having defended the spirituality of gorillas, he could hardly do less for the political virtue of Negroes. Resenting nothing so much as an accusation of sentimentality, he at once fired off a reply, duly published in the Pall Mall. Carlyle himself could not view the insignificance of the Negro with harder, more illusionless clarity. The question was not whether Gordon was "a Jamaica Hampden" or a "psalm-singing firebrand" or Eyre, an Odin or a Loki. Grant that Gordon was bad and Eyre was good, still "English law does not permit good persons, as such, to strangle bad persons, as such."[17] The letter concludes with sarcastic logic burning lambently beneath a thick ice of formal understatement.

The Jamaica affair very nearly caused a break between Huxley and Tyndall. "I am afraid that, if things had been pushed to an extremity over that unfortunate business," wrote Huxley after Tyndall's death, "each of us would have been capable of sending the other to the block. But the sentence would have been accompanied by assurances of undiminished respect and affection."[18] In the heat of battle he wrote, in a spirit little compatible with permanent bitterness, "If you and I are strong enough and wise enough, we shall be able to . . . [differ], and yet preserve that love for one another which I value as one of the good things of my life."[19] Tyndall was not the man to resist such an appeal.

Though they included the flower of English literary genius, neither the supporters nor the opponents of Eyre were capable of the artistic villainies which gave the Dreyfus case its brilliant reversal and climax. The agitation continued prosaically for a few years and then died away. Eyre was recalled but never tried.

This controversy appears to mark the time when Huxley ceased to take Carlyle seriously as a thinker. Ironically, Huxley faced the facts of human misery and human limitation with such desperate bravery that he tended, in some respects, to be as conservative as Carlyle himself. But as the stupidities of Gladstone and the liberals were later to make him very nearly a Tory, so now the stupidities of Carlyle and the conservatives kept him a liberal. He thought Carlyle lacked logic and good sense, as Carlyle probably thought he lacked soul and constructive power. Carlyle regarded society as an organism ruled by passion, instinct, and imagination, which expressed itself in various kinds of poetry and hero worship. Huxley regarded society as a body of individuals united by history, and ruled by reason and expediency, which are ideally embodied in science. Huxley's ultimate was truth. Carlyle's was rapidly becoming force and the fait accompli. He could never forgive Huxley *Man's Place in Nature*, yet by sudden, appalling Dr.-Jekyll-and-Mr.-Hyde transformations, his hero was coming to look more and more like Huxley's gorilla. Carlyle seemed simply to be traveling to the neo-Darwinian destination by a more romantic and picturesque route.

In his memorial essay on Tyndall, Huxley said that he regarded Carlyle not as a teacher but as "a great tonic."[20] In fact, Carlye had become a kind of solemn moral music which inspired him to feel religiously on atheistical subjects.*

No doubt Carlyle did not like his own qualities in Huxley, for Huxley also was a desperado of the intellectual life who went about always watchful and alert, with verbal pistols and cutlasses in his belt. Even the glances, coughs, and sneezes of such a man can become terrible. When, in W. H. Mallock's satirical *New Republic*, Dr. Jenkinson-Jowett reads the Athanasian Creed at Sunday morning service, Mr. Storks-Huxley creates consternation simply by blowing his nose. On another occasion,

---

* In 1866, while the Jamaica agitation was still going on, Huxley witnessed Carlyle's greatest personal triumph—his inauguration as Rector of Edinburgh University.

Early one morning, Tyndall called for his hard-bitten, sour-stomached hero of rhetoric in Chelsea, and having seen him drink his brown brandy and soda and embrace for the last time in this world his aged spouse, took him off on the journey northward. At Freystone, where Tyndall cured his friend's insomnia with a five hours' gallop through muddy fields, they were met by Huxley, and the three traveled on together. At Edinburgh Carlyle spread consternation among Scots by not writing out his address. The Rector's address had always been written out. Tyndall feared the frail old man might fail to sleep the night before the inauguration and wake up pallid and dumb. Back in London, Mrs. Carlyle feared that on seeing the great sea of faces he might fall down dead with excitement. On the crucial day, Huxley, Tyndall, and others were solemnly doctored, and then, nervously clasping the speaker's table and looking down earnestly at his audience, Carlyle began: "They tell me that I ought to have written

Mr. Storks turned sharply round, and, with an awful look in his eyes of contemptuous indignation, stared Mr. Saunders into silence. He held him fixed in this way for a few moments, and then said to him in a voice of grim unconcern, 'May I trouble you for the mustard.'[23]

Carlyle liked sweet, gentle men, like John Sterling.

When, some years later, Huxley saw the old man, near the end of his life, walking slowly and alone down the opposite side of the street, he crossed over and spoke. Carlyle looked at him, and observing, "You're Huxley, aren't you? the man that says we are all descended from monkeys," went on his way.[24]

History, on one extraordinary business or another, was always on Huxley's doorstep, furiously ringing the bell. Being a busy man, he sometimes slammed the door in her face. That was what he did when spiritualism importuned. How could one speak with authority about ghosts if one could not dissect them? Besides, the decerebrated frog was much more interesting:

If anybody would endow me with the faculty of listening to the chatter of old women and curates in the nearest cathedral town, I should decline the privilege, having better things to do. And if

---

this address, and out of deference to the counsel I tried to do so, once, twice, thrice. But what I wrote was only fit for the fire, and to the fire it was compendiously committed. You must therefore listen to and accept what I say to you as coming straight from the heart."[21] He then held his audience spellbound for an hour and a half, speaking with great power and fluency on his favorite themes.

There followed such a round of dinners and festivities as only the countrymen of Burns could provide. Mill's *Examination of the Philosophy of Sir William Hamilton* had just appeared, and Lord Neaves had, with happy inappropriateness, turned this unlikely material into a kind of drinking song. Tyndall remembered that Carlyle, wielding his knife as a baton, had led the refrain, which ran "Stuart Mill on Mind and Matter."[22]

About all this—so full of echoes out of his early intellectual life, so crowded with colorful personalities and memorable incidents—Huxley is completely silent. Great occasions found him a brilliant actor but a poor spectator.

the folk in the spiritual world do not talk more wisely and sensibly than their friends report them to do, I put them in the same category. The only good that I can see in the demonstration of the truth of "Spiritualism" is to furnish an additional argument against suicide. Better live a crossing-sweeper than die and be made to talk twaddle by a "medium" hired at a guinea a séance.[25]

But ultimately the opportunity to discover trickery drew him. One day in January, 1874, he received a request which he looked on as very nearly a command.

We had such grand fun, one afternoon [wrote Darwin from Erasmus's house in London], for George hired a medium, who made the chairs, a flute, a bell, and candlestick, and fiery points jump about in my brother's diningroom, in a manner that astounded every one, and took away all their breaths. It was in the dark, but George and Hensleigh Wedgwood held the medium's hands and feet on both sides all the time.[26]

Somewhat anticlimactically, Charles added that as the whole performance was very hot and tiring, he had retired before the miracles occurred. The company had been large, including Lewes and George Eliot, as well as Francis Galton. Lewes had been troublesome, making jokes and refusing to sit quietly in the dark. Though astounded by the whole proceeding, Charles was sure that spiritualism was all rubbish, and believed that the medium had freed himself by getting George and Hensleigh to join hands. But George and Francis Galton were curious and baffled. There must be another séance and Huxley must come to detect the imposture. Huxley came and saw and detected. Of course Darwin had once more absented himself, but his friend wrote him a full report:

My conclusion [he summed up] is that Mr. X is a cheat and an impostor, and I have no more doubt that he got Mr. Y to sit on his right hand, knowing from the turn of his conversation that it would be easy to distract his attention, and that he then moved the chair against Mr. Y with his leg, and finally coolly lifted [it] on to the table, than that I am writing these lines.[27]

Darwin declared that he felt vindicated before his whole family.

A few months later the two men joined forces against a more threatening folly. By 1875 the bitter agitation against vivisection had reached a climax. To acquire knowledge had long been felt by many Englishmen to be a somewhat reprehensible and unhealthy activity, but to acquire knowledge by dissecting live animals was a perversion of the heart as well as the mind. People lost their tempers and then looked around for good reasons for having done so. They found that very good reasons could be manufactured by slightly misquoting Huxley. A letter in The Record charged him with advocating that vivisection be conducted before children, if not by them, and cited passages from his Elementary Physiology, which, understood as referring to the subject discussed, made a very sinister impression. Thoroughly taken in, the Earl of Shaftesbury reiterated the accusation in a speech. Huxley fired off a letter to The Times straightening out the passages and accusing the Earl of ignorance and misrepresentation. Lord Shaftesbury, after expressing some astonishment that the vigorous language of the Physiology could have a meaning so little bloodthirsty, accepted Huxley's word in such simple good faith that the controversy was ended with an amicable exchange of private letters.

The result of this and other incidents was that Huxley found himself once more seated across the table from his theological enemies on a Royal Commission—appointed in this instance to report on vivisection. Though himself prevented by personal feeling from performing experiments on the higher animals, he felt obliged to assert the right of others to do so if for a worthy object and without inflicting unnecessary pain. He did not see why people should be allowed to eat meat and slaughter vermin, boys to use live bait, and ducks to swallow frogs whole and slowly crush them in their stomachs when scientists were forbidden to perform carefully limited dissections on anesthetized animals for the sake of increasing knowledge and saving lives.

In spite of the hideous gnashing of philanthropic teeth, Huxley was optimistic, though he relied more on the fox-hunting instincts of the Commons than on their respect for science to save England from sentimental obscurantism. For a time all went well. He began by collecting testimony from eminent scientists. And here Darwin was unexpectedly active and helpful. At once a famous biologist and a repentant snipe-shooter, he was passionately engaged on both sides of the question. If anything, he was more acutely sensitive than Huxley to human and animal suffering. The shrieks of tortured slaves in Brazil haunted his memory, particularly at night, even into old age. The sight of a horse ill-treated brought him back from a walk pale and shaken, and indeed coachmen hardly dared urge their horses to a moderate speed in the vicinity of Down for fear of "being abused" by Mr. Darwin.[28] Nevertheless, he was convinced that physiology can progress only by "experiments on living animals."[29] At Huxley's urging, he made pronouncements and signed testimonials, rising with un-Darwinian rashness to the epistolary heroism of a letter to The Times. In fact, even before the Royal Commission was appointed, he had been consulting with scientists in London and had helped his son-in-law Litchfield draw up a vivisection bill very similar to one partially approved by Huxley and brought before the House, unhappily without result, by Lyon Playfair.

Having gathered all possible testimony from the upper empyrean of Victorian science and then donned his robes of pontifical authority, Huxley began the work of illuminating, conciliating, and overawing his colleagues on the Royal Commission. It seemed as though even the tenderest philanthropic heart and the thickest philanthropic head could not hold out against him. But one day when he was absent at a Council meeting of the Royal Society, the Commission, apparently quite by accident, questioned a very benighted vivisectionist. "I am told," Huxley wrote Darwin, "that he openly professed the most entire indifference to animal suffering, and said he only gave anaesthetics to keep animals quiet."[30] Huxley himself was as shocked as any member of the Commission. "I declare to you I did not believe the man lived who was such an unmitigated cynical brute as to profess and act upon such principles, and I would willingly agree to any law which would send him to the treadmill."

Huxley still made heroic efforts. He even achieved a *deus ex machina*. Darwin would testify in person! "We expect you at 13 Delehay Street at two 'oclock to-morrow," wrote Huxley. "I have looked out the highest chair that was to be got for you."[31] But the course of mercy was not to be arrested. Deeply divided, the Commission reported cautiously and indecisively in 1876, and a few months later, somewhat to the astonishment of the Commission, Lord Carnarvon introduced a drastic anti-vivisection bill, which was duly carried.

Inevitably, so many and such varied activities left Huxley less time for scientific work, yet from 1864 to 1870 he published thirty-nine papers, of which three at least were extremely important—and particularly that which traced the development of birds from reptiles. Reptiles and birds had commonly been regarded as opposites. Reptiles crawled; they were heavy and cold-blooded. Birds flew; they were light and warm-blooded. Fresh from his studies of evolution and of man, Huxley was quite ready to accept paradoxes between ultimate origin and present adaptation. In 1864 he showed that many extinct reptiles had bird characteristics and many extinct birds, reptilian characteristics.³² He therefore proposed a threefold division of the vertebrates: (1) mammals, (2) sauroids (birds and reptiles), and (3) ichthyoids (fish and amphibia). The relationship between birds and reptiles has been universally acknowledged. In 1867 Huxley revolutionized the classification of birds themselves, finding salient differences not in webbed feet or aquatic habits, but particularly in certain small, seemingly insignificant bones of the palate. Animals are historical skeletons masquerading in the flesh and epidermis of changing adaptation.³³

15

The Metaphysical Society

As he now gradually turned from controversies arising out of the *Origin* to those involving the whole destiny of science in modern culture, Huxley inevitably became less of a scientist, more of a debater, a propagandist, and a statesman. In this period he developed his characteristic philosophy—one might almost call it his definitive plan of campaign. He also arrived at maturity as a prose and a platform artist.

The 1868 meeting of the British Association at Norwich was a great triumph for Hooker, who was president, a greater triumph for Huxley, who gave a lecture, and the greatest triumph of all for Darwin, who stayed at home and experimented with plants.

Huxley's lecture, the famous "On a Piece of Chalk," was addressed to the workingmen of Norwich as well as to the members of the Association. Once more Huxley discovers infinite riches in a little room. As Cuvier derived a whole *Megatherium* from a single bone, so from a piece of chalk Huxley brings forth not only half a continent and a whole sea bottom, but long vistas of evolution, geological and biological, and even a brief sermon against Moses, which leaves Darwin as the only alternative. "Either each species of crocodile has been specially created," says Huxley, "or it has arisen out of some pre-existing form by the operation of natural causes. Choose your hypothesis; I have chosen mine."[1]

"A Piece of Chalk" was a sample lesson, an illustration of what elementary scientific education should be. Another illustration, equally simple and eloquent in expression but much more complex in idea, was "The Physical Basis of Life," which Huxley delivered about the same time in the "holy city" of Edinburgh.

"The Physical Basis of Life" might be described as the philosophy of Hume expressed in the language of Macaulay, but it is also Huxley in a nutshell. His agnosticism, his materialism, some of his deepest contradictions and confessions, the ironic paradox of his later development—all are explicit or implicit in the apparently untroubled clarity of this brief essay. Even to the most liberal of Victorian Christians, it must have seemed very bold, a desperate attempt to cure superstition by administering one deadly spiritual poison and then counteracting it by another. To modern readers, it begins innocently enough with a fresh lesson—based on the contemporary researches of Max Schultze and others—in elementary science.

Appearing before a large audience with a bottle of smelling salts and other familiar, commonplace articles, Huxley declared that he had before him the essential ingredients of protoplasm —the physical basis of life. All life, from the amoeba up to man, is composed of this single substance, which uniformly exhibits the same properties and the same functions. Plants are distinguished from animals by the ability to generate organic matter from inorganic, but as there is no sharp distinction between simple plants and animals, so there is no distinction between simple protoplasm and nonliving matter except in a certain arrangement of molecules. In fact, mind itself is but "the result of molecular forces" in "the protoplasm which displays it."[2] Man is therefore, as Houston Peterson observes, brother not only to the monkey, but to the amoeba, even to the molecule and the atom.[3] Intellectual progress consists in the gradual victory of matter and causation over spirit and spontaneity. Unfortunately, religious leaders persist in regarding this glorious vision as a terrifying nightmare. "The advancing tide of matter threatens to drown their souls; the tightening grasp of law impedes their freedom; they are alarmed lest man's moral nature be debased by the increase of his wisdom."[4]

Having frozen his auditors with a terrible certainty, he now sought to revive them with an equally terrible skepticism. Following Hume, he asked what was matter but "the name for the unknown and hypothetical cause of states of our own consciousness?"[5] What was law but an observed uniformity, a mere *will* without any *must* of necessity? In a world full of evil and uncertainty we need only to believe that the order of nature is ascertainable to an unlimited extent, and that our volition—or as he emended in 1892, "the physical state of which volition is the expression"—"counts for something" in the course of events.[6]

No doubt Huxley sounded as though he were demonstrating a theorem in geometry. Actually, he was simply pointing up an old dilemma in metaphysics. If man is brother to the molecule, then presumably his will is subject to the mechanism— then thought to be very close knit—of molecular law. But if his will "counts for something," then he must only in a restricted sense be brother of the molecule. Huxley's position must be sought in his emphasis. He argues at length to show how mind is involved in the mechanism of matter, but offers only a few vague suggestions to indicate how it might in any sense be free.

Hume's skepticism was the fluid of uncertainty in which Huxley cushioned the shock of logical contraries. When pommeling religion, he emphasized the achievements of science and the omnipotence of matter and law. When intent on rescuing ethical responsibility from the consequences of his own offensive tactics, he declared, with equal gusto, that matter was an unknown and law a mere probability. In "The Physical Basis of Life" Huxley seems to enjoy all the pedagogical strength of dogmatism and all the polemical security of skepticism.

Having delivered this composition as a lecture, Huxley submitted it to the youthful John Morley, who in 1867 had taken over the languishing *Fortnightly Review* from G. H. Lewes. Morley published the essay with delight—and compared the sensation produced with that created by Swift's *Conduct of the Allies* and Burke's *French Revolution*.*

Nowadays man is awed not so much by the universe as by man's power to blow it up. But in the nineteenth century truth was neither a super-explosive, nor an angry newspaper statement, nor an edict of state, nor an objective of the thought police, nor even—in its most remembered form—a mathematical formula. It was not only abstract but human; not so much made as discovered. To be sure, it was sometimes more like a skeleton in the closet than a treasure in the earth, and in the human and religious sense, it had already been rent so desperately asunder by intellectual conflict that men like Carlyle seemed to think of it as a kind of poetic rubber which

---

* In "The Physical Basis" Huxley had declared that Comteism was "Catholicism *minus* Christianity" (*Methods and Results*, p. 156). This epigram brought a passionate reply from the leader of the English Comteists, Dr. Congreve, who, unable to associate hostility with anything but ignorance, accused Huxley of refuting the master without having read him. No charge could have been more dangerous. In "The Scientific Aspects of Positivism," duly published in *The Fortnightly* & later in *Lay Sermons, Addresses, and Reviews* (New York: D. Appleton & Company, Inc., 1870), pp. 147–173, Huxley made it clear that he had not only been familiar with Comte for some sixteen years but had read him with much greater care than had Dr. Congreve himself. Huxley sees no

could be stretched between any number of logical contraries. But at least it could be poetic; at least it was something people felt they should live by. And if the search was sometimes harrowing and terrible, it could also be joyous and spontaneous, even gay and convivial. One found truth while eating dinner or while smoking with friends by the fireside. Particularly, one found it in the "ingenious collision of divergent points of view."[7] If only an argument was big enough and lasted long enough, a considerable body of correct opinion was bound to emerge.

Consequently, debating societies were as common in Victorian life as psychiatrists and boosters' clubs are in our own. Every conceivable question was debated, but particularly the great question of religion vs. science. Since the publication of the *Origin*, the argument had been going strongly in favor of science, and Huxley's "Physical Basis of Life," which had carried *The Fortnightly* into a seventh edition, left the religious mind prostrate and quivering with horror. Something had to be done. In consultation with his friend Alfred Tennyson, James Knowles, famous as the editor of *The Nineteenth Century*, conceived the idea of bringing together in one society all the most distinguished men of the age genuinely concerned with religion. Dean Stanley demurred. The other side must be represented also. It was an appalling suggestion—a little like inviting the Devil to a debate on morality—but it was also in

reason to retract his epigram. He sets the father of positivism once more firmly down in the chair of St. Peter and then excommunicates him from the church of science. Comte shows too slight a grasp both of logic and of science to be a worthy representative of that reformed and purified community of reason. Neither his classification of the sciences nor his famous law of the three stages is consistent with the facts or with itself. What Huxley was here attempting to stamp out was the spirit of authority. He did so with a suspiciously pontifical air. "Pope Huxley," *The Spectator* dared to call him a little later, after a similar exhibition (January 29, 1870), pp. 135–136.

the most grandiose spirit of Victorian liberalism. A kind of Great Exposition of the contemporary mind would be held for the benefit of the contemporary mind. A whole culture—represented by those who had excelled in the highest competitions of the intellectual and spiritual life—would argue, illuminate, and persuade itself into greater truth and unity.

The Metaphysical Society was founded in 1869. Its membership of forty names reads like a muster roll of Victorian celebrity. Gladstone, Tennyson, Manning, Ward, Ruskin, Bagehot, Hutton, Lubbock, Tyndall, and Huxley were only among the most famous. Of those invited, only three refused—Newman, because he disapproved of religious argument with free thinkers; Spencer, because he feared overexcitement and head sensations; and Mill (who in "Liberty" had given the doctrine of discussion its classical formulation), because he feared the discussion would prove unprofitable: Socratic conversation among the few would accomplish far more than set lectures and general debate among the many. To be sure, eminent public men do not like to seek truth Socratically in private. The Metaphysicians were held together, partly at least, by the gravitational force of the sheer mass of their combined and diversified fame. A political statesman like Gladstone and an ecclesiastical statesman like Manning actually found time to attend these meetings. The Society lasted eleven years.

Respectable clergymen like the Bishop of Peterborough were probably a little apprehensive about being seen to descend at a common destination with such princes of darkness as Manning and such demons of illumination as Huxley and Tyndall. And the name—Metaphysical Society! One of the less notorious members was relieved when a hotel porter greeted him with, "A member of the *Madrigal* Society, sir, I suppose?"[8]

The first regular meeting was solemnly opened by James Knowles, who read Tennyson's recently completed poem, "The Higher Pantheism."

> The sun, the moon, the stars, the seas, the
>   hills and the plains,—
> Are not these, O Soul, the Vision of Him
>   who reigns?

asked Tennyson; and later he added, perhaps to indicate that
he had read "The Physical Basis of Life":

> Law is God, say some; no God at all,
>   says the fool,
> For all we have power to see is a straight
>   staff bent in a pool.

It was a somewhat tritely poetic statement of the intelligent,
well-informed half-belief which had characterized *In Memoriam*. Philosophical poems are not easily grasped on a first
hearing—especially after dinner. Some say "The Higher Pantheism" was received in silence. Others remembered that
Tyndall remarked with sacrilegious calm, "I suppose this is not
offered as a subject for discussion."[9] Having very appropriately
communicated with the Argonauts through his Mercury, Mr.
Knowles, Tennyson now subsided into the magnificent and
ornamental silence for which he had so much talent. On one
occasion, however, he did dumfound the undumfoundable
Huxley by asking if the sap rising in a plant did not suspend
the law of gravitation. Huxley tried in vain to see the joke.

After the poem had been read, R. H. Hutton, editor of *The
Spectator*, gave a paper "On Mr. Herbert Spencer's Theory
of the Gradual Transformation of the Utilitarian into Intuitive
Morality by Hereditary Descent." In a letter to Mill, Spencer
had explained the moral intuitions as utilitarian precepts which
had evolved into habits and instincts. Hutton objected that
moral habits separated from their rational authority would better account for a degeneration of the moral sense than for its
mystical extension and development. He also argued that, his-
torically, utilitarian justification has followed rather than preceded an ethical concept. The attack was a strong one, intended

to stimulate Spencer and propel him into the Society. Vigorously stimulated, he completely lost his temper, but at long
range, hotly replying two years later in a periodical.

The angels of light and the angels of darkness did not meet
face to face without some ruffling of wing feathers. Apparently
Manning was astounded to find that atheists did not really
believe in God. "It was a pathetic spectacle," wrote E. S.
Purcell, "to note the ill-disguised amazement with which
Manning listened to the ruthless and cold-blooded denials of
what to him were self-evident and eternal truths."[10] When it
was suggested that moral disapprobation should be avoided in
debate, there was a pause, and then the Catholic W. G. Ward
said, "While acquiescing in this condition as a general rule, I
think it cannot be expected that Christian thinkers shall give
no sign of the horror with which they would view the spread
of such extreme opinions as those advocated by Mr. Huxley."
There was another pause, no doubt expertly measured to equal
Ward's, and then Huxley replied, "As Dr. Ward has spoken,
I must in fairness say that it will be very difficult for me to
conceal my feeling as to the intellectual degradation which
would come of the general acceptance of such views as Dr.
Ward holds."[11] For a moment the Society, desperate and
gasping, clutched the torn roots of propriety above the abyss—
then drew itself up to safety. It was clear that hand-to-hand
fighting, however deadly, would have to observe the amenities.
Courtesy was at first cold, then almost too cordial.

Consorting for the first time with living representatives of
the age-old theological and philosophic positions, Huxley faced
a novel but Huxleyan embarrassment. Everybody else was some
kind of *ist* or *ite*; he alone was nothing, a fox without a tail, "a
man without a rag of a label to cover himself with."[12] He
therefore invented the term *agnostic*, which speedily became
famous and served to clothe him and a great many others in a
mantle of high-minded and surprisingly respectable infidelity.

In the first paper Hutton had set the issue which the Society was to debate to the end of its history: can truth be arrived at by the spirit as well as the senses, by intuition as well as experience? Does it reside in mind as well as in matter? The physiologist Carpenter read the second paper, in which, following the tradition of Paley, he made God accessory to the crime of a mechanistic universe. In the third paper, Huxley, with the aid of Hume, Kant, and Whately, once more demolished the immortality of the soul. In the fourth, Ward attempted to strike at the heart of empiricism by proving that memory, on which all science depends, is an intuition which cannot prove its validity in present experience. These papers were all clever, but perhaps a little disappointing. Sparks were produced in plenty, but they were the same old sparks; and in spite of the powerful chemicals present, there was no considerable precipitate of truth.

Quite apart from the vital question of correct tone, the exchange between Ward and Huxley was prophetic. From the brilliant, disorganized Homeric warfare of the early debates, these two men stood out as the opposing champions. Tall, dark, and intense, Huxley looked rather like a talkative mystic; and Ward, jovial, round, and rosy, looked very much like an equally talkative country squire. Both were clear-headed and quick-tongued. More the dialectician, Ward tended toward the subtle and self-conscious, combining great openness of mind and readiness for logical adventure with lighthearted assurance in the certainty of Catholic truth and the paradoxical freshness of extreme conservatism rationally defended. Questioned about Catholic doctrine on a point of conduct, he replied, "There are two views, of which I, as usual, take the more bigoted."[13]

Henry Sidgwick emphasized "the feeling one had that he gave himself up to the λογός like an interlocutor in a Platonic dialogue and was prepared to follow it to any conclusions to which it might lead." On the other hand, Sidgwick regarded

Huxley as perhaps unsurpassed "in the quickness with which he could see and express with perfect clearness and precision the best answer that could be made, from his point of view, to any argument urged against him."[14] He also remembered Huxley "as the most combative of all the speakers who took a leading part, . . . though always strictly within the limits imposed by courtesy."[15]

These two men learned to fight each other with rare cordiality, building a gay and even intimate comradeship on ruthless hostility and complete disagreement. Huxley combined a sincere respect for Ward's dialectic with a profound conviction that he was wrong. He was "a philosophical and theological Don Quixote," but one who was often extremely damaging to agnostic windmills. "And it all seemed to come so easily to him; searching questions, incisive, not to say pungent replies, and trains of subtle argumentation, were poured forth . . . [with] an air of genial good-humour, as if the whole business were rather a good joke."[16]

Ward was equally pleased with his new enemy. When they had first got on an easy footing, he drew Huxley aside after the meeting and began very confidentially, "You and I are on such friendly terms that I do not think it is right to let you remain ignorant of something I wish to tell you." With secret fears of impending salvation, Huxley begged him to go on. "Well, we Catholics hold that so and so and so and so (naming certain of our colleagues who were of less deep hue than mine) are not guilty of unpardonable error; but your case is different, and I feel it is unfair not to tell you so." Immensely relieved, Huxley replied, with a hearty handshake, "My dear Dr. Ward, if you don't mind, I don't."[17]

Sometimes the fascinations of intimate combat proved irresistible. "I do not ever remember my father's breaking in upon his regular hours at night," wrote Wilfred Ward, "except on occasion of one talk with Huxley, when each reached home alternately some five or six times, ending in a final parting very near cock-crow."[18] Ward found that though controversy with Catholics made him ill, controversy with skeptics and atheists invigorated and restored him. He took to inviting Huxley and other metaphysical desperadoes to dinner. The first occasion immediately followed a period in which Ward's inexorable logic, despite all the protests of his overflowing good nature, had led him to inflict cruel punishment on his scientific friend. Huxley went immediately to a window and stared out at the garden. Ward asked him what he was doing. "I was looking in your garden for the *stake*, Dr. Ward, which I suppose you have got ready for us after dinner."[19]

Though such picturesque warfare could not but enliven other members, Mill's prediction came true. The Society was too large and too little interested in metaphysics. When attendance was good, the discussion fell into triviality and irrelevance. When attendance was poor, it became keen, Socratic, and genuinely—though briefly—fruitful. But if no minds were changed, at least many were stimulated. Even Gladstone, who according to Huxley did not know the meaning of the word *metaphysics*, was said to have become so much interested in unpolitical problems that he lectured the Liberal Whip, impatient for instructions on an impending division, at Gladstonian length on the immortality of the soul.

In "The Metaphysical Society: A Reminiscence," R. H. Hutton, who had a talent for both reverence and drama, has compressed the whole of metaphysical history into a single ideal meeting. Before they fought, the Metaphysicians dined. Looking about him at the table, Hutton notices Ward chuckling "over the floundering of the orthodox clergy" in their criticism of Stanley's latitudinarianism, Tyndall discoursing in his "eloquent Irish voice" and perhaps with some failure of discretion, "on the proposal for a 'prayer-gauge,'" and Huxley "flashing out" with a skeptical defense of Bible teaching in

the Board Schools.[20] Huxley "always had a definite standard
for every question which he regarded as discussible at all, yet
made you feel that his slender definite creed in no respect
represented the cravings of his large nature."[21]

As speaker, Ward asked how mere experience can prove the
uniformity of nature—and therefore the impossibility of miracles—without examining every exception. A somewhat hack-
neyed, yet clever discussion followed, eliciting from almost
every man his own ingenious cliché or prejudice. Huxley broke
off short in a very graphic sketch he had been making on his
sheet of foolscap to declare that scientists "were too busy in
their fruitful vocation" to investigate every asserted case of
miracle. Besides, miracle-hunting gave scientists a bad professional reputation. Ruskin observed that if a second Joshua
caused the sun to stand still, he would not be in the least
surprised. The wonder to him was that it moved at all. Bagehot
admitted that as a child he may have expected such wonders
as stationary suns, but "the disillusioning character" of his
experience no longer permitted him to do so. Then the lawyer
Fitzjames Stephen, "in the mighty bass that always exerted a
sort of physical authority over us," laid down the laws of evidence by which miracles should be judged. "Looking at Mr.
Stephen with a benign smile," Archbishop Manning assured
him that in canonizing the Holy See went into evidence as
critically as even he could wish. The Archbishop then touched
on the undoubted authenticity of the miracles at Lourdes.
"Speaking with a singularly perfect articulation," Dr. Martineau disagreed with almost everybody, but particularly with
Archbishop Manning, whose views on the uniformity of nature, like St. Thomas's, could hardly be justified by Scripture.

Did Manning's benignity, Martineau's perfect articulation,
Huxley's invisible surplice, or Fitzjames Stephen's authoritative, slightly bullying bass ever get on anybody's nerves? The
definite and didactic Martineau certainly irritated Sidgwick,

and Sidgwick irritated Leslie Stephen, who exclaimed of him after a meeting, "A man has no right to be so fair to his opponents."[22]

Gradually, the Society became self-critical: each man developed an acute perception of his neighbor's faults. In 1873 Manning gave "A Diagnosis and a Prescription." In his opinion the Metaphysicians suffered from the disease of chronic anarchy which stemmed from the Renaissance and Reformation. A confusion of philosophic tongues and concepts had produced a paralyzing confusion of thought. He recommended closer logic and sharper definition—above all, a correct method and terminology. In short, he prescribed the scholasticism of St. Thomas. Manning's diagnosis was accurate, but his cure was somewhat heroic. Everybody wanted to be logical, but few were willing to admit that logic and St. Thomas were one. To encourage a greater sharpness of definition, the Society appointed a committee, but it accomplished little beyond spreading a gloomy, inquisitorial atmosphere.

Pushed by the attacks of Ward and his own pugnacity, Huxley became, in the later years of the Society, steadily more sarcastic and destructive. He was heavily ironic even in his second paper, "Has the Frog a Soul?" (1871), in which, early in its long martyrdom to science, he crucified the unredemptive batrachian on paraffin in order once more to crucify the immortality of the soul on the hard facts of physiology. In his last, "The Evidence of the Miracle of the Resurrection" (1876), he attempted, "in the style of a great criminal court advocate," to destroy the central case for the supernatural in Christianity.[23] These papers were bare abstracts rather than polished lectures such as he delivered to scientists and workingmen. Plainly, he reserved himself for the discussion, in which he was unrivaled. The presence of the immortals drew out the logic-fencer in him rather than the prose artist.

In the late seventies the Society began to change character.

Bagehot died in 1877, Tennyson ceased to attend after 1878, Ward was kept away by ill-health. Most important of all, James Knowles, that cool, daring ringmaster of hoop-jumping genius, resigned the secretaryship in 1879. Into the vacuum left by such men as Ward flowed the mighty bass voice of Fitzjames Stephen. Quite as formidable as its vocal instrument, his massive common sense, with acute, annihilating obviousness, ruthlessly depreciated the intricate impalpables of both science and religion. He was profoundly convinced of man's iniquity and therefore reluctant to give up hell, but he was less enthusiastic about heaven. He not only denied Darwin but failed to see the necessity of inventing him. In the words of Leslie Stephen, "Darwin was to his mind an ingenious person spending immense labour upon the habits of worms, or in speculating upon what may have happened millions of years ago. What does it matter? Here we are—face to face with the same facts."[24] Stephen probably made the Society more uncomfortable for everybody, but particularly for those who did not quite know what they were talking about.

For this reason, as well as for many others, the Metaphysical Society was becoming less and less a Victorian Olympus and more and more a seminar of professional philosophers. Discriminating newcomers were not impressed. John Morley described it to his sister as "an illustrious little club" which first confused itself with a bad dinner and then made "confusion worse confounded by bad metaphysics."[25] One evening in November, 1880, Martineau, as chairman, held up the mirror. With an unprecedented unanimity, the Metaphysical Society quietly voted itself dead.

It died, declared Huxley afterwards, "of too much love."[26] But more combat, in itself, could hardly have produced more agreement. Knowles was probably the more sagacious coroner. In his opinion, death supervened when everything had been said too many times. After a decade of discussion, the Metaphysicians finally understood, not each other, but the completeness of their fundamental disagreement. They were too old and too famous to learn anything new, much less to find common ground between Christian theology and the requirements for scientific truth, between faith in God and faith in evolutionary process.

But now old issues were taking new shapes. While scientists were explaining how dogma produced superstition and hatred, science itself was producing a new dogmatism and a new hedonism. Moreover, while the older empiricists were using the test of experience to refine truth into a rather dry and austere question mark, newer empiricists were using the same test to make it a tropical forest of abundance, variety, and vividness. Agnosticism is the reverse, and pragmatism the face, of the same coin.[27] Both creeds are undogmatic; but for one the criterion of belief is scientific evidence; for the other it is psychological need. William James held that a belief is true if it makes life more vivid and productive. Pragmatism was an ironic conclusion to an age of debate on fundamentals, but it was an even more ironic beginning to an age of persecution for ideas.

The long debates with Ward and others did for a time put Huxley at least in a posture of compromise. He was invited in 1870, as a kind of inspirational Professor Beelzebub, to address the Cambridge Y.M.C.A. His lecture "On Descartes' Discourse" is in part an attempt to extend the evolutionary point of view to the field of ideas. The history of thought is best symbolized not by a single great chain or an endless dialectic but by the ramifying branches of a tree or plant. Descartes, more than any other thinker, represents the main stem of modern science and philosophy. He "consecrated Doubt" as the primary duty of the scientific conscience and himself set the example, attempting to get rid of all preconceived notions. He did not entirely succeed, but he did succeed in pointing the way toward the two great modern traditions of thought. His doctrine that the mind can know nothing outside itself led directly to the idealism of Berkeley and Kant. His doctrine that, to our knowledge, thought invariably derives from a human machine ultimately reducible to matter and motion led with equal directness to the materialism of Priestley and De la Mettrie. These two systems are complementary rather than antagonistic; "and thought will never be completely fruitful until the one unites with the other."[28]

Even so, Huxley believes "that we shall, sooner or later, arrive at a mechanical equivalent of consciousness."[29] He speaks in a parenthesis of the human machine "adjusting itself within certain limits," but he follows immediately with the sentence, "I protest that if some great Power would agree to make me always think what is true and do what is right, on condition of being turned into a sort of clock and wound up every morning before I got out of bed, I should instantly close with the offer."[30] On the whole, the earnest Christians of the Cambridge Y.M.C.A. would have done well to fear Professor Beelzebub. His great evangelical earnestness made his horns and barbed tail seem the most superficial disguise, and he wore them in the sincere conviction that they were much less dangerous than a halo and a harp.

Much larger audiences than the Cambridge Y.M.C.A. were eager to hear Professor Huxley. In 1870 he gathered together the best known of his shorter writings, from the early reviews of the *Origin* to the "Descartes," and published them as *Lay Sermons, Addresses, and Reviews*. His first book since *Man's Place in Nature*, it was even more widely applauded than that work had been execrated seven years before. The difference was not altogether due to change in the public mind. *Lay Sermons* had, as its title portended, a strong moral tone. It was acclaimed not only by *The Westminster*, which praised alike its "sound common sense" and "brilliancy of literary treatment,"[31] but by such less radical journals as *The Contemporary*, which, though criticizing Huxley's interpretation of Descartes, regarded his attempt to reconcile science and religion as sincere, generous, and farsighted.[32]

As usual, *The Spectator* was more dubious. Huxley denied not only that religion was credible, but even that it conduced to virtue, which could best be achieved by treating self-denial, like everything else, as "a working hypothesis."[33] But, said *The Spectator*, one cannot "pray to a hypothesis."[34] As a matter of fact, by refining truth to such a thin probability, Huxley was undermining not only religion, but rationalism itself. When reason produces only a working hypothesis, many people cease to be reasonable.

Insomnia costs ordinary mortals much discomfort and waste of time. It provided Huxley with a very exact knowledge of English philosophy. He seemed to master difficult authors by sheer intellectual momentum. When Morley persuaded him to write a book on Hume for the English Men of Letters Series, he found the work already quite complete in his head. He needed only to consider the trouble of composition, and that was very little trouble. He "picked" at his task a little, early in the summer of 1878, and then, relaxing on vacation at Penmaenmaws, finished it off in the next six weeks.

Hume is such a book as a brilliantly gifted and educated man might write in six weeks. It is compact and well organized, sometimes witty and eloquent. It not only makes Hume clearer than Hume, but improves and corrects him in many important particulars. Yet a rather new kind of subject has not called forth new talents in Huxley. He had largely omitted Descartes from his essay on Cartesianism, but what is understandable in a brief essay becomes reprehensible in a three-hundred page book. The *Hume* required a biography, and biography implies character. Huxley shows little interest in either. His narrative is bare and rapid. He suggests that vanity led Hume to forsake philosophy for history. He touches swiftly on Hume's outer awkwardness and inner calm in the midst of a brilliant Parisian debut. But "success and wealth are rarely interesting"; Hume is hurried unceremoniously to his deathbed.[35] In a page, or a volume, or a dozen volumes, Carlyle would have painted his man to the life. Six-weeks' casual study hardly suggested the problem to Huxley.

If he produces only a superficial picture of the mind that thought Hume's ideas, he gives a splendid account of the ideas themselves. Abjuring metaphysical folly, Locke had peeled away from philosophical thinking layer after layer of unwarranted assumption. Hume laid open the bare bone of empiricism, reducing virtually all knowledge and thought to sense perceptions, the power to recall them, and the tendency to "associate" them according to similarity, succession, and co-existence.[36] Even our most familiar and trustworthy abstractions, like those of time, space, cause and effect, are apparently not innate or intuitive; they seem to arise from the association of particular impressions. We can never be sure—even when they have proved reliable guides to future experience—how far our ideas correspond to exterior reality. Empiricism recognizes no complete certainty.

But even Hume is not a perfect empiricist. He falls occasionally either into positive dogmatism, as when he maintains certain mathematical truths are necessary and independent of sense experience—or into negative, as when he maintains that the mind is nothing but a heap of impressions. It may be nothing but a heap of impressions, but again it may be highly unified according to a principle much less mechanical than that of association.

Huxley simplifies and modernizes Hume at some length, indicating, for example, how a subjective empiricism which analyzes mind in terms of impressions can be equated with an objective empiricism analyzing behavior in terms of nervous system. Hume himself was aware of this possibility, but did not, like Descartes, pursue it, except to argue animal intelligence from animal behavior. He also outlines an evolution of theology according to the expansion of thought and the refinement of feeling. These presages of nineteenth-century naturalism Huxley elucidates with admiration.

Coming to religion, Huxley reprehends his own faults in Hume with much acumen and considerable sternness. Empirical doubt is hardly a decisive weapon in theological controversy. Hume was therefore often very positive about the uniformity of nature, using it to destroy miracles on the one hand and to prove an intelligent Creator on the other. But we know that nature is uniform only so far as we have observed it. We cannot therefore be certain that miracles are a violation of natural law, or indeed that a partially intelligible universe indicates a perfectly intelligent Creator.

Huxley has nothing but approval for Hume's determinism: Hume defines free will as a belief or impression which springs from a consciousness of purpose and the sensation of having carried out that purpose. He does not deny that men make choices and act on them. He argues simply that those choices are part of the order of nature. Men are not free to love pain or to associate any emotion with any idea. The doctrine of free will leads to absurdity. The doctrine of necessity follows from the very rational view that men have always been governed by the same motives or causes. Huxley urges that it does not diminish, but increases, the sense of moral responsibility. "The very idea of responsibility implies the belief in the necessary

connexion of certain actions with certain states of mind."[37]
Rage, if sufficiently violent, causes an act of rage.

On Hume's ethics Huxley is sound and critical as far as he
goes. He once more praises Hume for his empirical approach
and traces his derivation of the good from the useful:

The moral approbation, therefore, with which we regard acts
of justice or benevolence rests upon their utility to society, because
the perception of that utility or, in other words, of the pleasure
which they give to other men, arouses a feeling of sympathetic
pleasure in ourselves. The feeling of obligation to be just, or of
the duty of justice, arises out of that association of moral approbation or disapprobation with one's own actions, which is what we
call conscience.[38]

He rightly observes that Hume takes too little account of the
reality of temptation and the difficulty of virtue.

The *Hume* volume also contains two separate essays.
"Bishop Berkeley on the Metaphysics of Sensation" (1871) is
another triumphantly lucid exposition of a philosophical system. It was meant eventually to grow into a new volume for
Morley's series, but Huxley was always too busy or too ill to
expand it. "On Sensation and the Unity of Structure of the
Sensiferous Organs" (1879) winds up the whole discussion of
idealism and materialism, of inward consciousness and the
outward unknown, with an inquiry into the mechanism of
sense. In the case of each organ, a wall of sensation intervenes
between the impression and its stimulus. How stimuli become
impressions is still a mystery. Sound metaphysics can teach us
only our essential ignorance. Science alone can teach us new
facts.

In the 1894 preface to this volume, Huxley gave his final
word on the historical positions of Hume and Berkeley. Both
are descendants of Descartes. The first carried Cartesian doubt
to its logical result; the second, the Cartesian principle that
we can be certain only of the facts of consciousness. It is sig-

nificant that Huxley consistently emphasizes Cartesian doubt rather than Cartesian rationalism. In one sense Hume was the complete negation of Descartes. Taking geometry as his model, Descartes insisted that true ideas must be logically connected. He never doubted that truth was rational because he never doubted that the universe was rational. What is not logical is not knowledge. Hume maintained that the reasoning faculty was simply a form of associative activity useful in ordering experience. The universe itself may be only superficially and incompletely logical. Descartes tries to explain everything by mathematics. Hume explains nearly everything but mathematics. Perhaps Huxley admired these two men too much to think them very different from each other, or from himself. One of them ministered to his impulse for clarity; the other, to his need for puritanically denying himself the luxuries of certainty.

16

THE EDUCATOR

By 1870 Huxley's scientific work was nearly at its minimum, while half the administrative business of English science traveled about under his hat. Within the last few years he had been president of the British Association, and of the Ethnological and Geological Societies. From 1871 to 1880 he was secretary of the Royal Society, a post of great strategic importance. As a member of the X, he belonged to the inner cabinet of science; and as a member of the Metaphysical, he was the chief spokesman for science in the exalted agora of the Victorian gods. During the next eight years he was on one Royal Commission after another, dealing with every problem from public schools to contagious diseases. He was several times asked to stand for Parliament, but always declined, feeling that he could perform more valuable service without political position.

The world was becoming a stage better and better suited to Huxley's particular talents and attainments, for while he was taking over science, science was taking over Victorian civilization. In a sense it had created Victorianism, having made possible the Industrial Revolution and the dominance of the middle class. Middle class victory had thrown into relief the antithesis, long latent in the middle class mind, between evangelical faith and utilitarian rationalism; and the second had already triumphed. Darwin had superseded Moses as an authority on origins and was beginning to be regarded as an authority on morals also. As a matter of fact, evangelicalism itself had, despite much excellent Christian rectitude, long since condoned laissez faire red in tooth and claw, and was even now listening with some tranquillity to Spencer's homilies on the virtuous and necessary starvation of failures.

Meanwhile prosperous Philistia had achieved an instant of monumental equilibrium which, in our present maelstrom of change, has become a majestic symbol of social permanence. By repealing the Corn Law and the Combination Acts, by improving factory conditions and restricting factory hours, it had won temporary allegiance from the working classes; and by voting peers into office and voting them out, by bullying them in the press and the pulpit and by browbeating them from the throne, it had converted the aristocracy into something nearly as respectable and unheroic as itself. If England had not quite solved her problems, at least she had stared them down. Impressively unified despite much latent contradiction, voluminously articulate in poetry and prose despite much muddleheadedness, splendid in energy and cautious in compromise, she had inspired herself with the wonders of the Exposition, frightened herself with nightmares of simian ancestry, and was now comforting herself with profits and progress that seemed as steady and inevitable as the flow of time itself.

Progress was no longer the precarious, sporadic result of genius and accident. It had become organized, methodized, even mechanized. The method and the mechanism were of course science and its instruments. A scientist with his instruments, like an Erewhonian millionaire with his capital, was a superhuman individual, bringing to bear Olympian faculties, luminously perspicacious and tremblingly sensitive, upon the twin abysses of the infinitely great and the infinitely small. Hypotheses were constantly reaching out into the darkness—slowly, almost inevitably refining and rectifying themselves through empirical contact with reality.

Necessity was rapidly ceasing to be the mother either of invention or of discovery. In fact, the practical old woman had all she could do to keep in sight of them. Maxwell's study of electromagnetic waves, for example, waited fifty years to be translated into Marconi's invention of the wireless. By industriously rubbing the lamp of science, the Victorians were evoking its slaves in such legions that only the feebler and more obvious could be put to work.

Yet even these weak and obvious few, keeping very busy, had been sufficient to launch the primal age of technology. Chiefly by the systematic application of steam power to his daily tasks, man had changed his physical environment more in a few decades than in as many centuries. He had also begun his weird Pilgrim's Progress in the mechanical forest. It was a forest which changed almost with the swiftness of illusion and, in which, more and more as time went on, man lived awfully in the presence of his powers and temptations, always in the crisis of his human dualism. Utopia smiled at him from one side and pandemonium threatened from the other.

In 1870, the perils of the forest were hardly suspected. Experience had shown that the machine could impoverish and oppress physically, creating the most savage paradoxes of abundance and want, paralysis and opportunity. Ruskin had attempted to show it could also impoverish and oppress spiritually, concentrating artistic skill and initiative in a few hands and imposing artistic silence and dehumanizing routine on everybody else. On the other hand, it had poured forth a deluge of cotton cloth. It hauled people in large numbers rapidly across land and sea. It permitted Europe and America to converse by means of a wire laid down on the bottom of the Atlantic. The steam engine, the gas light, the telegraph, the isolation of disease bacteria and the development of serums to combat them had both shrunk and complicated, lit up and cleansed the planet, which seemed likely to become as neat, intricate, and manageable, as a fine Swiss watch. What had solved so many old problems must eventually solve the new problems it had created.

In any case, mechanization had become a national necessity. The Americans promised heroic competition in a few decades; the Germans threatened dangerous competition at the moment. Prussia, that native country of clockwork conformity, had, after more than a hundred years, once more found in Bismarck a clockwinder of genius. Once more the wheels turned smoothly and the seconds ticked with fateful precision, and as the hours struck, empires fell like card houses and all Europe trembled. Germany, the land of quarreling princes and erudite visionaries, had suddenly become a super-Prussia—a great military state backed by a great industry and an unrivaled system of scientific and technological education.

In spite of their navy and their bank balances, thoughtful Englishmen were justly concerned. R. H. Hutton regretted that so great a people as the Germans should be ruled by a military caste so much below them in character and culture.[1] At the beginning of the war of 1870, Huxley was strongly sympathetic to the fatherland of his beloved Goethe and violently critical of Louis Napoleon. But the appalling destructiveness of modern warfare—and perhaps the martial ferocity of the German press—soon cooled his enthusiasm. "Bad days are, I am afraid, in store for all of us," he wrote his friend

Dohrn, "and the worst for Germany if it once becomes thoroughly bitten by the military mad dog."[2]

Romantic tradition painted the Germans as a combination of noble innocence and poetic profundity. History was even then demonstrating that they combined great practical energy and speculative power with a singular tractability to command. They peered curiously into the foundations of the universe and fell back in awe before a military cap and a pair of epaulettes. Discipline and system, joined with an illustrious intellectual tradition, had made German education a resource more valuable than all the iron and coal in the Ruhr. Germany was even more vigilantly and aggressively mobilized for discovery, and for the commercial exploitation of discovery, than for war.

Meanwhile, until well into the century, English education ignored science. Schools—particularly the public schools—were something between a ritual and a riot. They subjected young boys to jungle law on the playground and in the classroom they inculcated, by rote and rod, the Egyptian mysteries of a gentlemanly education. The survivors of this process usually possessed much stoicism, assorted vices more or less grave, some knowledge of Greek and Latin grammar, and a disagreeable acquaintance with fragments of classical literature. In 1828 Dr. Thomas Arnold founded a benevolent Christian despotism at Rugby, where students were taught to regard life as a grave moral responsibility, to read French and German, and to understand the classics as well as to translate them. Arnold's example produced some imitation and a great deal of criticism, particularly at Oxford, where Rugby men were much disliked for their priggishness.

In the early stages of the education controversy the chief spokesmen for science were F. W. Ferrar and Herbert Spencer. Ferrar, who had been a classical master at both Harrow and Winchester, was famous in his own time for writing very bad novels about very good little boys. His good little boys were not happy at school. Ferrar believed not only that the aristocratic institutions of England offered a poor moral environment, but that they taught the wrong things and taught them ineffectually. He maintained that the ideal curriculum should emphasize science, mathematics, and modern languages.

Spencer's theory was his own experience generalized for ordinary mortals, plus biological laissez faire—an impossible idealism modified by an even more impossible realism. Skillful, well-informed tutors like his father were lovingly to educe from commonplace little boys an original genius like Herbert's own for abstract reasoning and encyclopedic knowledge which might lead eventually to a million pounds or a synthetic philosophy. On the other hand, they were not to teach too lofty an idealism, lest little boys be unfitted for the aboriginal struggle which civilized life actually is. Finally, science is more liberal and more useful than classical literature: it provides the mind with facts and a method of thought rather than with mere standards of beauty and a training in taste.

By 1860 the increasingly sharp competition of Victorian life pointed an ungentlemanly finger at Victorian education. Having inherited the public schools along with everything else, the upper middle class had become increasingly dissatisfied with them. It did not object to the Egyptian mysteries as such. They conferred the authoritative mark of gentility. On the other hand, successful business men wanted their sons not only to be gentlemen, but to be successful gentlemen. The awful fact was that the Egyptian mysteries, as then taught, did not enable young men to do well with the competitive examinations for the army and the civil service. Men like Matthew Higgins and Henry Reeve declared that such an institution as Eton was run not for the moral and intellectual benefit of the students but for the financial benefit of the masters.

Mathematics and modern languages should be included in the curriculum. A Royal Commission should investigate the public schools.

The liberal attack was met by a flood of nostalgic conservative eloquence. Edmund Burke had not defended the British Constitution more grandly. The public schools are the majestic embodiments of long accumulated experience. The elaborate fabric of moral and material masonry which makes an Eton or a Winchester is so delicate and complex that the rude finger of reform might shatter it with a touch. But the indignant lowing of great Tory cattle beneath the British oak did not silence the importunate chink of liberal grasshoppers; and though Gladstone himself felt that a strict classical curriculum was at once a buttress of religion and a liberal exercise for the mind, a Royal Commission was duly appointed in 1861. It agreed with the liberal critics, recommending in effect that the public schools reform their governing bodies, give a large place to competitive examinations, and include music, drawing, history, geography, English composition, spelling, and above all natural science, in their curricula.

In 1867 Disraeli took his famous leap in the dark and by enfranchising the poor-rate payers gave the vote to the bulk of the middle class. Attention was thus dramatically focused on lower middle class schools, which for the most part were feeble and dingy imitations of such places as Eton and Harrow.

Having at this fateful moment been made principal of the South London Workingmen's College, Huxley delivered his inaugural address on "A Liberal Education; and Where to Find It," aiming drastic criticism at the whole English system, but particularly at the primary and secondary schools. The three R's are worth little if they serve only to make ignorance articulate. The classics are useless if they give no idea of ancient life and thought. Huxley protests that he would not deprecate the classics—they state "with grand simplicity . . . the everlasting problems of human life"[3]—though of their basic importance to European civilization he gives no adequate idea. English universities contain few great scholars, produce little significant research, and offer almost no opportunity for advanced study in the great field of modern science and culture.

England needs a broader, more realistic conception of a liberal education. Such education should develop and discipline the total man. It should make his body a strong and efficient "mechanism"; and his mind, "a clear, cold, logic engine."[4] It should cultivate a love of beauty, a tender conscience, healthy and vigorous passions, and a strong will with which to control them. It should also inform him, in so far as possible, with the totality of modern knowledge. Artificial education should take its cue from natural.

Nature is continually inculcating her truths with the long ferule of pain and pleasure. Or, as a hidden antagonist, she plays with each man a game of chess. Obviously, a good education should teach the rules of that game, for "nature's pluck means extermination."[5] Huxley implies here, as on other occasions, that the scientific method, not to say matter itself, is the key to nature both outside and within man. Moral law is as certain in its action as physical. "Stealing and lying are just as certain to be followed by evil consequences, as putting your hand in the fire, or jumping out of a garret window."[6] Apparently, moral education should expose the consequences of right and wrong with such scientific clarity that virtue would become a rational necessity. Huxley faces the unpleasant implications of his position with typical courage—some will call it typical complacency. If an occasional workingman must starve to death, he should have the satisfaction of knowing why.

Would it not be well to have helped that man to calm the natural promptings of discontent by showing him, in his youth, the necessary connection of the moral law which prohibits stealing with the stability of society—by proving to him, once for all, that it is better for his own people, better for himself, better for future generations, that he should starve than steal?[7]

Huxley rather hurriedly leaves these unpleasant alternatives and turns to a more cheerful future. The working class do not need religion to keep them quiet, but science to make their work effective. The middle class do not need Latin grammar to make them fashionable but economics to make them capable of retaining the industrial and commercial leadership which has been their great modern achievement.

Huxley's dichotomy between the useful and the fashionable is indicative. He understood much better the requirements of the new world than the virtues of the old education. His attempt to mediate between the two does not go very deep. He speaks of education a good deal in terms of breadth, humanity, happiness, beauty, and leisure; but his eloquence and his metaphors emphasize mechanism, determinism, strength, success, and extermination. By exaggerating the struggle of civilized man with nature or with his fellows, Huxley claims for the sciences a stronger sanction than they should have: education to save the skin must come before education to save the soul.

In 1869, at a dinner of the Liverpool Philomathic Society, Huxley made a speech on "Scientific Education," which he published from his notes. Here the strident accents of the Philistine are even more distinctly audible, though with some tribute of irony to more liberal values. Most Englishmen are devoted to the religion of "getting on." Very well! The mysteries of that religion are destined more and more to be scientific:

As industry attains higher stages of development, as its processes become more complicated and refined, and competition more keen, the sciences are dragged in one by one, to take their share in the fray; and he who can best avail himself of their help is the man who will come out uppermost in that struggle for existence, which goes on as fiercely beneath the smooth surface of modern society, as among the wild inhabitants of the woods.[8]

Huxley believes that a scientific education should accomplish two purposes: it should inculcate the idea of causality, and it should unfold the infinite panorama of the scientific universe. The student should grasp both the uniformity and the immensity of nature. But his training should not include all the sciences. Huxley counsels that the child should proceed from the concrete to the abstract, beginning with physical geography, and then studying with some thoroughness one science which deals predominantly with classification, such as botany, and one which deals predominantly with cause and effect, such as physics. Above all, he should get a grounding in the inductive method, which of all disciplines alone proceeds from facts to generalization, and so provides the best preparation for practical life. In this essay Huxley seems somewhat to fall into the utilitarian error of assuming that a rational subject matter generates a mind to deal with it.

By establishing a program of grants-in-aid, the Education Act of 1870 encouraged local school boards to offer universal free instruction. It also stipulated that national schools, built solely with state funds, should be undenominational. Huxley saw at once that if the school boards could stop wrangling about theology long enough to think about secular, and even nondenominational religious, education, they might strike an unparalleled blow against ignorance. He was in bad health and already had far too much to do. Nevertheless, he could not escape the logic of the situation. With a heavy heart and a clear conscience, he ran for the London School Board. He addressed several large meetings, wrote an article for *The Contemporary Review* which Knowles, the editor, circulated as an election manifesto—and finished second among the elected candidates.

The election article had a great effect. "The School Boards: What They Can Do and What They May Do" is a statesmanlike political pamphlet, full of sound compromise and even sounder appeal to the good sense of the voters. Huxley declares that religious education need not cause dispute. What has so much divided and embittered men is not religion itself but theology—the science, or pseudoscience, treating of "the nature of the Deity, and his relations to the universe."[9] Religion is basically awe and reverence, and these feelings are essential to morality. In England religion is best taught in the primary schools by nondenominational reading of the Bible, which has become "the national epic of Britain," and remains with all its faults, "a vast residuum of moral beauty and grandeur."

He lays down a broad elementary curriculum, which, besides reading, writing, and arithmetic, should include drawing, music, and the rudiments of physical science. He also emphasizes domestic economy. Poverty should in the first instance be solved by the poor themselves: prosperity begins at home— in the frugal efficiency of wife and husband. What argument could speak more eloquently to the hearts and pocketbooks of solid Victorian citizens?

Earnest Christians and dignified clergymen on the School Board awaited the advent of Professor Beelzebub with some trepidation. It was well known that he had devoured alive the worthy Bishop of Oxford almost before the eyes of his congregation, leaving nothing but a shovel hat and a pair of gaiters visible on the platform. But to the London School Board he bared his teeth only in courteous smiles. He arranged that pious members could use the committee room for prayer before meetings, and, refusing to align himself with the extreme secularists, strongly supported Bible instruction in the elementary schools.

However, Huxley's tact and diplomacy did not extend to Roman Catholics, though there were three on the Board. His experience with such men as Ward in the Metaphysical Society had taught him that the Church was as dangerous as it was benighted. It exercised intellect with consummate skill to defeat the natural purpose of intellect, which is the disinterested pursuit of truth. It was the "great antagonist," valuable only in keeping science and liberalism alert by its relentless warfare.[10] One could dine with Catholics, but one could never agree with them. Over the committee table, as in the forum, one must be ready at any moment to dispense with the amenities in order to thwart a plot or pursue a tactical advantage. When it was suggested that the Board should pay directly to denominational schools the fees for poor children, Huxley was bitterly opposed because public funds would thus be handed over to the Catholic Church.

As an educational statesman, Huxley fell short only through his old fault of attempting too much in too little time. Otherwise, he was a miracle of success. In the fourteen months he was a Board member, he put through a curriculum which endured many years and still remains the basic framework of instruction in London schools. What the schoolboy studied— English history, English grammar and composition, geography, drawing, elementary physical science—were what Huxley recommended in "A Liberal Education" and other essays. To be sure, being neither omnipotent nor omnipresent, he could not prevent some mismanagement. Ironically, science suffered most. In the elementary schools, Huxley's physical geography was whittled down to mere geography; and in the secondary, his physics and botany were replaced by chemistry badly

taught and badly tested. The memorization of chemical formulas was substituted for the memorization of Latin para-
digms. There was no romantic pursuit of knowledge in the
open air, no exciting rediscovery of truth in the laboratory.

Huxley knew that he could not turn the world upside down
from a committee armchair, nor win a victory simply with pen
and ink. Much as he emphasized the right curriculum, he
knew that the right curriculum well taught must be the ultimate goal. Science teaching would fail unless there were good
science teachers. In the summer of 1871, therefore, he gave a
six-week course in general biology for teachers. As a part of
the Victorian-Norman, grimly castellated vastness of the South
Kensington Natural History Museum had been placed at his
disposal for the purpose, he was able to do what he had not
been able to do in his cramped quarters in Jermyn Street: he
introduced, for the first time in biology, laboratory work together with instruction by lecture. Nature at first hand was
almost too much for some of his students. One clergyman, who
had taught textbook science for years, was shown a drop of his
own blood under the microscope. "Dear me!" he exclaimed,
"it's just like the picture in Huxley's *Physiology!*"[11] Despite
all of Huxley's efforts, science teaching in the schools was only
very gradually improved. In 1872, when the biological department of the School of Mines was transferred to South Kensington, Huxley made laboratory work a permanent part of all
his courses.

As a political operative, Huxley was devastatingly efficient.
On the School Board he accomplished a miracle more incredible than any he ever tried to discredit: he proved that he could
lead, as well as annihilate, clergymen. His memory long remained green and sweet among Board members, and several
of them, clerical and otherwise, wrote eulogies. "Towering as
was his intellectual strength and keenness above me . . . ,"
wrote the Reverend Benjamin Waugh gratefully, "he did not

"VANITY FAIR" IMMORTALIZES TWO MEN
OF SCIENCE IN THEIR "MEN OF THE DAY"
SERIES IN 1871: DARWIN (TOP) AND
HUXLEY (RIGHT).

condescend to me." In fact, what impressed Mr. Waugh most about Huxley was his "childlikeness." "There were no tricks in his talk. He did not seem to be trying to persuade you of something. What convinced him, that he transferred to others."[12]

One doubts that Huxley was quite so guileless as Waugh thought him. Nevertheless, he did not make the impression of a hardened veteran. After admiring his energy and practical sagacity, his ability to combine strong convictions with a readiness to enter into the thinking of others, Dr. J. H. Gladstone recollects with mild surprise that Huxley's only political weakness was a certain sensitiveness, a lack of that "pachydermatous quality" which enables one to sit comfortably while listening to personal abuse.[13] Several competent observers attested to his political ability. "I do not think," Sir Mountstuart Grant-Duff wrote Leonard Huxley in 1898, "that your father, if he had entered the House of Commons and thrown himself entirely into political life, would have been much behind Gladstone as a debater, or Bright as an orator."[14]

Huxley had so many opportunities to run for Parliament and refused them so steadfastly that some people thought he had no opportunities at all and was trying very hard to get them. Yet he never thought of himself as more nor less than a statesman of culture. Moreover, he did not desire power for its own sake, and preferred to be useful rather than merely prominent and illustrious. No one thought, when it became vacant in 1871, that he would accept the secretaryship of the Royal Society. It was known to be an anxious and laborious post, and he was overtaxed and in bad health. Moreover, he was certain before very long to be president. Nevertheless, feeling that he could be more useful as secretary, he let it be known that he was available. He served for the next ten years.

Throughout 1871, he continued as a matter of course to wage multifarious literary warfare, defending Darwin against biologists,* biology against clergymen, and state education against those who scarcely believed either in the state or in education. Much of the work was done at St. Andrews, to which he conducted a long and difficult migration of his entire family (but then collectively recovered from whooping cough), so that he could combine a summer holiday with proximity to the meeting of the British Association in Edinburgh. He relaxed characteristically, playing golf until his arms ached, astonishing the librarian by delving into the Latin works of Jesuit theologians in order to confute Catholic evolutionists, and devoting every remaining moment to the composition of papers. The most remarkable of these, "Administrative Nihilism," was aimed at the doctrinaire liberals.

Such people maintained that the government should not educate because it should not do anything, and that the poor should not be educated because they would thereby become discontent with their poverty. But the middle class had risen by their own efforts. Why should they favor a system which closed the door to ability? A nation should economize its brains by cultivating them to the utmost and allowing them to get easily to the top.

Misery is a match that never goes out; genius, as explosive power, beats gunpowder hollow. . . . What gives force to the socialistic movement which is now stirring European society to its depths, but a determination on the part of naturally able men among the proletariat to put an end . . . to the misery and degradation in which a large proportion of their fellows are steeped?[15]

In short, Huxley is for equality of opportunity, though never for equality of goods.

In Huxley's opinion, Mill's "Liberty" lays down too negative a doctrine for the modern world. If the individual is free

* See p. 241.

to do only what does not injure others he is not free to do very much. One cannot think or act without influencing the thought or action of others. An erroneous opinion or an ill-advised act is always an evil, never a good, in itself. A neighbor who neglects his drains is as dangerous to life and liberty as a neighbor who flourishes a pistol. In other words, a certain amount of government regulation is inescapable. How much is wise and expedient can only be determined by common sense and experience. Even Hobbes did not draw the line at mere security, and Locke boldly declared that "the end of government is the good of mankind."

What, then, is the good of mankind? Huxley defines it as "the attainment, by every man, of all the happiness which he can enjoy without diminishing the happiness of his fellow men."[16] And in such happiness Huxley would count all that flows from security, wealth, art, science, sympathy, and friendship. The last two benefits, Huxley felt, might be secured by an established church, whose "services should be devoted, not to the iterations of abstract propositions in theology, but to the setting before men's minds of an ideal of true, just, and pure living."[17]

Returning from the comparative idyll of St. Andrews, Huxley plunged once more with gusto into crushing routine. He had completed his term as president of the British Association, but in addition to all ordinary duties, he was of course still lecturing schoolmasters, still busy with the Royal Society and the School Board. He was serving on two Royal Commissions —one for contagious diseases and the other for aid to science— and he was turning out a stream of textbooks, both elementary and advanced: Vertebrate Anatomy in 1871, Elementary Biology in 1875, Invertebrate Anatomy in 1877, Physiography in 1877, and several others. His life had become a maze of official appointments, a melodrama of impossible deadlines; and yet, even while playing a little delicious hooky to lunch with Tyndall or week-end with Darwin, he carried everything off triumphantly, to the envy and admiration of all other busy and efficient men.

In December, 1872, Huxley changed his residence from 26 Abbey Place to No. 4 Marlborough Terrace, where he had enlarged a small house into something more ample and comfortable. He had purchased the property against the advice of his lawyer, who apparently feared trouble from the man next door. "There is something delightfully refreshing," he wrote his lawyer, "in rushing into a piece of practical work in the teeth of one's legal adviser." And he signed, "Yours willfully."[18] Meanwhile, the impossible grew daily easier. In December he told his wife that his mind had never been clearer or more vigorous. Yet within a week he had broken down, and could neither work nor think.

Dyspepsia descended upon him with all its Victorian horrors. He took a brief holiday without lasting benefit. "I've come back grunting and grumbling like an ungreased block," he complained to Hooker.[19] In the next summer he was once more seriously ill. "I begin to suspect," he wrote his friend Dohrn with remarkable innocence, "that I overworked myself last year. Doctors talk seriously to me, and declare that all sorts of wonderful things will happen if I do not take some more efficient rest than I have had for a long time."[20] At length, halfheartedly, he set out for Egypt. At Malta and Gibraltar, he stopped over to investigate for the Admiralty the continued and mysterious presence of a small grub in the sea biscuit. The culprit was apparently distasteful as well as elusive, and discontent among the men was becoming serious. After a rapid investigation, Huxley found large stores of unpurified cocoa near where the sea biscuit was being packed. Insect eggs were being blown into the naval stores. Huxley

340 APES, ANGELS, AND VICTORIANS

ordered that the sea biscuit be packed elsewhere, and the criminal was frustrated.

In Egypt, the fatherland of history, he observed that the top of Cephren's pyramid was limestone, not granite, and that the unbaked brick at Memphis was stratified exactly like Nile mud. Among his most vivid drawings was one of a vulture waiting impatiently while a jackal feasted on a carcass. His son declares that Egypt made a "profound impression" on him.[21] It may even have taught him a little patience, for there he decided to resign from the School Board and never to overwork again. Nevertheless, his letters from Italy were ominously full of volcanoes, ashes, and lava flows.

Huxley landed once more in England on April 6. He was sunburnt and heavily bearded, but not really well. English bustle and hurry soon brought a return of dyspepsia and melancholy. His physician, Sir Andrew Clark, put him on a strict diet, and for a time he retired to the depths of Devonshire. But fresh eminence and responsibility found him out. After a close contest he was elected Lord Rector of Aberdeen University, and about the same time he found himself defending Hooker from the renewed machinations of Sir Richard Owen.

He now occupied his new house in Marlborough Terrace—and his lawyer's warning proved justified. The dubious neighbor maintained that Huxley's drainage well made his basement damp. He attempted blackmail, then went to court. Although his suit failed and he was compelled to pay costs, the additional strain and worry had put Huxley once more in a serious condition. Sir Andrew Clark ordered him abroad but he had no money with which to go. In fact, he had accepted a loan from Tyndall to pay some of his building costs. The situation was humiliating. Two years before he had been triumphantly administering British science. Now he had not the means to restore himself to health. Then he received the following letter:

My Dear Huxley—I have been asked by some of your friends (eighteen in number) to inform you that they have placed through Robarts, Lubbock and Company, the sum of £2100 to your account at your bankers. We have done this to enable you to get such complete rest as you may require for the re-establishment of your health; and in doing this we are convinced that we act for the public interest, as well as in accordance with our most earnest desires. Let me assure you that we are all your warm personal friends, and that there is not a stranger or mere acquaintance amongst us. If you could have heard what was said, or could have read what was, as I believe, our inmost thoughts, you would know that we all feel towards you, as we should to an honoured and much loved brother. I am sure that you will return this feeling, and will therefore be glad to give us the opportunity of aiding you in some degree, as this will be a happiness to us to the last day of our lives. Let me add that our plan occurred to several of your friends at nearly the same time and quite independently of one another.—My dear Huxley, your affectionate friend,

Charles Darwin.[22]

The offer had been the result of a dark and devious conspiracy, as benevolence among good friends should be. Lady Lyell had first conceived the idea. She had whispered it to Emma Darwin, who had passed it on to Charles. He had caught at it eagerly and put it into execution. "He sent off the awful letter to Mr. Huxley today," Emma wrote Fanny Allen, "and I hope we may hear to-morrow. It will be very awful."[23] It was not awful at all. Deeply touched and somewhat humbled, Huxley accepted.

In the summer of 1873, he set out for France with Hooker as volunteer nurse and a heavy load of medical instructions as a guidebook. In spite of forced good spirits and a constant readiness to undertake more than his share of the travel arrangements, he obviously suffered, in Hooker's judgment, from "severe mental depression" until he happened in a Paris bookstall on a *History of the Miracles of Lourdes*, "which were then exciting the religious fervour of France and the interest of her scientific public."[24] The prospect of a little congenial destruction both raised his spirits and quieted his digestion. Plunging happily into a great pile of treatises, he soon reduced all visions and cures to natural causes. Hooker perceived that his friend had healed himself by an act of unfaith, and eager to consolidate this gain, threw himself into the trip with as light and boyish a heart as he could muster. He succeeded magnificently. Setting off on a geological odyssey of the Auvergne, they scaled extinct volcanoes, explored valleys for evidence of glaciation, smoked cigars, discovered the skeleton of a prehistoric man in a museum, gaily suffered an attack of diarrhea in Grenoble, and finally gave themselves up to mere naïve curiosity and idleness.

Toward the end of his trip, Huxley wrote his wife a remarkable letter.

I have been having a great deal of talk with myself about my future carer. . . . The part I have to play is not to found a new school of thought or to reconcile the antagonisms of the old schools. We are in the midst of a gigantic movement greater than that which preceded and produced the Reformation, and really only the continuation of that movement. But there is nothing new in the ideas which lie at the bottom of the movement, nor is any reconcilement possible between free thought and traditional authority. One or other will have to succumb after a struggle of unknown duration, which will have as side issues vast political and social troubles. I have no more doubt that free thought will win in the long run than I have that I sit here writing to you, or that this free thought will organise itself into a coherent system, embracing human life and the world as one harmonious whole. But this organisation will be the work of generations of men, and those who further it most will be those who teach men to rest in no lie, and to rest in no verbal delusions. I may be able to help a little in this direction—perhaps I may have helped already.[25]

Rarely, after this time, was he to express so much confidence in the future.

The two travelers now journeyed from the Auvergne to the Black Forest, and there separated. Hooker returned to his professional duties at Kew. Huxley was joined by his wife and his son Leonard, then twelve years old. He now had the leisure and the freshness to discover, with some surprise, that his son was a very clever, promising young fellow. "I began to tell him something of the glaciers the other day," he wrote Tyndall from Switzerland, "but I was promptly shut up with, 'Oh yes! I know all about that. It's in Dr. Tyndall's book.' "[26] At this point the loving father bursts out, "He is the sweetest little fellow imaginable"—and spends half the letter apologizing for his pride.

Returned home in good health at last, Huxley resumed his various careers—and particularly that in education. He had become an academic pluralist with a vengeance, being Lord Rector of Aberdeen, a Governor of Owen's College, as well as professor at the School of Mines.

Early in 1874 he delivered his belated inaugural address as Lord Rector of Aberdeen. "Universities: Actual and Ideal" begins with an intellectual history of Europe and ends with a sober estimate of the value of lectures and examinations. Practically, it proposes that the medical curriculum consist of fewer subjects more thoroughly studied. Botany and Zoology should be lopped off medicine and together constituted a separate faculty, with adequate facilities for teaching and research: if England is ever to catch up with Germany and France in science, investigators must be able to investigate. This paper, like other recent ones, continues Huxley's personal feud with the Pope. The Scholastic Philosophy, once the best available explanation of the universe, is still the strongest intellectual superstition in the world. It has absorbed into its school curriculum the new classicism, but not the new science, which is the voice of reason and therefore its "irreconcilable enemy."[27] Protestantism was simply a step toward reason and rationalism.

To the glitter and brilliance of this ceremonial year of high academic office, the Bristol meeting of the British Association added a still further, though somewhat baleful, glitter and brilliance. In his opening address as president, Tyndall expounded the victories of scientific discovery over theological error from Democritus to Darwin. He admitted there was as yet no bridge between consciousness on the one hand and molecular activity on the other, but he proclaimed matter, properly understood, the magic substance by which all mysteries would be penetrated and all contradictions resolved—the very principle and symbol of progress, uniting invisible atomicity with invisible intelligence and both with infinite possibility beyond. But science is not the whole of life. It must dominate the cognitive faculties, but religion will dominate "the creative," though the latter—whatever they are—disappear rapidly into "the infinite azure" of Tyndall's rhetoric.[28]

The speaker expressed these now familiar views with so much force and eloquence that he produced along clerical spines something of the authentic shivers of 1859. There was great excitement at the meeting and great indignation in the newspapers, both Irish and English. Huxley began to debate whether to give his own speech, scheduled for the third evening, "On the Hypothesis that Animals Are Automata, and its History." It was the kind of scruple which he loved to entertain and loved even more to dismiss. "I must grasp the nettle," he told his young friend and assistant Lankester—savoring his reluctance.[29] Of course there was an immense crowd in the auditorium. He gave them one swift, appraising glance, then turned down on the table his carefully prepared notes, and for ninety minutes spoke eloquently and extemporaneously on an extremely intricate subject.

"Animal Automatism" elaborates at length Tyndall's most offensive theme—with the firm optimism of a dentist assuring his patient that the drill is painless. Descartes, says Huxley, had maintained that animals are essentially machines without consciousness. With the discovery of reflex action in the nineteenth century, scientists had revived automatism and extended it to man. Under the formidable aegis of the decerebrated frog and its German student Goltz, Huxley expounds automatism in its boldest form, reducing consciousness to a mere reflection or echo of molecular movement: psychic events in the mind are caused by physical events in the nervous system. He thus seems to assert not only that thought cannot affect action, but that thought is impossible, for in recognizing only physical cause, he excludes causality from mental phenomena.

Some critics have felt that his educational achievements were thus reduced to a paradox. But not necessarily. He could still maintain with some logic that books, lectures, demonstrations, and other physical stimuli—being received into the nervous system and ingeniously combined and stored up there —may later result in useful behavior. The ultimate tendency of Huxley's views is to magnify the utilitarian and depreciate the liberal and aesthetic values of education. If the appreciation of poetry is a mere reflection of molecular movement, why cultivate poetry? That Huxley had no intention of undermining the intellectual life and its pleasures need hardly be pointed out. What he really wanted to do was to rescue psychology and morals from the sinister contamination of invisible influence. For how could causes be isolated, unless they could be weighed and described—unless in short they expressed themselves materially?

Huxley threw away the mind in order to preserve the brain in all the sharp, precise integrity which his faith and his appetite for clearness demanded. So one-sided a proceeding seldom leads to common sense. In a cogent chapter of his *Principles of Psychology*, William James points out—besides much else against "the automaton-theory"—that pleasures and pains would hardly be so intense if the former were not connected with truly beneficial and the latter with truly injurious events. If it were not the sensation of burning which causes a child to withdraw his finger from the flame, why should he be uselessly subjected to so much pain? Significantly, in *The Descent of Man*, published some three years before Huxley's paper, Darwin leans toward James's view. Though acknowledging that many actions are quite automatic, he has nothing to say of nerves and reflexes, and a great deal to say of pleasure and pain and the efficacy of purpose and choice. His whole discussion implies that consciousness is a salient utility existing not only in man but at least to some degree in animals as well. Darwin is as cautious and common sense as Huxley is bold and doctrinaire.

Inevitably, Huxley's propaganda for scientific education led him into conflict with Matthew Arnold. In 1869 Arnold had published *Culture and Anarchy*, and solved the education problem by solving all English problems. A Victorian prophet could do no less, and yet of all Victorian prophets Arnold was the least obviously prophetic. He was a seer who carried an umbrella, a Socrates who parted his hair fastidiously in the middle. He dared to contaminate prophecy with elegance, even with humor. Victorians were puzzled. They liked to hear their doom pronounced with a fitting awfulness of rage. They expected their Jeremiahs to lose their tempers.

At least Arnold's urbanity enabled him, in the midst of controversy, to solidify a fast friendship with Huxley. These two men offer the happy spectacle of antagonists who never fully realized how deeply they were at variance. In spite of much cordiality and even more agreement, they differed a little—and differed profoundly. Basically, one was a scientist and utilitarian and the other a poet and humanist, yet there was much of the scientist in the poet, something of the poet in the scientist, and a great deal of the moralist in both. One was too dogmatic about his science; the other, too dogmatic about his poetic and cultural intuitions. One was deficient in human and aesthetic insight; the other, in abstract thought and definition. Both were essentially stoics and at bottom unsympathetic to religion. Both hated the narrow and benighted complacency of the middle class and recognized the national need for more intelligence, a wider curriculum in education, and a greater state control over schools. In fact, Arnold's classicism was in many respects much like Huxley's science. The "prime direct aim" of a liberal education, wrote Matthew Arnold, "is to enable a man *to know himself and the world.*"[30] The definition is almost exactly the same as Huxley's in "A Liberal Education," except that, in application, Arnold stresses inwardness and self-knowledge and Huxley, action and a knowledge of the world and nature. This difference in emphasis presaged, among other things, a revolution in curriculum.

The two men had known each other at least since 1868, when Huxley, as president of the Geological Society, invited Arnold to the annual dinner. Apparently, they got along very well by secretly admiring each other's talents and openly mocking each other's hobbies and stratagems. As *Past and Present* had its heroic Abbot Samson, *Culture and Anarchy* had its oracular Bishop Wilson. Huxley declared he had never heard of this perspicacious ecclesiastic and insisted that Arnold had invented him, yet one day Arnold received the following letter:

My Dear Arnold—Look at Bishop Wilson on the sin of covetousness and then inspect your umbrella stand. You will there see a beautiful brown smooth-handled umbrella which is *not* your property.

Think of what the excellent prelate would have advised and bring it with you next time you come to the club. The porter will take care of it for me.

Ever yours faithfully,
T. H. Huxley.[31]

In Arnold's *St. Paul and Protestantism*, which appeared in 1870, Huxley saw his own ideas and an attack on puritanism. He tells Arnold he has been picking up many good things: "One of the best is what you say near the end about science gradually conquering the materialism of popular religion."[32] This idea he himself later used as a weapon against Christian orthodoxy. The rest of the letter is devoted to the narrowness of puritans. Huxley concludes, "I am glad you like my Descartes article. My business with my scientific friends is something like yours with the Puritans, nature being our Paul."

This friendship, like many others, indicates Huxley's great personal force and magnetism. No doubt Arnold exhibited his usual charm to gain his usual ends. Still, he seems to feel the weight of an imposing knowledge and authority. He is eager to agree and grateful for being agreed with. "It gave me strong pleasure," he wrote, "to find you so fully owning the charm and salutariness of J. C. [Jesus Christ] . . . The faults of Christianity come from its immense popularity, and from good and bad, fit and unfit, impelled to have dealings with it."[33] He also emphasizes that "the dictum about knowing 'the best that has been known and said in the world' was meant to include what has been done in science as well as in letters."[34] Inevitably, he appeals to Huxley for advice and for facts. How could he get a higher price for his books? Is the biology in a passage on Butler's arguments for a future state correct? Arnold's last letter concludes, "Ever yours, in spite of old age, poverty, low spirits and solitude."[35]

The end of this friendship was enlivened by a polite, yet significant disagreement. Speaking on "Science and Culture," Huxley gave on October 1, 1881, the inaugural address at the opening of Sir Josiah Mason's Science College in Birmingham. Mason was a practical man of business. He had made no provision for "mere literary instruction and education."[36] Huxley saw in the occasion an opportunity to sum up his whole campaign for scientific education in a swift, comprehensive maneuver against his two principal foes: the men of business who felt that rule of thumb was the best preparation for modern industry, and the "levites of culture" who maintained that the Greek and Latin classics were the best preparation for modern life. A science college founded by a practical man was in itself a refutation of practical men. Moreover, one cannot study applied science apart from pure science. One must be able to think scientifically before one can apply scientific thought to practical affairs.

But science had in fact already won its battle against rule of thumb. Huxley turned this victory into a terrible warning to classicists by boldly approving Mason's exclusion of literary instruction. A merely scientific education, though less liberal than one which contained some literature, was at least as liberal as one which contained nothing but literature, and infinitely more liberal than one which contained nothing but ancient literature in dead languages. The best training for life was the scientific study of nature; the best training for citizenship, the scientific study of society.

"Science and Culture" is moderate in statement, extreme in

tendency. It implies that a man had better know his environment than know himself, that he can acquire ethical and human knowledge more effectually through the general and impersonal language of science than through the concrete and moving language of literature, that science already has more to teach on humane subjects than do the humanities themselves, that the classics possess no peculiar sanity, no strategic centrality for the Western community.

Arnold's reply was telling. Addressing an American audience on "Literature and Science" (1883), he observed that scientists are inclined to overlook human nature. They do not relate knowledge to our sense of conduct or our sense of beauty. In fact, they hardly feel the need to do so. Darwin was content with biology and the domestic affections, and Faraday—was a pious Sandemanian. But men cannot live by formulas alone. Arnold went so far as to assert that the hairy quadruped which, according to Darwin, eventually became human, was not only "furnished with a tail and pointed ears,"[37] but with an ultimate and permanent necessity for Greek. Nowadays, even the most stalwart classicists are scarcely so confident. Wisdom may have been on Arnold's side, but the future was on Huxley's.*

Huxley was well aware that if England was to compete with such nations as Germany and the United States, she must have not only a corps of scientific experts but a great army of

---

* Perhaps Arnold's criticisms were made before Arnold made them, for in his address "On Science and Art in Relation to Education" (1882), Huxley protested with almost pathetic fervor that he was definitely and indubitably human and that he had never failed to take an interest in any work of art or field of knowledge simply because it was interesting and vivid. Even so, his criticism of life is still too much criticism and too little life, his education still too much a method of producing scientists and "clear, cold logic engines."

technicians. He opened his campaign for technical education in 1877 with a speech at the Workingmen's Institute and Club.*

"Technical Education" is another revelation of the adroit politician. It says very little, but says it with great skill and astuteness. Huxley's object was of course to convince working-men that they should have some scientific training. He begins by telling them that they are all really scientists and that all scientists, including himself, are really handicraftsmen. They must therefore bear the elegant scorn of fine literary men and armchair thinkers—and here he does not scruple to break philosophy mercilessly on the wheel of practical utility in order to buy a little democratic patronage for science: the "grovel-ling dissectors of monkeys and black beetles can [hardly] hope to enter into the empyrean kingdom of speculation."[38] He also contrives actually to enlist the British suspicion of mind in the service of mind itself. Most students should not be allowed to study too much, but a very few students can hardly study enough. Approximately one man in a million is a genius, and he is as likely to come from the laboring as from the upper classes. Such a man is invaluable to the nation. The educational system must be an intellectual laissez faire in which the genius can readily work his way to the top. Obviously, every working-man's son carries a test tube in his schoolbag.

Who could resist such talk? Inevitably, the movement for technical education formed itself around Huxley. He had been the leading spirit in the Government's Science and Art De-partment, which already offered technical instruction. He was now invited by a committee of the wealthy Clothmakers Company to draw up a plan for advancing the cause. Soon,

* Workingmen's Clubs, formed to discourage drink and encourage self-culture, had existed since the middle of the century.

under his guidance, the City and Guilds Institute had been established and was expending twenty-five thousand pounds a year to provide an adequate knowledge of the scientific principles involved in each trade. As President of the Royal Society, Huxley was from 1883 to 1885 a member of the Guilds Committee, and in that capacity once more exercised a wise and liberal influence upon the institution which he had formed.

The renewed spectacle of so much political flair led to another letter—this time from George Howell, M.P.—urging Huxley to enter public life. He replied once more that he felt he could be more effective outside: what he really wanted was to benefit science and to help the masses of the people to help themselves.

Huxley's later papers on education deal almost entirely with the professional and technical phases. His address on "The Connection of the Biological Sciences with Medicine" (1881) is a concentrated little history of medical thought, tracing how a modified mechanism gradually triumphs over animism based on trial and error. His "The State and the Medical Profession" (1884) proposes—with almost a Burke's resource in disguised innovation—some sweeping new practical measures to be grafted on old principles and existing institutions. It also indicates his reluctance to entrust to the state an educational function which might be performed by a private agency. His last word on this subject—an address on technical education delivered in 1887—indicates the grim pressures behind revolution in the curriculum.[39] England cannot feed herself with what she produces on her own soil. Therefore, she must produce efficiently and sell cheaply—or perish. Her only hope is in superior technical and scientific knowledge, and she must grow in such knowledge as she grows in population. Malthus with his flaming sword stands guardian before any Eden of classical dilettantism or idyllic simplicity. Only a scientific people can survive in a scientific future.

17

Triumphal Progress

In the autumn of 1876, Huxley gave ultimate proofs at once of his genius and his liberalism by discovering America. Few distinguished Europeans have been so little disillusioned by the adventure. Huxley was extremely polite, instinctively sympathetic, somewhat reticent, perhaps not very deeply interested. What was to be for his grandson a terrifying glimpse into the future was for the eminent scientist himself a mild surprise and a great personal triumph. America had long since discovered Huxley. An indefatigable champion of truth and progress, a monumental embodiment of rational energy and moral force, he was something better than a great Englishman. He was a great Englishman with American virtues, a mirror in which Americans might admire themselves in the most flattering light—and as a matter of fact, they were throughout his visit so ecstatically intent upon their own reflections that they took little note of the properties of the glass itself. Even before he had ever reached its shores, the continent was rocked with thunders of applause. Huxley was astonished and genuinely moved. He responded by behaving precisely as a celebrity should, making brilliant speeches, acknowledging plaudits, uttering memorable words on memorable occasions, and above all refraining from that strange and ungrateful perversity of criticism which the contemplation of the American scene had produced in Dickens and Mrs. Trollope.

The rigors of an American Welcome were to reveal that there were limits to Huxley's strength. Had he entered politics, he might have failed, as Grant-Duff had declared, for the lack of a sound digestion.

Huxley had at first intended simply to visit his elder sister and early confidant "Lizzie," who had settled with her husband in Tennessee. Some months before his departure an American who had named his son Thomas Huxley sent through Frederic Harrison a startling message: "The whole nation is electrified by the announcement that Professor Huxley is to visit us next fall. We will make infinitely more of him than we did of the Prince of Wales and his retinue of lords and dukes."[1] Shortly after, American adulation took the substantial form of an offer of one hundred pounds to deliver the ceremonial address at the opening of Johns Hopkins University.

After some hesitation, Huxley accepted the invitation, though he refused the honorarium. He already knew the future president of Johns Hopkins, having met him at Sir Lauder Brunton's and at one of the gay, conspiratorial dinners of the X. Daniel Coit Gilman belongs to the heroic age of American college presidents, when a series of farsighted Yankees, armed with a few resolute millions, were buying up some of the best young brains of Europe. Gilman had appealed to Huxley for a biologist, and the latter had recommended his former demonstrator H. U. Martin, who was then with signal success to establish the first biological laboratory, as well as the methods of his chief, in the United States.

A migration of the entire family seemed out of the question and therefore, leaving such children as were still unmarried under the care of Sir William and Lady Armstrong at Craigside, Huxley and his wife set out on what he liked to call his "second honeymoon." Then, as now, America was not only a house of glass, but a house of magnifying glass. A crowd of reporters came on board as the *Germanic* pulled into harbor. Standing on the deck, wrote Mr. Smalley, London correspondent of the *New York Tribune*, the great scientist enjoyed to the full the "marvellous panorama" of the New York skyline, for he was at all times "on intimate terms with Nature and also with the joint work of Nature and Man."[2] As they drew near the city, "he asked what were the tall tower and tall building with a cupola, then the two most conspicuous objects." "The Tribune and Western Union Telegraph buildings," replied Smalley. "Ah," said Huxley, "that is interesting; that is American. In the Old World the first thing that you see as you approach a great city are steeples; here you see, first, centres of intelligence." Surely at that moment the buttons on Mr. Smalley's waistcoat grew taut with pride. Surely he swore silent allegiance to science in her warfare against religion.

After the tall buildings, the busy tugboats aroused Huxley's attention. He watched them earnestly for a long time and said at last, "If I were not a man I think I should like to be a tug." For "they seemed to him," explained Mr. Smalley somewhat chemically, "the condensation and complete expression of the energy and force in which he delighted."

The Huxleys' welcome was hearty, sincere, spectacular, and exhausting. Mr. Appleton the publisher seized them at the dock and carried them off to his country house at Riverdale. From there Mrs. Huxley was hastened to the great summer resort at Saratoga, while Huxley was taken to Yale University. There his guide was Professor O. C. Marsh, a charming early example of the New England gentleman crossed with the scientist and the frontiersman, who had risked his scalp in Indian country many times to establish the genealogy of the horse. Conventional in spite of his romantic exploits and as a provincial somewhat in awe of the great Englishman, Marsh proposed the accepted academic ritual of looking over the buildings. Again came the masterly reply, cutting straight through American ceremony to the American heart. "Show me what you have got inside them," said Huxley; "I can see plenty of bricks and mortar in my own country."[3] With a will Marsh led the way to the fossils.

And what fossils! "Brontotheres, pterodactyls, mosasauers and plesiosauers, . . . perissodactyls and artiodactyls," chants *A Century of Science in America.*[4] Now at last Huxley had sailed into his own particular New York harbor. He was a little surprised to find that the New World was so very old. "The most wonderful thing I ever saw!" he wrote his wife.[5] Meanwhile, he could not escape the Great American Welcome, nor did he really want to. Installed in the luxurious apartments of Marsh's uncle, "the millionaire Peabody," he was promptly called on by the Governor and interviewed by a reporter, who noted with surprise very little of the "highfalutin" philosopher and much of "the commercial or mercantile" type.[6] Marsh collected notables for him to meet, took him to teas and dinners, told him Western stories, and drove him up and down New Haven, whose stately avenues, roofed and bordered with tall elms, pleased him very much. "I assure you I am being 'made of,' " he wrote Mrs. Huxley with jovial satisfaction, "as I thought nobody but the little wife was foolish enough to do."

But lionizing was restricted to leisure hours. Each day from nine to six was devoted to the serious business of several hundred thousand years ago. Marsh had brought forth his prehistoric horses only after some hesitation because they did not fit into Huxley's published theories. But Huxley was shortly to give a lecture on the subject in New York, and he must know the facts. He was equal to them. Point by point, bone by bone, the two men argued their way back into hippian history. And now the apostle of method received a lesson in methodology from his provincial colleague. Time and again Huxley demanded proof, and each time Marsh simply asked his assistant to fetch box number so and so. The right bone always appeared to illustrate the right point. "I believe you are a magician," exclaimed Huxley at last. "Whatever I want, you just conjure it up."[7] At the end of two days he capitulated. The horse, unknown to the New World when Columbus landed, had indeed originated there rather than in the Old. It had evolved from a small, four-toed animal* to the large, hoofed animal we now know. But, as Marsh tells the story, his own discoveries were less remarkable than Huxley's magnanimity in accepting them.

Huxley was grateful to Marsh for an intellectual, even more for a moral, benefit: now at last he could believe in evolution with a good conscience: he had the ultimate proofs which his intensely scrupulous nature had so long demanded. "No collection which has been hitherto formed," he wrote shortly after this time, "approaches that made by Professor Marsh, in the completeness of the chain of evidence by which certain existing mammals are connected with their older tertiary ancestry."[8] He left Yale with regret.

Once more reunited, he and Mrs. Huxley went on to Boston, conversed with the daughters of Longfellow and Hawthorne, attended a scientific meeting at Buffalo, and then, as befitted second honeymooners, spent a week at Niagara. Huxley was at first disappointed by the Falls, but after observing them from below and passing behind the wall of water into the Cave of the Winds, he yielded to the spell of this thundering manifestation of nature's energy. He liked to sit of an evening and listen to the low sound, distinctly audible despite the water's

* *Orohippus.* Marsh shortly after discovered a five-toed horse (*Eohippus*).

roar, of the grinding of great stones at the foot of the cataract.

From Niagara they went on to Nashville, Tennessee, where Huxley's elder sister, Mrs. Scott, awaited them at the house of her son. As the train pulled in, Henrietta at once spotted the old lady among the crowd on the platform by her piercing black eyes and strongly Huxleyan features. "Tom" was then fifty-one, with spectacles, side-whiskers, a great reputation, and long experience in ways of command and responsibility. "Lizzy" was sixty-two, with deep lines and gray hair and the memory of a great civil war in which her sons had fought and been defeated. What did these two feel and think, and what did they say to each other? On this intensely personal point, as so often, Huxley is silent in his letters.

As a matter of fact, he had very little time for thought, feeling, or words, for in Nashville he experienced for the first time the full and unabated rigors of welcome. A performing pterodactyl or a domesticated dinosaur could hardly have aroused a more lively curiosity among the citizens of Nashville than the great English thinker and evolutionist. He was exhibited and observed at every possible opportunity, and his every breath and action were recorded in the newspapers. No fascinating fossils in the cool privacy of the laboratory this time. In the moist, sweltering heat of a Southern summer, he visited a public school, the new Vanderbilt University, the state capitol. He spoke to children on the street and exchanged heavy witticisms with the head of a theological seminary. At his nephew's house, a continual stream of visitors rapidly wore him down and finally drove him to his room. A deputation then waited on him, begging that he either deliver an address, be entertained at a public dinner, or "state his views"—presumably to a reporter. Faced with these terrible alternatives, Huxley chose the address, and leaving his wife to receive callers, retired for the greater part of a day to prepare a few notes on the geology of Tennessee. Because of the heat, he spoke in the evening.

Professor Huxley was greeted last night by the best people of Nashville [explained *The Daily American* the next morning]. The professional men, the solid business men, and the beauty and fashion of the city, and with them the curiosity seekers, who paid their tribute to the great scientist whose fame had preceded him. The audience was not only select. It was a public demonstration which showed the deep interest which all classes feel in the progress of modern investigation.[9]

The best people of Nashville did not escape without actually contemplating some of the fruits of modern investigation. Huxley was utterly exhausted and in very poor voice, yet, speaking of slow geological changes such as that illustrated by Niagara Falls, he could not refrain from uttering the defiant whisper:

During that vast time the population of the earth has undergone a slow, constant and gradual change, one species giving way to another. . . . I need not say that this view of the past history of the globe is a very different one from that which is commonly taken. It is so widely different that it is impossible to effect any kind of community, any kind of parallel, far less any sort of reconciliation between these two. One of these must be true. The other is not.[10]

He insisted no more on this unpleasant issue; and when he had finished speaking, the crowd applauded wildly. Perhaps they thought strange opinions quite normal for a domesticated dinosaur. Perhaps they felt there might even be something in evolution, for, as an editorial hopefully pointed out, "devout Roman Catholics, like Prof. Jerome Cochrane of Mobile, and distinguished Presbyterian divines, like Atkinson of Virginia, hold the views of Darwin and Huxley."[11] But apparently, in its enthusiasm for progress and enlightenment, Nashville failed to carry along the rest of Tennessee, for after nearly fifty years of further progress and enlightenment a Mr. Scopes was found guilty in a spectacular court trial of violating a state law which forbade the teaching of evolution in the public schools.

The visitors now journey to Cincinnati and finally to Baltimore for Huxley's address at the opening of the Johns Hopkins University. Here the profits of the Baltimore and Ohio Railroad seemed actually to have called into being a utopia of the mind. Johns Hopkins was to be not a club, a mausoleum, or a clotheshorse for the latest architectural fad, but a place of learning, a professors' and students' university. After half had been subtracted for a hospital, its considerable endowment was to be devoted to faculty salaries and the financing of research.

Surely, here was a theme to call forth the fire of Huxley's enthusiasm. Unfortunately, his fire was still guttering desperately under ever increasing gales of hospitality. The day before the address was to be given, he had gone off to see Washington and returned very tired, only to be told that he must attend a formal dinner and a reception that evening. "I don't know how I shall stand it!" he exclaimed.[12]

Shutting himself up in his room, he took two hours' rest, but then had to dictate his lecture before going out. He had planned to deliver it from notes; in that case, reporters had explained, they would have to take it down as well as they could and then telegraph it to the Associated Press, so that it could be published in New York papers the following morning. This procedure summoned up such a nightmare vision of possible error piled on error that, undergoing a fresh and heroically inconspicuous martyrdom for truth, Huxley dictated "to a stenographer, in cold and irresponsive seclusion the speech which he expected to make before a receptive and hospitable assembly."[13] The stenographer promised to return a fair copy early the next morning, but it did not come until the last moment before the ceremony. Glancing at it on his way to the lecture hall, Huxley discovered with horror that it was written on "flimsy," from which he could not possibly read with any effect. He wisely resolved once more to speak *ex tempore* and did so with fluency, though what was recorded in Baltimore differed inevitably from what was published in New York. Huxley liked to say afterwards that though both versions represented the speaker's words, a future historian might reasonably pronounce them spurious and conclude that the address had never really been given.

As a finished essay, "University Education" is somewhat disappointing. A new world had apparently brought very little new illumination, or perhaps in that moment of exhaustion nothing could illuminate him. He confines himself pretty much to education, emphasizing the importance of theory to a nation obviously too much devoted to practice. Significantly, he expresses cautious sympathy for many tendencies now dominant in the American university system. He disapproves of entrance requirements, prefers course examinations to comprehensive examinations, and maintains that research is best pursued in combination with teaching. With regard to medical training, he insists that it should be strictly professional, without liberal frills. A doctor should know what is useful to his patients, not what is pleasant and broadening to himself. He strongly approves of Johns Hopkins for preferring brains to architecture and, in terms which must have delighted the crowd, advises the governing body of the university to build it a sumptuous façade a hundred years hence, when it has provided everything necessary to study and learning.

Only at the very end of his speech does Huxley turn to the

larger theme of the United States itself. He begins with a handsome compliment:

> To an Englishman landing upon your shores for the first time,
> travelling for hundreds of miles through strings of great and
> well-ordered cities, seeing your enormous actual, and almost in-
> finite potential, wealth in all commodities, and in the energy and
> ability which turn wealth to account, there is something sublime
> in the vista of the future.[14]

But then, taking one lens from Arnold's spectacles and another
from Malthus's, he gives the American future a long, scrutiniz-
ing look.

> I cannot say that I am in the slightest degree impressed by your
> bigness, or your material resources, as such. Size is not grandeur,
> and territory does not make a nation. The great issue, about which
> hangs a true sublimity, and the terror of overhanging fate, is
> what are you going to do with all these things? . . . Forty millions
> at your first centenary, it is reasonably to be expected that, at
> the second, these states will be occupied by two hundred millions
> of English-speaking people, spread over an area as large as that
> of Europe, and with climates and interests as diverse as those of
> Spain and Scandinavia, England and Russia. You and your de-
> scendants have to ascertain whether this great mass will hold
> together under the forms of a republic, and the despotic reality
> of universal suffrage; whether state rights will hold out against
> centralisation, without separation; whether centralisation will get
> the better, without actual or disguised monarchy; whether shifting
> corruption is better than a permanent bureaucracy; and as popu-
> lation thickens in your great cities, and the pressure of want is
> felt, the gaunt spectre of pauperism will stalk among you, and
> communism and socialism will claim to be heard. . . . The one
> condition of success, your sole safeguard, is the moral worth and
> intellectual clearness of the individual citizen.[15]

As these words were spoken, there crept over the huge auditorium, crowded as usual "with the beauty, wealth, and intelligence of a great American city," a somewhat tenser silence.[16]
The great evolutionist had confronted confident Americans

with un-American possibilities of evolution. He went no further, but concluded with a congratulatory glance into the future of the university itself, when students "wander hither from all parts of the earth, as of old they sought Bologna, or Paris, or Oxford."[17] There was immense applause—partly, perhaps, the applause of relief. He had not meant to scold.

Huxley's blessing did not particularly help the new university. A sensational letter appeared in a New York religious weekly complaining that not only had Huxley been included, but the prayer had been omitted, from the Hopkins inaugural program. Another letter, which came into President Gilman's hands, put the point even more forcefully: "It was bad enough to invite Huxley. It were better to have asked God to be present. It would have been absurd to ask them both."[18] For several years the spoken address and the unspoken prayer hung like two dark clouds over the university's future.

Ignorant of the theological lightning he had drawn down, or ignoring it, Huxley went on to New York, where he was to give three lectures on evolution. For three nights he was a front-page sensation. Jenny Lind herself could not have packed Chickering Hall any tighter. An immense crush, wrote the New York Tribune, but "a highly respectable crush."[19] At exactly eight o'clock the first evening Professor Huxley appeared on the platform amid great applause. "He laid a copy of Milton's Paradise Lost upon the reading desk; nothing else, neither manuscript nor notes."[20] Leaning slightly forward over the desk, he began to speak in low, measured tones. He did not gesture, though sometimes he grasped the desk with both hands and leaned over it even more intently. There was deep silence throughout the hall.

These "Lectures on Evolution" are models at once of expository and polemical economy. By adroit Voltairean arrangement and maneuver, he tears down the Pentateuch with one hand and builds the new gospel of evolution beside its ruins with the other. In his first lecture he presents three hypotheses of terrestrial history: either present conditions have always existed, or they were specially created some five thousand years ago—Huxley illustrated from Milton rather than Moses—or they have evolved gradually by a natural process. In the subsequent lectures he demolishes the first and second hypotheses by demonstrating that the third is the only one which fits the facts of science, and then, setting up an opposition between morals and orthodoxy, he insists that loyalty to truth must come before loyalty to creed. He also enlists national pride against Christian orthodoxy, using American scenery to batter Hebrew cosmogony. By the sheer weight of superior grandeur and antiquity the geological past of the United States belittles and discredits the theological past of the Old Testament. The Connecticut Sandstone is a great manuscript recording events many hundred times older than the oldest events recorded in the Bible. Niagara Falls is a kind of sublime waterclock measuring out thirty thousand years between us and certain insignificant shellfish whose remains are to be found in the region.

The last two lectures marshal recent discoveries to fill out two important gaps in the geological record—the development of birds from reptiles and the long and intricate history of the horse. In large degree these lectures are Marsh's facts expressed in Huxley's style. They were enthusiastically received by the audience and by all newspapers except the *Sun*, which was determined in misapprehension and disapproval. The first lecture was in its opinion too discreet. "Instead of attacking Moses over the shoulders of John Milton, he should strike at Moses, face to face."[21] The second lecture was too rudimentary. "It is evident . . . that Professor Huxley believes his audience to be totally lacking in scientific knowledge."[22] Actually, of course, the "Lectures," apparently written during his sojourn in the United States, were an impressive compliment to his audience. Clearly, he thought America well worth making safe for Darwinism. But respect does not imply interest or understanding. Characteristically, he had, even for a scientist, a great deal to say of America's extinct animals and very little to say of her living human population.

He returned to England with a firm belief in the paleontological significance of *Orohippus* and *Hesperornis Regalis* and a humorous and somewhat rueful perception into the fallibility of the American reporter. "I had a very pleasant trip in Yankee-land," he announced to Professor Baynes, "and did *not* give utterance to a good deal that I am reported to have said there."[23] Of course he lost no time trumpeting *Orohippus* and *Hesperornis* to a London audience, and shortly after wrote to Marsh, thanking him once more and complimenting him on the recent discovery of *Eohippus*, a still older equine.

And now Huxley's whole life was becoming a triumphal progress through a world of fame and achievement. In 1877 he published his *American Addresses*, *Physiography*, and *Manual of Invertebrate Anatomy*; in 1878, his *Hume* and an *Introductory Primer* for the Science Primer Series. In 1878 also he was made president of the new Association for Liberal Thinkers and, by way of contrast, a Governor of Eton College. In the same year—just two years after he had soundly lectured her on the occasion of Darwin's degree—he received an LL.D. from Cambridge. Orthodoxy was bowing to the heretic. "I find 53," he wrote Dohrn a little later, "to be a very youthful period of existence. I have been better physically, and worked harder mentally, this last twelve-month than in any other period of my life."[24]

In 1881, when the School of Mines was absorbed by the new Normal School in Kensington, he was made Dean of the College and Professor of Biology. He bore his new responsibilities with irrepressible high spirits, and was much amused by his new title. "I am astonished," he wrote Sir John Donnelly, his immediate superior in the Education Department, "that you don't know that a letter to a Dean ought to be addressed 'The Very Revd.' I don't generally stand much upon etiquette, but when my sacred character is touched I draw the line."[25]

His official life had now migrated from the cramped, downtown bustle and noise of Jermyn Street to the newly constructed splendor and spaciousness of the Normal School, known from 1890 as the Imperial College of Science. The vast institution at the edge of Kensington Gardens—fabulous symbol of the marriage between Victorian wealth and Victorian science—was then just beginning to unfold its wild and eclectic grandeur, a nightmare yet undreamed save by its architects. But there already rose in red brick and rich mosaic the ornate Gothic spire of the Albert Monument, where Arthurian romance mingled suggestions with the Arabian Nights, and the pomp of India mysteriously joined hands with the primness of England. There expanded also the giant, squat, Georgian rotundity of Albert Hall, where Wagner was hissed and Bright applauded. And all around, more and more extensively as time went on, rose the Imperial College itself—a wilderness of red brick, five stories of Victorian suburbia, blossoming at the sixth—into the turrets of Camelot and the minarets of Bagdad. Here the Huxley Building presents the comparatively modest and rational suggestion of a prosperous nonconformist church surmounted by a Venetian palace or an arcade from the Alhambra. There the Natural History Museum raises acres of striped yellow and brown brick in Moorish ladrillado up into whole forests of early Norman spires populated by whole zoos of guardian wolves and lions.

In this Victorian Nineveh Huxley gave lectures, conducted examinations, and did all the dignified and august things that deans do. His letters betray no unwonted excitement, no sense of architectural bewilderment or artistic prostration. He simply accepted these buildings, as he accepted the mastodon and the emu.

One gets a vivid picture of Huxley at this almost legendary period. He was by no means lost in his setting. To curious visitors and casual hero-worshipers, to flustered assistants and awe-stricken students, the Dean of the College of Science must have seemed at least as impressive as the façade of the Natural History Building—and sometimes nearly as uninviting. Oliver Lodge remembered all his life the cold eye which Huxley bent upon him when as a young man he had, even though with good reason, ventured for the first time on a few friendly words.[26] Above many a relatively innocuous social occasion, the Dean hung like a poised avalanche, likely at any moment to come down with a terrible crashing and splintering of the amenities upon the head of some minor offender. Where there was so much rectitude, discipline, and dedication, there could be little sympathy for weakness, little reluctance in castigation. In fact, there was no reluctance whatever. When Duncan Darroch, apparently a technician, wrote him that Professor Frankland never showed his face in the chemistry laboratory, and authorized him to do what he saw fit with the letter, Huxley replied, "Exercising the discretionary power you gave me, I will forward it to Dr. Frankland."[27] When his brother-in-law Joseph B. Heathorn wrote that in turning over his father's papers, he had found a note bequeathing a gold watch to Huxley's eldest son, Huxley answered in the following words, "So many years have elapsed since your father's death, that his unregarded wishes had better so far as my son is concerned go unfulfilled; and I must beg leave on my son's behalf to decline the watch."[28] What lay behind this need to sacrifice ordinary people so ruthlessly on the altar of his own high principles?

An illuminating impression of Huxley at this time was recorded by Beatrice Potter, later Mrs. Sidney Webb. She sought an interview with him regarding Herbert Spencer, who wanted her to be his literary executor. Under May 6, 1886, she wrote in her diary:

Throughout the interview, what interested me was not Huxley's account of Spencer but Huxley's account of himself. . . . How as a young man, though he had no definite purpose in life he felt power; was convinced that in his own line he would be a leader. That expresses Huxley: he is a leader of men. I doubt whether science was pre-eminently the bent of his mind. He is truthloving, his love of truth finding more satisfaction in demolition than in construction. He throws the full weight of thought, feeling, will, into anything that he takes up. He does not register his thoughts and his feelings: his early life was supremely sad, and he controlled the tendency to look back on the past and forward into the future. When he talks to man, woman, or child he seems all attention and he has, or rather had, the power of throwing himself into the thoughts and feelings of others and responding to them. And yet they are all shadows to him: he thinks no more of them and drops back into the ideal world he lives in. For Huxley, when not working, dreams strange things: carries on lengthy conversations between unknown persons living within his brain. There is a strain of madness in him; melancholy has haunted his whole life. 'I always knew that success was so much dust and ashes. I have never been satisfied with achievement.' None of the enthusiasm for what is, or the silent persistency in discovering facts; more the eager rush of the conquering mind, loving the fact of conquest more than the land of the conquered. And consequently his achievement has fallen far short of his capacity. Huxley is greater as a man than as a scientific thinker. The exact opposite might be said of Herbert Spencer.[29]

Perhaps he seemed to Beatrice Potter a little more mystical than he actually was. Perhaps he was a little more mystical in the presence of a striking young woman than in that of aldermen or gamekeepers. Even so, the passage is full of hints and suggestions. One notes particularly the sadness in early life, the want of purpose coupled with a sense of power, the tendency to look forward and back, the need always to be destroying and conquering in the name of truth. Clearly, there were things which he dared not face. One suspects in Huxley—despite his dedicated optimism and his demonstrations of clockwork harmony—a deep sense that the universe is hostile. Darwinism provided that sense of hostility with a rationale, which in such essays as "The Struggle for Existence" Huxley had already begun to develop. And now other authors confirmed him. "Butler's 'Analogy' is unassailable," he wrote Darwin, "and there is nothing in theological dogmas more contradictory to our moral sense, than is to be found in the facts of nature."[30] One thinks of the calm, strong angel in "Science and Education," with his threat of "nature's pluck," which is extermination.

Perhaps, also, Huxley was afraid to face himself. He had found in life no satisfying constructive purpose, no human or intellectual end large enough for the working of his whole mind and spirit. Yet he could not live with that haunting vacancy. He had devoted himself to demolition, gladiatorial combat, desultory presidencies—to achievements that seemed to promise peace but always turned to "so much dust and ashes." No less in his fastidious pride could he be content with himself morally. Some sense of guilt or impurity—hinted at perhaps in the famous letter to Kingsley*—kept him always at his treadmill of self-discipline. Mere human nature he could not accept, either in himself or others. "The great thing in the world," he wrote on the occasion of Leonard's eighteenth birthday, "is not so much to seek happiness as to earn peace and self-respect."[31] He tried strenuously for a lifetime to earn them. More and more through these years his triumphal progress looks like a flight from reality.

---

* "Kicked into the world a boy without guide or training, or with worse than none, I confess to my shame that few men have drunk deeper of all kinds of sin than I." (Leonard Huxley, *Life and Letters of Thomas Henry Huxley*, New York: D. Appleton & Company, 1901, I, 237.) The statement is of course exaggerated.

But what the world saw in the Dean of the College was of course "the leader of men." Huxley's rule, writes Professor T. Jeffery Parker,

was characterised by what is undoubtedly the best policy for the head of a department. To a new subordinate, "The General," as he was always called, was rather stern and exacting, but when once he was convinced that his man was to be trusted, he practically let him take his own course; never interfered in matters of detail, accepted suggestions with the greatest courtesy and good humour, and was always ready with a kindly and humorous word of encouragement in times of difficulty. I was once grumbling to him about how hard it was to carry on the work of the laboratory through a long series of November fogs, "when neither sun nor stars in many days appeared." "Never mind, Parker," he said, instantly capping my quotation, "cast four anchors out of the stern and wish for day."[32]

In the classroom Huxley was clear, precise, austerely eloquent, with occasional flashes of epigram and caustic humor, but with no hint of the facetiousness or small jocularity in which many lecturers indulge. "As one listened to him," wrote Jeffery Parker, "one felt that comparative anatomy was indeed worthy of the devotion of a life, and that to solve a morphological problem was as fine a thing as to win a battle."[33] In the laboratory, which he seldom visited in later years, he was a sudden and rather terrible presence, but not without occasional declensions into humor, or even into humanity. Professor H. F. Osborn recalled that he once appeared at the elbow of an Irish student notorious for his anatomical drawings in watercolor. Turning over the pages of the young man's drawing book, Huxley paused at a large blur which was carefully labeled, "sheep's liver." "I am glad to know that is a liver," he observed with a gentle smile; "it reminds me as much of Cologne cathedral in a fog as of anything I have ever seen before."[34] At an examination he passed a country boy who had declared the mitral valve to be on the right side of the heart. "Poor little beggar!" exclaimed Huxley, "I never got . . . [it] correctly myself until I reflected that a bishop was never in the right."[35]

Despite his austerity, there was that in Huxley which lifted the mind to admiration and filled the heart with loyalty. He left a stir of feeling and wonder behind him when he passed. Cabmen refused to accept his fare, and messengers asked him for a chance signature on an envelope. Fathers wrote him after their sons' deaths how much their sons had owed him, and after his own death, his former victim St. George Mivart was proud to write an essay of laudatory recollection and anecdote.[36] His assistants—prosaic, critical men hardened in the academic routine—broke into poetry at the thought of him. Professor E. Ray Lankester wrote:

> There has been no man or woman whom I have met on my journey through life, whom I have loved and regarded as I have him, and I feel that the world has shrunk and become a poor thing, now that his splendid spirit and delightful presence are gone from it. Ever since I was a little boy he has been my ideal and hero.[37]

Meanwhile, Huxley's eldest son Leonard, then eighteen and a student at St. Andrews, had won a scholarship for Oxford. As one academic potentate to another, his father wrote a letter to Benjamin Jowett. To youthful Oxonians and to many eminent personages who had once been youthful Oxonians, the Master of Balliol was something in the way of a Delphic Oracle. In fact, "the voice was the man"—a "cherubic chirp," which emerged from terrible silence under the auspices of a "commanding forehead" and an "infantile smile."[38] Viceroys were uneasy in his presence because viceroys had been his students; nor did tutorial conferences necessarily cease with graduation. In a sense, Jowett counseled an empire as Delphos counseled a civilization.

Like most mysteries, Jowett was full of contradictions. He despised learning and research, yet he introduced Hegel to Oxford and by his elegant translations reintroduced Plato to England. He sneered at logic as a dodge, yet he wanted to set Christian doctrine on a sound logical and scientific basis. He apparently believed in a personal God and in the teachings of Jesus, yet in his writings and public utterances he seemed so broad and liberal a churchman that agnostics like Leslie Stephen thought he should take off his surplice and give up the protection of Balliol. Above all, Jowett was a schoolmaster. As such, he employed the method of Socrates to achieve the results of the sophists. The Socratic question led first to clarity of thought but ultimately to worldly success. Too shy and timid, beneath his pedagogical façade, to go out into the world himself, he urged his students to do so and was as ambitious for them as he was for Balliol herself.

Toward ladies and toward men of genius, this eccentric and rather awful academic personage was meek and amicable. To Tennyson he was a properly deferential admirer; to Browning, a delightful breakfast companion who preached surreptitiously on Sunday; to Mrs. Huxley, an engaging bachelor who wrote arch answers to arch invitations. To Huxley himself, Jowett was something between an awed hero-worshiper and a sagacious tutor in disguise. He was also a comrade-in-arms. Friendship had been almost inevitable between one of the authors of *Essays and Reviews* and the author of *Man's Place in Nature*.

I am trying to introduce or rather to persuade others to introduce [Jowett wrote Huxley in 1877] more physical science into the university. I am inclined to think that some kind of it (as of Arithmetic) should be one of the requirements for a degree. Some scientific men appear to be opposed to this on the ground that it will lower the character of such studies. I cannot agree with them; no study can reach a very high standard with the mass of students. Yet it may do them great good and gain something from them in return.[39]

Huxley could have confidence in such a man. When Leonard came to Oxford in 1880, Jowett took his career in charge. A shrewd judge of character, and an even shrewder judge of success, he quickly decided that Leonard should be a barrister: he had a very clear, cool head. But Leonard wanted to get married. "The nearest way to attain that happiness," Jowett wrote Mrs. Huxley with distaste, "would be to become a Schoolmaster."[40] The clear, cool head was not dominant. Leonard became a schoolmaster and got married.

Meanwhile, Jowett was occupied with the father:

It is a good thing [he wrote in 1885] to have been P.R.S. [President of the Royal Society] and a good thing to have resigned and have the remaining years of life free for study and reflection. All the past may be gathered up in them and there is no reason to fear that the powers of reflection will fail. I have a sort of faith that the last ten years of life may be the best, if only undisturbed, and the calmest and the wisest and the fullest of invention and creation and the freest from illusion.[41]

Jowett now attempted to take Huxley's last ten years in hand. To be sure, he was only a very courteous and indirect adviser. It was a delicate and fearful task to direct so large and powerful "a logic engine" along fruitful paths. "What a tremendous controversialist he is!" Jowett wrote Mrs. Huxley, with an involuntary shudder. "Such smashing blows! I who am a coward and a man of peace admire his heroic qualities, but I should like also to hear without controversy what he would say on some of the Ethical and Philosophical Problems of the day."[42] By insinuation, by compliment, by gentle deprecation, by confidential indoctrination of Mrs. Huxley, he tried to deflect the logic engine from shattering creeds and occupying

presidential chairs, and to set it once more to making discoveries, not only scientific but ethical and philosophical. "In the
present state of the world," he observed inconspicuously at the
end of a more sententious passage, "the decomposing process
goes on fast enough generally whereas there is little or nothing
done."[43] One may be a little surprised that he hoped for so
much constructive action from Huxley. To be sure, his attitude
reflects the growing superstition about science. Science had
produced physical miracles—why not moral?

> I am . . . pleased [wrote Jowett] that you do not altogether
> throw cold water on the suggestion, which seems to have occurred
> to your own mind, that you should try to find a new basis for
> morals now when it seems likely to be buried under physics.
> There is no subject which it is more natural to consider in the
> late years of life or one of which the consideration is more needed
> than at the present time. All men are asking on what principle
> they must live and they want an answer independent of the
> traditional theology: Will you lend them a helping hand? My
> impression is that the answer will come with more effect from
> you than from any theologian.[44]

Very late, perhaps too late—Huxley began to do what Jowett
wanted. Had he lived longer, he might even have followed
Jowett's advice.

In a progressive country, even orthodoxy is only liberalism
a little behind the times. In 1881 Oxford considered Huxley
for two of her most important posts. He was sounded with
regard first to the Linacre Professorship of Physiology and
then to the Mastership of University College. His own respectability astonished him. "I begin to think," he wrote
Leonard, "I may yet be a Bishop."[45] He refused both offers.
Huxley at Oxford would have been Huxley incessantly at war.
It was easier to convert England than to convert Oxford.

When offered a Fishery inspectorship, however, he promptly
accepted—and without vacating any of his other posts. As one

of the two inspectors of the realm, Huxley had both practical and scientific duties. He had to study fish and fish diseases, investigate weirs and salmon runs, settle disputes, pass on local by-laws, and write reports. The veteran of several Fishery commissions and principal author of one of "the ablest and most exhaustive" reports on the subject ever laid before Parliament, Huxley was thoroughly at his ease with the work and looked forward cheerfully to combining his two favorite pleasures of discovering new scientific truth and "jamming" it "down the throats of fools."[46] As a matter of fact, he did work out the life cycle of the salmon disease *Saprolegnia ferax*, and amassed much valuable information about the herring and the cod. He also conveyed this, and doubtless much other, truth either gently or forcefully down the throats of politicians and fishermen. But the old savor was gone. If the advantage of his new post was much walking in the open air, its disadvantages were heavy dinners and interminable hearings. At first he was tolerant. A gala exhibition of fish and fishing tackle evoked mild approval. "Afterwards," he wrote, "a mighty *dejeuner* in the St. Andrew's Hall—a fine old place looking its best. I was just opposite the Princess, and could not help looking at her with wonderment. She looked so fresh and girlish. She came and talked to me afterwards in a very pleasant simple way."[47] But fat aldermen and talkative poachers were far more frequent than royal princesses. Within a few months Huxley had come to loathe dinners and abhor meetings. "Will you tell me what all this has to do with my business in life," he wrote Flower, "and why the last fragments of a misspent life that are left to me must be frittered away in all this drivel?"[48]

In fact, behind its stately façade of political and oratorical achievement, his life was becoming an ever swifter melodrama of looming deadlines and paralyzing frustration. He seldom had time to finish anything—and least of all his scientific researches, which after 1870 became more feverish and

more fruitless. Ironically, at the very time when the multiplicity of official duties prevented him from achieving anything
considerable, his powers of intellectual concentration seem to
have reached their heights. When he studied crayfish, he ate,
drank, slept, and breathed crayfish. In 1878 he was so deep in

COURTESY OF SIR JULIAN HUXLEY

T. H. HUXLEY AND HIS WIFE, HENRIETTA, TAKEN IN 1882.

the invertebrate complexities of the rare creature spirula that
when one of the demonstrators came to him with a question
about the brain of a codfish, he looked up blankly and replied,
"Codfish? That's a vertebrate, isn't it? Ask me a fortnight

hence, and I'll consider it."[49] But something always intervened to render concentration useless. Spirula lay on his worktable for months and even years.

Interruptions did not always spring from official business. In 1878 diphtheria invaded his family and brought his daughter Madge to such a crisis that poor Huxley, for all his discipline, could think of almost nothing else. In the midst of an after-dinner speech, he broke down for the first time in his life, and for one painful moment forgot what he had to say.

All permanence seemed to be disappearing from his life. In 1882 he lost both a master and a disciple. In April, Darwin died at Down; in the summer, Francis Balfour fell from a precipice while ascending one of the peaks of Mont Blanc. Both blows struck home, but Darwin's career was full and complete, whereas Balfour's had scarcely begun. Moreover, he was Huxley's scientific heir, the alter ego who was to have completed Huxley's work. Now that work might never be done. "A Paper 'On the Characters of the Pelvis' . . . in 1879, is full of suggestive thought," says Sir Michael Foster, "but its concluding passages seem to suggest that others . . . were to carry out the ideas."[50]

After Balfour's death, Huxley made redoubled efforts. Often, after a long afternoon at a public hearing, he would snatch a half hour at his laboratory bench before going home. Yet when in 1883 the opportunity offered, he became temporary President, and then in 1884 duly elected President of the Royal Society. He was obviously too busy, perhaps already too ill, to assume additional burdens. But to earn, and then refuse, the crown of an official scientific career—Huxley was in this respect very human; he dearly loved a presidency.

And now the gap between what he wanted to do and what he had to do, even between what he had to do and what he had strength to do, grew wider and wider. He was physically and spiritually exhausted. The universe seemed less and less rational, life less and less permanent and meaningful. No wonder that he found himself longing for the immortality which in years past he had so firmly rejected.

It is a curious thing [he wrote Morley] that I find my dislike to the thought of extinction increasing as I get older and nearer the goal.

It flashes across me at all sorts of times with a sort of horror that in 1900 I shall probably know no more of what is going on than I did in 1800. I had sooner be in hell a good deal—at any rate in one of the upper circles, where the climate and company are not too trying.[51]

From the later portraits his sharp, alert features look out with a settled and persistent sadness.

A succession of illnesses now followed. "In reply to your letter . . . ," he wrote Donnelly, "I have the honour to state . . . that I have (a) had all my teeth out; (b) partially sprained my right thumb; (c) am very hot; (d) can't smoke with comfort."[52] He could also eat nothing but gruel, he had developed a liver complaint, and his hand was like lead, so that he could scarcely hold a scalpel. Worst of all, he was so utterly exhausted that the thought of the day's work very nearly nauseated him. His only consolation was Gordon's stand against the Sudanese. "I should like to see him lick the Mahdi into fits," he declared, "before Wolseley gets up."[53] The exhausted man took several brief vacations without benefit. Finally, Sir Andrew Clark informed him that he would suffer a real breakdown if he did not take a prolonged rest.

Convinced that he had betrayed South Kensington and the Royal Society, exposed England to a civil war between the rod men and the net men, and condemned himself, as the culmination of his career, to professional oblivion—Huxley set out for Italy. At the railway station in London he received news that his daughter Marion had been stricken with a slow and treacherous disease which, as he rightly feared, was to prove fatal. "I am a tough subject," he wrote afterwards, "and have learned to bear a good deal without crying out, but those four-and-twenty hours between London and Luzern have taught me that I have a good deal to learn in the way of grinning and bearing."[54] It was his second recuperative exile, destined to be much longer than the first. In fact, his symptoms resembled much more those of the desperate melancholia which as a young man he had suffered on board the *Rattlesnake*. He was full at once of deadly lassitude and nervous irritability, of eagerness to hide away from his fellow men and to hate them at a moment's notice. Once more, also, he distracted himself with literature. He even resumed his study of Italian and discovered *The Autobiography of Benvenuto Cellini*. The very thought of science disgusted him.

Full of heavy fears for his daughter, Huxley refreshed himself with Lido air, endured Verona, battled with cholera-closed hotels in Naples. Ravenna was a wonderful "deadly lively sepulchre of a place."[55] It illustrated that art too had an evolution, and itself contained one great phase of that evolution in little. He regarded Rome as young Matthew Arnold had regarded the elderly George Sand—as a fabulous old woman still fascinating in advanced decay and the shadows of a long and sinister past. In the shadows of that long past, however, he found his cure and the way back to science. He began by sneering puritanically at papal ceremonies, with much talk of "man-millinery" and "bedizened dolls."[56] From the aesthetic point of view, he would "destroy everything except St. Paolo fuor Le Mure of later date than the fourth century."[57] On the other hand, he felt easy in the Catacombs. They were congenial both to his mood and his temperament. Gradually he became interested in Pagan Rome and then—with the first symptoms of returning health—in Roman geology and prehistory. One month later he was writing the preface for a new edition of the *Lessons in Elementary Physiology*, which he was bringing out in collaboration with Sir Michael Foster.

His wife had shared all but the first three weeks of this vacation with him. Early in the spring of 1885, they began to move northward. They "broke their backs and enlarged their minds" in the art galleries of Florence, shivered in Venice, thawed out in San Remo, and finally landed at Folkestone on April 8.[58]

Huxley had by no means recovered. The lightest task cost him infinite labor. He had developed "a perfect genius for making mountains out of molehills."[59] After some tentative exertions, with immediate consequences of lassitude and blue devils, he resigned his professorship, his deanship, and at length the presidency of the Royal Society.

In the midst of the negotiations incident to his retirement, he received news he was to be awarded the D.C.L. degree by Oxford. "It will be," he wrote, "a sort of apotheosis coincident with my official death, which is imminent. In fact, I am dead already, only the Treasury Charon has not yet settled the conditions upon which I am to be ferried over to the other side."[60] His pension caused nearly as much secret turning of official cogs as the financing of his early monographs on the oceanic hydrozoa. Eventually, Huxley continued at the college as professor and honorary dean, with a pension equal to his salary of fifteen hundred pounds and no duties except that of a general superintendence over scientific work.

18

The Pleasant Avocation of War

Huxley found health at last not in the sunshine of Italy nor in the offices of a physician but in the pages of a review. In the leading article of *The Nineteenth Century* for November, 1885, Gladstone descended on Dr. Réville's scientific *Prolégomènes de l'Histoire des Religions* like a thick and aggressive fog. Skillfully hiding his forest in his trees, the great man declared for nearly everything—he was for science and for religion, for Moses and for Darwin. Yet he had no doubt that, with all respect for the high intellectual activity which it involved, science had done little but footnote the text of Genesis. The opening verses of that book were simply a compressed and poetic account of the nebular hypothesis and of biological and paleontological study up to the death of Cuvier. In his conclusion Gladstone paid Darwin a ceremonious but extremely vague compliment, as in parliamentary battle he might suavely hail a dubious ally with a view to producing a convenient silence of acquiescence.

There was to be no convenient silence. Huxley slammed down *The Nineteenth Century* and began to blaspheme about the house with a vigor and heartiness that astonished his family.

The angrier he became the better he felt. Gladstone had administered the electric shock which finally precipitated the clouds of melancholy, setting off a splendid storm of polemical thunder and lightning.

The storm lasted more than half a decade. There is something heroic about so prolonged a commotion; and in his courage and daring, in the magnitude of what he defended and what he attacked, in the sheer quantity and inveteracy of his secondary virtues—in common sense, alertness, energy, and learning—Huxley was an heroic, if not always a brilliant, controversialist.

Probably no one quite understood Gladstone's article. Huxley did not quite understand it, but he understood enough to know that Gladstone had trimmed and pounded science outrageously to make it fit the needs of orthodoxy. That the greatest political leader of his time could hold so lightly the most brilliant epoch in the history of biology, was shocking and infuriating to Huxley. The Grand Old Man was really a Grand Old Anachronism. Gleefully, insidiously, Huxley decided to modernize him a little. He had never shared Darwin's admiration for Gladstone. He respected the man's ability to succeed without respecting the abilities which made him a success. Sometimes he was quite harsh. "Gladstone I see," he had written Hooker many years before, "is pumping himself up at Whitby. Some of these days he will turn himself inside out like a blessed Hydra, and I daresay he will talk just as well in that state as in his normal condition."[1]

"The Interpreters of Genesis and the Interpreters of Nature" appeared in the December issue of The Nineteenth Century. "Do read my polishing off of the G.O.M.," Huxley wrote Spencer. "I am proud of it as a work, and as evidence that the volcano is not yet exhausted."[2] As a health certificate, the essay is impressive, but as a literary composition it is rather wordy and pedestrian. Huxley explains, politely, but firmly and insistently, that neither the phrases of Genesis nor the theories of science can be stretched into any easy agreement.

The antagonism of science is not to religion [he concludes], but to the heathen survivals and the bad philosophy under which religion herself is often well nigh crushed. And for my part, I trust that this antagonism will never cease; but that, to the end of time, true science will continue to fulfil one of her most beneficent functions, that of relieving men from the burden of false science which is imposed upon them in the name of religion.[3]

Gladstone was at this time prime minister and almost on the eve of introducing his first Home Rule Bill. Irishmen were more unreasonable and Tories more perfidious than ever. If the aged statesman was not, as in former years, doing the work of ten men, at least he was doing the work of five. Nevertheless, he found time to dash off a reply to Huxley, which appeared in *The Nineteenth Century* for January, 1886.[4] With unruffled courtesy, he listed all of Huxley's most telling blows, turned a majestic cheek, and then proceeded to reconcile Genesis not only with Cuvier but with the latest textbook writers in geology and paleontology. If in some trifling details the Mosaic author did not always agree with up-to-date scientific authority, he wrote in obedience to the peculiar purpose of the Deity, which was not to lecture mankind on science but to instruct it in morals and religion. Moreover, Gladstone gently concluded, religion was a rather more serious matter than Professor Huxley seemed to realize.

The effect of this stately evasion on Huxley may be imagined. Never was his digestion better; never was his temper worse. He felt that he had nothing more to say on the subject, but that a reply was essential. He replied at length.[5] His editor returned the manuscript in alarm. "I spent three mortal hours this morning taming my wild cat," wrote Huxley of his revision. "He is now castrated; his teeth are filed; his claws are cut; he is taught to swear like a 'mieu'; and to spit like a cough; and when he is turned out of the bag you won't know him from a tame rabbit."[6] In fact, he had become a wild cat in rabbit's clothing. Huxley referred to "the cloud of argument" which had emanated from the great parliamentarian. He showed that Gladstone did not always agree with Gladstone, that he sometimes did not agree with the "Mosaic writer," and that he never agreed, basically, with the modern scientific authorities whom he quoted so confidently. Huxley also wanted to know what the nebular hypothesis had to do with such statements as "And the spirit of God moved on the face of the waters."[7]

Lesser champions now entered the battle, which echoed and reechoed at Homeric length through the pages of *The Nineteenth Century*. Huxley, bidding a farewell to arms in his second article, now vanished like a mythological hero into the starry vault of scientific detachment: in "The Evolution of Theology: An Anthropological Study" (1886) he contemplates religion as "a natural product of the operations of the human mind."[8] The Bible is not a book but a whole literature —a series of "stratified deposits (often confused and even with their natural order inverted) left by the stream of the intellectual and moral life of Israel during many centuries."[9] Analyzing religious beliefs in *Judges* and *Samuel*, he finds them at the stage of monolatry, or the worship of a tribal deity, which stood midway between the refined monotheism of the prophets —into which it was to develop—and the animism characteristic of all primitive cultures—from which it had clearly arisen.

But Huxley was always most dangerous when he seemed most scientific. "The Evolution of Theology" was another

Man's Place in Nature—or rather, *Theology's Place in Nature*. Huxley levels religion to its origins as he had leveled man to his, and undermines supernatural causes by showing how satisfactorily natural causes could take their places. He concludes with a panoramic picture, indicating how Egyptian and Babylonian influences determine the evolution of Judaism, and philosophic and scientific influences that of Christianity. One of the functions of science is to purify religion of its theology, for religion is advanced and elevated in proportion as it approaches pure ethics, and primitive and debased in proportion as it develops dogmas and ceremonies.

Exhilarating as it had been, the massacre of Gladstone did not completely restore the melancholy Comanche. In the next two years, Huxley fled before his blue devils to Yorkshire, to Bournemouth, even to the Alps, where, during a really happy summer, he made a valuable study of gentians. When he was cheerful he pursued science. When he was despondent, he "chewed" theology. In general, he found that as long as he could walk ten miles a day or gobble up an occasional statesman or philosopher, he kept in reasonably good spirits.

In the intervals of sending batches of autobiography for criticism, Spencer slyly threw him a philosopher. Had he noticed that W. S. Lilly had published in the *Fortnightly* for November, 1886, an article on "Materialism and Morals," in which, of course, he proved that Spencer and Huxley were materialists and therefore not moral? Huxley read—and yielded to his instincts.

The result was "Science and Morals," which appeared in the next number of the *Fortnightly*. This essay says nothing new, but says it with greater skill than ever before. It actually turns apologetics into a mode of attack. Huxley comes before his readers in the sackcloth and ashes of scientific skepticism and takes his leave—in sackcloth that has become strangely like the papal regalia of his most confident dogmatism. He begins with a gentle protest against the harsh word materialism. Materialism, according to Büchner, explains the universe in terms of matter and force. But science does not try to reduce consciousness to matter and force. Moreover, it recognizes that matter and force themselves are immaterial unknowns. How can an indivisible atom occupy space? How can it affect other atoms by a force resident in nothingness?

On the other hand, Huxley maintains that mind is certainly dependent on physical causes. Changes in physiology certainly precede changes in consciousness, as muscular contraction precedes a movement of the arm. Again, he acknowledges a belief in "determinism," for the opposite of determinism is spontaneity, and to believe in complete spontaneity is to believe in utter chaos. Yet he feels that he is no more a determinist than Thomas Aquinas and Bishop Berkeley, and though a materialist, no less free to believe in an intelligent Deity. Lilly must have read this essay with some bewilderment, the more so as Huxley nowhere concedes that mental phenomena really affect physical phenomena. He ends with the famous metaphor in which science is Cinderella, and theology and philosophy are the two ugly sisters:

She lights the fire, sweeps the house, and provides the dinner; and is rewarded by being told that she is a base creature, devoted to low and material interests. But in her garret she has fairy visions out of the ken of the pair of shrews who are quarreling down stairs. . . .
    She knows that the safety of morality lies . . . in a real and living belief in that fixed order of nature which sends social disorganisation upon the track of immorality, as surely as it sends physical disease after physical trespasses.[10]

The editor of the *Fortnightly* declared that the article "simply made the December number."[11]

A sermon by Canon Liddon brought Huxley once more into

theological controversy. The distinguished preacher had asserted that catastrophies—and particular sacred catastrophies—represented suspensions of lower laws of nature by higher. In "Pseudo-Scientific Realism" Huxley explained that such thinking was plainly a survival of medieval realism, which conceived universals as actual existences. Physical laws are not agents or forces in themselves. They do not bind nature in any way, nor can they counteract or supersede each other. They are simply generalized records of experience and therefore a means by which, with a high degree of probability, future experience can be predicted.

This essay is remarkable both for its sweep and its verve. Huxley sketches out the history of metaphysical thought in a few strokes, disposing of the medieval cosmos in a single sentence:

From the centre of that world, the Divine Trinity, surrounded by a hierarchy of angels and saints, contemplated and governed the insignificant sensible world in which the inferior spirits of men, burdened with the debasement of their material embodiment and continually solicited to their perdition by a no less numerous and almost as powerful hierarchy of devils, were constantly struggling on the edge of the pit of everlasting damnation.[12]

He concedes that the scholastic philosophers were human, even that they were intelligent: they kept thinking alive, but they thought about nonsense.

Huxley had shot an arrow in the direction of Canon Liddon, but it was the Duke of Argyll who shouted "ouch!" His outcry, full of metaphysics and moral reprobation, covers some twenty pages of the Fortnightly for March. He was not only in pain; he was very angry, and quite naturally he attributed all of Huxley's calm to himself and all of his own anger to Huxley. "The Professor" was on the whole right, but he had made an unseemly and vituperative attack on the pulpit. The Duke proceeded to explain what the Canon meant and what the professor meant in such a way that it became very unclear what anybody meant. Finally, Darwin's great reputation had established a scientific "Reign of Terror," against which, his Grace predicted, Huxley himself would rebel.

Huxley soon guessed, and after scanning the Duke's *Reign of Law* clearly ascertained, that the noble author had been defending his own confusion in the Canon's name. Responding in "Science and Pseudo-Science," Huxley neatly traced the concept of natural law from Bacon's time to his own, showing that the law of the conservation of energy indicates, throughout organic and inorganic nature, a uniformitarianism in the succession of events which permits no shuffling of "higher" and "lower" laws. Finally, he did not spare the Duke, whose presumptuous ignorance and hopeless confusion had put him, Huxley declared, to the trouble of writing a good deal of very elementary exposition.

Huxley expected the Duke to subside into silence. Instead, he ascended to the stratosphere. In "A Great Lesson," published in the September *Fortnightly*, he rhapsodically expounded first Darwin's coral reef theory and then the counter-theory which John Murray had developed while on the *Challenger* expedition. Clearly, even Darwin could err, yet such was the awe in which he was held that Murray, influenced by other scientific men, hesitated two years before making public his results.

Huxley did not deign to make a deliberate reply, but at the end of "An Episcopal Trilogy" he pointed out that Murray had by no means proved Darwin wrong about coral reefs. After an exhaustive study, the American Dana had decided that Darwin's theory still accounted best for all the facts.

Huxley's essay, published in the *Fortnightly* for November, 1887, deals principally with speeches made by three enlightened bishops at a meeting of the British Association. Huxley agrees with them that science and religion are not essentially in conflict. The spiritual essence of Christianity could be saved intact if only the miraculous husk could be cast away. The author's language is full of the generosity of concession and understanding. He grants that prayer may certainly be efficacious, in a psychological and even in a practical sense. He acknowledges that scientists have their "full share of original sin."[13] Astronomy does not teach them greatness of soul nor microbiology, meekness. But when he comes to speak of the achievement of science, his real feeling becomes clearer:

Theological apologists who insist that morality will vanish if their dogmas are exploded, would do well to consider the fact that, in the matter of intellectual veracity, science is already a long way ahead of the Churches; and that, in this particular, it is exerting an educational influence on mankind of which the Churches have shown themselves utterly incapable.[14]

Now his melancholy returned and drove him into fresh exile in the hotels of Yorkshire and Switzerland. He had become a familiar figure in certain foreign and provincial breakfast rooms —a celebrated man with sad eyes and white sideburns, who filled obscure physicians with rapturous enthusiasm and clerical old maids with indignant and vituperative piety. Huxley was too much preoccupied to notice the stir he caused. Henrietta had been ill of late, and in 1887 his second daughter Marion, Mrs. John Collier, died of pneumonia. She had been ill for three years. Huxley had hoped and not hoped.

Indeed [he wrote to Hooker in a revealing letter] . . . I have feared the gradual supervention of dementia. . . . She was a brilliant creature with a faculty for art, which some of the best artists have told me amounted to genius: she was married most happily to a man who has throughout shown the most utter devotion to her, and all the world seemed . . . open to her young life. But after her last confinement more than three years ago, melancholy set in (of the worst type).[15]

Huxley must have seen some of the deep horror of heredity in this. Providentially, he had almost at once to travel four hundred miles to make a speech on technical education to a large crowd in a hot, stuffy room. He returned reinvigorated, if not comforted.

At best, these were sad years. He complained that as often as he fled to Yorkshire or Switzerland, he returned to find some old friend gone. In 1888 Matthew Arnold died in a Liverpool hotel. Huxley could not but think of his own end. "Poor Arnold's death has been a great shock—rather for his wife than for himself . . . ," he wrote Foster. "I have always thought sudden death to be the best of all for oneself, . . . but terrible for those who are left. Arnold told me years ago he had heart disease."[16] Huxley had just learned that he also had heart trouble. A "weakness and some enlargement of the left ventricle." Luckily, the valves were all right. "I do not suppose there is any likelihood of an immediate catastrophe in my own case. I should not go abroad if there were. Imagine the horror of leaving one's wife to fight all the difficulties of sudden Euthanasia in a Swiss hotel!"[17]

The X Club—once the gay, conspiratorial cabinet of science —had by this time dwindled into a knot of ailing, overworked old men, who were just a little tired of each other and perhaps just a little too delicate for the fare they sat down to.

It has long been too obvious to me [Huxley wrote Hooker as early as 1883], that the relations of some of us at the X have been very strained. Strong men as they get old seem to me to acquire very much the nature of apes [?], and tend to become dangerous to one another and run amuck at everything that does not quite suit their fancy. I am conscious of the tendency myself. It is hateful to me and where I have time to think I put it down at all costs.[18]

In 1888 Huxley contributed to *The Proceedings of the Royal Society* "An Obituary" of Charles Darwin. Obituaries are probably never easy, and Huxley was more in the mood to write his own than Darwin's. Yet he had splendid materials at his disposal—not only the rich personal experience of a lifelong friendship but Darwin's own revealing "Autobiography" and Francis Darwin's newly published *Life and Letters*. He took infinite pains, but succeeded only in performing the standard miracle of Victorian biographical piety—a Pygmalion metamorphosis in reverse, in which a living friend is turned into a marble statue—or rather, a kind of memorial whetstone on which to grind moral axes. Darwin's youthful indifference to his studies, for example, demonstrates how little ordinary classical education could awaken the interest of a first-rate mind. What Huxley wrote in personal letters at this time was much more alive and vivid: "Exposition was not Darwin's *forte*," he confided to his younger colleague Foster, "and his English is sometimes wonderful. But there is a marvellous dumb sagacity about him—like that of a sort of miraculous dog—and he gets to the truth by ways as dark as those of the Heathen Chinee."[19]

In 1888, twelve months after his old friend Hooker, Huxley was awarded the Copley Medal by the Royal Society. So often Darwin's visible and vocal vicar at gala dinners Darwin could not eat, Huxley now could not eat his own. He received the medal at the preliminary meeting and then retired. That autumn he also resigned his seat on the Eton Board of Governors. He had not been able to attend a meeting for a year and a half.

The minor tribulations of old age—earache and mufflers and extra heavy overcoats—were fast falling to his share. He even had to face the consequences of his own liberalism. He had always urged as a matter of simple common sense that a man might marry his deceased wife's sister. In January, 1889, he learned that his youngest daughter Ethel was going to marry

John Collier, the widower of Marion. Abruptly Huxley realized he had always hoped none of his own daughters would
make this common-sense experiment. Yet "whatever annoy-
ances and social pin-pricks may come in Ethel's way," he told
Hooker, "I know nobody less likely to care about them."[20]

The Victorians were so serious that a book did not need to
be good to stagger them. It needed only to be serious. Mrs.
Humphrey Ward's *Robert Elsmere* was very serious: she had
succeeded in translating her uncle Matthew Arnold's *Literature and Dogma* into the clichés of contemporary moral melodrama. To recuperate from Oxford and the fever, Robert
Elsmere, a young cleric whose virtues are as romantically handsome as the muscles of a more obvious kind of hero, comes to
a sequestered valley of Westmoreland. Here he falls in love
with the beautiful and saintly Catherine Leyburn, who compromises sufficiently with her own lofty Christianity to return
his love. He becomes a rector in Surrey. They marry, have a
child, and live happily ever after until Robert grows friendly
with a sinister squire, who, instead of keeping a mad wife in
the garret, reads Gibbon and Hume in the library. The squire
touches on miracles, and Robert's faith collapses like a house
of cards. He renounces his Christian ministry, goes with his
wife to London, founds a new faith of humanity, and dies a
martyr to feeding orphans and comforting cripples.

Mrs. Ward's novel did not cause a revolution, but it advertised a revolution that had already occurred. Novel readers who
had never opened such books as the *Origin* or *Literature and
Dogma* awakened to the ideas they contained with a shock.
Probably Gladstone never read the *Origin*, but he certainly
read *Robert Elsmere* and wrote one of his most perceptive articles about it. Its aim, he noted, was "to expel the preter-
natural element from Christianity, to destroy its dogmatic
structure, yet to keep intact the moral and spiritual results."[21]

History shows that a religion cannot long survive its deity, nor a type of character, the religious dogmas out of which it grew. Moreover, miracles lie at the very basis of Christianity. They are inseparable, on the one hand, from the miraculous biography which embodies the divinity of Christ and on the other, from the dogmas according to which that divinity may be worshipped. The Christian type was not likely to be preserved without the Christian scheme.

Not only the state but the church took notice of *Robert Elsmere*. The Church Congress, meeting in the fall of 1888, regarded it as the latest symptom of a very old disease, and in a special afternoon set aside for the purpose, rather recklessly applied the modern name *agnosticism*. The Bishop of Peterborough, amid wild cheers, denounced "cowardly agnosticism," and Dr. Wace, the Principal of King's College, exclaimed that an agnostic is a man who, on the plea that he has no scientific knowledge of the unseen world, refuses to accept the authority of Jesus Christ. His real name is infidel.

Of course Huxley read the *Official Report of the Church Congress*. In *The Nineteenth Century* for February, 1889, he replied with a long and somewhat acidly illuminating article on "Agnosticism." He failed to see that agnostic and infidel were interchangeable words. Dr. Wace did not accept the authority of Mohammed. Mohammedans would therefore consider him an infidel, no matter how uncritically he believed in his own religion. In short, his definition of an agnostic expressed a prejudice rather than a principle. But was not his loyalty to Christianity a prejudice also? Rational belief, as the author of *Robert Elsmere* had said, depended on the value of testimony. Now the story of the Gadarene swine rested on very dubious evidence. Like much else in the New Testament it varied considerably from one gospel to another. Again, the destruction of valuable livestock reflected a carelessness unworthy and uncharacteristic of Jesus. The transference of demons from men to swine involved a superstition common to all barbarous peoples and productive of the grossest error and cruelty. Did Jesus believe in such a superstition, and if so, could he be divine? Finally, Christianity was not even a coherent unity recognized by all Christians. Not only the Buddhist and the Mohammedan, but the modern Catholic and the ancient Nazarene would consider Dr. Wace an infidel.

On the other hand, no one would consider him an agnostic:

Agnosticism, in fact, is not a creed, but a method, the essence of which lies in the rigorous application of a single principle. That principle is of great antiquity; it is as old as Socrates; as old as the writer who said, "Try all things, hold fast by that which is good"; it is the foundation of the Reformation, which simply illustrated the axiom that every man should be able to give a reason for the faith that is in him; it is the great principle of Descartes; it is the fundamental axiom of modern science. Positively the principle may be expressed: In matters of the intellect, follow your reason as far as it will take you, without regard to any other consideration. And negatively: In matters of the intellect, do not pretend that conclusions are certain which are not demonstrated or demonstrable.[22]

As Huxley had first used the term in Metaphysical Society days, an *agnostic* had indeed followed reason, but he had maintained that even reason could not carry him very far, that the ultimate reality behind appearances can never be known. To get Socrates, Luther, and Descartes all on his side and to underline the ancient lineage of the free inquiry from which agnosticism grew, Huxley has here plainly done violence to a valuable word.

His article concluded with a digression on Frederic Harrison's "The Future of Agnosticism," published in the *Fortnightly* for January. Huxley was wonderfully courteous, admiring Harrison's intelligence in the abstract and reducing it to the wildest insanity in the concrete. Yet through the

polemical skyrockets and Roman candles, one notices again
the dark background of sadness.

I know of no study which is so unutterably saddening as that
of the evolution of humanity, as it is set forth in the annals of
history. Out of the darkness of prehistoric ages man emerges with
the marks of his lowly origin strong upon him. He is a brute, only
more intelligent than the other brutes, a blind prey to impulses,
which as often as not lead him to destruction; a victim to endless
illusions, which make his mental existence a terror and a burden,
and fill his physical life with barren toil and battle. He attains
a certain degree of physical comfort, and develops a more or less
workable theory of life, in such favourable situations as the plains
of Mesopotamia or of Egypt, and then, for thousands and thousands of years, struggles, with varying fortunes, attended by infinite wickedness, bloodshed, and misery, to maintain himself at
this point against the greed and ambition of his fellow-men. He
makes a point of killing and otherwise persecuting all those who
first try to get him to move on; and when he has moved on a
step, foolishly confers post-mortem deification on his victims. . . .
And the best men of the best epochs are simply those who make
the fewest blunders and commit the fewest sins.[23]

In short, history is, for the most part, so much inductive evidence of original sin. It records the slow retreat of the natural
man, the repetitious tragedy of the nonconformist and the
innovator. The rationalist-Protestant view has seldom been
more eloquently or gloomily expressed.

"Agnosticism" produced a double-headed counterattack
from Dr. Wace and the Bishop of Peterborough.[24] The Bishop
squared off only to subside into the most gracious controversial
amenities, but Dr. Wace proved surprisingly firm, both in the
head and in the spine. Not in the least overawed, he calmly
explained himself into good sense and Huxley into something
very like nonsense. He was perfectly aware that infidel was a
relative term and he had used it so. He knew that Christian
testimony presented a complex problem and that some parts

of the New Testament were more suspect than others. In fact, he corrected Huxley on some finer differences among the higher critics. The Gadarene story might or might not be true, but it was not essential to Christian faith. The Passion, the Lord's Prayer, and the Sermon on the Mount were essential. They constituted not a scientific but a moral authority which compelled the assent of sensitive and reverent consciences.

Mrs. Ward answered Wace indirectly with a long and very un-Platonic dialogue called "The New Reformation."[25] What struck her imagination were the patient, courageous investigations of the German critics and the splendid drama which emerged so luminously from the dark wilderness of variant readings. The Germans had uncovered the human being in the Christ, the human history in the miracles and the theology. They had shown how history had prepared for Jesus long before he was born so that he could mold it long after he was dead, how in fact he was a supremely happy combination of l'homme, le moment, et le milieu. In short, Mrs. Ward argued that Dr. Wace's moral authority arises from the historical process.

Naturally Huxley was enthusiastic about Mrs. Ward's article. She maintained that "all history is one," as he maintained that all life is one.[26] She likewise showed that a union of science and religion had already taken place and she had provided it with the splendid title of the New Reformation. "If it should be possible for me to give a little shove to the 'New Reformation,'" he wrote Knowles, "I shall think the fag end of my life well spent."[27]

His "Agnosticism: A Rejoinder" was something decidedly more vigorous and less polite than "a little shove." Dr. Wace had asserted that the Sermon on the Mount and the Lord's Prayer formed the center of Christian teaching. Huxley now proceeded to remove that center: there is no real agreement among the gospels on the Lord's Prayer and the Sermon on the Mount. He devoted the latter part of his article to proving that the "universal Christianity" of Paul differed widely from the earlier Nazarene Christianity of James and Peter, inasmuch as it freed Gentiles from the ceremonial and dietary restrictions of the Jewish law. He concluded by explaining once more the absurdity of the Gadarene story and the absurdity of Dr. Wace in believing it.

One cannot but regard this article as an elaborate and mistaken attempt to make Christianity a needle in a haystack of conflicting evidence. Huxley kept himself so busy picking at facts and fictions that he never felt obliged to inquire whether they contained any truth. His matter was never thinner nor his manner rougher, and never was he more pleased with himself. "I am possessed by a writing demon," he declared on beginning the article; and a little later, "You can't think how I enjoy writing now for the first time in my life."[28] No doubt easy victories were more relaxing. Huxley seems to have taken Dr. Wace and Christianity as medicine.

In "Christianity and Agnosticism,"[29] Wace renewed his accusations of quibbling and evasion, and challenged Huxley to respond either with an acknowledgment or a refutation.

In "Agnosticism and Christianity" Huxley responded with further variations on his old arguments. He persisted in seeing contemporary religious controversy entirely as a battle between agnosticism and ecclesiasticism, between critical honesty and the uncritical acceptance of a comforting illusion. To believe in the Passion, the Lord's Prayer, and the Sermon on the Mount is simply to believe in angels and fiends, a savior and a devil, a heaven and a hell—in short, in a great deal of worn-out metaphysical furniture. Cardinal Newman had shown that the miracles of the Bible rest on no stronger ground than those of Church history. He inferred that therefore all Christian miracles must be accepted. Huxley inferred that therefore no Christian miracles need be accepted.

My article, he told Hooker, is "as full of malice as an egg

is full of meat, and my satisfaction in making Newman my accomplice has been unutterable."[30] He had a scandalized admiration for Newman's wit and eloquence, his "subtlety and acuteness";[31] but he failed to see how so intelligent a man could believe in Catholicism. Only one explanation was possible. "I have been reading some of his works lately, and I understand now why Kingsley accused him of growing dishonesty. After an hour or two of him I begin to lose sight of the distinction between truth and falsehood."[32] Huxley's scientific zeal led him to judge men's morals by their cosmogonies. He did not see how a churchman could be so devoted to a spiritual truth as to accept all the dubious metaphysics in which it was wrapped.

Huxley resembled Newman considerably and misunderstood him almost completely. Both had much in common with Hume. Both doubted the reality of the physical world—Huxley at least theoretically, Newman instinctively and from earliest childhood. Both also doubted its rationality—and saw that the way of the critical intellect leads to skepticism, which both used chiefly as a weapon in controversy. Huxley sought truth by reasoning on the evidence of the senses, Newman, by reasoning on the intimations of conscience; and as Newman aspired to produce a *Novum Organum* for religion in terms of spiritual psychology, so Huxley looked forward to a *Novum Organum* for morals in terms of physical science.

Huxley was a Protestant who had long ago ceased to believe in God. Newman was a Protestant whom the need for more tangible grounds for hope had made a Catholic. Huxley found temporary exaltation in man's rapidly growing scientific power and knowledge. Newman found comfort at last in a universal church which, evolving logically and authoritatively from a divine mission and a divine revelation, seemed to represent reason in an unreasonable world.

Whatever he thought of Newman or indeed of contem-

porary Protestantism, Huxley protested that he did not mean
to oppose Christianity itself: he was attempting only to clear
away idolatrous accretions, to uncover truth by removing error.
In one passage at least, he very nearly removes Jesus: Apparently "you conceive," he wrote in thanking the Reverend Estlin
Carpenter for The First Three Gospels,

. . . that the personality of Jesus was the leading cause—the
conditio sine qua non—of the evolution of Christianity from
Judaism.

I long thought so, and having a strong dislike to belittle the
heroic figures of history, I held by the notion as long as I could,
but I find it melting away.

I cannot see that the moral and religious ideal of early Christianity is new—on the other hand, it seems to me to be implicitly
and explicitly contained in the early prophetic Judaism and the
later Hellenised Judaism. . . . It is quite true that the new vitality
of the old ideal manifested in early Christianity demands "an adequate historic cause." . . . Platonic and Stoical philosophy—
prophetic liberalism—the strong democratic socialism of the Jewish political system—the existence of innumerable sodalities for
religious and social purposes—had thrown the ancient world into
a state of unstable equilibrium. With such predisposing causes
at work, the exciting cause of enormous changes might be relatively insignificant. The powder was there—a child might throw
the match which should blow up the whole concern.

I do not want to seem irreverent, still less depreciatory, of
noble men, but it strikes me that in the present case the Nazarenes
were the match and Paul the child.[33]

In short, here as elsewhere, Huxley shows himself a determinist. The grandeur of historical forces leaves little room for any
human—or superhuman—grandeur.

On the other hand, his growing disgust for sentimentalism
in politics and theology led him to express guarded approval
for old-fashioned Calvinism:

The doctrines of predestination; of original sin; of the innate
depravity of man and the evil fate of the greater part of the race;
of the primacy of Satan in his world; of the essential vileness of

matter; of a malevolent Demiurgus subordinate to a benevolent Almighty, who has only lately revealed himself, faulty as they are, appear to me to be vastly nearer the truth than the "liberal" popular illusions that babies are all born good and that the example of a corrupt society is responsible for their failure to remain so; that it is given to everybody to reach the ethical ideal if he will only try; that all partial evil is universal good; and other optimistic figments, such as that which represents "Providence" under the guise of a paternal philanthropist, and bids us believe that everything will come right (according to our notions) at last.[34]

This passage indicates the kind of criticism Huxley was capable of when he could get his mind off Gadarene pigs. His study of Rousseau at this time had obviously sharpened his eye for contemporary romanticism.

In 1890 Huxley was obliged once more to annihilate Canon Liddon, who had defended the Old Testament as divinely accurate because it was essential to the Christian system. In "The Lights of the Church and the Light of Science," Huxley agreed that certain Old Testament stories were indeed unhappily essential to Christian theology. He then opened up on the Deluge fabrication first with his old scientific guns and afterward with a splendid new masked battery assembled from Babylonian archeology. The latter part of the essay he devoted to hunting the Deluge, universal or partial, not only out of the pulpit but out of Christian textbooks and encyclopedias.*

That fall Gladstone gathered his articles on the Bible into a book which he published as *The Impregnable Rock of Holy*

---

* Another essay, "Hasisadra's Adventure" (1890), tells the ancient Babylonian version of the Deluge as it appears on the clay tablets of Assurbanipal. Huxley builds up the relative restraint and probability of this account only to descend upon it with the combined weight of geology, archeology, and common sense—and so strike a concentrated blow not only at the more exaggerated Hebrew variant but at the misguided people who deceive themselves into swallowing such nonsense. None deceives himself more than the modern theological "reconciler," who feels that a miracle is proved fact when it is proved a bare possibility.

Scripture. He explained all biblical criticism as irrelevant, reiterated all his former arguments as unanswerable, predicted the rapid decline of skepticism, and concluded with a gibe at Huxley, to whom, after two thousand years of discussion, it

PRESS PORTRAIT BUREAU

HUXLEY IN 1890, AFTER THIRTY YEARS OF DEDICATION.

was reserved to discover from an analysis of the incident of the Gadarene swine that our Lord was "no better than a law-breaker and an evil-doer."[35] Gladstone explained that Gadara was a Jewish city. The swineherds should not have been raising pork any more than they should have eaten it. Jesus was therefore perfectly justified in destroying their property. Apparently, no rock was quite so impregnable as the cranium of the Grand Old Man himself.

Huxley was so delighted at the prospect of further battle with the G.O.M. that he was almost grateful for being insulted. In "The Keepers of the Herd of Swine,"[36] he was full of gaiety and metaphorical scalps, peace pipes, and tomahawks. Only after some pages did he assume the sternness appropriate to the reprehension of perfidy and ignorance. Needless to say, he proved that Gadara was an Hellenic city, and that to question the truth of an incident in the New Testament was not to impugn the character of Jesus.

But Huxley's strategy of attacking Christianity at its weakest point had begun to work against him. Demonology in the Gospels is a fairly important question. The character of Jesus is a very important one. But two eminent men cannot argue about pigs indefinitely without becoming ridiculous. It was observed in the press that they might be better occupied at their age. Although Huxley was inclined to agree, nevertheless the controversy continued. In *The Nineteenth Century* for February, 1891, Gladstone apologized so haughtily for his accusations that, thinking the whole matter over at leisure, Huxley decided he was very angry, and published an indignant article on "Mr. Gladstone's Controversial Methods." Unfortunately, he could not get away from pigs. At the very end, he tried desperately to give them metaphysical significance. Religion, ethics, progress—everything hung on how people felt about the Gadarene pigs. But people were tired of Gadarene pigs. The controversy died of its own grotesqueness.

Apparently, the older and tireder he grew, the harder he fought. At this time he was also waging voluminous warfare against the Salvation Army. A lady about to subscribe one thousand pounds to General Booth's *Darkest England* scheme had paused to ask Huxley his opinion. He had taken one look at the Salvation Army, another at Booth's *In Darkest England, and the Way Out*—and suddenly realized with horror that he had discovered a grave national danger. Enthusiastic religion with "corybantic" rites was bad. Religious fanaticism with military organization was infinitely worse. Huxley communicated his ideas to *The Times* in a series of letters eloquent with warnings against Franciscan corruption and Jesuitical machination.[37]

He was in the habit of taking a rather sentimental view of himself in such warfare.

Attacking the Salvation Army may look like the advance of a forlorn hope [he wrote his son Leonard], but this old dog has never yet let go after fixing his teeth into anything or anybody, and he is not going to begin now. And it is only a question of holding on....

The *Times*, too, is behaving like a brick. This world is not a very lovely place, but down at the bottom, as old Carlyle preached, veracity does really lie, and will show itself if people won't be impatient.[38]

His campaign was neither spectacular nor successful. The letters, swift and brisk at first with the excitement of denunciation and historical discovery, soon stagnated among the muddy technicalities of allegation and counterallegation. Huxley tried several times to bow hmiself out, only to discover a new antagonist in the next morning's issue. Meanwhile, the Salvation Army continued to flourish, and General Booth lived to be officially invited to the coronation of Edward VII.

As literature, such essays as "Agnosticism" and "Agnosticism and Christianity" are less compact, less brilliant, and less permanently interesting than such earlier, less controversial essays as "A Piece of Chalk" and "A Liberal Education."

But destruction is always spectacular; and warfare against

heaven, however perfunctorily and hastily waged, always rather satanically impressive. Therefore Huxley the bishop-eater has tended to be more famous, though less read, than Huxley the teacher and the statesman of science.

To be sure, controversy is a highly perishable art. History settles most disputes with a finality that makes almost any argument seem unnecessarily long-winded and contentious. Yet some disputes repeat themselves, and eventually they find a great man to argue them and a posterity not too wise after the event. Obviously, a controversialist should be concerned with the truth and understand what he is arguing against as well as what he is arguing for. But if he cannot be very just, he should be very partial. He should possess the patient malice, the hate-sharpened insight, the loving artistry of invective, the vivid sense of minds and characters in conflict which turn debate into drama. The most interesting argument is the *ad hominem*: the artistic controversialist does not so much annihilate as bring to life. Hazlitt immortalized Gifford by the sheer intensity and eloquence of his hatred. Butler created a Darwin whom he could refute and conquer. To be sure, a few supreme artists, like Burke, possess both the intellectual and the literary virtues of their craft: they can understand an opponent as profoundly as they hate him, and argue a great issue with a skill and indignation equal to the justice of their cause.

Huxley was deficient both in vividness and in openness of mind. He had too little insight into character to be tempted to personalities and—in any case—too much Victorian propriety to be really malevolent. He never attacked a foible instead of a fallacy, and of his opponents only Gladstone emerged as an individual. Again, Huxley's attitude toward religion and other important questions was often negative. Basically, he believed that if he could make everybody tell the truth about everything, a great many problems would be solved. No doubt the change would be startling. But obviously one cannot seize truth simply by pursuing error with a police club. One must pursue the truth itself.

Yet, at his best, he was clear, logical, well-informed, dexterous, and often brilliant. He had a quick eye for fundamental absurdities, as when he said that Comteism was "Catholicism minus Christianity."[39] He was admirable when waging terse, clear-cut expository argument, as in "The Physical Basis of Life," where idealism grows dim in the clarity of materialism; or when bringing to bear a large and many-sided knowledge, as in "Mr. Darwin's Critics," where he quoted Mivart's authority to demolish Mivart's ideas; or when exploiting complexly the opportunities of a dramatic situation, as in "Science and Culture," where he contrived to read the same sermon to all his opponents at once.

19

"Il Faut Cultiver Notre Jardin"

Huxley continued to fight, but now, for a time at least, he found something new to fight about. The issue was politics.

In 1886 Gladstone split the Liberal Party in an attempt to carry Home Rule for Ireland. Revolution began to flow into the vacuum. A Joshua wrapped in the Mosaic authority of Bentham, John Stuart Mill had already quietly led the Utilitarians through a wilderness of compromise, from laissez faire individualism to something like Fabian socialism. The Marxist Democratic Federation had risen to something more than Hyde Park notoriety, and made a convert of William Morris. Henry George had conducted his fiery campaigns for the Single Tax, and made a convert of Wallace. In 1889 the Fabians published their *Essays*. In 1892 the Labour Party was to be formed

Huxley was as cautious about politics as he was extreme about religion. As a thinker in the utilitarian tradition, he was a firm believer in democratic government, valuing freedom of speech and conscience above everything else. Yet, admiring Hobbes quite as much as Locke, he distrusted the masses and abhorred the vague, emotional oratory that sways them. Above all, he abhorred politicians. As a scientist, he favored more government because he favored more sanitation, research, education, more scientific posts for scientific men. He also remained the exponent of a special knowledge and a special method, using anthropology to explode social contract and biology to refute the labor theory of value.

Publicly, Huxley held aloof from partisan politics, feeling that he thereby spoke more authoritatively for science; but in his private letters he expressed contempt for Gladstone and despair at Irish Home Rule, which he thought would critically weaken English defenses, virtually dispossess English property owners in Ireland, and launch a poor and ignorant people on a reckless adventure. He seems to have believed in a strong empire as well as a strong government, and sometimes gave cautious and guarded approval to such Conservatives as Salisbury, Chamberlain, and—from an earlier generation—Shaftesbury.

Huxley began his political excursus in 1888, with "The Struggle for Existence in Human Society," a moral and sociological footnote to the *Origin*. Huxley does not see much justice in natural selection. It means progress and death; but the progress is very remote, and the death very immediate. "It is not clear what compensation the *Eohippus* gets for his sorrows in the fact that some millions of years afterward, one of his descendants wins the Derby."[1] Civilization puts limits to man's struggle for existence, but what those limits are, and what the relation of Darwinism is to society, Huxley does not explain, nor does he refer to such books as Bagehot's *Physics and Politics*, which deal with the subject.

Nevertheless, he suggests, though in a very practical and restricted setting, Bagehot's primary concept—that there is a natural selection of societies. In spite of his civilization, man is bound by nature. When he multiplies beyond the limit of his food supply—as he nearly always does—he is exposed to the struggle for existence, and therefore to poverty. And not only individuals but nations. For England, the struggle is particularly vital and desperate, because she must undersell competitors to buy food with which to live. England's problem is to maintain standards of living and culture without losing the war of competitive costs. Huxley finds the solution first, as formerly, in technical education and second, in state services and state aid. "The Struggle for Existence" clearly looks forward to "Evolution and Ethics."

This essay led to a quarrel with Spencer, which in turn led, rather deviously, to Huxley's four political articles of 1890. Despite head sensations, an attitude of permanent invalidism, and the continued and evident preparation of social alibis against the descent of sudden illness—Spencer had an extraordinary capacity for enjoyment and companionship. He had never been young all at once, but he was permanently young at intervals. "Spencer was here an hour ago as lively as a cricket," Huxley marveled to Hooker from a convalescent retreat at Bournemouth. "He is going back to town on Tuesday to plunge into the dissipations of the metropolis."[2] When the philosopher's head was not full of speculations and polysyllables, it was full of plans for picnics and excursions. What about a yachting trip? "With Mrs. Tyndall and your wife, and Beatrice Potter (supposing that does not entail any danger of domestic perturbation!) we might form a sufficiently lively party. . . . I suppose I should only need to let the fact leak out, and Valentine Smith would probably lend us his steam yacht."[3] The friendship between Huxley and Spencer seems to have been a convivial warfare in which they fought clergymen and idealists—usually *in absentia*—about fundamentals, and each other about details.

But warfare cannot always tend to harmony. Reading "The Struggle for Existence in Human Society," Spencer detected, as he told his old friend in a letter, both a borrowing and a criticism of his own ideas. Huxley had not only discovered these ideas late; he had made poor use of them. In spite of the struggle for existence, Spencer denied that poverty was any longer a problem for England, or that such a problem, if it existed, could be solved by state aid. In fact, he would have liked to write an answer but desisted in order to save his strength—presumably for more important work—and to prevent a coolness between himself and Huxley.

The whole letter was disagreeable and offensive in tone; but with the discrimination of a controversialist, Huxley lost his temper only at the implication that he might lose his temper over criticism. "It is not agreeable to me to be told that criticism is withheld because it may cause a coolness on my part toward the critic. I do not hold old friendship quite so lightly, nor would any severity of criticism have affected me so unpleasantly as the confession of intent to which I refer."[4] Temporarily cowed, Spencer explained himself in softer terms, and a fragile peace was made. Within two years, however, it was shattered when Spencer offered to send the latter half of his *Autobiography* manuscript unceremoniously through a stranger. Huxley took offense at once. There was a curt note from Spencer, a cold and stately reply from Huxley, and then nothing on either side for several weeks. Meanwhile, in support of his old friend, Huxley entered a lengthy debate on the nationalization of land in *The Times*. At one point he playfully observed that Spencer would probably try to cure cholera by deduction. Thereupon, Spencer wrote Hooker offering to resign from the X Club. "Huxley, besides causing me a serious relapse," he complained, "has done me irreparable damage by making me look like a fool to a hundred thousand readers."[5] After some mediation from Hooker, Huxley wrote Spencer:

I desire you to understand that when I wrote the letters of which you complain I had not the slightest intention of holding you up to ridicule by a repartee no sharper than you have often laughed at—or of taking up a position of greater antagonism to your views, than I have always taken in private—and on at least ten [?] occasions, in public.[6]

Even a calm and sensible man might have found it hard to forgive anyone so righteous. And Spencer—as mutual friends reminded Huxley throughout the quarrel—was far from being either calm or sensible. But apparently he once more bowed before superior moral force: the correspondence between them continued in a vein of rather careful cordiality.

Huxley availed himself of the dignified pages of *The Nineteenth Century* for a long last word on land nationalization. This, as well as all forms of socialism, he regarded as utopian illusion rendered dangerous by grave and widespread poverty. Apparently he had read neither Marx nor the Fabians, and saw Henry George as the most significant contemporary spokesman for revolution. "Did you ever read Henry George's book 'Progress and Poverty'?" he asked Knowles. "It is more damneder nonsense than poor Rousseau's blether. And to think of the popularity of the book."[7] Huxley believed that by guaranteeing a sound elementary education—and perhaps the opportunity to profit from such education afterwards—the state should help the poor to help themselves. Though he had condemned extreme laissez faire as nihilism, Huxley now upheld private enterprise as essential to real justice and healthy initiative.

In "The Natural Inequality of Men" Huxley explains contemporary revolutionists by going back to the arch-revolutionary and equalitarian Rousseau. The *Discourse on the Origins of Inequality* implies that by abolishing private property, civilized man might regain the perfect freedom and equality which his primitive ancestors enjoyed in a state of nature. For "the state of nature," on which Rousseau's whole argument depends, Huxley had all of a scientist's scorn. Its author hardly believed in it himself. If it never existed, he observes, it ought to have existed. Huxley recognizes here, together with a contemptible intellect, a fumbling attempt at an ideal standard. From this point, his essay becomes the *Discourse on Inequality* as it should have been written. Following Sir Henry Maine, he traces the theory of a state of nature back to Stoic elements in Roman law, where the concepts of natural liberty and equality served as convenient legal fictions. They were never anything more. Newborn children are not free and only in a negative sense equal. Moreover, all the evidence indicates that land was at first held in part communally and in part individually. As societies progressed, private ownership drove communal ownership out, being a better adaptation to civilized environment and to civilized, industrious human nature. As population increases, land cannot belong to all because there is not enough for all. It cannot belong to the human race because it belongs to nations.

Huxley is contemptuous of the qualities that made Rousseau influential. He feels that he has disposed of Rousseau when he has refuted him. In fact, he denies not only the competence, but the importance, of the common people in politics. He is not an optimistic but a peremptory rationalist. Though politics are not rational at the moment, they should be made so without delay. But how? Huxley would not have Comte's priesthood of scientists. He wants the freedom of democracy without its folly and stupidity.

When "The Natural Inequality of Men" came out, Huxley was derided for having slain a dead revolutionary. He determined at once to kill a live one. His victim was Henry George, who, as Huxley pointed out, was a Rousseauist in his abstract a priori approach and in his confusion of natural with political rights. Natural rights permit a man or an animal to do whatever conduces to individual advantage or enjoyment. Political rights permit a man to do whatever does not injure his fellow man in society. Natural rights imply the struggle for existence;

political rights, a polity based on a degree of justice and co-operation. Huxley insists on this distinction with great ferocity of illustration. "It is admitted that a tiger has a natural right to eat a man; but if he may eat one man, he may eat another, so that a tiger has a [natural] right of property in all men, as potential tiger-meat."[8] Through these years Huxley was obviously exploring the iniquity of nature from many points of view.

His refutation of Henry George's economics is rather facile. Distinguishing sharply between wealth created by labor and wealth derived from land or the bounty of nature, George declares that a man may own as private property only what he actually produces. Huxley replies that a man has only a partial right to the fruits of his own labor because he did not produce the mental and physical endowments which performed that labor—the contribution of nature cannot be practically separated from the contribution of man. That any case could be made out for taxing an "unearned increment" in private property, Huxley is angrily unwilling to grant. Once more he has attempted to refute revolution rather than to understand it.*

Writing in his next article on "Government: Anarchy or Regimentation" Huxley condemns the two extremes by tracing their history. Regimentation, identified in modern times with socialism, begins with Hobbes and finds its most influential and characteristic expression in Rousseau's *Social Contract*. (Apparently Huxley finds nothing really new or significant in socialism after Rousseau.) Individualism begins with Locke, proceeds through the Physiocrats to the Benthamites and ends

---

* "Capital—The Mother of Labour" is a further attack on George's labor theory of value. Labor is inevitably dependent on capital. A laborer cannot complete any useful product unless he has food to sustain him and materials to work with. Moreover, food, or vital capital, is produced not only by human labor applied to land, but by animal and plant labor applied to nature's accumulated capital.

in the anarchism of Bakunine. Both schools of thought are hopelessly a priori, deducing rules for civilized life from a state of nature which anthropology shows to be utterly unreal. Both fail to reckon with the infinite reproductive power of man. Socialists do not see that production can never keep up with population; individualists do not see that the pressure of numbers tends to turn every kind of competition into a ruthless struggle for existence. Too much regimentation destroys initiative; too much individualism produces a type of character ill fitted for civilized life. The analogy of the family shows that governments should regulate neither too much nor too little. Huxley stood doubtful between the ruthlessness of capitalists and the incompetence of politicians. There is no real solution to the problem of poverty because there is no humane way to keep population down.

Accompanied by his younger son Harry, who had just finished medical school and was soon to be married, Huxley visited the Canary Islands in 1889, repeating the first leg of the voyage which, as a surgeon's assistant, he had begun in 1846. His letters contain almost no reflections about early times except an ironic reference to "Portuguese progress," inspired by the sight of Madeira after forty-four years.[9] He rode horseback, walked twelve to fifteen miles a day, longed for letters, and came home with his skin burned to a deep sienna and his controversial appetite whetted to a fine edge. The Linnean medal had been awarded him in his absence.

As a residence, London had now become impossible for the same reason that it had once been indispensable. It was too much the exciting, fascinating center of things. After some looking around, Huxley purchased a plot of land in Eastbourne and built a house, into which he moved in December, 1890. A fairly restrained example of the flamboyant contemporary style, it was a large, steep-gabled, red-brick affair, with a tiny Norman

choirhouse for his books at one end, a white-timbered glass-
house for his gentians at the other, and a short hexagonal
Romanesque tower squatting on the roof. The garden, coming
down from an eminence in a broad, steep terrace, looked public
and rather ill at ease with itself. As Eastbourne houses were
named, he called his Hodeslea, an approximation of the Anglo-
Saxon for Huxley. This word, with its hint at once of modern
philology and of a primitive, rural remoteness, heads most of
his final letters.

Gentians had made Huxley a botanist; Hodeslea made him
a gardener. Puttering a little each day, he discovered with
astonishment that the mere growth and existence of trees and
flowers were strangely absorbing. He raised saxifrages, rejoiced
in a conservatory, looked forward to flower shows, found new
significance in Voltaire's *"Il faut cultiver notre jardin,"* and
argued with his gardener. "Books? They'll say anything in them
books," declared that dignitary, and while the white-maned
sage strode about the garden, hose in hand, continued to de-
nounce the watering of plants in any weather as a learned
prejudice.[10] Here is a plant, jested Hooker, "which will flourish
on any dry, neglected bit of wall, so I think it will just suit
you."[11] Huxley responded with statistics of progress. His flowers and creepers remained a heart-warming comfort down to
the last bleak spring of his life.

Children and grandchildren were frequent visitors at Hodeslea. No doubt Huxley had been a rather formidable father.
"We felt our little hypocrisies shrivel before him," writes
Leonard; "we felt a confidence in the infallible rectitude of his
moral judgements which inspired a kind of awe."[12] But in any
case they felt confidence. Both as a father and grandfather,
Huxley was touchingly, reassuringly eager to win affection. Far
from requiring children to develop the virtues convenient to
parents, he admired rebellion. "I like that chap!" he exclaimed
of his little grandson Julian. "I like the way he looks you straight

in the face and disobeys you."[13] He attempted to captivate a little granddaughter with such an extraordinary amount of nonsense that at length she remarked, very deliberately and with much astonishment, "Well, you are the curious'test old man I ever seen."[14] When Julian read Kingsley's *Water Babies*, he found his grandfather's name listed among the authorities on these fascinating creatures. He looked into the matter at once.

Dear Grandpater—Have you seen a Waterbaby? Did you put it in a bottle? Did it wonder if it could get out? Can I see it some day?—Your loving

Julian[15]

To this he received a prompt reply, neatly printed and blessedly legible.

My dear Julian—I never could make sure about that water baby. I have seen babies in water and babies in bottles; but the baby in the water was not in a bottle and the baby in the bottle was not in water.

My friend who wrote the story of the water baby, was a very kind man and very clever. Perhaps he thought I could see as much in the water as he did—there are some people who see a great deal and some who see very little in the same things.

When you grow up I dare say you will be one of the great-deal seers and see things more wonderful than water babies where other folks can see nothing.

Give my best love to Daddy and Mammy and Trevenen—Grandmoo is a little better but not up yet—

Ever your loving Grandpater[16]

Always the prodigious performer, Huxley fascinated his children so completely with the illustrated adventures of a bull terrier that Leonard, falling asleep at the beginning of an afternoon's episode, regarded the loss as one of the bitter disappointments of his early life. Huxley drew special pictures and told special stories when children were ill, and when they sat with glazed eyes and full stomachs after Christmas dinner, he annually astonished them by carving wonderful beasts, usually pigs, out of orange peel. Pigs became sacred to the occasion, and when Jessie was compelled by her marriage to be absent, her father wrote:

The specimen I enclose, wrapped in a golden cerecloth, and with the remains of his last dinner in the proper region, will prove to you the heights to which the creative power of the true artist may soar. I call it a "Piggurne, or a Harmony in Orange and White."

Preserve it, my dear child, as evidence of the paternal genius, when those light and fugitive productions which are buried in the philosophical transactions and elsewhere are forgotten.[17]

Huxley *Pater* does not seem to differ altogether from Huxley *Iconoclastes* and Huxley *Episcopophagous:** he must throughout life have exerted on those more terrible Huxleys a softening and humanizing influence.

In 1892 Huxley published his articles on agnosticism and Christianity as *Controverted Questions*, later *Science and Christian Tradition*. By far the best essay in the volume, both in form and content, is the "Prologue," which very nearly renders the volume unnecessary. It is a careful and deliberate attempt, when the heat and hurry of battle are over, to review and understand—at least from his own point of view—what the battle had been about. "It cost me more time and pains," he wrote a friend, "than any equal number of pages I have ever written."[18] Science and religion, he declares, have been perennially at war. The one studies nature and produces progress. The other explores supernature and produces confusion and darkness. In fact, progress is directly proportionate to the victory of naturalism over supernaturalism. Huxley then plunges into a brilliant and compact history of Protestantism from the

* "Bishop-eating," an epithet invented by Huxley.

fourteenth to the nineteenth century. Arguing from the authority of an infallible scripture, Protestants invoked critical
reason to destroy the papacy. But reason, once invoked, could
come to rest neither on an infallible scripture nor on a selection
of infallible scriptures. It could base itself permanently only on
the unyielding facts of nature.

What are the facts of nature that scientific reason has discovered? They form themselves, says Huxley, into the great
truth of evolution. First adumbrated in solar astronomy, then
clearly evident in embryology and paleontology, a principle of
development now seems discernible in chemistry and is obviously fundamental to the study of all terrestrial life, which in
many instances has progressed from very simple to increasingly
complex forms, producing consciousness, intelligence, and
morality as emergent values along the way. What heights development may somewhere have reached, science of course
cannot know. It denies, not that a supernature may exist, but
that such existence has yet been proved.

> Looking at the matter from the most rigidly scientific point of
> view, the assumption that, amidst the myriads of worlds scattered
> through endless space, there can be no intelligence, as much
> greater than man's as his is greater than a blackbeetle's; no being
> endowed with powers of influencing the course of nature as much
> greater than his, as his is greater than a snail's, seems to me not
> merely baseless, but impertinent.[19]

The emphasis on physical space is noteworthy. In effect,
Huxley refuses to recognize the existence of any reality apart
from matter, or the validity of any method apart from the
scientific. A Supernature cannot yet be proved by induction
from the phenomena of nature. Therefore, there is no honest
refuge except in agnosticism.

If people frankly admitted their ignorance and became genuinely truthful in all their relationships, "a reformation would be
effected such as the world has not yet seen, an approximation

to the millennium."[20] Apparently, truthtelling would encourage a detached, scientific attitude toward morals. "The rules of conduct . . . are discoverable—like the other so-called laws of nature—" he wrote in a private letter at this time, "by observation and experiment, and only in that way."[21] And in a letter of 1894:

There is much need that somebody should do for what is vaguely called "Ethics" just what the Political Economists have done. Settle the question of what will be done under the unchecked action of certain motives, and leave the problem of "ought" for subsequent consideration. . . .

We want a science of "Eubiotics" to tell us exactly what will happen if human beings are exclusively actuated by the desire of well-being in the ordinary sense. Of course the Utilitarians have laid the foundations of such a science, with the result that the nicknamer of genius called this branch of science "pig philosophy," making just the same blunder as when he called political economy "dismal science."

"Moderate well-being" may be no more the worthiest end of life than wealth. But if it is the best to be had in this queer world —it may be worth trying for.[22]

In 1892 Huxley became a president for the last time. Since 1887 there had been strong feeling that the many colleges scattered through the metropolis should be gathered together in the University of London, then merely an examining body. Everybody agreed there should be unity; the question was— what kind? Huxley tried to remain aloof, but inevitably he had opinions and inevitably people asked him to express them. He believed that medical schools should not be domineered over by scientists who wanted to use them as recruiting stations, nor scientific schools domineered over by *littérateurs* who had no use for them at all. He believed that there should be schools of art and literature and that literary professors should teach literature and not philology. The reform association seemed to have similar ideas. Therefore he joined it. Therefore it elected him president. His leadership was bold and vigorous, but apparently the whole movement, as so often in academic politics, suffered from too much light. Too many people had too many ideas, and for the time being London University continued unreformed.

At this time Huxley also added a modest cupola to the utilitarian edifice of his career.

I was present at a small party of scientific men [wrote Huxley's immediate chief Donnelly to Lord Spencer] when Huxley . . . was asked if he had ever heard of Darwin having been offered any honour during his lifetime by the Crown. Huxley said he was pretty sure no offer of any kind had been made to him adding that 50 or 100 years hence it would seem absolutely incredible that the state had in no way recognized his transcendent services to science. . . .

And after a laugh at the struggle of some, who were known to us, to secure bits of ribbon, Huxley said, "Well I don't mind saying what is the only kind of honour I should care about as a Man of Science—for there is not the *slightest fear* of its being offered me—and that is a Privy Councillorship. There is a possible appropriateness in that—a kind of fiction that one was called to the Councils of the State on behalf of Science." Now the object of my writing is to ask Your Excellency to consider whether this honour is so entirely out of the question.[23]

It proved by no means to be out of the question. Huxley's name duly appeared on the list of Her Majesty's new appointments. He complained of having to get out his old court dress and make the journey down to Osborne, but actually he was much pleased. He described the ceremony of "kissing hands" to his wife with the gusto of rational superiority:

Then we were shown into the presence chamber where the Queen sat at a table. We knelt as if we were going to say our prayers, holding a testament between two, while the Clerk of the Council read an oath of which I heard not a word. We each

advanced to the Queen, knelt and kissed her hand, retired backwards, and got sworn over again (Lord knows what I promised
and vowed this time also). Then we shook hands with all the
P.C.'s present, including Lord Lorne, and so exit backwards. It
was all very curious.[24]

While on his knees, he glanced up to have a close look at the
Queen. Her eyes were fixed upon him. She was taking advantage of the same opportunity.

Meanwhile, the restless traveler in search of health had given
place to a delicate old man much threatened and beleaguered,
beyond the windows of his study, by cold east winds, chill
night air, and other eventualities of weather and season. A
dinner at the X was a perilous and desperate adventure to be
undertaken only after much anxious weighing of the pleasures
of conviviality against the dangers of influenza. His old friendship with Hooker was sometimes reduced to a few lines about
symptoms sent from one invalid bed to the other. And then
there were the funerals of old friends. "Neither you nor I have
any business to commit suicide," he admonished Hooker on
the eve of Hirst's funeral, "for that which after all is a mere
sign of the affection we have no need to prove for our old
friend, and the chances are that half an hour cold chapel and
grave-side on a day like this would finish us."[25]

Tennyson's funeral he did attend. Who would miss the
Battle of Waterloo or the surrender at Sedan? Huxley had also
admired Tennyson as the most genuinely scientific poet of the
age. The funeral was a pageant of Victorian history and Tennysonian autobiography. The solemn music, the sober grandeur
of the Abbey, the Union Jack upon the coffin, the soldiers of
the Light Brigade in the nave, the scarce departed presence
of the Victorian Laureate himself stirred Huxley so deeply
that he composed the one poem of his discreeter years.[26] It is
not a very good poem. It simply indicates his patriotism, his
moralism, and his admiration for German literature. The short

lines of the early stanzas suggest Goethe; the repeated line is paraphrased from Schiller's *"Gib diesen Todten mir Heraus"*:

> *Bring me my dead!*
> *To me that have grown*
> *Stone laid upon stone,*
> *As the stormy brood*
> *Of English blood*
> *Has waxed and spread*
> *And filled the world,*
> *With sails unfurled;*
> *With men that may not lie*
> *With thoughts that cannot die.*

The poem concludes:

> *and all around*
> *Is silence: and the shadows closer creep*
> *And whisper softly: All must sleep.*

Two old friends and one ancient enemy died soon after Tennyson. The ancient enemy was Sir Richard Owen. But Huxley found he had long since forgotten all resentment, and at a public meeting actually seconded the motion for a statue. Characteristically, he was tickled by the irony of the situation, and spoke so eloquently in Owen's behalf that the latter's grandson asked him to write an anatomical chapter for *The Life of Richard Owen*. Huxley complied. The essay is a model of tact and magnanimity. "If I mistake not," he wrote, "the historian of comparative anatomy and paleontology will always assign to Owen a place next to, and hardly lower than that of Cuvier, who was practically the creator of those sciences in their modern shape."[27] And as he toiled away at the essay, he wrote with some surprise to Hooker, "The thing that strikes me most is, how he and I and all the things we fought about belong to antiquity. It is almost impertinent to trouble the modern world with such antiquarian business."[28]

But much antiquarian business was being wound up. "You see Jowett is going or gone," he wrote Hooker.[29] Almost to the end the prophetic schoolmaster had tranquilly continued to influence famous men, receive old students, pen graceful notes to married ladies, edit Plato, utter epigrams in a doze, and supervise the building at Balliol. He became seriously ill just before a much anticipated visit to a country house. His doctor was reluctant to let him go, but the Master was not to be denied—and passed away with great resignation a few weeks later, a martyr to the consolations of a bachelor's life, at the home of Sir Robert Wright. Almost his last coherent words were encouragement to a favorite pupil. Almost his last bit of wire-pulling had been an attempt to persuade Tennyson to resolve all contemporary philosophical and religious differences with a universal poetic prayer.

But Huxley's gravest loss was Tyndall. In 1875, while poised on the utmost verge of bachelordom, that solemn Irishman had proposed to the daughter of Lord Claud Hamilton, a charming and intelligent lady some twenty years his junior. The necessity of taming Tyndall to an approximation of the reason and sanity of conjugal life filled his friends with apprehension for the prospective bride. It worried Tyndall too. "You do not know what a devil's advocate I made of myself," he told Huxley, "before I permitted a word that could compromise her to pass the lips of that brave girl. And one of the many things she had to face and contemplate was the inexorable fact of my years."[30] She had resisted his pleas against himself, however, and they had since lived in strenuous and scientific felicity, traveling, climbing mountains, and geologizing together. Their American lecture tour had been as brilliant as the Huxleys' own. Quite recently, Tyndall had been forced by ill-health to retire as Director of the Royal Institution, and devotedly cared for by his wife, seemed to be declining into a prosaic and elderly decrepitude. For years he had dosed himself incessantly for headaches, insomnia, and stomach pains. Late one December night in 1893, he awoke violently ill and sent his wife for magnesia. Bewildered with sleep and the midnight crisis, she gave him chloral by mistake. The mistake was discovered too late, and some hours later Tyndall died.

The newspapers insisted relentlessly on the circumstances of his death. Huxley was concerned for Lady Tyndall. "That poor woman was to my mind in a somewhat dangerous condition—the exaltation of grief which is apt to precede a sudden breakdown."[31] Partly to exonerate her, he wrote an obituary. It was full of melancholy recollections of the old days. Four survivors—Hooker, Huxley, Lubbock, and Frankland—attended the cold December funeral. "It was we four who stood, pondering over many things, in Haslemere Churchyard the other day."[32] That was the last meeting of the X Club.

Having spent nearly a lifetime in thinking about the religious problem, G. J. Romanes established in 1892 an annual lecture at Oxford encouraging other people to think about everything else—except politics. Rather oddly, under these conditions, Gladstone was asked to give the first lecture and Huxley, the second. Huxley always found it difficult to resist an invitation to lecture. He found it impossible to resist an invitation to follow Gladstone. Nor was the G.O.M. unwilling to precede. Clad in the red magnificence of his doctor's robe, he spoke on the relatively safe subject of the Odyssey, luncheoned and dined indefatigably, and disappeared in a cloud of his own splendid and ebullient conversation. Equally high-spirited, Huxley offered to lecture the following year in court dress. He told Romanes that his title would be "Evolution and Ethics" and though promising to avoid contemporary religious controversy, must have hinted with his usual gusto at dire and electrifying overtones, for Romanes wrote back in great alarm and had to be soothed in haste. Huxley sent him an advance copy of the lecture. Both Mrs. Romanes and Mrs. Huxley agreed that it exuded not the slightest whiff of heresy.

Throughout 1892 Huxley read, meditated, wrote, revised, cut, and polished. His subject was a bit of unfinished business, a problem old and familiar to himself and to his century: what is the relation of nature to morality and justice? In the eighteenth century, nature had for the most part been an ingenious mechanism devised by a benevolent Creator to increase human comfort and self-esteem. For Bishop Butler indeed, it had been not so much a machine to be understood as a mystery to be accepted with resignation, embracing much that seemed cruel and wasteful to merely human comprehension. In the nineteenth century, it was found to be an endless, divinely inspired picture gallery and symphony concert in which the lonely enthusiast, escaping from the restraints of city life, might dreamily commune with God and recover the primitive innocence of freedom and spontaneity. Toward the middle of the nineteenth century, Tennyson, deep in Lyell and personal bereavement, had seen that nature's pictures were hung in a charnel house and that her music was played in a tomb.

In 1859 Darwin had of course discovered that the charnel house was a factory of progress. Mid-century optimists were delighted to learn that nature moved forward on the sound business principles of laissez faire. The question of justice seemed hardly relevant. To be sure, it became painfully relevant for Darwin; and even more so for his pupil Romanes, who, writing in a mood of bitter skepticism, had not like his master been comforted for the cruelties of nature either by the excitement of having explained them or the conviction that they led to genuine progress. After millions of years of evolution

we find that more than half of the species which have survived the ceaseless struggle are parasitic in their habits, lower and insentient forms of life feasting on higher and sentient forms; we find teeth and talons whetted for slaughter, hooks and suckers moulded for torment—everywhere a reign of terror, hunger, and sickness, with oozing blood and quivering limbs, with gasping breath and eyes of innocence that dimly close in deaths of brutal torture![33]

The impact of Darwinism on the humanitarian conscience had inevitably produced pessimism. But Romanes' *Candid Examination of Theism* (1876) had also drawn heavily from Mill's posthumous *Three Essays on Religion* (1873), which, in oddly un-Darwinian terms, summed up the case against nature both as a model for morality and an argument for theism.

In 1860, shortly after a brief and sudden illness had carried away his eldest son,* Huxley had declared that nature was neatly and precisely just. He had reiterated that conviction on several later occasions, but as early as 1871, in "Administrative Nihilism," he had begun to maintain the opposite, and in this he was doubtless encouraged by such works as Tennyson's *In Memoriam* and Butler's *Analogy*, which he admired.

The Romanes lecture represents the culmination of Huxley's pessimism. As usual, he is all courage and decision, and expresses the new truth, however unwelcome, so starkly that he very nearly pushes it into falsehood. The cosmic process, he declares, is a welter of incessant change and for sentient beings, a scene of struggle, suffering, and death. The ethical process, in part at least, substitutes cooperation and curtails suffering. Man has learned to live in comparative harmony with his fellow man and has thus become the dominant animal of the planet. Yet he is only partially emancipated from nature. He still suffers pain, is still struggling against the ape and tiger within him. Naturally he wonders whether there is any ultimate justice or reason for suffering. Jewish culture replies with

* See p. 155.

the counsel of resignation, Greek culture with a moral order administered by gods and goddesses, Indian culture with the doctrine of Karma, by which, through the transmigration of souls, every living creature in one existence or another eventually reaps as he has sown.

Huxley is impressed with the positive and critical character of Indian thought. He emphasizes that the doctrine of transmigration, like that of evolution, had

its roots in the world of reality. . . . The sum of tendencies to act in a certain way, which we call "character," is often to be traced through a long series of progenitors and collaterals. So we may justly say that this "character"—this moral and intellectual essence of a man—does veritably pass over from one fleshly tabernacle to another.[34]

From the Indian system, "the supernatural, in our sense of the term, was entirely excluded. There was no external power which could affect the sequence of cause and effect which gives rise to karma; none but the will of the subject of the karma which could put an end to it."[35] In fact, Buddha perceived possibilities of skeptical economy of which Berkeley himself was unaware. It cannot be proved that mind, any more than matter, exists. Therefore Gautama reduced the cosmos "to a mere flow of sensations, emotions, volitions, and thoughts,"[36] in which karma was the only reality. Though full of admiration for the almost scientific method with which Buddha treats moral phenomena, Huxley cannot sympathize with what seems the ultimately negative character of his system. That life is a dream, that man's object should be to end that dream by deadening desire and sensation, no sound Victorian could grant. Huxley is extremely severe with Indian mysticism as a practical way of life. "No later monachism has so nearly succeeded in reducing the human mind to that condition of impassive quasisomnambulism, which, but for its acknowledged holiness, might run the risk of being confounded with idiocy."[37]

Continuing with his survey of philosophies, Huxley rejects Stoicism, and therewith something very like the faith in which he began his career. In passages reminiscent of Mill's *Three Essays*, he points out that Stoicism simply does not recognize the evil in nature.

That there is a "soul of good in things evil" is unquestionable; nor will any wise man deny the disciplinary value of pain and sorrow. But these considerations do not help us to see why the immense multitude of irresponsible sentient beings, which cannot profit by such discipline, should suffer; nor why, among the endless possibilities open to omnipotence—that of sinless, happy existence among the rest—the actuality in which sin and misery abound should be that selected.[38]

Man's tragedy is that he must find ethical greatness in negation. "By the Tiber, as by the Ganges, ethical man admits that the cosmos is too strong for him; and by destroying every bond which ties him to it by ascetic discipline, he seeks salvation in absolute renunciation."[39]

Huxley's solution involves fresh heroism of the will and the intellect. It is "to pit the microcosm against the macrocosm."[40]

Ethical nature may count upon having to reckon with a tenacious and powerful enemy as long as the world lasts. But, on the other hand, I see no limit to the extent to which intelligence and will, guided by sound principles of investigation, and organized in common effort, may modify the conditions of existence, for a period longer than that now covered by history.[41]

In short, with the aid of science man may hope so to improve his own nature and his immediate social and physical environment as to create a friendly, rational world inside the hostile, irrational universe.

What is fundamental in this essay? There is an insistence

on change which, in certain passages, almost reduces nature to an illusion and which, together with the emphasis on the inwardness of moral experience, suggests mysticism. There is also—despite the rejection of Stoicism—Stoic melancholy about the present and Stoic optimism about the future. Finally, there is a Hardyesque hostility to the cosmos as a place of slaughter and suffering. All of these elements, in greater or less degree, are native to Huxley and to the *Zeitgeist*. That they are all present in a single essay may indicate a renewed expansion or illumination of mind. Old age is sometimes a period of rapid learning.

Huxley was afraid his lecture might be misunderstood. As a matter of fact, it was scarcely heard. Shortly before the event he attended a meeting of doctors which proved to be an even bigger meeting of influenza microbes. They robbed him of his voice, raised pimples on his nose, caused it to run furiously, and so inflamed and swelled his visage that he began to look like a particularly disreputable Captain Costigan. Captain Costigan gradually subsided into Professor Huxley, however; and when, before a packed audience in the Sheldonian Theatre, he rose in his red robes, tall and white-maned—his square, aggressive features frosted over with the pallor and thoughtfulness of age—he seemed no less than the legendary champion who, thirty-three years before, had won the great victory over Bishop Wilberforce at the same university. But alas! he was an orator without a voice. Through the first half of the discourse his voice was so low that there were cries of "Speak up!" and the undergraduates began to press down from the galleries. He finished in stronger tones, but on the whole, he was an inaudible wonder. There was a wave of somewhat bewildered applause, and he was carried off to a luncheon.

Huxley described his lecture as an "egg-dance."[42] As a matter of fact, it was not only an extremely dexterous, but a some-

what puzzling maneuver among breakables and unmention-
ables. It was full of talk about Indian mysticism and of protest
against the cruelties of evolution. It set up a sharp antithesis
between the ethical and the cosmic process, yet failed to define
very clearly what the ethical process was. Inevitably, it was
much misunderstood. Mivart expected Huxley to become a
Roman Catholic. Spencer did not know what to expect, but
he felt quite sure that Huxley's errors had been invented by
Huxley and that his truths had been discovered some forty
years before by Herbert Spencer. Perhaps he also suspected
that Huxley was simply continuing *The Times* controversy
from the shelter of a red robe. In a review entitled "Evolutionary Ethics," Spencer quoted at length from his early works
to show how long ago he had emphasized that only the ethical
process results in progress and a survival of the "best." On
the other hand, the ethical process is part of the cosmic; and
if so, "how can the two be put in opposition?"[43] Some people
think, wrote Spencer in effect, that the professor meant to
read me a lesson, but "it is scarcely supposable that he deliberately undertook to teach me my own doctrines." In a spirit
of particular cordiality, he sent an autographed copy of the
review to his old friend, and was "quite startled" to receive a
stiff reply in the third person.[44] "As if the fellow had not
sucked my brains for thirty years!" snorted Huxley.[45] He wondered how he had ever put up with such "a long winded
vanitous pedant of a kill-joy."[46] But Spencer answered him
with such pathetic, crestfallen surprise that a few days later
Huxley found himself writing a letter of comfort.

However, the public record must be set straight. He saw
that his lecture needed a preface. The preface, or "Prologmena," turned out longer than the lecture itself. The ethical
process, he declared, was indubitably part of the cosmic process, but was nonetheless in opposition to it. He spelled out
his point with an elaborate analogy to gardening. In a state of

nature, plants are selected by a competition of each against all. Those survive which are best adapted to natural conditions. In a garden, plants—many perhaps quite foreign to the region— are chosen by the gardener according to his taste and need. They flourish because his skill and foresight create conditions favorable to them. The horticultural process is part of the cosmic, but runs counter to it and may be superseded by it whenever the gardener relaxes his efforts.

The ethical process depends on a victory of "the organized and personified sympathy we call conscience"[47] over unlimited self-assertion. Civilized man tends like every kind of organism to overpopulate his environment. He could improve himself as a species only by ruthlessly exterminating the socially unfit But he does not know who the socially fit are; and even if he did, the practice of exterminating them would corrupt and disintegrate his whole society. As a matter of fact, he does not compete so much for survival as for pleasures. He progresses by social rather than biological evolution, creating, like the gardener, conditions which will facilitate "the free expansion of the innate faculties of the citizen."[48] Huxley's ultimate position was thus not very different from Darwin's.

The "Prologmena" is obviously not a very precise or thorough analysis of social evolution. Huxley says that civilized men are, and are not, subject to the struggle for existence.[49] Of course they must in some manner be subject to it, since their numbers increase more rapidly than their food supply. But how? In his last years Huxley seems to have thought a good deal about this problem. After his death, two series of comments on "Evolution and Ethics" were found among his papers. In civilized life, he declares, the competition between individuals is drastically modified and in large part replaced by a competition between societies, in which the ethically superior tend to survive. "The ethical process and the cosmic process work in harmony in respect of the external relations of each society."[50] Clearly, he was thinking along the lines of Bagehot's *Physics and Politics*.

The influenza microbes had the last word. They once more became very active, and from his bed Huxley sent cartoons of them to Hooker. When he recovered he had a last summer stay at Majola in Switzerland. The mountains, the tiny blue lake of Sils, the narrow path around it, Herr Walther at the hotel, and the Oxford professor Campbell and his wife, who came there every summer—were all old friends now. Huxley was once more restored by brisk walks and Alpine air, but not so wonderfully as before. By the next summer, Majola had become too distant. "Will you tell Herr Walther," he wrote Professor Campbell, "we are only waiting for a balloon to visit the hotel again?"[51]

But he didn't need a balloon to reach Oxford for the meeting of the British Association. Just a third of a century had passed since his now legendary victory over Bishop Wilberforce. Huxley rightly guessed that the occasion would be interesting. Once more the Sheldonian Theatre was packed with an audience on the alert for history. Once more, white haired and red robed with the insignia of age and honors, Huxley sat on the platform. The presidential address was delivered by the Marquis of Salisbury, leader of the Tory Party, a former Prime Minister, and Chancellor of the University. As a gentleman-politician habituated to understatement and practical affairs, Lord Salisbury was not likely to become embroiled in heated argument on a metaphysical subject. As an enlightened patriot dedicated to the applause of British achievement, he felt obliged to accede to majority opinion and regard Darwinian evolution as firmly legislated into the constitution of the universe. As a Tory elegantly skeptical of the value of all novelty and progress, however, he regarded Darwinism as a particularly disagreeable form of liberalism and therefore still essentially a party question. Expatiating on the progress of science and ranging gracefully from astronomy to physics and chemistry, he came at length to biology and evolution, a principle which was now "disputed by no reasonable man."[52] He dwelt with delicate irony on "that comforting word, evolution," and then touched on the current controversy over acquired characteristics in a way that seemed to put the whole subject in doubt.

The attack was skillfully veiled, and surely a Chancellor, a Marquis, an ex-Prime Minister could deliver with impunity a parliamentary thrust against even the constitution of the universe. As Lord Salisbury spoke, many a glance fell on Huxley, and none more intently than that of Henry Osborn, an American professor and former student, who had come full of a sense of having moved from the periphery to the center of history. He noticed that though the venerable countenance showed no sign of wrath, Huxley sank deeper into his chair and his foot tapped restlessly on the platform.

As a matter of fact, he was in a difficult position. Entrusted —at his own request for a slight and humble role—with seconding the vote of thanks to the Chancellor, he was condemned to praise. The problem was how to make praise carry a reprimand. He had read Lord Salisbury's speech in proof on the previous day and had been deep in thought ever since. No doubt the tapping of the foot indicated temptation. "The old Adam, of course, prompted the tearing of the address to pieces, which would have been a very easy job."[53] The physicist Lord Kelvin rose amid mild applause and moved the vote of thanks without a murmur of protest. Apparently he had no wish to defend the universe against Lord Salisbury.

There was tremendous, and no doubt hopeful, applause when Huxley rose. In a voice now clear and resonant, he spoke of the reconcilers of the twenties and thirties who tried "to keep their scientific and other convictions in two separate logic-tight compartments."[54] Such people wanted to allow science no broad general concepts but to keep her "grinding at the mill of utility." The "pax Baconiana" of the reconcilers was ended forever by the publication of The Origin of Species. With dangerously edged reiteration, Huxley then quoted those passages in the Chancellor's speech that gave full recognition to the evolutionary principle. He concluded by quoting very pointedly from a German scientist to show that Darwinian controversies imply no doubt of essential Darwinism. To be sure, great evolutionary problems remain to be solved, but no great subject was ever exhausted in thirty-five years. He sat down amid a fresh pandemonium of applause. History had repeated itself by innuendo.

Through 1893 and much of 1894 Huxley was engaged in editing the nine volumes of his Collected Essays, for each of which he wrote a brief preface. The prefaces form an interesting commentary on himself and what he stood for. He made no great pretensions to careful craftsmanship. "Written for the most part, in the scant leisure of pressing preoccupations, or in the intervals of ill-health, these essays are free neither from superfluities in the way of repetition, nor from deficiencies which, I doubt not, will be even more conspicuous to other eyes than they are to my own."[55] His fault had always been that he did too many things too rapidly. Moreover, he had never been able to write without the stimulus of an immediate occasion and he had to finish before the occasion had lost its dramatic effectiveness. He found discipline not in the critical eye of scholarly posterity but in the somewhat dull ear of the contemporary workingman or lecture-goer. "The task of putting the truths learned in the field, the laboratory, and the museum, into language which, without bating a jot of scientific accuracy shall be generally intelligible, taxed such scientific and literary faculty as I possessed to the uttermost."[56]

Part of this discipline was that he had no illusions about the average audience. "I venture to doubt if more than one in ten . . . carries away an accurate notion of what the speaker has been driving at."[57] Huxley's strength is that, in the last analysis, he did not level his ideas down to dullness. He drove a wedge of clarity into it. His concessions were all in language and form—in vivid and dramatic illustration, in short, simple paragraphs, in direct, familiar, and colloquial phrasing.

The intelligent workingman was very nearly Huxley's ideal auditor. He not only evoked, both early and late, some of Huxley's best lectures, but was to have been his final court of appeal in scriptural controversy. In the last years of his life Huxley was planning to sum up the results of scientific biblical study in a series of workingmen's lectures. When lecturing was obviously out of the question, he thought of a primer or popular history for young people. But the time was too short.

Some years before, a "Darwin Medal" had been established, to be awarded biennially for biological research. The first award went very appropriately to Wallace and the second, to Hooker. Huxley approved of both choices but felt that in the future the honor should fall to younger men, on whom it would act as a spur. Instead, it fell to himself. He tried to scold the guilty conspirators, but in vain. "One gets chill [in] old age," he wrote his old student Foster, "and it is very pleasant to be warmed up unexpectedly even against one's injunctions."[58] The medal was presented at the Royal Society anniversary dinner, which he attended with trepidation, paid for with illness—and enjoyed thoroughly. In fact, it was the occasion of one of his wittiest speeches. He protested that he was at a loss to explain why he had been awarded the medal. His scientific services were in no way comparable to those of Wal-

lace or Hooker. But "they also serve who only stand and wait."
To be sure, his standing and waiting had been "of a somewhat
peculiar character."[59] He then told the story of a Quaker
passenger on a ship which was attacked by pirates. The captain
put a pike in his hands and bade him take part in the action.
The Quaker replied that he could not fight, but was willing to
stand and wait at the gangway.

He did stand and wait with the pike in his hands, and when the
pirates mounted and showed themselves coming on board he
thrust his pike with the sharp end forward into the persons who
were mounting, and he said, "Friend, keep on board thine own
ship." It is in that sense that I venture to interpret the principle
of standing and waiting to which I have referred.[60]

The cold, dreary February of 1895 was enlivened by a remarkable event. A Tory politician published a book on metaphysics. The author was A. J. Balfour, an urbane, languid,
clever young man whose habit of sitting on his spine had
awakened the permanent suspicion of Disraeli. A book on
metaphysics would have ruined a politician in Disraeli's day.
In Balfour's, it simply caused a sensation. To be sure, *The
Foundations of Belief* was a very political work on metaphysics
—in fact, like Lord Salisbury's effort at the British Association,
a kind of prolonged speech from the Opposition benches
attacking the fashionable scientific-utilitarian universe and
urging the Tory universe in its stead. The right honorable
author did not openly disparage the critical intellect, but he
did exercise his own intellect with considerable skill to show
that intellect should not be exercised too much or too critically.
Too much thinking divides people in practical affairs and
reduces them to absurdity in speculation. Mere mind cannot
arrive at its own fundamental data. It should reason cautiously
on data provided by custom and tradition.

The strongest part of the book is the attack on the naturalistic or agnostic position: naturalism is inconsistent with itself

and with man's practical situation in the universe. The scientific naturalist declares "we may know only 'phenomena' and the laws by which they are connected,"[61] yet makes such knowledge tenuously dependent on a long sequence of causes extending backward into an essentially unknown outer world on the one hand and forward on the other to the "dark chasm"[62] which separates neural changes from intelligent thought. He argues as though he believed in determinism and behaves—like everybody else—as though he believed in free will. He is a zealot for Christian morals, yet builds up a vast, mechanistic, essentially irrational universe in which the Christian God and the Christian system cannot live. Without mentioning any names, Balfour is particularly acid about such scientific exponents of moral force as Huxley.

Their spiritual life is parasitic: it is sheltered by convictions which belong, not to them, but to the society of which they form a part; it is nourished by processes in which they take no share. And when those convictions decay, and those processes come to an end, the alien life which they have maintained can scarce be expected to outlast them.[63]

Balfour's prediction was already coming true as he wrote.

As a matter of fact, he had provided Huxley with several shoes which might have fit remarkably well. Wilfred Ward— once Huxley's pleasant enemy in the Metaphysical Society, now his jolly neighbor in Eastbourne—was quite aware of this, and when, after lunch one afternoon, Huxley dropped in full of high spirits and eager talk about Erasmus, insidiously offered to lend him *The Foundations of Belief*.

You need not lend me that [said Huxley, becoming "extremely animated"]. I have exercised my mind with it a good deal already. Mr. Balfour ought to have acquainted himself with the opinions of those he attacks. An attack on us by some one who understood our position would do all of us good—myself included. No human being holds the opinions he speaks of as "naturalism." He is a good debater. He knows the value of a word. The word "Naturalism" has a bad sound and unpleasant associations. It would tell against us in the House of Commons, and so it will with his readers.[64]

Suspecting a hostile audience, Huxley was reluctant to enter on particulars, but was encouraged to do so by degrees.

Balfour uses the word *phenomena* [he declared] as applying simply to the outer world and not to the inner world. The only people his attack would hold good of would be the Comtists, who deny that psychology is a science. . . . All the empiricists, from Locke onwards, make the observation of the phenomena of the mind itself quite separate from the study of mere sensation. No man in his senses supposes that the sense of beauty, or the religious feelings (this with a courteous bow to a priest who was present), or the sense of moral obligation, are to be accounted for in terms of sensation, or come to us through sensation.

But no doubt, answered Ward, Mr. Balfour had described not so much what naturalists thought as what they logically ought to think. "Mill was almost the only man on their side in this century who had faced the problem frankly, and he had been driven to say that all men can know is that there are 'permanent possibilities of sensation.'" Huxley merely replied that empiricists were not bound by all of Mill's theories. He thought Balfour's book a brilliant literary effort, but "as a helpful contribution to the great controversy, the most disappointing he had ever read."

"There has been no adverse criticism of it yet," ventured Ward innocently.

"No!" he answered with emphasis. "*But there soon will be.*"

At Knowles's request, Huxley was already writing a reply. He seems to have approached the *Foundations* with some respect, hoping to prove that the enlightened Tory was an agnostic at heart; but the more he read, the more fallacies he found. Balfour was simply another proof that politicians were fundamentally irrational. "I am inclined to think," Huxley wrote Knowles, "that the practice of the methods of political leaders destroys their intelligence for all serious purposes."[65]

Meanwhile, the cold weather continued and influenza spread in Eastbourne. Huxley shivered before his fire, expected influenza, and detected so many errors in Balfour's book that he had to divide his reply into two installments. He sent off the first, very nearly finished the second—and then went to bed with influenza.

The first installment of "Mr. Balfour's Attack on Agnosticism," was duly published in The Nineteenth Century for March, 1895. It was essentially an old defense against a rather new attack. Balfour's naturalism, Huxley insisted, was something very different from either his own agnosticism or Locke's empiricism. Agnosticism does not deny that a supernatural world may exist. It simply denies that verifiable knowledge of such a world has thus far been established. Empiricism does not restrict itself to material phenomena. It deals also with mental phenomena, and so—one gathers—may eventually discover a scientific basis for the moral life. Attacked for his more dogmatic position, Huxley once more escaped by defining his more skeptical position.

He very aptly described his first article as a "cavalry charge."[66] His second was to bring the bayonets and heavy artillery into play. It was not published until 1932, when—still a bare, preliminary draft—it appeared in the Appendix of Houston Peterson's Huxley: Prophet of Science. One can see what Huxley meant by bayonets and heavy artillery. He attacked Balfour's summing-up against naturalism, proposition by proposition. When he had finished, hardly a word or an idea was left standing. Huxley denied that the agnostic regards the universe as irrational. A tadpole is a rationally constructed organism, rationally adapted to his environment in the universe. Therefore, the forces which formed him and the universe are rational. Again, Huxley insisted that the agnostic believes in a moral law. That law will not change so long as human nature and social conditions remain what they are. But social conditions—and men's ideas—were even at that moment revolutionizing the moral law. Huxley had refuted Balfour without entirely understanding him.

Huxley concludes with one of his few criticisms of Christianity as a moral ideal:

To believe against the dictates of the carnal reason; to refuse to listen to the impulses of affection tainted by sin, and principles, the offspring of self-righteousness; to withdraw from all human interests, renounce volition, and sink into a quietistic machine driven by the Spirit—these are the counsels of perfection accepted in theory, though happily more or less ignored in practice, by the great majority of Christians.[67]

And again: "They have recognised in themselves and others only one object—the salvation of their souls; to attain that they have been as ready to trample down every consideration of patriotism or social welfare."[68] He also took the opportunity to sum up his disagreement with Spencer: he did not approve of Spencer's a priori method, of his formulation of the evolutionary principle, or of the ethical and political deductions which he made from that principle.

Huxley's illness grew worse. He watched its progress with wry amusement, almost with detachment. At the outset, the doctor had pronounced the influenza "a mild type."[69] Huxley wondered what a severe type would be like. "I find coughing continuously for fourteen hours or so a queer kind of mildness." He survived the influenza, as well as the bronchitis which accompanied it. But now heart and kidney disease set in. His doctor became fearful. "I am carried down to a tent in the garden every day," the invalid wrote Hooker, "and live in the fresh air all I can." When his son Leonard asked him how he was, he replied with brisk impatience, "A mere carcass, which has to be tended by other people." Leonard found him thin, but sunburnt, alert, and cheerful. He remained eagerly interested in the garden to the end, and when he could no longer get out, asked daily after certain flowers and plants.

Though recognizing the gravity of his case, he was determined to live. He told his nurse that the doctors could not be right about the kidney ailment; for if they were right, he ought to be in a state of coma. As a matter of fact, they were surprised that he was not. In a very shaky hand, he wrote Hooker that the newspaper reports were unnecessarily alarming. Three days later his heart began to fail, and on the same evening—June 29, 1895, at the age of seventy—he passed quietly away.

He was buried at Finchley, beside his little son Noel. Both graves were shaded by a stately young oak. It had been a sapling when, thirty-five years before, he had stood, heartbroken, over Noel's grave. By Huxley's own wish, three lines from a poem by his wife were inscribed on his tombstone:

> Be not afraid, ye waiting hearts that weep;
> For still He giveth His beloved sleep,
> And if an endless sleep He wills, so best.

NOTES

1. Revolution in a Classroom

1. Leonard Huxley, *Life and Letters of Thomas Henry Huxley* (New York: D. Appleton & Company, Inc., 1901), I, 194; also see "The British Association," *The Athenaeum*, July 14, 1860, pp. 59–68.
2. See a review of Darwin's *Origin of Species*, *The Edinburgh Review*, CXI (1860), 487–532.
3. "On the Zoological Relations of Man with the Lower Animals," *The Natural History Review*, I (1861), 67–84.
4. *Life and Letters of Huxley*, I, 202.
5. *Ibid.*, p. 195.
6. *Loc. cit.*
7. *Ibid.*, p. 196.
8. "A Grandmother's Tales," *Macmillan's Magazine*, LXXVIII (1898), 433.
9. *Ibid.*, p. 434.
10. *Life and Letters of Huxley*, I, 202.
11. *Loc. cit.*

2. A Scientific Odyssey

1. Thomas Henry Huxley, *Methods and Results*, authorized ed. (New York: D. Appleton & Company, Inc., 1897), p. 4.
2. Huxley, "Autobiography," *Methods and Results*, p. 5.

3. Leonard Huxley, *Life and Letters of Thomas Henry Huxley* (New York: D. Appleton & Company, Inc., 1901), I, 6.

4. See Sir William Hamilton's review of Cousin's *Cours de Philosophie: Introduction à l'Histoire de la Philosophie, The Edinburgh Review,* I (1829), 194–221.

5. Houston Peterson, *Huxley: Prophet of Science* (London: Longmans, Green & Co., Ltd., 1932), p. 14.

6. "Autobiography," *Methods and Results,* p. 8.

7. Julian Huxley, ed., *T. H. Huxley's Diary of the Voyage of H.M.S. "Rattlesnake"* (New York: Doubleday, Doran & Company, Inc., 1936), p. 38.

8. *Life and Letters of Huxley,* I, 237.

9. *Ibid.,* I, 18.

10. "Obituary: Thomas Wharton Jones," *The British Medical Journal,* II (1891), 1176.

11. "Autobiography," *Methods and Results,* p. 9.

12. *Loc. cit.*

13. *Diary of the Rattlesnake Voyage,* p. 48.

14. Notebook 13, written in 1899 in Mrs. Huxley's hand, Huxley Papers: Scientific and General Correspondence (London: Imperial College of Science and Technology), LXII, 4.

15. *Loc. cit.*

16. *Life and Letters of Huxley,* I, 41.

17. *Diary of the Rattlesnake Voyage,* pp. 242–243.

18. Notebook 13, in Mrs. Huxley's hand, Huxley Papers, LXII, 1–2.

19. *Diary of the Rattlesnake Voyage,* p. 136.

20. *Ibid.,* p. 135.

21. *Ibid.,* p. 136, n.1.

22. "The Evolution of Theology: An Anthropological Study," *Science and Hebrew Tradition,* authorized ed. (New York: D. Appleton & Company, Inc., 1897), pp. 317–318.

23. T. H. Huxley, "Science at Sea: Narrative of the Voyage of the *H.M.S. Rattlesnake,*" *The Westminster Review,* LXI (1854), 117–118.

24. *Diary of the Rattlesnake Voyage*, p. 166.

25. *Ibid.*, p. 203.

26. *Ibid.*, p. 208.

27. *Ibid.*, p. 232.

3. A Prophet in His Own Country   pages 30–48

1. Leonard Huxley, *Life and Letters of Thomas Henry Huxley* (New York: D. Appleton & Company, Inc., 1901), I, 74.

2. *Ibid.*, p. 68.

3. *Loc. cit.*

4. *Ibid.*, p. 73.

5. *Ibid.*, p. 67.

6. *Ibid.*, p. 68.

7. *Ibid.*, p. 75.

8. *Ibid.*, pp. 69, 95.

9. Herbert Spencer, *An Autobiography* (New York: D. Appleton & Company, Inc., 1904), I, 462.

10. "A Theory of Population Deduced from the General Law of Animal Fertility," *The Westminster Review*, n.s. I (1852), 501.

11. *Ibid.*, p. 500.

12. Spencer, *Autobiography*, I, 467.

13. *Life and Letters of Huxley*, I, 88.

14. *Ibid.*, p. 91.

15. *Ibid.*, p. 129.

16. *Ibid.*, p. 118.

17. *Ibid.*, p. 119.

18. *Ibid.*, p. 120.

19. *Ibid.*, p. 138.

20. Notebook 13, written in 1899 in Mrs. Huxley's hand, Huxley Papers: Scientific and General Correspondence (London: Imperial College of Science and Technology), LXII, 31, 84.

21. *Life and Letters of Huxley*, I, 140.

22. Notebook 13, in Mrs. Huxley's hand, Huxley Papers, LXII, 1–2.
23. *Loc. cit.*
24. *Ibid.,* p. 86.
25. *Life and Letters of Huxley,* I, 162.
26. *Ibid.,* pp. 106–107.
27. *Ibid.,* pp. 94–95.
28. See "On the Educational Value of the Natural History Sciences," *Science and Education,* authorized ed. (New York: D. Appleton & Company, Inc., 1897), p. 65.
29. *Ibid.,* p. 63.
30. *Ibid.,* p. 65.
31. *Ibid.,* p. 62.
32. Michael Foster and E. Ray Lankester, eds., *The Scientific Memoirs of Thomas Henry Huxley* (London: Macmillan & Co., Ltd., 1903), I, 311, 310.
33. Unpublished letter to Edward Forbes, Huxley Papers, XVI, 172.
34. *Life and Letters of Huxley,* I, 105–106.
35. Sir Arthur Keith, "Huxley as Anthropologist," Supplement to Nature, May 9, 1925, p. 720.
36. *Life and Letters of Huxley,* I, 102.
37. *Ibid.,* p. 106.

4. *The Tale of an Unlikely Prince*   pages 49–67

1. Francis Darwin, ed., *The Life and Letters of Charles Darwin,* authorized ed. (New York: D. Appleton & Company, Inc., 1896), I, 473.
2. *Ibid.,* p. 484.
3. *Ibid,* pp. 477–478.
4. *Ibid.,* p. 492.
5. *Ibid.,* p. 495.
6. *Ibid.,* p. 53.
7. From an unpublished portion of Charles Darwin's "Auto-

biography," Darwin Papers (Cambridge: University Library), p. 2.

8. *Life and Letters of Darwin*, I, 30.

9. *Ibid.*, p. 38.

10. Francis Darwin and A. C. Seward, eds., *More Letters of Charles Darwin, A Record of His Work in a Series of Hitherto Unpublished Letters* (New York: D. Appleton & Company, Inc., 1903), I, 7.

11. *Life and Letters of Darwin*, I, 44.

12. *Ibid.*, p. 147.

13. *Ibid.*, p. 49.

14. *Ibid.*, p. 50.

15. *Ibid.*, pp. 53–54.

16. "The Tamworth Reading Room," *Discussions and Arguments on Various Subjects*, 3d ed. (London: Pickering & Co., 1878), p. 299.

17. *Works and Life* (London: Longmans, Green & Co., Ltd., 1915), II, 191.

18. The first edition was published as Vol. III of the *Narrative of the Surveying Voyages of His Majesty's Ships Adventure and Beagle*. Later editions were published as *Journal of Researches into the Natural History and Geology of the Countries Visited during the Voyage of the H.M.S. Beagle Round the World, under the Command of Capt. Fitz Roy, R.N.*, authorized ed. (New York: D. Appleton & Company, Inc., 1896).

19. *More Letters of Darwin*, I, 12.

20. *Journal of Researches*, pp. 374–375.

21. Nora Barlow, ed., *Charles Darwin and the Voyage of the Beagle* (London: Pilot Press, 1945), p. 247.

22. "Autobiography," *Life and Letters of Darwin*, I, 67.

23. *Darwin and the Voyage of the Beagle*, p. 66.

24. *Ibid.*, p. 96.

25. *Ibid.*, p. 116.

26. *Life and Letters of Darwin*, I, 207.

27. *Ibid.*, p. 55.
28. "Charles Darwin and Psychotherapy," *The Lancet*, January 30, 1943, p. 131.
29. Unpublished letter to W. D. Fox, October 5, 1833, Darwin Papers (Cambridge: University Library).
30. Unpublished letter to W. D. Fox, November 17, 1831, Darwin Papers (Cambridge: University Library).
31. Unpublished letter to W. D. Fox, February 15, 1836, Darwin Papers (Cambridge: University Library).
32. *Life and Letters of Darwin*, I, 47.
33. Francis Darwin, "Reminiscences of My Father's Everyday Life," *Life and Letters of Darwin*, I, 89–90.
34. "The Life of the Shawl," *The Lancet*, December 26, 1953, p. 1354.
35. *Life and Letters of Darwin*, I, 275.
36. "The Life of the Shawl," *The Lancet*, December 26, 1953, p. 1351.
37. W. C. Alvarez, *Nervousness, Indigestion, and Pain* (New York and London: Paul B. Hoeber, Inc., Medical Department of Harper & Brothers, 1943), pp. 240–243.
38. R. B. Litchfield, *Tom Wedgwood, the First Photographer, etc.* (London: Duckworth, 1903), pp. 21, 23–24; quoted by Alvarez, *op. cit.*, p. 242.
39. Unpublished portion of Darwin's "Autobiography," Darwin Papers (Cambridge: University Library), p. 78c.
40. *Loc. cit.*
41. *Life and Letters of Darwin*, I, 63.
42. *Loc. cit.*

5. A Premeditated Romance   pages 68–81

1. Henrietta Litchfield, ed., *Emma Darwin, Wife of Charles Darwin: A Century of Family Letters* (London: John Murray, 1915), II, 1.
2. *Ibid.*, I, 277.

3. *Ibid.*, p. 278.
4. See p. 106.
5. *Emma Darwin*, I, 58.
6. *Ibid.*, p. 155.
7. *Ibid.*, II, 6.
8. *Loc. cit.*
9. *Ibid.*, pp. 5, 6.
10. *Ibid.*, pp. 9–10.
11. *Ibid.*, I, 42. This passage is from an earlier, privately printed edition (Cambridge: University Press, 1904); hereafter I shall refer to this edition as the "privately printed edition."
12. *Ibid.*, II, 13.
13. An unpublished portion of Charles Darwin's "Autobiography," Darwin Papers (Cambridge: University Library), pp. 73B–73C.
14. *Emma Darwin*, II, 15.
15. *Ibid.*, pp. 23–24.
16. *Ibid.*, p. 24.
17. *Ibid.*, p. 37.
18. *Ibid.*, p. 34.
19. *Ibid.*, pp. 40–41.
20. *Ibid.*, p. 48.
21. *Loc. cit.*
22. Unpublished letter of Charles Darwin to Caroline Darwin, 1839, Darwin Papers (Cambridge: University Library).
23. *Loc. cit.*
24. *Emma Darwin*, II, 65–66.
25. *Ibid.*, p. 76.
26. Unpublished letter to Susan Darwin, April 27 [1842], Darwin Papers (Cambridge: University Library).
27. Unpublished letter to Catherine Darwin, Saturday [1842], Darwin Papers (Cambridge: University Library).
28. Unpublished letter to Catherine Darwin, Friday [1842], Darwin Papers (Cambridge: University Library).
29. *Emma Darwin*, II, 87.

30. *Ibid.*, p. 119.
31. *Ibid.*, p. 186.
32. "The Life of the Shawl," *The Lancet*, December 26, 1953, p. 1352.

6. *Barnacles and Blasphemy*   pages 82–100

1. Francis Darwin, ed., *The Life and Letters of Charles Darwin*, authorized ed. (New York: D. Appleton & Company, Inc., 1896), I, 259.
2. Published as Parts I and II respectively of the *Geology of the Voyage of the Beagle*.
3. Unpublished letter to Sir Charles Lyell, December 4, 1849, Charles Darwin Papers (Philadelphia: American Philosophical Society).
4. Francis Darwin and A. C. Seward, eds., *More Letters of Charles Darwin, A Record of His Work in a Series of Hitherto Unpublished Letters* (London: John Murray, 1903), I, 38.
5. *Life and Letters of Darwin*, I, 317.
6. *Ibid.*, p. 345.
7. Unpublished letter to Joseph Hooker, May 10, 1848, Darwin Papers (Cambridge: University Library).
8. *Life and Letters of Darwin*, I, 66.
9. *Ibid.*, p. 315.
10. *Loc. cit.*
11. *Ibid.*, p. 18.
12. Henrietta Litchfield, ed., *Emma Darwin, Wife of Charles Darwin: A Century of Family Letters, 1792–1896* (London: John Murray, 1915), II, 119–120.
13. *Life and Letters of Darwin*, I, 117.
14. *Ibid.*, p. 131.
15. "On the Reception of the 'Origin of Species,'" *Life and Letters of Darwin*, I, 549–550.
16. *More Letters of Darwin*, I, 41.

17. *Ibid.*, p. 63.
18. *Life and Letters of Darwin*, I, 368.
19. *Ibid.*, p. 126.
20. *Ibid.*, p. 125.
21. *Ibid.*, p. 68.
22. *The Principles of Geology, Being an Attempt to Explain the Former Changes of the Earth's Surface, by Reference to Causes Now in Operation*, 1st ed. (London: John Murray, 1830–1833), II, 132.
23. *Life and Letters of Darwin*, I, 369.
24. *Ibid.*, p. 368.
25. *Ibid.*, p. 68.
26. *Ibid.*, p. 69.
27. See *The Foundations of the Origin of Species: Two Essays Written in 1842 and 1844*, Francis Darwin, ed. (Cambridge: University Press, 1909).
28. *Life and Letters of Darwin*, I, 370.
29. *Ibid.*, p. 354.
30. *Ibid.*, p. 99.
31. *Ibid.*, p. 354.
32. *Ibid.*, p. 394.
33. *Ibid.*, p. 461.
34. *More Letters of Darwin*, I, 199.
35. *Life and Letters of Darwin*, I, 431.
36. *Ibid.*, pp. 501, 502.
37. *Ibid.*, p. 509.
38. Unpublished letter, May 3 [1856], Charles Darwin Papers (Philadelphia: American Philosophical Society).
39. *Life and Letters of Darwin*, I, 453.
40. *Ibid.*, p. 466.
41. *Ibid.*, p. 474.
42. *Ibid.*, pp. 474, 475.
43. *Ibid.*, p. 476.
44. *Ibid.*, p. 483.
45. *Ibid.*, p. 482.

7. The Most Important Book of the Century

pages 101–122

1. See Arthur O. Lovejoy, *The Great Chain of Being, A Study of the History of an Idea, The William James Lectures delivered at Harvard University, 1933* (Cambridge, Mass.: Harvard University Press, 1936), p. 55.
2. *Ibid.*, pp. 67–99.
3. Charles Darwin, "Historical Sketch," *The Origin of Species by Means of Natural Selection, or the Preservation of Favoured Races in the Struggle for Life*, authorized ed. (New York: D. Appleton & Company, Inc., 1896), I, xiv.
4. Francis Darwin, ed., *The Life and Letters of Charles Darwin*, authorized ed. (New York: D. Appleton & Company, Inc., 1896), I, 34.
5. Lamarck, *Philosophie zoologique, ou expositions des considérations relatives à l'histoire naturelle des animaux à la diversité de leur organisation et des facultés qu'ils en obtiennent*, etc., Nouvelle Edition, Revue et Procédée d'une Introduction Biographique (Paris: Librairie F. Savy, 1873), I, 233–236.
6. Mrs. Lyell, ed., *Life, Letters and Journals of Sir Charles Lyell, Bart.* (London: John Murray, 1881), I, 168.
7. See *Ibid.*, p. 174.
8. *A History of the Thirty Years' Peace, A.D. 1816–1846* (London: George Bell & Sons, 1877), II, 334.
9. *Life, Letters and Journals of Lyell*, I, 328.
10. Quoted by André Maurois, *Disraeli: A Picture of the Victorian Age* (New York: D. Appleton & Company, Inc., 1928), p. 130.
11. *The Origin of Species*, I, 36.
12. *Ibid.*, pp. 77–78.
13. *Ibid.*, p. 136.
14. *Ibid.*, p. 96.
15. *Ibid.*, p. 131.
16. *Ibid.*, II, 305–306.

17. *Religion and Science*, Home University Library (London and New York: Geoffrey Cumberlege, Oxford University Press, 1935), pp. 72–73.

18. See Erik Nordenskiöld, *The History of Biology: A Survey*, trans. from the Swedish by L. B. Eyre (New York: Tudor Publishing Co., 1949), pp. 461–476.

19. See J. H. N. Sullivan, *The Limitations of Science*, A Mentor Book (New York: The New American Library, 1940), p. 187.

20. See George G. Simpson, *The Meaning of Evolution: A Study of the History of Life and of Its Significance for Man*, The Terry Lectures (New Haven, Conn.: Yale University Press, 1949).

21. T. H. Huxley and Julian Huxley, "The Vindication of Darwinism," *Touchstone for Ethics, 1893–1943* (New York: Harper & Brothers, 1947), p. 167.

22. *The Meaning of Evolution*, p. 118.

23. See Julian Huxley, *Evolution: A Modern Synthesis* (New York: Harper & Brothers, 1943).

8. Convulsions of the National Mind   pages 123–154

1. *Life of Charles Darwin*, "Great Writers," E. S. Robertson, ed. (London: Walter Scott, n.d.), p. 102.

2. Francis Darwin, ed., *The Life and Letters of Charles Darwin*, authorized ed. (New York: D. Appleton & Company, Inc., 1896), II, 24.

3. Charles Darwin Papers (Philadelphia: American Philosophical Society).

4. *Life and Letters of Darwin*, I, 83.

5. Leonard Huxley, *Life and Letters of Thomas Henry Huxley* (New York: D. Appleton & Company, Inc., 1901), I, 102.

6. Mrs. Lyell, ed., *Life, Letters and Journals of Sir Charles Lyell, Bart.* (London: John Murray, 1881), II, 212.

7. *Life and Letters of Huxley*, I, 171.

8. *Ibid.*, p. 178.

9. *Ibid.*, p. 183.
10. *Ibid.*, p. 188.
11. *Life and Letters of Huxley*, I, 189.
12. *Life and Letters of Darwin*, II, 23.
13. *Ibid.*, I, 7, 10.
14. *Ibid.*, II, 37.
15. Quoted by Sir Francis Darwin and A. C. Seward, eds., *More Letters of Charles Darwin, a Record of His Work in a Series of Hitherto Unpublished Letters* (London: John Murray, 1893), I, 190, n.2.
16. "Design versus Necessity," *Darwiniana*, authorized ed. (New York: D. Appleton & Company, Inc., 1876), pp. 75–76.
17. *Life and Letters of Darwin*, I, 277.
18. An unpublished portion of Charles Darwin's "Autobiography," Darwin Papers (Cambridge: University Library), p. 60.
19. *Ibid.*, pp. 63–64.
20. *Ibid.*, p. 69.
21. *More Letters of Darwin*, I, 260–261.
22. *Life and Letters of Darwin*, I, 282.
23. *More Letters of Darwin*, I, 169.
24. *Life and Letters of Darwin*, II, 131.
25. *Ibid.*, p. 39.
26. Mrs. Kingsley, ed., *Charles Kingsley: His Letters and Memories of His Life* (London: Macmillan & Co., Ltd., 1899).
27. *Ibid.*, p. 44.
28. "Objections to Mr. Darwin's Theory of the Origin of Species," *The Spectator*, March 24, 1860, p. 285.
29. *The Life and Letters of Darwin*, II, 44.
30. *Ibid.*, p. 106.
31. *Ibid.*, p. 32.
32. *Ibid.*, p. 155.
33. *Ibid.*, p. 12.
34. *Ibid.*, p. 35.
35. *Ibid.*, p. 38.

36. *Ibid.*, p. 78.
37. *Ibid.*, p. 33.
38. In the London *Times*, December 26, 1859, pp. 6–7; see Thomas Henry Huxley, *Darwiniana*, pp. 1–21.
39. *Life and Letters of Darwin*, II, 47–48.
40. *More Letters of Darwin*, I, 140.
41. Quoted by Eric Nordenskiöld, *The History of Biology, A Survey*, trans. from the Swedish by L. B. Eyre (New York: Tudor Publishing Co., 1949), p. 511.
42. Quoted in *Life and Letters of Darwin*, II, 77.
43. *Ibid.*, p. 78.
44. *Ibid.*, p. 29.
45. *Loc. cit.*
46. *Ibid.*, p. 158.
47. Henrietta Litchfield, ed., *Emma Darwin, Wife of Charles Darwin: A Century of Family Letters, 1792–1896* (London: John Murray, 1915), II, 173.
48. *Ibid.*, p. 174.
49. *Ibid.*, p. 181.
50. *Ibid.*, p. 172.
51. *More Letters of Darwin*, I, 204–205.
52. Major Leonard Darwin, "Memories of Down House," *The Nineteenth Century*, CVI (1929), 119–120.
53. *Life and Letters of Darwin*, I, 112.
54. *Emma Darwin*, II, 145.
55. *Ibid.*, p. 157.
56. Unpublished letter to W. E. Darwin, Wednesday [n.d.], Darwin Papers (Cambridge: University Library).
57. *Emma Darwin*, II, 167.
58. *Ibid.*, p. 166.
59. Unpublished letter to W. E. Darwin, April 27, Darwin Papers (Cambridge: University Library).
60. Unpublished letter, October 3, 1851, Darwin Papers (Cambridge: University Library).
61. *Emma Darwin*, II, 169–170.

62. *Life and Letters of Darwin*, I, 113.
63. Major Darwin, "Memories of Down House," *The Nineteenth Century*, CVI (1929), 119.
64. *Emma Darwin*, II, 163.
65. Major Darwin, "Memories of Down House," *The Nineteenth Century*, CVI (1929), 120.
66. Unpublished letter to Susan Darwin, March 9, 1849, Darwin Papers (Cambridge: University Library).
67. Gwen Raverat, *Period Piece: A Cambridge Childhood* (London: Faber & Faber Ltd., 1952), p. 122.
68. *Life and Letters of Darwin*, I, 110.
69. *Ibid.*, p. 111.
70. *Emma Darwin*, II, 136–137.
71. *Life and Letters of Darwin*, II, 61.
72. *Ibid.*, p. 59.

9. *An Interlude: Huxley, Kingsley, and the Universe*
pages 155–163

1. Leonard Huxley, *Life and Letters of Thomas Henry Huxley* (New York: D. Appleton & Company, Inc., 1901), I, 163.
2. The entire letter is quoted in *ibid.*, pp. 233–239.
3. "The Language of Values in Carlyle and Huxley."
4. "A Liberal Education; And Where to Find It," *Science and Education*, authorized ed. (New York: D. Appleton & Company, Inc., 1897), p. 82.
5. *Life and Letters of Huxley*, II, 240–241, n.
6. *Ibid.*, I, 259.
7. "Thomas Henry Huxley," *The Drift of Romanticism, Shelburne Essays* (Boston: Houghton Mifflin Company, 1913), VIII, 210–214.
8. *Life and Letters of Huxley*, I, 261.
9. *Ibid.*, p. 262.
10. *Ibid.*, p. 263.
11. *Ibid.*, I, 264.

10. *Human Skeletons in Geological Closets*

pages 164–183

1. *Autobiographic Memoirs* (London: Macmillan & Co., Ltd., 1911), I, 283.
2. Francis Darwin and A. C. Seward, eds., *More Letters of Charles Darwin, A Record of His Work in a Series of Hitherto Unpublished Letters* (London: John Murray, 1903), I, 231.
3. Leonard Huxley, *Life and Letters of Thomas Henry Huxley* (New York: D. Appleton & Company, Inc., 1901), I, 223.
4. *Ibid.*, p. 254.
5. *Ibid.*, p. 213.
6. *Ibid.*, p. 255.
7. Francis Darwin, ed., *The Life and Letters of Charles Darwin*, authorized ed. (New York: D. Appleton & Company, Inc., 1896), II, 56.
8. *Ibid.*, p. 60.
9. *Life and Letters of Huxley*, I, 184.
10. *Ibid.*, p. 205.
11. See Houston Peterson, *Huxley, Prophet of Science* (London: Longmans, Green & Co., Ltd., 1932), p. 145.
12. See Professor Huxley, "On the Zoological Relations of Man with the Lower Animals," *The Natural History Review*, n.s. I (1861), 67.
13. "On the Relations of Man to the Lower Animals," *Evidence as to Man's Place in Nature*, authorized ed. (New York: D. Appleton & Company, Inc., 1897), p. 155.
14. "On Some Fossil Remains of Man," *Man's Place in Nature*, p. 199.
15. Mrs. Charles Kingsley, ed., *Charles Kingsley: Letters and Memories of His Life* (London: Macmillan & Co., Ltd., 1899), p. 254.
16. *The Athenaeum*, February 28, 1863, p. 287.
17. Lady Hooker and Leonard Huxley, eds., *Life and Letters of*

    Sir Joseph Dalton Hooker (London: John Murray, 1918),
    II, 32.
18. Mrs. Lyell, ed., *Life, Letters and Journals of Sir Charles
    Lyell, Bart.* (London: John Murray, 1881), II, 366.
19. *More Letters of Darwin*, I, 237.
20. *Life and Letters of Darwin*, II, 62.
21. *Life, Letters and Journals of Lyell*, II, 325.
22. *Ibid.*, II, 361–362.
23. *Ibid.*, p. 361.
24. Unpublished letter to Sir Charles Lyell, April 17, 1862, The
    Charles Darwin Papers (Philadelphia: American Philosophi-
    cal Society).
25. *Life and Letters of Darwin*, II, 130.
26. *Ibid.*, p. 133.
27. *More Letters of Darwin*, I, 155–156.
28. *Ibid.*, p. 155.
29. *Ibid.*, p. 154.
30. *Loc. cit.*
31. *Life and Letters of Darwin*, II, 119.
32. *Ibid.*, p. 137.
33. *Ibid.*, p. 157.
34. *Ibid.*, p. 100.
35. *Ibid.*, p. 193.
36. *The Geological Evidences of the Antiquity of Man, with
    Remarks on the Theories of the Origin of Species by Varia-
    tion*, 2d ed. (London: John Murray, 1863), p. 468.
37. *Ibid.*, pp. 494–495.
38. *Ibid.*, p. 506.
39. *Life and Letters of Darwin*, II, 194.
40. *Ibid.*, p. 196.
41. *Ibid.*, p. 198.
42. *Ibid.*, p. 199.
43. *Loc. cit.*
44. *Ibid.*, p. 218.
45. *More Letters of Darwin*, I, 243.
46. *Ibid.*, I, 205.

47. *Life, Letters and Journals of Lyell,* II, 254.
48. *More Letters of Darwin,* I, 205.
49. *Life and Letters of Darwin,* II, 166–167.
50. *More Letters of Darwin,* I, 240.
51. *Charles Kingsley: Letters and Memories,* p. 253.
52. *More Letters of Darwin,* I, 243.
53. "Criticisms on 'The Origin of Species,'" *Darwiniana,* authorized ed. (New York: D. Appleton & Company, Inc., 1897), p. 98.
54. *Life and Letters of Darwin,* II, 214.

11. Orchids, Politics, and Heredity   pages 184–216

1. Francis Darwin, ed., *The Life and Letters of Charles Darwin,* authorized ed. (New York: D. Appleton & Company, Inc., 1896), II, 225.
2. Unpublished letter to George Darwin, September 13, 1875, Darwin Papers (Cambridge: University Library).
3. Unpublished letter to Reginald Darwin, April 8, 1879, Darwin Papers (Cambridge: University Library).
4. *Life and Letters of Darwin,* II, 175.
5. *Ibid.,* p. 216.
6. *Ibid.,* pp. 215–216.
7. *Ibid.,* p. 232.
8. *Ibid.,* I, 73.
9. *Ibid.,* p. 95.
10. *Ibid.,* p. 90.
11. Francis Darwin and A. C. Seward, eds., *More Letters of Charles Darwin, A Record of His Work in a Series of Hitherto Unpublished Letters* (London: John Murray, 1903), II, 270–271.
12. *Ibid.,* II, 279.
13. *Ibid.,* p. 278.
14. Unpublished letter, May 17, 1868, Darwin Papers (Cambridge: University Library).
15. *More Letters of Darwin,* II, 285.

16. *Ibid.*, p. 286.
17. *Life and Letters of Darwin*, II, 175.
18. *More Letters of Darwin*, I, 202.
19. *Ibid.*, p. 203.
20. *Life and Letters of Darwin*, II, 429.
21. *More Letters of Darwin*, I, 202.
22. *The Various Contrivances by Which Orchids Are Fertilized by Insects*, 2d ed., revised (New York: D. Appleton & Company, Inc., 1889), pp. 285–286.
23. *Life and Letters of Darwin*, II, 448.
24. *Ibid.*, p. 462.
25. *Ibid.*, p. 213.
26. Mrs. Lyell, ed., *Life, Letters and Journals of Sir Charles Lyell, Bart.* (London: John Murray, 1881), II, 384.
27. Unpublished letter, December 4 [1864], Darwin Papers (Cambridge: University Library).
28. *Life and Letters of Darwin*, II, 219.
29. *Ibid.*, I, 36.
30. Henrietta Litchfield, ed., *Emma Darwin, Wife of Charles Darwin: A Century of Family Letters, 1792–1896* (London: John Murray, 1915), II, 185.
31. *Life and Letters of Darwin*, II, 443.
32. *Ibid.*, pp. 443–444.
33. *Ibid.*, p. 444.
34. *Life and Letters of Darwin*, II, 485.
35. *Loc. cit.*
36. *Ibid.*, p. 486.
37. *Ibid.*, p. 487.
38. *Ibid.*, p. 488.
39. *Ibid.*, p. 489.
40. *Ibid.*, p. 474.
41. *More Letters of Darwin*, II, 322–323.
42. *Ibid.*, p. 327.
43. *Ibid.*, p. 328.
44. *Loc. cit.*
45. *Ibid.*, pp. 331–332.

46. "Charles Darwin and Psychotherapy," *The Lancet*, January 30, 1943, p. 130.
47. *Life and Letters of Darwin*, I, 341.
48. *Ibid.*, II, 238.
49. *Loc. cit.*
50. *Ibid.*, I, 92.
51. *Loc. cit.*
52. *Ibid.*, p. 93.
53. *Ibid.*, p. 101.
54. *Ibid.*, p. 81.
55. *Ibid.*, II, 219.
56. *Ibid.*, pp. 188–189.
57. *Life and Letters of Darwin*, II, 239.
58. Unpublished letter, October 2, 1866, Darwin Papers (Cambridge: University Library).
59. *Life and Letters of Darwin*, II, 178.
60. *Ibid.*, p. 166.
61. *Ibid.*, p. 169.
62. Jane Loring Gray, ed., *Letters of Asa Gray* (Boston and New York: Houghton Mifflin Company, 1893), II, 474.
63. *Life and Letters of Darwin*, II, 173–174.
64. *Ibid.*, p. 174.
65. Unpublished letter to Asa Gray, January 22 [1862], Darwin Papers (Cambridge: University Library).
66. *More Letters of Darwin*, II, 177.
67. *Ibid.*, pp. 476–477.
68. *Ibid.*, p. 183.
69. Unpublished letter to Asa Gray, January 19 [1863], Darwin Papers (Cambridge: University Library).
70. Unpublished letter, April 20, 1863, Darwin Papers (Cambridge: University Library).
71. Unpublished letter to Asa Gray, August 4, 1864, Darwin Papers (Cambridge: University Library).
72. Unpublished letter to Asa Gray, Sept. 13 [1864], Darwin Papers (Cambridge: University Library).
73. *Letters*, II, 537.

74. Unpublished letter to Asa Gray, August 15 [1870?], Darwin Papers (Cambridge: University Library).

75. *Life and Letters of Darwin*, I, 82.

76. *More Letters of Darwin*, I, 270.

77. *Life and Letters of Darwin*, II, 255.

78. *Ibid.*, p. 228.

79. Leonard Huxley, *Life and Letters of Thomas Henry Huxley* (New York: D. Appleton & Company, Inc., 1901), I, 289.

80. *Life and Letters of Darwin*, II, 228.

81. *Life and Letters of Huxley*, I, 289.

82. *Life and Letters of Darwin*, II, 228–229.

83. *Ibid.*, p. 248.

84. *The Variation of Animals and Plants under Domestication*, authorized ed. (New York: D. Appleton & Company, Inc., 1896), I, 456.

85. *Ibid.*, II, 178.

86. *Ibid.*, p. 398.

87. *Life and Letters of Darwin*, II, 256.

88. *Ibid.*, p. 260.

89. *Ibid.*, p. 263.

90. *Ibid.*, p. 266.

91. "Autobiography," *Life and Letters of Darwin*, I, 10–11.

92. *Loc. cit.*

93. *Ibid.*, p. 12.

94. *Ibid.*, p. 19.

95. *Ibid.*, p. 13.

96. *Ibid.*, p. 11.

12. The Subject of Subjects   pages 217–246

1. Leonard Huxley, *Life and Letters of Thomas Henry Huxley* (New York: D. Appleton & Company, Inc., 1901), I, 386.

2. Francis Darwin, ed., *The Life and Letters of Charles Darwin*, authorized ed. (New York: D. Appleton & Company, Inc., 1896), II, 278.

3. "The Origin of Human Races and the Antiquity of Man

Deduced from the Theory of Natural Selection," *The Anthropological Review*, II (1864), clviii-clxx.

4. *Life and Letters of Darwin*, II, 271–272.

5. *Ibid.*, p. 276.

6. *Ibid.*, p. 273.

7. *Ibid.*, p. 274.

8. Henrietta Litchfield, ed., *Emma Darwin, Wife of Charles Darwin: A Century of Family Letters, 1792–1896* (London: John Murray, 1915), II, 191.

9. *Ibid.*, p. 192.

10. *Life and Letters of Darwin*, II, 274.

11. Unpublished letter, April 27, 1867, Darwin Papers (Cambridge: University Library).

12. Unpublished letter, May 5, 1867, Darwin Papers (Cambridge: University Library).

13. James Marchant, *Alfred Russell Wallace: Letters and Reminiscences* (New York: Harper & Brothers, 1916), p. 131.

14. Francis Darwin and A. C. Seward, eds., *More Letters of Charles Darwin, A Record of His Work in a Series of Hitherto Unpublished Letters* (New York: D. Appleton & Company, Inc., 1903), I, 304.

15. Marchant, *Wallace*, p. 152.

16. *Ibid.*, p. 183.

17. *Ibid.*, p. 185.

18. *Ibid.*, p. 186.

19. *Ibid.*, p. 189.

20. *More Letters of Darwin*, II, 39.

21. *The Quarterly Review*, CXXVI (1869), 391–392.

22. As quoted in *More Letters of Darwin*, II, 40.

23. "Sir Charles Lyell on Geological Climates and the Origin of Species," *The Quarterly Review*, CXXVI (1869), 381.

24. *Life and Letters of Darwin*, II, 296.

25. *Ibid.*, II, 294–295.

26. *Life and Letters of Darwin*, II, p. 291.

27. *Ibid.*, II, 298.

28. *Ibid.*, p. 299.

29. *Ibid.*, p. 301.
30. *Ibid.*, pp. 305–306.
31. *Ibid.*, p. 294.
32. Unpublished letter, December 10, 1864, Darwin Papers (Cambridge: University Library).
33. Walter Bagehot, "Physics and Politics," *Works and Life* (London: Longmans, Green & Co., Ltd., 1915), VIII, 34.
34. *More Letters of Darwin*, II, 41; *Life and Letters of Darwin*, II, 297–298.
35. *Ibid.*, p. 43.
36. *Ibid.*, p. 30.
37. Friedrich Nietzsche, "Der Antichrist," *Werke: Auswahl in zwei Bände* (Stuttgart: Alfred Kröner, 1938), II, 223.
38. *Macmillan's Magazine*, XXIII (1870–71), pp. 353–357, reprinted in Francis Galton, *Inquiries into Human Faculty and Its Development* (London: Macmillan & Company, 1883), pp. 68–82.
39. *Fraser's Magazine*, LXXVIII (1868), 353–362.
40. *The Descent of Man, and Selection in Relation to Sex*, authorized ed. (New York: D. Appleton & Company, Inc., 1896), p. 133.
41. *Emma Darwin*, II, 202.
42. *Ibid.*, pp. 196–197.
43. "George Paston" [Emily Morse Symonds], *At John Murray's; Records of a Literary Circle*, with a Preface by the Rt. Hon. Lord Ernle (London: John Murray, 1932), p. 232.
44. *The Descent of Man*, p. 70.
45. *Ibid.*, pp. 564–565.
46. *Emma Darwin*, II, 203.
47. "Mr. Darwin's Critics," *Darwiniana*, authorized ed. (New York: D. Appleton & Company, Inc., 1897), pp. 120–121.
48. "Philosophy and Mr. Darwin," *The Contemporary Review*, XVIII (1871), 281.
49. *Life and Letters of Darwin*, II, 311.
50. "Mr. Darwin's Critics," *Darwiniana*, p. 122.
51. *Life and Letters of Huxley*, I, 392.

52. *Life and Letters of Darwin*, II, 327.
53. *Ibid.*, p. 329.
54. *Life and Letters of Huxley*, I, 458.
55. H. E. Litchfield, ed., *Emma Darwin, Wife of Charles Darwin: A Century of Family Letters*, Privately Printed (Cambridge: University Press, 1904), II, 237–238.
56. *Emma Darwin* (London: John Murray, 1915), II, 203.
57. *Ibid.*, p. 196.
58. *Ibid.*, pp. 247–248.
59. Gwen Raverat, *Period Piece: A Cambridge Childhood* (London: Faber & Faber Ltd., 1952), p. 121.
60. *Emma Darwin*, II, 208.
61. *Life and Letters of Darwin*, II, 373.

13. "I Am Not the Least Afraid of Death"

pages 247–280

1. James Marchant, *Alfred Russell Wallace: Letters and Reminiscences* (New York: Harper & Brothers, 1916), p. 228.
2. Francis Darwin, ed., *The Life and Letters of Charles Darwin*, authorized ed. (New York: D. Appleton & Company, Inc., 1896), II, 494, 495.
3. Francis Darwin and A. C. Seward, eds., *More Letters of Charles Darwin, A Record of His Work in a Series of Hitherto Unpublished Letters* (New York: D. Appleton & Company, Inc., 1903), II, 381.
4. Marchant, *Wallace*, p. 233.
5. *The Various Contrivances by Which Orchids Are Fertilized by Insects*, 2d ed. rev. (New York: D. Appleton & Company, Inc., 1889), p. 351.
6. *Life and Letters of Darwin*, II, 504.
7. *Ibid.*, p. 467.
8. *Ibid.*, p. 507.
9. *Life and Letters of Darwin*, II, 507
10. *More Letters of Darwin*, II, 434.
11. *Life and Letters of Darwin*, I, 25.

12. *Loc. cit.*
13. *Ibid.*, p. 86.
14. Unpublished passage of the "Autobiography," Darwin Papers (Cambridge: University Library), p. 73b, 2.
15. *Life and Letters of Darwin*, I, 71.
16. Unpublished passage of the "Autobiography," Darwin Papers (Cambridge: University Library), p. 74.
17. *Ibid.*, p. 78I.
18. *Ibid.*, pp. 78M–78N.
19. *Ibid.*, p. 78I.
20. *Ibid.*, p. 78J.
21. *Loc. cit.*
22. *Ibid.*, p. 78L.
23. Leonard Huxley, ed., *Life and Letters of Thomas Henry Huxley*, authorized ed. (New York: D. Appleton & Company, Inc., 1901), I, 388.
24. *Life and Letters of Darwin*, I, 60.
25. Mrs. Lyell, ed., *Life, Letters and Journals of Sir Charles Lyell, Bart.* (London: John Murray, 1881), II, 436.
26. *Life, Letters and Journals of Lyell*, II, 459.
27. *Life and Letters of Darwin*, II, 374–375.
28. *Loc. cit.*
29. John Morley, *The Life of William Ewart Gladstone* (New York: The Macmillan Company, 1904), II, 562.
30. *Loc. cit.*
31. Henrietta Litchfield, ed., *Emma Darwin, Wife of Charles Darwin: A Century of Family Letters, 1792–1896* (London: John Murray, 1915), II, 211.
32. *Ibid.*, p. 224.
33. Gwen Raverat, *Period Piece: A Cambridge Childhood* (London: Faber & Faber Ltd., 1952), p. 187.
34. *Ibid.*, p. 209.
35. *Emma Darwin*, II, 215.
36. *Ibid.*, p. 218.
37. *Ibid.*, p. 221.

38. *Ibid.*, p. 211.

39. *Ibid.*, p. 218.

40. *Ibid.*, p. 216.

41. *Ibid.*, pp. 225–226.

42. *Loc. cit.*

43. *Ibid.*, p. 227.

44. *Ibid.*, p. 225.

45. *Life and Letters of Darwin*, I, 112.

46. *Emma Darwin*, II, 228, n. 3.

47. *Ibid.*, p. 229.

48. *Ibid.*, pp. 236–237.

49. Thomas Carlyle, *Reminiscences*, Charles Eliot Norton, ed. (London: Macmillan & Co., Ltd., 1887), p. 173.

50. *Emma Darwin*, II, 230.

51. Unpublished letter, Sunday [1864], Darwin Papers (Cambridge: University Library).

52. Henry Festing Jones, *Samuel Butler, Author of Erewhon: A Memoir* (London: Macmillan & Co., Ltd., 1919), I, 157.

53. Samuel Butler, "Unconscious Memory," *Works*, Shrewsbury ed., H. F. Jones and A. T. Bartholomew, eds. (New York: E. P. Dutton & Co., Inc., 1924), VI, 20.

54. Ernst Ludwig Krause, *Erasmus Darwin*, trans. *from the German by W. S. Dallas, with a Preliminary Notice by Charles Darwin* (London: John Murray, 1879), p. 216.

55. Henry Festing Jones, *Charles Darwin and Samuel Butler, A Step towards Reconciliation* (London: A. C. Fifield, 1911), p. 14.

56. *Life and Letters of Darwin*, II, 527.

57. *Ibid.*, p. 404.

58. *More Letters of Darwin*, I, 395.

59. *Emma Darwin*, II, 247.

60. *Life and Letters of Darwin*, II, 529.

61. *Emma Darwin*, II, 251, 253.

62. *Ibid.*, p. 251.

63. *Ibid.*, p. 253.

64. Unpublished letter from Francis Darwin to Thomas Henry Huxley, Huxley Papers, Scientific and General Correspondence (London: Imperial College of Science and Technology), XIII, 10.
65. Geoffrey West, *Charles Darwin, A Portrait*, 2d ed. (New Haven: Yale University Press, 1938), p. 316.
66. *Life and Letters of Darwin*, II, 531.
67. "Charles Darwin," *Darwiniana*, authorized ed. (New York: D. Appleton & Company, 1897), p. 246.

14. An Eminent Victorian   pages 283–300

1. Leonard Huxley, *Life and Letters of Thomas Henry Huxley* (New York: D. Appleton & Company, Inc., 1901), I, 524.
2. *Ibid.*, p. 328.
3. *Ibid.*, p. 237.
4. *Ibid.*, p. 242.
5. *Ibid.*, p. 477.
6. *Ibid.*, p. 324.
7. *Ibid.*, II, 86.
8. *Ibid.*, p. 83.
9. Herbert Spencer, *An Autobiography* (New York: D. Appleton & Company, Inc., 1904), II, 9.
10. David Duncan, *Life and Letters of Herbert Spencer* (New York: D. Appleton & Company, Inc., 1908), I, 118.
11. "The Scientific Aspects of Positivism," *Lay Sermons, Addresses, and Reviews* (New York: D. Appleton & Company, Inc., 1870), pp. 168–169.
12. *Life and Letters of Huxley*, I, 272.
13. "Emancipation—Black and White," *Lay Sermons*, p. 22.
14. *Ibid.*, p. 25.
15. Unpublished letter, March 17, 1860, Charles Darwin Papers (Philadelphia: American Philosophical Society).
16. *Life and Letters of Huxley*, I, 416.
17. *Ibid.*, p. 301.

18. "Professor Tyndall," *The Nineteenth Century,* XXXV (1894), 4.
19. *Life and Letters of Huxley,* I, 305.
20. "Professor Tyndall," *The Nineteenth Century,* XXXV (1894), 3.
21. *Ibid.,* pp. 363–364.
22. *Ibid.,* p. 365.
23. *The New Republic: or, Culture, Faith and Philosophy in a Country House,* J. Max Patrick, ed. (Gainesville: University of Florida Press, 1950), p. 88.
24. *Life and Letters of Huxley,* I, 297.
25. *Ibid.,* p. 452.
26. Francis Darwin, ed., *The Life and Letters of Charles Darwin,* authorized ed. (New York: D. Appleton & Company, Inc., 1896), II, 364–365.
27. *Life and Letters of Huxley,* I, 455.
28. *Life and Letters of Darwin,* II, 378.
29. *Ibid.,* p. 380.
30. *Life and Letters of Huxley,* I, 473.
31. *Loc. cit.*
32. See Theodore Gill, "Huxley and His Work," *Annual Report of the Board of Regents of the Smithsonian Institute Showing the Operations, Expenditures of the Institution,* 20 July, 1895 (Washington: Government Printing Office, 1896), pp. 772–773.
33. Sir Michael Foster and E. Ray Lankester, eds., *The Scientific Memoirs of Thomas Henry Huxley* (London: Macmillan & Co., Ltd., 1901), II and III, 239–297.

15. The Metaphysical Society   pages 301–321

1. *Discourses Biological and Geological,* authorized ed. (New York: D. Appleton & Company, Inc., 1897), p. 35.
2. *Methods and Results,* authorized ed. (New York: D. Appleton & Company, Inc., 1897), p. 154.

3. *Huxley: Prophet of Science* (London: Longmans, Green & Co., Ltd., 1932), p. 162.
4. *Methods and Results*, p. 160.
5. *Ibid.*, p. 160.
6. *Ibid.*, p. 163.
7. Thomas Carlyle, *The Life of John Sterling*, Works, H. D. Trail, ed. (New York: Charles Scribner's Sons, 1897), XI, 36.
8. Alan W. Brown, *The Metaphysical Society: Victorian Minds in Crisis, 1869–1880* (New York: Columbia University Press, 1947), p. 29.
9. A.S. and E.M.S., *Henry Sidgwick: A Memoir* (London: Macmillan & Co., Ltd., 1906), p. 220.
10. *Life of Cardinal Manning, Archbishop of Westminster* (New York and London: Macmillan & Co., 1896), II, 513.
11. *Life and Letters of Huxley*, I, 340–341.
12. "Agnosticism," *Science and Christian Tradition*, authorized ed. (New York: D. Appleton & Company, Inc., 1897), p. 239.
13. A.S. and E.M.S., *Henry Sidgwick*, p. 222.
14. *Ibid.*, p. 221.
15. *Ibid.*, p. 223.
16. Wilfred Ward, *William George Ward and the Catholic Revival* (London: Macmillan & Co., Ltd., 1893), pp. 314–315.
17. *Loc. cit.*
18. *Ibid.*, p. 317.
19. *Ibid.*, p. 316.
20. *The Nineteenth Century*, XVIII (1885), 180–181.
21. *Loc. cit.*
22. Noel Annan, *Leslie Stephen: His Thought and Character in Relation to His Time* (Cambridge: Harvard University Press, 1952), p. 206.
23. Frederic Harrison, *Autobiographic Memoirs* (London: Macmillan, 1911), p. 301.

24. *Life of Sir James Fitzjames Stephen, Bart., K.C.S.I., A Judge of the High Court of Justice* (New York: G. P. Putnam's Sons, 1895), p. 375.
25. F. W. Hirst, *Early Life and Letters of John Morley* (London: Macmillan & Co., Ltd., 1927), II, 8, 56.
26. *Life and Letters of Huxley,* I, 340.
27. See Noel Annan, *Leslie Stephen,* p. 187.
28. "On Descartes' 'Discourse Touching the Method of Using One's Reason Rightly and of Seeking Scientific Truth,'" *Methods and Results,* pp. 169–191.
29. *Ibid.,* p. 191.
30. *Ibid.,* pp. 192–193.
31. "Science," *The Westminster Review,* XCIV (1870), 501.
32. H. Calderwood, "Professor Huxley's Lay Sermons," *The Contemporary Review,* XV (1870), 205–206.
33. "Science in a Condescending Mood," *The Spectator,* October 1, 1870, pp. 1170–1171.
34. *Ibid.,* p. 1171.
35. *Hume, With Helps to the Study of Berkeley,* authorized ed. (New York: D. Appleton & Company, Inc., 1897), p. 43.
36. *Ibid.,* p. 81.
37. *Ibid.,* p. 222.
38. *Ibid.,* p. 235.

16. The Educator   pages 322–352

1. "The Politics of the War: Bismarck and Louis Napoleon," *The Contemporary Review,* XV (1870), 170.
2. Leonard Huxley, *The Life and Letters of Thomas Henry Huxley* (New York: D. Appleton & Company, Inc., 1901), I, 361.
3. *Science and Education,* authorized ed. (New York: D. Appleton & Company, Inc., 1897), p. 98.
4. *Ibid.,* p. 86.
5. *Ibid.,* p. 85.

6. *Ibid.*, p. 88.
7. *Ibid.*, p. 89.
8. "Scientific Education: Notes of an After-dinner Speech," *Science and Education*, p. 114.
9. "The School Boards: What They Can Do and What They May Do," *Science and Education*, pp. 394–389.
10. "Scientific Education: Notes of an After-dinner Speech," *Science and Education*, pp. 120–121.
11. *Life and Letters of Huxley*, I, 407.
12. *Ibid.*, pp. 378–379.
13. *Ibid.*, pp. 364–365.
14. *Ibid.*, p. 381.
15. *Methods and Results*, authorized ed. (New York: D. Appleton & Company, Inc., 1896), p. 256.
16. *Ibid.*, p. 281.
17. *Ibid.*, p. 284.
18. *Life and Letters of Huxley*, I, 412.
19. Unpublished letter, December 31, 1871, Huxley Papers, Scientific and General Correspondence (London: Imperial College of Science and Technology), II, 187.
20. *Life and Letters of Huxley*, I, 395–396.
21. *Ibid.*, p. 398.
22. *Ibid.*, pp. 394–395.
23. Henrietta Litchfield, ed., *Emma Darwin, Wife of Charles Darwin: A Century of Family Letters, 1792–1896* (London: John Murray, 1915), II, 212.
24. *Life and Letters of Huxley*, I, 421.
25. *Ibid.*, pp. 427–428.
26. *Ibid.*, p. 426.
27. *Science and Education*, p. 210.
28. John Tyndall, "The Belfast Address," *Fragments of Science* (New York: D. Appleton & Company, Inc., 1892), II, 201.
29. Houston Peterson, *Huxley: Prophet of Science* (London: Longmans, Green & Co., Ltd., 1932), p. 197. See also *Life and Letters of Huxley*, I, 444.

30. *Schools and Universities on the Continent, Works,* de luxe ed. (London: Macmillan & Co., Ltd., 1903–1904), XII, 386.
31. *Life and Letters of Huxley,* I, 335.
32. *Ibid.,* p. 353.
33. Unpublished letter, January 13, 1872, Huxley Papers, Scientific and General Correspondence (London: Imperial College of Science and Technology), X, 158.
34. Unpublished letter, October 17, 1880, Huxley Papers, X, 163.
35. Unpublished letter, February 9 [no year], Huxley Papers, X, 165.
36. "Science and Culture," *Science and Education,* p. 140.
37. "Literature and Science," *Discourses in America, Works,* IV, 347.
38. "Technical Education," *Science and Education,* p. 408.
39. "Address on Behalf of the National Association for the Promotion of Technical Education," *Science and Education,* pp. 427–451.

17. *Triumphal Progress* pages 353–380

1. Leonard Huxley, *Life and Letters of Thomas Henry Huxley* (New York: D. Appleton & Company, Inc., 1901), I, 493.
2. *Ibid.,* p. 495.
3. *Ibid.,* p. 495.
4. Edward S. Dana and others, *A Century of Science in America, with Special Reference to the American Journal of Science, 1818–1918* (New Haven, Conn.: Yale University Press, 1918), p. 233.
5. *Life and Letters of Huxley,* I, 496.
6. *Loc. cit.*
7. *Ibid.,* p. 495.
8. *Ibid.,* p. 497.
9. Quoted by Houston Peterson, *Huxley: Prophet of Science* (London: Longmans, Green & Co., Ltd., 1932), p. 204.

10. *Loc. cit.*

11. *Loc. cit.*

12. *Life and Letters of Huxley*, I, 500.

13. Quoted by Peterson, *Huxley*, p. 206.

14. "Address on University Education," *Science and Education*, authorized ed. (New York: D. Appleton & Company, Inc., 1897), pp. 259–260.

15. *Ibid.*, pp. 260–261.

16. Quoted from Abraham Flexner, *Daniel Coit Gilman, Creator of the American Type of University* (New York: Harcourt, Brace & Company, Inc., 1946), p. 84.

17. "University Education," *Science and Education*, p. 261.

18. Fabian Franklin, *Life of Daniel Coit Gilman* (New York: Dodd, Mead & Company, Inc., 1910), p. 221.

19. "Evidence of Evolution," September 19, 1876, p. 1.

20. *Loc. cit.*

21. "Prof. Huxley's Evasion," *New York Sun*, September 19, 1876, p. 1.

22. "Huxley's Second Lecture," *New York Sun*, September 21, 1876, p. 1.

23. *Life and Letters of Huxley*, I, 502.

24. *Ibid.*, II, 3.

25. *Ibid.*, p. 38.

26. Unpublished letter from Oliver Lodge to T. H. Huxley, July 17, 1893, Huxley Papers, XXII, 2.

27. Unpublished letter, May 5, 1883, Huxley Papers, XIII, 8.

28. Unpublished letter, March 11, 1881, Huxley Papers, XVIII, 97.

29. Beatrice Webb, *My Apprenticeship* (New York and London: Longmans, Green & Co., 1926), p. 28.

30. *Life and Letters of Huxley*, I, 505.

31. *Ibid.*, p. 539.

32. *Ibid.*, pp. 434–435.

33. *Ibid.*, p. 435.

34. *Ibid.*, pp. 436–437.

35. *Ibid.*, p. 439.

36. "Some Reminiscences of Thomas Henry Huxley," *The Nineteenth Century*, XLII (1897), 985–998.
37. *Life and Letters of Huxley*, II, 447.
38. The Hon. Lionel A. Tollemache, *Benjamin Jowett, Master of Balliol* (London: Edward Arnold & Co. [1895]), pp. 2, 3.
39. Unpublished letter, April 13, 1877, Huxley Papers, Scientific and General Correspondence (London: Imperial College of Science and Technology), VII, 9.
40. About 1882, Huxley Papers, VII, 49–50.
41. Dec. 2, 1885, Huxley Papers, VII, 58.
42. Feb. 26, 1889, Huxley Papers, VII, 66.
43. Feb. 9, 1892, Huxley Papers, VII, 83.
44. Feb. 9, 1892, Huxley Papers, VII, 83.
45. *Life and Letters of Huxley*, II, 34.
46. *Ibid.*, pp. 23, 24.
47. *Ibid.*, p. 29.
48. *Ibid.*, p. 53.
49. *Ibid.*, I, 526.
50. *Ibid.*, p. 429.
51. *Ibid.*, II, 67.
52. *Ibid.*, p. 78.
53. *Ibid.*, p. 80.
54. *Ibid.*, p. 88.
55. *Ibid.*, p. 92.
56. *Ibid.*, pp. 95, 97.
57. *Ibid.*, p. 98.
58. *Ibid.*, p. 108.
59. *Ibid.*, p. 111.
60. *Ibid.*, p. 118.

18. The Pleasant Avocation of War   pages 381–405

1. Unpublished letter, Sept. 11, 1871, Huxley Papers, Scientific and General Correspondence (Imperial College of Science and Technology), II, 181.
2. Leonard Huxley, ed., *Life and Letters of Thomas Henry*

Huxley (New York: D. Appleton & Company, Inc., 1901),
II, 123.

3. *Science and Hebrew Tradition*, authorized ed. (New York:
   D. Appleton & Company, Inc., 1897), pp. 162–163.
4. "The Proem of Genesis."
5. "Mr. Gladstone and Genesis," *Science and Hebrew Tradition*, p. 164.
6. *Life and Letters of Huxley*, II, 125.
7. *Science and Hebrew Tradition*, p. 189.
8. *Ibid.*, p. 288.
9. *Ibid.*, p. 289.
10. *Evolution and Ethics and Other Essays*, authorized ed.
    (New York: D. Appleton & Company, Inc., 1897), p. 146.
11. *Life and Letters of Huxley*, II, 156.
12. *Science and Christian Tradition*, authorized ed. (New York:
    D. Appleton & Company, Inc., 1897), p. 64.
13. *Ibid.*, p. 140.
14. *Ibid.*, pp. 141–142.
15. Unpublished letter, November 21, 1887, Huxley Papers, II,
    299.
16. *Life and Letters of Huxley*, II, 209–210.
17. *Ibid.*, p. 210.
18. Unpublished letter, June 30, 1883, Huxley Papers, II, 250.
19. *Life and Letters of Huxley*, II, 203.
20. *Ibid.*, p. 231.
21. W. E. Gladstone, " 'Robert Elsmere' and the Battle of Be-
    lief," *The Nineteenth Century* (1888), XXIII, 773.
22. Thomas Henry Huxley, "Agnosticism," *Science and Chris-
    tian Tradition*, pp. 245–246.
23. *Ibid.*, pp. 256–257.
24. Henry A. Wace and The Bishop of Peterborough, "Agnos-
    ticism, A Reply to Professor Huxley," *The Nineteenth Cen-
    tury*, XXV (1889), 351–371.
25. *Ibid.*, pp. 454–480.
26. *Ibid.*, p. 473.
27. *Life and Letters of Huxley*, II, 237.

28. *Ibid.*, p. 237.

29. *The Nineteenth Century*, XXV (1889), 700–721.

30. *Life and Letters of Huxley*, II, 240.

31. "Agnosticism and Christianity," *Science and Christian Tradition*, p. 343.

32. *Life and Letters of Huxley*, II, 240.

33. *Ibid.*, pp. 282–283.

34. "An Apologetic Irenicon," *The Fortnightly Review*, n.s. LVIII (1892), 569.

35. *The Impregnable Rock of Holy Scripture* (Philadelphia: J. D. Wattles, 1896).

36. *The Nineteenth Century*, XXVIII (1890), 967–979.

37. Republished in *Evolution and Ethics and Other Essays*, pp. 237–334.

38. *Life and Letters of Huxley*, II, 289.

39. "The Physical Basis of Life," *Methods and Results*, authorized ed. (New York: D. Appleton & Company, Inc., 1893), p. 156.

19. *"Il Faut Cultiver Notre Jardin"*   pages 406–440

1. *Evolution and Ethics and Other Essays*, authorized ed. (New York: D. Appleton & Company, Inc., 1897), p. 199.

2. Leonard Huxley, ed., *Life and Letters of Thomas Henry Huxley* (New York: D. Appleton & Company, Inc., 1901), II, 198.

3. Unpublished letter, March 19, 1886, Huxley Papers, Scientific and General Correspondence (London: Imperial College of Science and Technology), VII, 172–175.

4. Unpublished letter, February 9, 1888, Huxley Papers, VII, 211.

5. Unpublished letter, December 5, 1889, Huxley Papers, VII, 243.

6. Unpublished letter, December 9, 1889, Huxley Papers, VII, 244.

7. *Life and Letters of Huxley*, II, 261.

8. *Methods and Results*, pp. 346–347.
9. *Life and Letters of Huxley*, II, 271.
10. *Ibid.*, p. 470.
11. *Loc. cit.*
12. *Ibid.*, p. 456.
13. *Ibid.*, p. 460.
14. *Ibid.*, pp. 460–461.
15. *Ibid.*, p. 461.
16. *Ibid.*, pp. 462–465.
17. *Ibid.*, pp. 457–458.
18. *Ibid.*, p. 317.
19. "Prologue," *Science and Christian Tradition*, authorized ed. (New York: D. Appleton & Company, Inc., 1897), p. 39.
20. *Ibid.*, p. 40.
21. *Life and Letters of Huxley*, II, 324.
22. *Ibid.*, pp. 407–408.
23. Unpublished letter of Sir John Donnelly to Lord Spencer, May 15, 1885, Huxley Papers, XXX, 131–133.
24. *Life and Letters of Huxley*, II, 348.
25. *Ibid.*, p. 353.
26. "To Tennyson: The Tribute of His Friends," *The Nineteenth Century*, XXXII (1892), 831–832.
27. Richard Startin Owen, *The Life of Richard Owen, with the Scientific Portions Revised by C. Davies Sherborn and an Essay on Owen's Position in Anatomical Science by the Right Hon. T. H. Huxley, F.R.S.* (London: John Murray, 1894–1895), II, 312.
28. *Life and Letters of Huxley*, II, 395.
29. *Ibid.*, p. 387.
30. Unpublished letter, February 20, 1876, Huxley Papers, I, 145.
31. Unpublished letter to Sir Joseph Hooker, December 15, 1893, Huxley Papers, II, 438.
32. "Professor Tyndall," *The Nineteenth Century*, CCIII (1894), 6.
33. "Physicus" [G. J. Romanes], "Supplementary Essay in Reply

to a Recent Work on Theism," *A Candid Examination of Theism* (London: Kegan Paul, Trench, Trubner & Co., 1892), p. 171.

34. *Evolution and Ethics and Other Essays*, p. 61.
35. *Ibid.*, p. 64.
36. *Ibid.*, p. 67.
37. *Ibid.*, p. 64.
38. *Ibid.*, p. 72.
39. *Ibid.*, p. 77.
40. *Ibid.*, p. 83.
41. *Ibid.*, p. 85.
42. *Life and Letters of Huxley*, II, 381.
43. *The Athenaeum*, August 5, 1893, pp. 193–194.
44. Duncan, *Life and Letters of Spencer*, II, 36.
45. Unpublished letter to Hooker, October 20, 1893, Huxley Papers, II, 433.
46. Unpublished letter to Hooker, September 26, 1890, Huxley Papers, II, 365.
47. *Evolution and Ethics and Other Essays*, p. 30.
48. *Ibid.*, p. 43.
49. See John Dewey, "Evolution and Ethics," *The Monist*, VIII (1897–1898), 321–341.
50. Huxley Papers, Philosophy and Ethics, XLV, 47.
51. *Life and Letters of Huxley*, II, 402.
52. *Ibid.*, pp. 397, 399.
53. *Ibid.*, pp. 401–402.
54. Thomas Henry Huxley, "Past and Present," *Nature*, LI (1894), 1–3. Leonard Huxley (*Life and Letters of Huxley*, II, 400) says that this article contains the substance of his father's speech of thanks.
55. Preface, *Methods and Results*, pp. v–vi.
56. Preface, *Discourses Biological and Geological*, authorized ed. (New York: D. Appleton & Company, Inc., 1897), p. v.
57. *Ibid.*, p. vi.
58. *Life and Letters of Huxley*, II, 410.
59. *Ibid.*, p. 412.

60. Ibid., p. 412.
61. A. J. Balfour, The Foundations of Belief, Being Notes Introductory to the Study of Theology (New York and London: Longmans, Green, 1895), pp. 6–7.
62. James Martineau, "The Foundations of Belief," The Nineteenth Century, XXXVII (1895), 554.
63. The Foundations of Belief, p. 83.
64. Life and Letters of Huxley, II, 419–420.
65. Ibid., p. 421.
66. Loc. cit.
67. Peterson, Huxley, p. 326.
68. Ibid., p. 327.
69. Life and Letters of Huxley, II, 423–425.

INDEX

Abbéville, finds at, 168, 174
Aberdeen University, 340, 343
Adaptation, Darwin on, 93; of insectivorous plants, 248–249; Lyell on, 57
Agassiz, Alexander, 139, 224, 287
Agnosticism, 308, 394–397, 403; Balfour's attack on, and Huxley's reply, 436–439; controversy between Huxley and Ward on, 315, 392–396; Huxley on, 417–418, 438–439; pragmatism and, 315
Aivas, David G., 158
Alvarez, Walter C., 64
Animals, automatism in, 344–345; breeding of, and variations, 91, 93, 109–110, 112, 211–212; color in, and sexual selection, 226, 227; distinction of plants from, 302; distribution and classification of, 116, 117; selection process in, 110
Anthropology, finds of early human skulls, 168; Huxley's writings on, 26–27, 170–173
Apes, similarities between man and, 170–173
Appendicularius, classification of, 18
Aquinas, Thomas, 242, 386
Argyll, Duke of, 180; controversy with Huxley, 387–388; on Darwin's study on orchids, 191
Aristotle, 57, 101
Arnold, Matthew, 346–350, 379, 390, 392
Arnold, Thomas, 326
Artificial selection, 110, 129, 234
Australia, *Rattlesnake* expedition to, 13, 16–29
Automatism, 344–345

Bacon, Francis, 90, 238
Bagehot, Walter, 56, 141, 232–233, 238, 306, 312, 314, 407, 431

Bain, Alexander, 238
Bakunine, Mikhail, 413
Balfour, A. J., 435–438
Balfour, Francis, 377
Bär, Karl Ernst von, 129, 182
Barnacles (Cirripedia), Darwin's studies on, 83–84, 96
Barzun, Jacques, 86
Bates, H. W., 161, 182
Beagle, Darwin's voyage on, 51, 54–62, 85
Behavior, variations in, 115
Bentham, George, 180
Bentham, Jeremy, 119
Berkeley, Bishop, 316, 320, 386, 426
Bettany, G. T., 123
Birds, relationship of reptiles with, 299–300, 364
Bismarck, Otto, Prince von, 325
British Association, 1–6, 32, 34, 78, 301, 322, 337, 338, 344, 352, 431
Brown, Robert, 66, 78, 187, 250, 254
Büchner, Ludwig, 386
Buckle, Henry Thomas, 203–204
Buffon, Georges Louis Leclerc, 103, 210, 213, 269, 272
Bulwer, Sir E. Lytton, 84
Burke, Edmund, 119, 304, 328, 352, 404
Butler, Joseph, Bishop of Durham, 424, 425
Butler, Samuel, 86, 103n., 124, 254, 269–274
Byron, Lord, 219

Calvinism, Huxley on, 399–400
Cambridge University, 52, 54, 63, 85, 135, 180, 231, 266–267, 274, 276, 315–316
Carlyle, Thomas, 161, 179, 219, 318, 403; Darwin on, 66–67, 266; inauguration as Rector of Edinburgh University, 294–295n.; influence on Huxley, 13, 43, 159; meeting with Emma Darwin, 73; relations with Darwin, 265–266; relations with Huxley, 293–295; on science and religion, 108
Carpenter, W. B., 139, 287, 309
Carus, Victor, translation of Origin of Species, 186
Catastrophist theory, 57–58, 97
Cellini, Benvenuto, 379
Chambers, R. W., 4, 106, 108, 125, 126
Chance, natural selection and, 131–134
Chandler, 14
Characteristics, acquired, and heredity, 213; useless, in classification, 114
Cirripedia, 83–85, 96
Clark, Sir Andrew, 198, 248, 276, 285, 340, 378
Classification of plants and animals, 117
Coelenterates, 18
Colenso, Bishop J. W., 202, 262, 287
Color and sexual selection, 226, 227
Competition, Darwin on nature of, 92, 220; in economic theory, 94, 219; natural selection and, 122

Comte, Auguste, 108, 304–305n., 405

Congreve, Richard, 304n.

Convergence, concept of, 117

Cooke, Dr., 14

Copernicus, Nicolaus, 129

Coral reefs, Darwin's theory on, 59, 65, 82, 388

Creation theory, 58, 107

Cross-fertilization, as invigorating offspring, 249–250; mechanism of, 186, 189, sex and, 111–112

Cuvier, Georges Leopold, 381, 383; evolution according to, 57; Huxley's attitude toward doctrine of, 44–46, 165, 301, 381, 383

Dana, James Dwight, 388

Darwin, Anne Elizabeth, 79, 152–153

Darwin, Caroline, 51, 69

Darwin, Charles: characterization, 1–2, 51–52, 87–88, 95, 123–124, 252–253, 391; compared with Huxley, 8, 86–87, 112, 283–284; courtship and marriage, 71–79; Cuvier's influence on, 57–58; death and burial, 277–280; degrees, membership in learned societies, decorations and medals, 54, 192–194, 266–267; early life, 51–54; family life and children, 78–81, 85–86, 95, 144–154, 199–201, 243–245, 248, 253–254, 259–269; health, 54–55, 63–65, 69, 86, 151–152, 198, 276–278;

obituary by Huxley, 391; opinions on American Civil War, 204–208; opinions on automatism, 346; opinions on ethical problems, 237–238; opinions on religion, 53–54, 61, 73, 133–138; opinions on spiritualism, 296–297; opinions on vivisection, 298; relationship with Butler, 270–271; relationship with Carlyle, 265–266; relationship with Falconer, 182; relationship with Gray, 89, 136, 189–190, 204–208; relationship with Huxley, 46, 88, 89, 128, 166, 173, 188, 232, 341; relationship with Lyell, 55, 65–66, 91–92, 173–181, 257; relationship with Wallace, 49, 98–99, 209, 222, 224–228, 229, 230; studies on barnacles, 83–85, 96; studies on climbing plants, 194–195, 248; studies on earthworms, 262; studies on heredity, 121–122n., 186, 209, 211–214; studies on orchids, 161, 187, 189–192; theory on coral reefs, 59, 65, 82, 388; theory of pangenesis, 209–210, 213, 214, 230; voyage on the Beagle, 54–62

BOOKS: Coral Reefs, 83, 248; Descent of Man, 217, 235–240, 243, 245, 247, 248; automatism in, 346; criticism and comments on, 240–243; Effects of Cross- and Self-fertilization, The, 249–250;

Darwin, Charles—(Continued)
Books—(Continued)
Expression of the Emotions in Man and Animals, The, 235, 245, 246, 249; Forms of Flowers, The, 250; Geological Observations on South America, 83, 248; Geological Observations on the Volcanic Islands, 83, 248; Insectivorous Plants, 248–249; Journal of Researches . . . during the Voyage of the H.M.S. Beagle, 56, 82; Origin of Species, The, 55, 57, 89, 91, 94, 98, 101, 109–118, 174, 180–181, 305, 392, 407, 433; competition in, 220; criticism of, 123–132, 147, 167, 182–183, 184, 208–209, 231, 241, 270, 272; editions and translations of, 154, 186, 224, 229, 230, 247; genetics in, 112; Huxley's impression of, 128–129; influence of, 101; influences on, 58; reaction to publication of, 118–121, 123–124, 132, 137, 144, 145; reception by clergy, 37; writing of, 96–98; Power of Movement in Plants, The, 249, 250; Variation of Plants and Animals under Domestication, 210, 222, 223, 235, 248; Various Contrivances by which Orchilds Are Fertilized by Insects, The, 189–191
Articles and Shorter Pieces: "Autobiography," 133, 251–254, 266, 391; "Erasmus Darwin," 269; "Movements and Habits of Climbing Plants, The," 195; Statement of 1844, 94, 95

Darwin, Elizabeth, 85
Darwin, Emma Wedgwood, 341; biographical notes, 69–71; courtship and marriage, 71–79; in Darwin's Autobiography, 253–254; family life, 78–81, 151, 152, 243, 259, 260, 267, 278, 279; religious attitudes and Darwin's theories, 145–147, 243, 261–262
Darwin, Erasmus (Charles Darwin's brother), 64, 72, 73, 145, 153, 154, 223, 275–276, 296
Darwin, Erasmus (Charles Darwin's grandfather), 59, 64, 103, 268–269, 272
Darwin, Francis, 84, 85, 148, 249, 259, 262, 263, 270, 271, 275, 278, 391
Darwin, George, 85, 223, 242, 259, 260, 296
Darwin, Henrietta, 85, 147, 189, 216, 235, 243, 244–245, 248, 261, 262, 275, 277
Darwin, Horace, 147, 152, 262–263, 274
Darwin, Leonard, 146, 151, 223, 259, 260
Darwin, Mary, 85
Darwin, Robert, 261; in family life, 51, 63, 64, 85–86; relationship with Charles Darwin, 51, 63, 80, 81, 90, 215–216
Darwin, Susan, 65–66, 151

Darwin, William Erasmus, 79, 148–150, 151, 263, 263–265, 276, 279

Darwin Medal, 434

Daubenny, Charles Giles, 2

De Candolle, Alphonse, 92n., 139, 182

Descartes, René, 254, 315–317, 320–321, 345

Descent, principle of, 117

Descent of Man (see under Darwin)

Design, concept of, 133–135, 214

Des Perthes, Boucher, 168, 174

Determinism, 386

De Vries, Hugo, 114, 212, 214

Disraeli, Benjamin, 109, 258, 328, 435

Divergence, concept of, 117

Dohrn, Anton, 326, 339

Domestic animals, breeding of, and variations, 91, 110, 112, 212; selection process in, 111; and species question, 92–93

Donnelly, Sir John, 285, 378, 419

Draper, John W., 4

Drosera, Darwin's studies on, 248, 258

Dyer, Thiselton, 251

Earthworms, Darwin's studies on, 262

Edinburgh, University of, 37–38, 52, 291, 294n.

Education, 326–329, 330–331; controversy between Huxley and Matthew Arnold on, 346–350; Huxley's activities in, 328–336, 343–344, 350–352;

Huxley's essay "University Education," 361

Ehrenberg, Christian Gottfried, 193

Eliot, George, 34, 296

Elwin, Whitwell, 235

Embryology, 170

Empiricism, 318–320

Engis skulls, 171, 178

Environment, analogical resemblances as effect of, 117; human mind as adaptation to, 237; influence of, 213; instinct resulting from, 114; types differentiated to cope with, 58

Epicurus, 241

Ethics, Darwin on, 237–238; Huxley on, 417–418, 426–430

Eton College, 365, 391

Evolution theory: Darwin's approaches and explanations, 51, 59, 86–96, 109–110, 118; history of, 101–105; Huxley's position on, 35, 126–127, 363–364; Lyell's position on, 57, 65, 91, 104–106, 256; spread and acceptance of, 182–183, 220–221

Extinction, Darwin on, 58, 92

Eyre, Governor, 292–293

Fabian Society, 406, 410

Falconer, Hugh, 50, 139, 180–182, 254

Farrer, T. N., Lord, 188, 274, 276

Ferrar, F. W., 326–327

Fertility, pressure of, and selection, 111

Fertilization, cross-, 111, 186–187, 190, 249–250; of orchids, 186–187, 190

Fish, Huxley's studies on, 375

Fitzroy, Captain Robert, 54, 61, 62, 82, 83

Flaubert, Gustave, 224

Flourens, M. J. P., 183

Flower, Sir William, 167, 168, 169, 375

Forbes, Edward, 30, 37–38, 45, 50, 97

Foster, Sir Michael, 285, 380, 434

Fox, W. D., 62, 89

Frankland, Sir Edward, 286, 367

Frere, John, 168

Galton, Sir Francis, 133n., 233–234, 280, 296

Geology, Darwin's studies on, 55, 59, 60–61; Huxley on, 364; Lyell's *Principles of Geology*, 55, 57, 66, 91, 92, 105–106, 126, 202, theory of coral islands, 60–61, 65, 83, 388; Wallace's paper on Lyell, 228

George, Henry, 226, 406, 410–412

Gilman, Daniel Coit, 354, 363

Gladstone, Dr. J. H., 336

Gladstone, William Ewart, 106, 124, 328, 336, 406, 407; article on *Robert Elsmere*, 392–393; on education, 328; member of Metaphysical Society, 306, 311; theological controversies with Huxley, 381–384, 400–402; visit to Darwin, 258–259

Goethe, Johann Wolfgang von, 47, 130, 325, 421

Gould, George M., 15n.

Grant-Duff, Sir Mountstuart, 336, 354

Gray, Asa: on climbing plants, 194; crusade for evolution theory, 136–137; on divine intent in nature, 190; on natural selection, 131–132; relationship with Darwin, 50, 89, 177–178, 194–195, 197, 204–208, 214–215, 241, 248, 250, 287

Gray, F. E., 131

Greg, W. R., 235

Grote, George, 66

Gully, Dr., 151, 198

Haeckel, Ernst, 142–143, 236, 284

Hamilton, Sir William, 11, 157, 295n.

Harrison, Frederic, 165, 354, 394

Harvey, William, 129

Heathorn, Henrietta (see Huxley, Henrietta Heathorn)

Hegel, Georg Wilhelm Friedrich, 105, 107, 372

Helmholtz, Hermann Ludwig Ferdinand von, 108, 287, 289

Hennell, Charles, 107–108n.

Henslow, J. S., 4, 53, 54, 55, 61, 78, 139, 180, 231

Heredity: cross-fertilization and, 249–250; Darwin on, 121–122n., 186–187, 209, 211–215; Galton on, 233–234; Huxley on, 129–130; Mendel's studies of, 211; variation and, 110, 112–113

Herschel, Sir John, 131, 132, 279

Hobbes, Thomas, 218, 338, 406, 412

Hooker, Joseph Dalton, 174, 408, 409, 434; biography of, 32–33; on pangenesis, 214; receives Darwin Medal, 434; receives Royal Medal, 38; relationship with Darwin, 50, 84, 89, 98, 99–100, 124–125, 128, 130, 138–141, 179, 185, 187, 188, 192, 206, 214, 217, 226, 246, 251, 253–257, 275, 279; relationship with Huxley, 4, 6, 16, 41, 173, 174, 242, 286, 339, 341–343, 391, 414, 420, 421, 422, 423, 431, 439, 440; speech before British Association, 6

Hooker, Richard, 119

Holland, Henry, 145

Horse, evolution of, 356–357, 364

Hubble, Douglas, 61, 63–64, 198

Humboldt, Alexander von, 16, 54, 66, 179

Hume, David, 238, 302, 303, 309, 317–321

Hutton, R. H., 306, 307, 311, 325

Huxley, Ethel, 391–392

Huxley, Harry, 413

Huxley, Henrietta Heathorn, 202, 372, 373; courtship and marriage, 19–21, 36, 38–40; Journal, quotations from, 29, 39; married life, 161, 284–286, 342–343, 380, 425, 440; Spencer's admiration for, 40; trips to Europe and United States, 355–364

Huxley, Jessie, 284

Huxley, Julian, 121, 415

Huxley, Leonard, 161, 336, 343, 369, 371, 373, 374, 440

Huxley, Marion, 378–379, 389, 392

Huxley, Noel, 155, 161, 440

Huxley, Thomas Henry: answer to Mivart's attacks on Darwin, 241–242; answer to Wilberforce at British Association, 5–6; on automatism, 346; characterization of, 9–11, 14, 87, 283–284, 289, 367–369, 404–405; compared with Darwin, 8, 87, 283–284; as a controversialist, 382, 404–405, 409; controversies on agnosticism, 393–397; controversy with Arnold on scientific education, 346–350; controversy with Congreve, 304–305n.; controversy with Gladstone, 382–383, 400–402; controversy with Liddon, 386–388, 400; controversy with Lilly and the Duke of Argyll, 385–388; controversy with Spencer, 408–410; correspondence with Kingsley, 155–163; courtship and marriage, 19–21, 36, 38–40; Darwin on, 231–232, 255; Darwin Medal awarded to, 434; debates in Metaphysical Society, 309–313; degrees, recognition, and membership in learned societies, 15, 16, 31–32, 37, 41, 166, 186, 322, 331–336, 343, 365–367, 377, 380, 391, 418–420; early life, 10–15; educa-

Huxley, T. H.—(Continued)
tional activities, 328–337,
343–352, 360–362; family
life, 284–286; 413–416, 419–
420; health, 12, 15–16n.,
24, 339–343, 377–379, 428,
438–440; offers to enter
Parliament, 336, 352; official
positions, 16, 38, 331–332,
338, 340, 343, 352, 366–
373, 374, 391, 418; opin-
ions on American Civil War
and race question, 289–290,
292–293; opinions on conflict
between science and religion,
7–8, 10–13, 156–163, 317,
319–320, 331–332, 364, 385–
386, 398–402, 404–405;
opinions on Darwinism and
campaign for it, 125–130,
140–141, 164–166, 336–337;
opinions on Henry George's
economics, 411–412; opin-
ions on politics, 406–408;
opinions on religion, 10–12;
opinions on Salvation Army,
402–403; opinions on social
problems, 336–338, 407–413;
opinions on spiritualism, 296;
opinions on vivisection, 297–
299; opinions on women, 290–
291; opposition to theories
of, 363; on pangenesis theory,
214; philosophy of life, 425–
428; plan for future, 41–42;
poem on death of Tennyson,
421; relationship with Carlyle, 293–295; relationship
with Darwin, 39, 84, 89, 166,
214, 241–242, 254–255, 273,
277, 278, 279–280, 287, 296–
299, 336–337, 338, 340–341,
377, 388; relationship with
Hooker, 420; relationship
with Jowett, 373–374; relationship with Owen, 2–3, 17,
30, 45; relationship with
Spencer, 33–35, 288–289,
408–410; relationship with
Tyndall, 33, 293–294; reply
to Balfour's Foundations of
Belief, 436–439; scientific
work, 15, 18, 22, 299–300,
324, 375–377; transmutation
hypotheses, 125–129; travels
in Egypt, France, Switzerland, and Italy, 340–343,
379–380; travels in United
States, 355–364; voyage on
the Rattlesnake, 16–29
Books: Collected Essays, 433;
Elementary Physiology, 297;
Evidence of Man's Place in
Nature, 48, 164–170, 172–
174, 294, 316, 372, 385;
Hume, 317–321; Lay Ser-
mons, Addresses, and Re-
views, 304n., 316; Science
and Christian Tradition, 416
Articles and Lectures: "Administrative Nihilism," 332,
337; "Agnosticism," 393–
395; "Agnosticism: A Re-
joinder," 396–397; "Agnosticism and Christianity," 397;
"Bishop Berkeley on the
Metaphysics of Sensation,"
320; "Connection of the Biological Sciences with Medicine," 352; "Emancipation

Huxley, T. H.—(Continued)
ARTICLES AND LECTURES—
(Continued)
—Black and White," 290; "Episcopal Trilogy, An," 388; "Evidence of the Miracle of the Resurrection," 313; "Evolution and Ethics," 423–428; "Prolegomena," 429–430; "Evolution of Theology, The: An Anthropological Study," 384–385; "Government: Anarchy or Regimentation," 412; "Has the Frog a Soul?," 313; "Hasisadra's Adventure," 400n., "Interpreters of Genesis and the Interpreters of Nature, The," 382; "Keepers of the Herd of Swine, The," 402; "Lectures on Evolution," 363–364; "Liberal Education, A: and Where to Find It," 328; "Lights of the Church and the Light of Science, The," 400; "Mr. Balfour's Attack on Agnosticism," 438; "Natural Inequality of Men, The," 410–411; Obituary of Charles Darwin, 280, 391; "On a Piece of Chalk," 301–302; "On the Anatomy and the Affinities of the Family of the Medusae," 22; "On Descartes' Discourse," 315; "On the Educational Value of the Natural History Sciences," 43; "On the Hypothesis That Animals Are Automata and Its History," 344–345; "On Natural History as Knowledge, Discipline and Power," 44; "On Our Knowledge of the Causes of the Phenomena of Organic Nature," 165; "On Science and Art in Relation to Education," 350n.; "On Sensation and the Unity of Structure of the Sensiferous Organs," 320; "On the Theory of the Vertebrate Skull," 47–48; "Phenomena of Organic Nature, The," 165; "Physical Basis of Life, The," 302–305; "Pseudo-scientific Realism," 387; "Relation of Man to the Rest of the Animal Kingdom," 169; "School Board, The: What They Can Do and What They May Do," 332; "Science and Culture," 349–350; "Science and Morals," 385–386; "Science and Pseudo-science," 388; "Scientific Education," 330; "State and the Medical Profession, The," 352; "Struggle for Existence in Human Society," 407–408; "Technical Education," 351; "Universities: Actual and Ideal," 343–344; "University Education," 361–362

Hybrids, characters in, 213; relative immutability of, 91

Imperial College of Science in South Kensington, 41, 334, 366, 378

Insectivorous plants, Darwin's studies on, 248–249

Jamaica Affair, 292–293
James, William, 315, 346
Jellyfish, Huxley's studies on, 22
Johns Hopkins University, Huxley's visit to, 285, 360–361
Jones, Wharton, 15
Jowett, Benjamin, 294, 372–374, 422

Kant, Emanuel, 104, 309, 316
Keith, Sir Arthur, 170
Kelvin, William Thomson, Lord, 134–135, 259
Kennedy, Edmund, 23
Kingsley, Charles, correspondence with Huxley, 155–163, 284; on evolution, 137, 415; on similarities between man and ape, 172
Knowles, James, 306, 307, 314, 331, 437
Kölliker, R. A., 182
Krause, Ernst, 142, 268, 272–273

Laissez faire theory, 218–219
Lamarck, Jean Baptiste P. A., Chevalier de, 35, 57–58, 97, 104, 131, 180, 182, 213, 253, 270, 271, 272, 274
Lankester, E. Ray, 344, 371
Lecky, W. E. H., 202, 204
Leibnitz, Gottfried Wilhelm, 102n., 254
Liddon, Canon, 386–388, 400
Lilly, W. S., 385–386
Litchfield, R. B., 244, 277
Locke, John, 338, 406, 412, 438
Lodge, Oliver, 367

Lubbock, John, Lord Avebury, 4, 96, 175, 203, 257–258, 278, 279, 286, 306, 423
Luther, Martin, 394
Lyell, Charles, 31, 68, 73, 78, 125, 193, 290; attitude toward religion, 174–175, 176; biography, 256–257 on evolution of man, 168–169, 173–182; on Huxley's Man's Place in Nature, 174; on invariability of species, 57, 91; on natural causes and geological evolution, 104–106; relationship with Darwin and attitude toward evolution theory, 49, 55, 65–66, 88–92, 97–100, 105–106, 124–125, 130, 136, 140, 173–182, 202, 228–229, 256–257; Wallace's paper on, 227–228
BOOKS: Antiquity of Man, The, 173, 178; Principles of Geology, 55, 57, 65, 66, 91–92, 105, 106

Macaulay, Thomas Babington, 9, 66, 302
Macgillivray, John, 17, 22, 26
Mackintosh, Sir James, 52
McLennan, John, 232
Maine, Henry, 221–222, 232
Mallock, W. H., 294
Malthus, Thomas Robert, 93–94, 110, 352, 362
Man, origin and evolution of, 167, 220–222; Darwinian theory and, 218; in Darwin's Descent of Man, 235–240; Huxley on, 170–173, 302, 303; Lyell on, 178; and primitive society,

Man—(Continued)
232–233; Wallace on, 227–228

Manning, Archbishop, 306, 308, 312, 313

Man's Place in Nature (see under Huxley; Evidence of Man's Place in Nature)

Marconi, M. G., 324

Marcus Aurelius, 238

Marsh, O. C., 355–357, 364, 365

Martineau, James, 312, 314

Marx, Karl, 219, 406, 410

Mason, Sir Josiah, 349

Matter: Huxley on, 162, 165–166, 302–304, 386; Tyndall on, 344

Matthew, Patrick, 106, 184–185

Maurice, F. D., 163, 172

Mayer, J. R., 165

Maxwell, J. C., 324

Medusae, Huxley's studies on, 24

Mendel, Gregor, 121, 129, 210–211

Metaphysical Society, 306–315, 322, 333, 394

Mill, John Stuart, 108, 220, 238, 251, 290, 295n., 306, 307, 311, 337, 406, 425, 427, 437

Milman, H. H., 107–108n.

Milton, John, 252, 363–364

Mimicry, 182

Mines, School of, 37, 38, 46, 365

Miracles, debates on, 312

Mivart, St. George, 241–242, 254, 271, 371

Mollusks, Huxley's studies on, 18

More, P. E., 162

Morley, John, Lord, 258, 259, 287, 304, 314, 317, 378

Murray, John (geologist), 388

Murray, John (publisher), 154, 235, 240

Mutations, 94, 114, 129

Napoleon, Louis, 325

Natchez remains, 178

Natural selection: and competition, 218–219; Darwin on, 93, 94, 110, 177; and evolution from general to complex form, 191; in human evolution, 226, 237, 238; Lyell on, 57, 180; Malthus on, 110; opinions of contemporary scientists on, 121–122; opposition to, 131–132; in plants, 191; priority question, 184–185; related to variations, 112, 212; in societies, 407; Wallace on, 225, 228, 230

Naturalism: Balfour on, 436; Descent of Man encouraging trend toward, 239; Huxley on natural laws, 388, 437, 438

Neanderthal man, 168, 171, 178

Newman, Cardinal, 1, 104, 106, 135, 306, 398

Newton, Isaac, 7, 118, 120, 129, 147, 279

Nietzsche, Friedrich, 234, 235

Norton, Charles Eliot, 264

Oceans and continents, 116

Orchids, Darwin's studies on, 187–192

Origin of Species, The (see under Darwin)

Osborn, H. F., 370, 432

Ouless, W., 246

Owen, Sir Richard, on Darwinism, 2; on evolution and crea-

Owen, Sir Richard—(Continued) tionism, 107; Huxley and, 2, 45–48, 107, 109, 169, 174, 178, 254, 421
Owen's College, 343, 349
Oxford, 1, 2, 332, 363, 372–373, 374, 431

Paleontology, 115, 120, 171
Paley, William, 52, 177
Pangenesis, theory of, 209–210, 213, 214
Parker, T. Jeffrey, 370
Pasteur, Louis, 165
Peterborough, Bishop of, 306, 393, 395
Peterson, Houston, 12–13, 303, 438
Plants: cross-fertilization in, 186–187, 249–250; Darwin's studies of, 186–192, 194–195, 212; distinguished from animals, 302; distribution and classification of, 116, 117; Mendel's studies of, 211; natural selection in, 191; revolving movements of, 249; sterility in, 198
Plato, 102, 372, 422
Playfair, Lyon, Lord, 258, 298
Positivism, 304–305n., 405
Potter, Beatrice (Mrs. Sidney Webb), 368, 408
Pragmatism, 315
Primitive society, books on, 232–233
Principles of Geology (see Lyell)
Progress, 323–325, 424
Protestantism, 398–399

Quatrefages, J. L. A. de, 230

Race differentiation, 239–240
Rattlesnake expedition to Australia, 16–18, 22–28, 379
Raverat, Gwen, 260
Religion, 348, 372, 393, 425, 436, 439; Darwin's attitude toward, 53–54, 59–61, 133, 135; Huxley's attitude toward, 10–12, 317, 319, 332, 364, 385, 398–402, 404–405; Lyell's attitude toward, 174–175, 176
Religion vs. science: Carlyle on, 108; Darwin on, 53; discussions in debating societies, 305; in Gladstone-Huxley controversy, 383–384; Huxley on, 156–163, 363, 364, 416–418; Mrs. Ward on, 396; various scientists on, 106–108, 131–133
Reptiles, relationship of birds with, 299–300, 364
Reymond, Du Bois, 165
Rich, Anthony, 274
Roman Catholic Church, 1, 308, 310, 311, 333, 359; Huxley's attitude toward, 304–305n., 333
Romanes, G. J., 199, 276, 423–425
Rousseau, Jean Jacques, 410–411
Royal College of Science, 366
Royal Institution, 41, 141
Royal Navy, 17, 30, 35–36
Royal Society, 31, 32, 36, 99–100, 192, 253, 257, 336, 338, 377, 378, 391, 434

Royal Society of Edinburgh, 193
Royal Zoological Society, 63
Royer, Mlle. C., 230
Rugby, 326
Ruskin, John, 306, 312, 324
Russell, Bertrand, 119

Sabine, General Sir Edward, 192
Salisbury, Marquis of, 407, 431–432
Savigny, Friedrich Karl von, 221
Schaafhausen, H., 168
Schelling, Friedrich Wilhelm Joseph von, 119
Schultze, Max, 302
Science, in education, 326–327, 349–351; Huxley's views on, 42–44, 157, 386; progress of, in England, 323–324 (see also Religion vs. science)
Scott, Elizabeth, 14, 354, 358
Scott, John, 196–197
Scott, Sir Walter, 193
Sedgwick, Adam, 53, 138, 147, 231
Sedgwick, Sara, 264–265
Seebright, Sir John, 242
Selection, principle of (see Artificial selection; Natural selection; Sexual selection)
Self-fertilization, Darwin on, 249
Seward, Anna, 268–269
Sexual selection, Darwin on, 94, 111–112, 239–240; in Wallace-Darwin correspondence, 224–226, 227, 239–241
Shaftesbury, third Earl of, 238
Shaftesbury, seventh Earl of, 297, 407
Sidgwick, Henry, 309
Simpson, George, 121

Smith, Adam, 119, 218, 238
Social evolution, Bagehot on, 233; and human evolution, 238–239; Spencer's theory of, 35
Socrates, 280, 346, 372, 394
Species: Darwin's definition of, 110; diversification of, 111; of domestic animals, 92–93; Lyell on, 91, 179
Speech, man in relation to, 179
Spencer, Herbert, 101, 105, 209, 226, 232, 237, 280, 306, 307–308, 323, 368; Darwin on, 203, 254–255; in education controversy, 327; Hutton's arguments against, 307; relationship with Huxley, 33–36, 288–289, 385, 408–409, 429; relationship with Mrs. Huxley, 40; at X Club meetings, 287–288
WRITINGS: Autobiography, 34, 409; "Development Hypothesis, The," 35; Psychology, 246, 287, 288; "Theory of Population Deduced from the General Law of Animal Fertility, A," 34
Spiritualism, 296
Sprengel, C. C., 187
Stanley, Dean, 305
Stanley, Owen, 17, 18, 27–28, 29
Stephen, Fitzjames, 312–314
Stephen, Leslie, 144, 313, 314, 372
Stephen (Woolf), Virginia, 260
Strauss, David, 107
Suarez, Francisco, 242
Survival, struggle for, 93, 209, 218, 329, 337, 407–408, 409, 424–427

Tennyson, Alfred, 78, 202, 223, 261, 284, 290, 306–307, 314, 420–421, 424, 425

Tory party, 383, 431, 435

Transmutation hypothesis, 92, 126

Tunicates, Huxley's studies on, 18

Tylor, E. B., 134, 202

Tyndall, John, compared with Huxley, 33, 144; marriage and death, 422–423; member of Metaphysical Society, 311; opening address as president of British Association, 344; relations with Huxley, 286–287, 292, 294, 294–295n., 343, 344–345

Universe, concept of, 134, 155–163

Variations: and external conditions, 94; in natural selection, 212; possible causes of, 112, 129; selection of, 93, 112–113; small, Darwin's emphasis on, 121

Victoria, Queen, 420

Victorianism, 322–326

Vivisection question, 297–299

Voltaire, François Marie Arouet de, 10

Wace, 393–394, 395–397

Wagner, Moritz, 246

Wales, Prince of, 193–194, 354

Wallace, Alfred Russell, 16, 254, 406, 434–435; Darwin Medal awarded to, 434; on Darwin's *Descent of Man*, 241; on pangenesis theory, 214; pri-

ority question and paper on evolution, 98–100, 253; relations and correspondence with Darwin, 49, 89, 98–100, 128, 154, 209, 222, 224–229, 230, 241–242, 247, 249, 275

ARTICLES: "Malay Archipelago," 229; "Origin of Human Races, The," 222; "Sir Charles Lyell on Geological Climates and the Origin of Species," 227–228

Ward, Mrs. Humphrey, 392–393, 396

Ward, Wilfred G., 306, 308–311, 333, 436–437

Watson, H. C., 131, 138

Waugh, Benjamin, 334–336

Webb, Mrs. Sidney (see Beatrice Potter)

Wedgwood, Elizabeth, 153, 261

Wedgwood, Emma (see Darwin, Emma Wedgwood)

Wedgwood, Hensleigh, 251, 296

Wedgwood, Josiah, 52, 54, 61, 261

Wedgwood, Thomas, 65

Weismann, August, 246

Wells, W. C., 185

Westminster Abbey, 279

White, Gilbert, 113

Wilberforce, Bishop Samuel, 5–8, 160, 332

Wild species, variability in, 91

Woolner, T., 224

Wordsworth, 252

X Club, 286–287, 322, 390, 409, 420, 423

Yale University, 355–356

A NOTE ABOUT THE PRODUCTION OF THIS BOOK

The text of this special edition of *Apes, Angels, and Victorians* was set in Electra, a typeface created by the great American designer William Addison Dwiggins and first used in 1937.

✗

The cover was printed by Livermore and Knight Co., a division of Printing Corporation of America, in Providence, Rhode Island. Cover stock was supplied by the Plastic Coating Corp. of Holyoke, Massachusetts. The paper is TIME Reading Text, by The Mead Corporation of Dayton, Ohio.